SHAKING THE FOUNDATIONS

200 Years of Investigative Journalism in America

Edited by Bruce Shapiro

THUNDER'S MOUTH PRESS/NATION BOOKS
NEW YORK

In Memory of
Frank Donner

SHAKING THE FOUNDATIONS:
200 Years of Investigative Journalism in America

Published by
Thunder's Mouth Press/Nation Books
An Imprint of Avalon Publishing Group Incorporated
161 William St., 16th Floor
New York, NY 10038

Nation Books is a co-publishing venture of the Nation Institute and Avalon Publishing Group Incorporated.

Library of Congress Cataloging-in-Publication Data is available.

ISBN 1-56025-433-5

9 8 7 6 5 4 3 2

Book design by Paul Paddock
Printed in the United States of America
Distributed by Publishers Group West

CONTENTS

II. MUCKRAKERS AND THE ERA OF REFORM: 1900–1920

III. FACTORIES, FIELDS, AND FASCISTS: INVESTIGATIVE JOURNALISM'S FORGOTTEN DECADES, 1920–1960

IV. A FORCE TO BE RECKONED WITH: 1960–1990

FOREWORD

By Pete Hamill

The reporter is the member of the tribe who is sent to the back of the cave to find out what's there. The report must be accurate. If there's a rabbit hiding in the darkness it cannot be transformed into a dragon. Bad reporting, after all, could deprive people of shelter and warmth and survival on an arctic night. But if there is, in fact, a dragon lurking in the dark it can't be described as a rabbit. The survival of the tribe could depend upon that person with the torch.

In certain basic ways, the modern investigative reporter is only a refinement of that primitive model. The tools of the trade are now extraordinary: the astonishing flood of documents on the Internet, the speed of other forms of communication, local and international, and, perhaps most important, the existence of a tradition.

Much of that tradition comes from work done over many decades in the United States, where a splendid variety of men and women took advantage of the First Amendment to the Constitution and made that specific freedom real by practicing it. In many ways, they had a simple task: to note the difference between what the United States promised and what the United States delivered. Those reporters were the first to dig into the system that seemed beyond any laws. They took their torches to the back of the cave and in newspapers and magazines they told the citizenry what they had found.

Their basic search was for an explanation of what all could plainly see: rotting city slums, child labor, widespread prostitution, exploitation of immigrant labor. They knew that thousands were dying in cities like New York because there was not enough water. There were not enough hospitals. There were few schools. There were no libraries open to the poor. Thousands died each summer of cholera and smallpox. Others, broken in spirit, found degraded refuge in alcohol or petty crime. Clearly, the gaudy promises of America were not being kept, and those early investigative reporters saw a common root to all our ills: corruption.

This was not a case of a few isolated thieves. Much corruption was systemic. When the *New York Times* brought down William M. Tweed in 1871 (with the immense help of *Harper's Weekly* cartoonist Thomas Nast), it was by publishing documents that showed the way the system worked. The records were provided by an unhappy low-level politico who had been bypassed in his own quest for some of the swag. On one level, they proved what almost everybody suspected: Boss Tweed and his Ring were stealing millions through a system that involved kickbacks from municipal contractors. But they also showed that the system was wider than anyone had thought. Tweed was corrupt, but his corruption had a purpose beyond personal enrichment: as a New York Democrat he needed cash to bribe the upstate Republicans who controlled the city from Albany. If he wanted to get water to his constituents, or build a school in the Five Points (services essential to maintaining his personal power), Tweed needed cash to bribe the Republicans. That was the system he had inherited from his predecessors; when he was gone, the system persisted, in newer, subtler, more respectable clothing.

The reporters and their editors understood that one victory was not the end of the campaign. Exposure in the press was soon an essential part of a process that all knew must continue for as long as there was a United States. After the Civil War, the cycles were established: corruption, then exposure, then reform, followed by a slow drift back into corruption. They continue today. In a way, those cycles are an almost comforting expression of the eternal American verities. They are infuriating, and can certainly hurt human beings, but they remind us of the endless capacity of human beings for larceny and folly, and assure us that the nation will never achieve the dubious perfection of utopia. In the twentieth century, we all learned that the promise of utopia almost always leads to mounds of corpses.

Across the years from the 1870s to the present, investigative reporters have become a mainstay of American journalism, and this book provides a splendid set of examples of the craft. They are a special breed. They don't require the indifference to physical danger of the great war correspondents (although they do, in fact, sometimes risk their lives). They don't need the instinct for celebration that is essential to the greatest sportswriters. They don't often display the entertaining cynicism of veteran police reporters. But they share one absolutely essential quality: an almost obsessive tenacity.

That sometimes ferocious tenacity is what serves as the motor for all of their other skills. Day after day, they go on. They batter at closed doors and they gnaw away at hidden redoubts. The quarry is often clever and always elusive. They examine documents designed to be obtuse, studying them like archaeologists examining Mayan hieroglyphs, looking for patterns, for buried facts, for implied verbs. Most of us would see such work as tedium; they do it with growing excitement. They meet in remote coffee shops with people who might be persuaded to tell the real story. They go back to sources once fruitlessly interviewed, hoping for illumination on the second, third, or fifth try. They go on and on.

They are not, of course, cops. They carry no guns. They have no subpoena power. Sometimes they are helped by good cops who suspect felonies that they cannot prove in court. Sometimes they are in pursuit of the cops themselves. But like the best police detectives, they have a gift for imagining themselves into the minds of felons. They try to think the way the bad guys think, imagining their strengths and weaknesses, creating a number of possible scenarios. They're not simply clerking crimes against the citizens; they must first imagine them.

They pick up the spoor of stories in a variety of ways. They see the announcement of some major municipal contract—school books, parking meters, road construction—and experience urges them to examine the fine print. They search the names of contractors, dig out past records, match names with campaign contributions, demand lists of subcontractors. They always suspect that some piece of the cost to taxpayers will include payoffs to hoodlums, or diversions of money to personal bank accounts. The investigation begins.

On other occasions, they receive anonymous phone calls, whispering of nefarious schemes. Or they are in a bar with reporters and lawyers and they pick up a rumor. They begin to check out these tips, knowing, as one great newspaper editor told me years ago, "If you want it to be true, it usually isn't." Sometimes the rumors turn out to be false, planted by political opponents or personal enemies. The reporters acknowledge that they've hit a "dry hole," from which nothing will flow, and they close the file. More often, they follow the trail of one possible story and discover that it leads to a completely different destination, much richer or more nefarious than the first.

In that sense, most investigative reporters resemble prosecutors. Indeed, their labors often force previously indifferent prosecutors to actually prosecute, that is, to put the right people in jail. But there are many investigators who also serve as unofficial counsel for the defense. They work valiantly to get the wrongfully accused out of jail. They use their tenacious gifts to defend the weak from those with careless power. They go after union leaders who make sweetheart deals at the expense of their members, while looting the pension plans on the side. They go after vicious slumlords who create misery among their poor tenants. They expose businesses that defraud investors and employees.

But they are also surprising people. In my experience, most of today's investigative reporters have vague politics. In that sense, they don't resemble the great generation of muckrakers at the turn of the nineteenth and twentieth centuries, who were men and women with an idealistic, mainly socialist vision of the America that would emerge from their labors. Today's investigators have an almost permanent skepticism about human virtue, political or otherwise. If they are pursuing a crooked judge, they don't much care whether he is a Democrat or a Republican, a liberal or a conservative, or a man who gives alms to orphans and bellows "God Bless America" most loudly on the fourth of July. If he's a crook, they want to nail him. As the great Washington columnist Lars-Erik Nelson once said to me, "The enemy isn't liberalism. The enemy isn't conservatism. The enemy is bullshit."

To be sure, however, most investigative journalism—no matter what the personal politics of its practitioners—aids the progressive side of American politics. It's part of the process of reform, of improving the lot of at least some citizens, incrementally leading toward the goal of elemental social justice that has always belonged to the left. Exposure of corruption usually leads to punishment of big shots (not always, of course). Sometimes the ratholes are actually plugged by legislation. Sometimes (again, not always) there is even a clear moral lesson: power does not always guarantee immunity. Many of us have lived through a time when even a president of the United States fell before the tenacity of investigative reporters.

In this country, and in most others, there is no great tradition of right-wing investigative reporting (William Safire of the *New York Times* is an exception). Most right-wing governments, from that of Francisco Franco to that of Saddam Hussein, have smothered all attempts at exposure, sometimes with violence. The Soviet Union, in spite of all its official socialist rhetoric, was essentially a right-wing state, and feared a free press almost as much as it feared its own citizens. Reporters for *Pravda* and Tass were chosen on the basis of ideological rigidity, and such people make poor reporters. They substitute dogma for curiosity, certainty for doubt. Skepticism, of course, was a crime. In the service of the armed Stalinist bureaucracy, the Soviet reporters asked no questions. Asking questions, after all, could lead to the basement of the Lubyanka prison.

Communism failed for a number of reasons, but one was certainly the absence of an independent press. There was no pain-in-the-ass reporter shining a light upon the slippery privileges of the nomenklatura. There was no fearless weekly making sardonic fun of the difference between what was said by the leadership and what was actually delivered. No Soviet reporter cast a word of doubt or rage on the processes of the Purge Trials or asked why the Kulaks died or raised arguments against the pact with Hitler. Forgive the apparent absurdity, but there was no Soviet equivalent of the *Wall Street Journal,* explaining that a certain ball-bearing plant in Minsk was inefficient because the managers were relatives of some big shot in Moscow and were essentially thieves or brutes or both. Soviet inefficiency and corruption were never scrutinized in public. Finally, the whole wormy structure crumpled into the rubbish heap of history.

That dismal, murderous example should remind us of how crucial the press is to our own imperfect system. Without criticism, no modern society can endure, and investigative journalism is essentially a form of criticism. Every journalist knows that great journalism is impossible without great publishers; no Katharine Graham, no Woodward and Bernstein. Publishers must provide both money and patience while their reporters do their work, and then they must publish their findings. That truth has to be learned again in every generation. When newspapers and magazine publishers turn timid—usually out of fear of the readers or fear of the advertisers—the news package itself gets softer and flabbier. One result: the readers become increasingly indifferent. Worse, the larger society itself becomes stagnant, and the thieves and scoundrels get bolder.

But even timidity is part of the recurring American cycle of advance and retreat. As I write, there's an atmosphere of triumphant right-wing vindication in the air over the war in Iraq, and a sneering dismissal of those who refuse to embrace the conventional pieties. But even the story of the war remains hidden, incomplete, buried behind the image-mongering. We should be reassured by one thing: investigative reporters are at work, methodically separating myth from fact, propaganda from actuality. The full story will come out, as it always does, because someone is heading into the cave with a torch.

INTRODUCTION: STRIKING THROUGH THE MASK

By Bruce Shapiro

Top administration officials denied it. The president's allies in Congress howled, denouncing the exposé that appeared in the newspaper that October morning as a seditious lie. But finally there was no denying the facts: public funds misappropriated for the president's personal use. And there was no denying the source: the administration's own account books, furnished by a pseudonymous informant.

This sounds like the most contemporary of media-drenched political scandals. But the year was 1795; the president was George Washington; the newspaper was the *Philadelphia Aurora and General Advertiser,* edited by Benjamin Bache, grandson and caustic protégé of Benjamin Franklin.

To read Bache's *Aurora* today is to inhale the crisp wind that was journalism inventing itself. Congress had barely blotted the ink on the First Amendment. Only a few years earlier, colonial editors had risked prosecution for criticism of the Crown's agents. Yet here was the pugnacious editor of a six-day-per-week sheet rifling the new government's ledgers and correspondence, subjecting the revered first chief executive to relentless scrutiny and passionate diatribes, cramming contentious dispatches onto the front page beside the shipping news. James Madison and other framers of the Constitution may have encoded freedom of the press, but it was Bache's generation of journalists who gave it breath with pent-up fury.

Newspapers in those days were ardently partisan, and Bache was a particularly ardent anti-Federalist and Jeffersonian. Yet he also published congressional debate reports so accurate that his paper was required reading for his most bitter enemies. He ran detailed dispatches from revolutionary France and rebellious Ireland. He won notoriety with a series of scoops that would do credit to any journalist today. In 1794 Bache printed a leaked draft of the contentious Jay Treaty with Britain. A year later came his Washington financial exposé. In 1798 Bache obtained and published secret dispatches between the government of France and the Adams administration in the XYZ Affair. That disclosure so infuriated Bache's opponents that 170 years before Richard Nixon formed his

White House "plumbers" squad to plug media leaks, the Federalist-dominated Congress attempted its own plumbing job by passing the short-lived Sedition Act and indicting Bache. (He continued to edit his newspaper while out on bail, only to die in a yellow fever epidemic.)[1]

The *Aurora* dispatches are among the first intimations of what would, in just a few decades, emerge as a powerful stream of American reporting and political literature, a stream unfortunately neglected by historians and critics. Over the two centuries since Bache, other inquisitive and relentless American writers—some celebrated, many undeservedly forgotten—have hammered out factual revelations that have evicted from office the highest-level leaders, freed the incarcerated innocent, challenged the logic of wars, exposed predatory corporations. Their work has pushed the boundaries of free expression and lent momentum to social reform. These writers have defined a distinct tradition of inquiry and exposé: an American tradition of investigative journalism.

This is the first anthology to collect two hundred years of that tradition. It represents one reporter's encounter with a few dozen master practitioners, their stories chosen sometimes for historical importance, sometimes for thematic resonance, sometimes simply for a gripping read. Gathered as much for the general reader as for the student of journalism or American culture, these magazine articles, newspaper dispatches, and book chapters—all unabridged—convey the thrill of the chase after facts, and are united by smoldering outrage. Some rise to a high level of literature. Some lay bare the varied configurations of power of their eras. The investigative tradition becomes a prism through which can be delineated American social issues as they appeared to contemporaries and partisans: slavery and financial trusts, immigration and war, witch-hunts and government corruption.

Note that I call this a tradition, not a genre: journalism has evolved too rapidly and too haphazardly for familiar contemporary labels such

1 Rosenfeld, R. N. 1997. *American Aurora: A Democratic Republic Returns.* New York, St. Martin's. There have been several books on Bache and the *Aurora,* but Rosenfeld's account, told through the imagined voice of Bache's real protégé and successor, William Duane, is both the most comprehensive and the most accessible.

as "feature" or "news analysis" to have more than transient meaning. So what, exactly, is the tradition of investigative journalism, and where did it come from?

Lincoln Steffens first talked about "journalistic investigations" in 1906,[2] but the notion of professionally distinct "investigative reporting" would probably have mysified most journalists before the 1960s. When a small network of daily newspaper reporters founded the professional association Investigative Reporters and Editors in 1977, they spent hours arguing about what it all meant. Even today, with "investigative teams" at every major newspaper and television station, a precise definition remains elusive. Bob Greene, former investigative editor of *New York Newsday* and one of the country's most influential journalism educators, insists that investigative reporting has to involve "uncovering something somebody wants to keep secret"—the Watergate standard.[3] Others say secrecy is irrelevant, that investigative journalism can expose social conditions or patterns of institutional conduct that are there for anyone to see but have been ignored—as *Chicago Tribune* reporters have done over the past several years by dissecting death-row convictions and innocence cases.

The selections in this book make clear an investigative impulse that goes beyond any narrow definition. Some of these writers reported for newspapers, some worked at magazines, and some wrote books. They occupy no fixed position on the political compass. But characteristic of all their work is determination to speak documented truth to lying power, preference for methodical ferreting of undisclosed fact over ideological bombast, and fierce belief in the ability of readers to effect change.[4]

2 Kaplan, J. 1974. *Lincoln Steffens: A Biography.* New York, Simon and Schuster.

3 Weinberg, S. 1996. *The Reporter's Handbook: An Investigator's Guide to Documents and Techniques.* New York, St. Martins.

4 Protess, D., et al. 2000. *The Journalism of Outrage: Investigative Reporting and Agenda Building in America.* New York, Guilford Press. The phrase "investigative impulse" is coined by Protess, though he does not use it as broadly.

It's also clear that the investigative tradition's history is in desperate need of revision. As conventionally recounted, the story of investigative journalism starts with the muckrakers, the Progressive-era crusaders who burst upon the mass-magazine scene in the first half-decade of the twentieth century. The muckrakers were, certainly, an extraordinary cohort: among them Ida Tarbell, who chronicled the rise of Standard Oil; Lincoln Steffens, who detailed urban corruption; Upton Sinclair, whose novel *The Jungle* exposed the filth and horrific working conditions in slaughterhouses. The muckrakers exhausted their reform movement after less than a decade, their influence waning well before World War I sucked up all the journalistic oxygen.

After the muckrakers, goes the conventional view, came decades of silence. The crusading investigative press was "all but stomped out during the Great Depression and World War II," as James AuCoin, one of the few historians to attempt an overview of the investigative literature, puts it.[5] Buried by generations of conservative newspaper publishers and complacent reporters, investigative reporting would not experience a revival until the end of the 1960s, beginning with skeptical reporting on the war in Vietnam and culminating just a few years later in the Watergate disclosures of Woodward and Bernstein, which suddenly gave new muckrakers the status of celebrities.

That is the standard version of the story: the muckrakers and Watergate, with little before and less in between. The currency of this view probably owes something to deservedly influential chronicles of the Progressive era by historian Richard Hofstadter. It also owes something to the muckrakers themselves, who were not only hard-hitting reporters but prolific memoirists. It's easy to see why the muckrakers are a touchstone—though few of the journalists who know the muckrakers' names have read their exhaustive (and, I fear, sometimes exhausting) magazine stories and books.

5 AuCoin, J. 1995. "The Re-emergence of American Investigative Journalism 1960–1975." *Journalism History 21.*

But that standard version of history leaves too much out of the picture. For one thing, the investigative tradition's roots go back further than the muckrakers. Northwestern University journalism professor David Protess identifies elements of crusading inquiry in pre-Revolution newspapers in New England, such as early reports questioning Massachusetts Bay Colony leaders' handling of a smallpox epidemic.[6] (The Puritan legacy seems closely tied up with reform journalism: Both the ideal of the city on a hill and the yearning to expose the sin that subverts it run throughout investigative literature. The witch-hunter and the reform crusader are not necessarily far apart in temperament.) Post-Revolutionary editors like Bache and Phillipe Freneau began the gradual shift from speculative and invective journalism to documentation. In the early nineteenth century, abolitionists and the African-American press systematically set out to expose conditions in the slaveholding South, compiling the kind of first-person eyewitness accounts that 150 years later would turn up in human-rights reporters' revelations of death camps in the Balkans. After the Civil War, critics of railway trusts and other emerging corporate combines meticulously detailed manipulation of the financial markets. In the same decades a new generation of such antiracist reformers as Ida B. Wells documented the emergence of lynching and the Ku Klux Klan to enforce Jim Crow laws. Meanwhile, American novelists—Herman Melville, Mark Twain, William Dean Howells, and Frank Norris—were bringing elements of documentary exposé to subjects ranging from the flogging of sailors to Mary Baker Eddy's then-new Christian Science sect, some in their fiction and some in nonfiction essays.

The nineteenth century also brought the first professional reporters, spawned by evolving printing technology and the emergence of the competitive mass-market daily newspaper. Exposés—sometimes high-minded, sometimes sensationalist—sold papers. By the 1880s, the *New York Times* had brought down the city's notorious Boss Tweed; Nellie

6 Protess, ibid.

Bly invented herself as the first celebrity undercover reporter; the iconoclastic newspaper editor John Swinton had abandoned a successful career at the *New York Sun* to start his own labor weekly aimed at the exposure of industrial serfdom. Jacob Riis's *How the Other Half Lives,* published in 1892, triggered the first great crusade against slums. In other words, it turns out that when the muckrakers built their short-lived reform movement, they built it on a well-established investigative foundation.

It turns out, too, that the presumably fallow decades after the muckraking magazines collapsed were alive with vigorous, inquiring reporters who deserve to be remembered. Popular women's magazines kept muckraking progressivism alive, so that in the 1920s a reporter like Vera Connolly could spend months at a time unearthing the details of degrading conditions on Indian reservations and in juvenile jails. Beginning with the 1930's a generation of radical journalists—such as George Seldes and Stetson Kennedy, in these pages—adopted investigative methods with a passion. And even the late 1950s and early 1960s, usually dismissed as a period of journalistic complacency, look barren only because of a crabbed equation of journalism with daily newspapering. During the 1950s a writer like Fred J. Cook could move from broadsheet exposés of mobsters to magazine exposés of J. Edgar Hoover's FBI. McCarthyism, seeming to marginalize dissent, gave impetus to Jessica Mitford and I. F. Stone. And no definition of investigative journalism could exclude the vastly influential book-length exposés by Rachel Carson and Ralph Nader, *Silent Spring* and *Unsafe at Any Speed.* Conceived in the late 1950s and published within months of each other in 1962, these books meet any standard for the journalism of exposure. Both resurrect what historian Robert Miraldi calls the "evangelical crusader" mode of the early muckrakers: Carson and Nader explicitly define environmental depredation and auto-company profiteering not just as dangers to the public but as fundamental usurpations of democracy. It's more than arguable that Carson and Nader—their investigations radically altering public consciousness, inspiring environmentalism and anticorporate consumerism—fulfilled the muckrakers' early promise more fully than the muckrakers themselves.[7]

This revisionist thumbnail suggests that the investigative impulse—the factual pursuit of corruption and inequity—moved like a tide beneath the surface of American politics and letters from the very beginning. It took the rebellion against British press-silencing laws and seditious libel prosecutions—a rebellion embodied in the First Amendment—to foster a journalism of inquiry, which ebbs and flows with the commercial publishing market, with political movements and technological changes, with the whims of media owners, with literary trends and journalistic fashion. Certain themes consistently rise to the surface in these varied dispatches: electoral corruption; slavery, Jim Crow, and the legacy of racism; workplace exploitation; the concentrated power of corporations and financiers. From post–Civil War reformers and pre–World War I progressives emerges the sense of good American democratic order undone by corporate boardrooms and political machines. From African-Americans and immigrants and labor and feminists springs the challenge that the old order was not so great to begin with, that the egalitarian promise of the Revolution always wrote certain constituencies out of the story.

Thus the subjects of investigative journalism turn out to be not just individual elected thieves, or singular corrupt corporations. Rather, what has always been at issue are the fundamental contradictions in American history. The work of these reporters so profoundly and consistently threatened the accepted order that by my count more than one-third of the writers in this volume were jailed, indicted, beaten, burned out of their offices, or otherwise threatened for their accurate exposés. Yet the role of investigative writers remains, curiously, the subject of relatively little scholarship.

It is no exaggeration to say that at their most potent, investigative writers' documentary encounters with human greed, cruelty, and suffering

7 Miraldi, R., ed. 2000. *The Muckrakers: Evangelical Crusaders.* Westport, CT, Praeger.

have altered language, journalism, the terms of public debate, even the self-definition of American society, in profound and enduring ways. Consider just one example. On November 13, 1969, residents of thirty U.S. cities—among them Boston, St. Louis, and San Francisco—opened their morning newspapers to a startling dispatch. Seymour Hersh's story began like this: "Lieutenant William L. Calley Jr., twenty-six, is a mild-mannered, boyish-looking Vietnam combat veteran with the nickname 'Rusty.' The Army is completing an investigation of charges that he deliberately murdered at least 109 Vietnamese civilians in a search-and-destroy mission in March 1968 in a Viet Cong stronghold known as 'Pinkville.'" In that initial article and several subsequent stories, Hersh documented how on March 16, 1968, American soldiers in Charlie Company of the Twentieth Infantry Division's First Battalion, under Calley's direct command, massacred 567 men, women, and children, out of a total population of 700 in a hamlet listed on maps as My Lai 4. As Hersh later reported, Calley and Charlie Company were acting under orders to destroy the village. In the weeks and months that followed, My Lai became a synonym for war crimes and a metaphor for American conduct in Southeast Asia and provoked a spasm of national conscience-searching. Hersh's revelation of the My Lai massacre was widely and immediately recognized as a significant moment in the history of the Vietnam War.[8]

In retrospect, Hersh's account was also a key moment in the history of journalism. For one thing, he single-handledly brought to war reporting the language of war-crimes trials. Vietnam correspondents who had witnessed but never reported atrocities suddenly recognized that the killings of civilians counted as news. Frank McCullough of *Time* magazine, for instance, covered the war for four years without reporting on American atrocities. But after My Lai broke, he felt moved to recall seeing Viet Cong prisoners pushed from airplanes by American troops, shot with their hands tied behind their backs, and devoured by

8 Hersh, S. 1970. *My Lai 4: A Report on the Massacre and Its Aftermath.* New York, Random House.

Dobermans unleashed by interrogators. Many other reporters told similar stories: it was as if the press suddenly had official sanction to report a previously suppressed government secret—when in fact the only suppression had been by the reporters themselves, of their own moral vocabulary and news judgment.

A few years later, the veteran *Times* Vietnam correspondent Neil Sheehan—to whom a former Pentagon analyst named Daniel Ellsberg entrusted the Pentagon Papers—described the thinking of American war reporters before My Lai. Sheehan recalled that in 1966, three years before Calley's court-martial, he witnessed U.S. troops wiping out five Vietnamese fishing villages, killing as many as 600 civilians. The raids "seemed unnecessarily brutal" but "it did not occur to me that I had discovered a possible war crime." He went on: "I had never read the laws governing the conduct of war, though I had watched the war for three years in Vietnam and written about it for five. . . . The Army field manual says it is illegal to attack hospitals. We routinely bombed and shelled them. . . . Looking back, one realizes the war crimes issue was always present." Hersh's stories changed the underlying presumption of reporters and editors about what counts as news.[9]

And the impact of that single investigative series did not end with Vietnam. Hersh's My Lai exposé apparently marks the first instance on record in which investigative reporting did the spadework of documenting large-scale mass murder. As historian Walter Lacquer points out, nothing like that had happened with the Holocaust, in either the American or British press. Nor did it happen in the early cold war, when contending superpowers and their surrogates piled up corpses from Southeast Asia to Latin America. Hersh's My Lai report—defining not just a criminal act of mass murder but a specific chain of responsibility—pointed the way. The years since 1969 have seen the rise of human-rights investigative reporters, some of whose work in Central America in

9 Knightley, P. 1976. *The First Casualty: From the Crimea to Vietnam: The War Correspondent as Hero, Propogandist and Myth Maker.* New York, Praeger.

the 1980s and the Balkans in the past decade appears in these pages. Educated in the language of war-crimes trials, inspired by the standards of Nuremberg and the Genocide Convention, all of them look over their shoulder at My Lai. That pivotal story of November 1969 teaches a central lesson: how a single compelling investigative report can, like Hersh's Pinkville exposé, radically alter the terms of public discourse for years forward.

Looking over two centuries of investigative reporting, it also becomes evident that journalists have had to be literary and intellectual innovators, constantly creating the techniques of research and storytelling and analysis for a democratic and unregulated press. How can enticing, even thrilling writing be made from account ledgers, court exhibits, forensic notes—and all on deadline and in limited space? The selections in this volume are filled with invention. Who until Ida Tarbell even thought to write the biography of a corporation? Who until I.F. Stone thought to patiently use public documents to expose public lies about war? Who until Rachel Carson thought to turn scientific studies into a vivid warning of environmental destruction? No storytellers in history had ever contended with such questions.

Investigative reporters tend to think of themselves as journalistic John Waynes, mapping a solitary quest on the frontier of exposure. But taking their work together, one is struck by how these journalists seem engaged in an unconscious conversation with distant, long-dead colleagues whose writing or name the contemporary reporter may not know but whose themes and craft still resonate. Read Steve Mills and Ken Armstrong of the *Chicago Tribune* on falsely convicted Illinois death-row inmates alongside Ida Wells's work on victims of lynching one hundred years before; Jack Anderson's disclosure of corruption in the Nixon Justice Department alongside the *New York Times* on the Tweed Ring; Marvel Cooke's "infiltration" of the 1950s Bronx domestic-work market alongside Nellie Bly's ten days in the madhouse (and in turn alongside Barbara Ehrenreich's recent best-seller *Nickel and Dimed*); William Greider's dissections of contemporary corporate autocracy alongside Henry Adams and Lincoln Steffens.

All those "conversations" are finally about how the story of democracy—the story of those who have power and those who don't—gets told. It seems especially urgent to ask that question at the present moment. As I write, American journalism is beset by two alarming developments. One is an administration in Washington that is more hostile to journalistic inquiry than any in decades. The George W. Bush presidency may be transient, but it has bred a culture of secrecy—and specific measures, including squelching of the Freedom of Information Act—that will outlive it and sooner or later spread beyond the beltway to the states, making reporters' jobs at every level more difficult.

The second trend—part of the much larger story of corporate globalization—is the concentration of media ownership into an ever-shrinking handful of megacorporations. Corporate media predators profoundly threaten investigative reporting. A generation and more ago, interference from publishers was often unvarnished and direct, as a youthful George Seldes found out in 1909, when on his first reporting job he wrote about sexual harassment in a Pittsburgh department store that happened to be a major advertiser at his paper. Seldes was nearly fired, and the story landed on the spike.[10] In today's media environment, such overt censorship is rare. The threat is more likely to the budget, the freedom, the resources needed to conduct investigative reporting, the willingness of corporate news managers to hire reporters who might rock the boat or to free them from constrictive beats.

Yet to review the biographies of troublemaking reporters is also to recognize that investigative journalism has shown enormous resilience in the face of business pressure. Media critics like Mark Crispin Miller and Robert McChesney—themselves notable muckrakers of corporate concentration—tend to focus on "the media" in monolithic, institutional terms, as nothing more than vehicles for communicating the agenda of the world's elites. Ownership, goes the argument, determines content.

10 Seldes, G. 1987. *Witness to a Century: Encounters with the Noted, the Notorious and the Three SOBs.* New York, Ballantine Books.

But the history of investigative reporting suggests something more complicated: a constant push-and-pull between media owners' interests and the quiet determination of reporters to subvert them. It is a mistake to underestimate the ability of reporters working even in corporate-owned media to document abuses of power, and an even bigger mistake to underestimate the ability of news consumers to get the message.

This book emerged from a seminar on investigative journalism I have taught since 1993 at Yale University. The class is a practical and hands-on introduction to the craft, but when I first conceived of the seminar I also wanted to give my students examples of provocative and influential investigative literature. I remembered my excitement as a teenager following the breaking Watergate scandal and the sense of stunned revelation I felt at my first reading of *Silent Spring.* I wanted readings that would inspire my students in the same way. I wanted material to illustrate essential reporting and narrative techniques. I wanted selections that would give some sense of the historical evolution of investigative journalism as well as its formal breadth, from daily newspaper and monthly magazine stories to book-length inquiries. I found to my astonishment that no such collection exists. So at first out of frustration, then with increasing enthusiasm, I began assembling my own reading list.

Historians of journalism will probably find no end of omissions: I'll preemptively mention Paul Anderson's reporting on the Teapot Dome scandal, Frank Norris's reportage on the stock market, Charles Edward Russell's wide-ranging and principled muckraking, Phillip Meyer's pioneering use of sociological research in the *Detroit Free Press* accounts of that city's 1967 riots, Don Bartlett and Jim Steele's innovative computer-assisted investigation of Philadelphia prisons in the early 1970s. All these, and others, are important to the history of investigative reporting, but I decided with regret that for one reason or another they don't work well in this anthology. So I leave readers to the investigative exercise of tracking down those stories in a research library. I found that some investigative books I love—among them Peter Mattheissen's *In the Spirit of Crazy Horse* and J. Anthony Lukas's incomparable *Common Ground*—simply do not lend themselves to excerpting in ways that would make sense in the context of this book. I have found myself favoring magazine and book reporting over newspapers for pragmatic literary reasons: some of the most important newspaper investigations are written in concise shorthand that doesn't hold up to rereading (perhaps a warning to investigative reporters too absorbed in research methods at the expense of the yarn). I have sharply limited selections from the muckraking era because the muckrakers are amply documented elsewhere. I direct readers who want to explore the full range of this movement to a superb anthology, decades out of print but still on library shelves (and richly deserving of republication), Arthur and Lila Weinberg's *The Muckrakers*; and to an excellent recent biography, *The Pen Is Mightier: The Muckraking Life of Charles Edward Russell* by Robert Miraldi.

Finally, I have deliberately limited my choices from the last decade to three selections that announce key themes facing journalists headed into this new, disorienting century. Anyone looking for recent reporting on Enron or transnational terrorism will have to wait for the judgment of history.

The tradition of investigative journalism is diverse, contentious, and deeply connected to the most enduring themes of American politics and culture. Draft all the contributors in this volume into an investigative journalists' hall of fame, and more than a handful would probably resign in protest at some of the other choices. But all of them, any of them, would probably feel a tremor of recognition at the great and terrifying moment when Melville's Captain Ahab tries to convince his crew to join his quest for the White Whale. Seizing the shrouds, peg leg driven into the wood of the Pequod's quarterdeck, he nails to the mast a doubloon: reward for the first sailor who spots his nemesis. As the Pequod's sailors cheer the hunt in atavistic frenzy Ahab turns to his prudent, cerebral first mate, Starbuck, who sees nothing but pursuit of a dumb beast. Listen, says Ahab: this is more than just a whale hunt; it is pursuit of both evil and truth: "All visible objects, man, are but as pasteboard masks. But in each event—in the living act, the undoubted deed—there, some unknown but still reasoning thing puts forth the mouldings of its features from behind the unreasoning mask. If man will strike, strike through the mask!"

"Strike through the mask!" is the exhortation and ambition of every journalist in this book. Great reporters like Hersh, Wells, Bache, or Carson are about more than just exposing singular abuses and wrongdoings. In their voices we hear a distinct echo of Melville's obsessed captain: the immovable conviction that beneath the surface of public events—"in the living act, the undoubted deed"—lies a deeper and darker tale that must be hunted down and wrenched to daylight.

BRUCE SHAPIRO
New Haven, Connecticut
February 2003

I.

THE INVENTION OF EXPOSURE: 1798–1900

Benjamin Franklin Bache

The grandson of Benjamin Franklin, Benjamin Bache (1769–1798) accompanied Franklin to Europe and was educated under his supervision. In 1793 Bache used his inheritance from Franklin to start a newspaper, the Philadelphia Aurora and General Advertiser. *Bache's journalism was both personal and partisan; he was a close ally of Thomas Jefferson and a relentless critic of the Federalists. His network of friends and informants provided Bache with a series of controversial scoops, culminating in 1798 when he published leaked dispatches concerning the XYZ affair. Enraged Federalists in Congress passed the Alien and Sedition acts and secured the indictment of Bache for seditious libel. Before he could be tried Bache died in a yellow-fever epidemic.*

In this Aurora *dispatch, dating from 1795, "A Calm Observer" opens the Washington administration's account books to scrutiny. It is the earliest journalistic allegation of political corruption to directly and thoroughly quote a leaked government document. "A Calm Observer" was actually the clerk of Congress, who had access to the administration's records—a post-Revolutionary Deep Throat.*

A CALM OBSERVER

From the *Philadelphia Aurora and General Advertiser,* 1795

To Oliver Wolcott Esq. late Comptroller, now Secretary of the Treasury of the United States.

Sir,

When a man who has been advanced from an inferior to a superior station in the Government and called upon to execute a high and responsible public office, deliberately violates every obligation of duty, overleaps the barriers of the constitution, and breaks down the fences of the law, contemning and despising every principle which the People have established for the security of their rights and to restrain the arbitrary encroachments of power, what, I ask, Sir, is the degree of guilt of such a man? And to you, is the enquiry particularly addressed, for as Nathan said unto David 'Thou art the man,' and by your own acts shall you be condemned.

Attend then, Sir, to the following particulars and state of facts.

On the 30th day of April 1789, the President of the United States qualified into office and took the following oath: "I do solemnly swear that I will faithfully execute the office of President of the United States; and will to the best of my ability, preserve, protect and defend the Constitution of the United States."

By a clause in the 1st section of the 2d article of the Constitution, it is declared, "that the President shall, *at stated times,* receive, for his services, a compensation, which shall neither be encreased nor diminished during the period for which he shall have been elected, and he shall not receive, within that period, any other emolument from the United States, or any of them."

By the 3d Section of the same Article it is directed "that the President of the United States shall take care that the laws be faithfully executed."

By a clause in the 9th Section of the first Article it is declared "that no money shall be drawn from the Treasury, but in consequence of appropriations made by law."

By the act of Congress to establish the Treasury department passed the 2d of September 1789 it is made the duty of the Secretary of the Treasury "to grant under the limitations therein established or thereafter to be established, all warrants for money to be issued from the Treasury in pursuance of appropriations by law."

By the same act it is made the duty of the Comptroller of the Treasury, "to countersign all warrants drawn by the Secretary of the Treasury *which shall be warranted by law.*"

By the act of Congress, supplemental to the act establishing the Treasury department passed the 3d day of March 1791, it is directed that every officer in the said department shall take an oath "well and faithfully to execute the trust committed to him."

By the act of Congress for allowing a compensation to the President, passed the 24th of September 1789, there is allowed to the President *at the rate of* 25,000 dollars per annum, *for his services* to commence with the time of entering on the duties of his office, to continue as long as he should remain in office, and to be paid *quarterly* out of the Treasury of the United States.

By an annual act of Congress, provision is made for the President's compensation by a specific appropriation of the sum of 25,000 dollars and no more.

Between the 30th of April 1789, the day on which the President qualified into office and the 30th of April 1790, which completed the first year of his Presidency he drew by warrants from the late Secretary of the Treasury countersigned by the Comptroller the sum of 25,000 dollars and no more.[1]

Between the 30th of April 1790 and the 30th of April 1791 being the second year of his service the President drew by like warrants the sum of 30,150 dollars, being an excess beyond annual compensation made by law and the appropriation thereof by Congress of 5,150 dollars.

Between the 30th of April 1791 and the 30th of April 1792, being the third year of his service the President drew by like warrants the sum of 24,000 dollars which being 1,000 dollars less than his annual compensation reduced the excess that he received the year before to 4,150 dollars.

Between the 30th of April 1792 and the 30th of April 1793 being the fourth year of his service the President drew by like warrants the sum of 26,000 dollars which again made up the excess of his second year's compensation to 5,150 dollars more than the law allows.

On the 4th of March 1793 when the first term of four years for which the President was elected into office expired, he had drawn from the public Treasury by warrants from the late Secretary of the Treasury, countersigned by the Comptroller the sum of 1,037 dollars beyond the compensation allowed him by law estimating from the day he qualified into office.

The evidence of the sums drawn and of the truth of the facts here stated, will be seen in the official reports made to Congress of the annual

1 Mr. Eveleigh was then Comptroller

receipts and expenditures of the public monies, signed by you as Comptroller of the Treasury, and which have been published for the information of the people.

But, Sir, as if it had been determined by the late Secretary of the Treasury, and yourself as Comptroller, to set at defiance all law and authority, and to exhibit the completest evidence of servile submission and compliance with the lawless will and pleasure of a President, attend to the following facts:

On the 4th of March 1793, the President qualified into office and commenced the second term of four years for which he was re-elected.

On the 18th February 1793 Congress passed an act providing "that from and after the 3d day of March in the present year (1793) the compensation of the President of the United States shall be *at the rate of 25,000 dollars per annum, in full for his services, to be paid QUARTER YEARLY at the Treasury.*"

Between the 4th day of March 1793, and the 4th day of June following, being the first quarter after the passing of the last mentioned act, there was paid to the President out of the public Treasury by warrants from the late Secretary of the Treasury, countersigned by you as Comptroller, the sum of eleven thousand dollars, being an excess of 4,750 dollars in one quarter beyond the compensation allowed by law, and making at the same rate a compensation of 44,000 dollars per annum instead of the 25,000 dollars, fixed by Congress.

Upon you, Sir, the late Secretary of the Treasury and the President must rest the responsibility of these extraordinary outrages upon the laws and Constitution of our country; since it remains to be seen how far the independent & impartial justice of the National Legislature will be exercised in punishment of the offence already committed as well as to prevent the repetition of it hereafter. In vain, Sir, are the numerous prohibitions of the Constitution and of the laws; in vain, Sir, are all the obligations of oaths and duty, and in vain will be all future precautions of the Legislature to guard the chastity of the public treasury from lawless violation and abuse, if one man can exalt himself above the law and with impunity disregard those high restraints which the people have ordained.

Is there any other man in the government of the United States who would have dared to ask, or to whom you and your predecessor in office would have presumed to grant the like favour?

Is it or is it not a small favour to receive 4,750 dollars of the public money in one quarter beyond the amount of legal salary, and in addition to the former excess of 1,037 dollars, already in hand and not refunded?[2]

If the precedent which this donation from the treasury furnishes, were to be followed in favour of other public officers, how many hundred thousand dollars per annum would thus be lawlessly taken from the public treasury and saddled upon the people? Was it or was it not the duty of the late Secretary of the Treasury and of yourself as Comptroller to have checked and restrained the abuse of power that has been stated, and why, instead of doing so, did you become, obedient like, the servile and submissive instruments of it?

Can the people feel respect for the constituted authorities of their country, when those very constituted authorities are the first to trample upon the laws and Constitution of their country?

What will posterity say to the man who has acted in the manner I have stated, after having thus solemnly addressed the Legislature of his country: "When I was first honoured with a call into the service of my country, then on the eve of an arduous struggle for its liberties, the light in which I contemplated my duty required that I should renounce every pecuniary compensation. From this resolution I have in no instance departed; and, being still under the impressions which produced it, I must decline as inapplicable to myself any share in the personal emoluments which may be indispensably included in a permanent provision for the executive department, and must accordingly pray that the pecuniary estimates for the station in which I am placed, may, during my continuance in it, be limited to such actual expenditures as

2 It will hereafter be seen whether the excess of compensation has been continued up to the present time, and to what amount?

the public good may be thought to require"? Will not the world be led to conclude that the mask of political hypocricy has been alike worn by a CESAR, a CROMWELL and a WASHINGTON?

A CALM OBSERVER.

John Barber

In 1839 residents of the Connecticut shoreline reported seeing a "long low black schooner," "full of Negros," in Long Island Sound. The schooner was the Amistad—a Spanish vessel that was transporting a cargo of Mendi slaves, taken captive in Sierra Leone and purchased at auction in Cuba. On the third day of the voyage from Havana to a Cuban plantation, the slaves rebelled, led by Sengbe Pieh, whom the Spaniards called Joseph Cingue. The slaves ordered the crew to steer toward the rising sun—back to Africa—but at night the crew changed direction up the North American coast. Captured in Long Island Sound by a U.S. Navy ship, the Amistad slaves were jailed in New Haven, and the Spaniards who had purchased them in Havana went to court to demand their return.

New Haven newspaper editor, novelist, and religious essayist John Warner Barber (1798–1885) was a member of the Amistad Committee, a group of prominent abolitionists who organized the captives' defense. His A History of the Amistad Captives *told their story, incorporating newspaper accounts, court transcripts, and the words of the captives themselves, made possible only when New Haven linguist Josiah Gibbs painstakingly located a translator on the New York docks. This passage is a notable early attempt at the documentation of human-rights abuse through direct accounts by its victims—a technique that echoes in contemporary reporting on genocide and mass murder.*

The Amistad case eventually reached the U.S. Supreme Court, which ordered the captives sent home to Sierra Leone.

FROM A HISTORY OF THE AMISTAD CAPTIVES (NEW HAVEN, 1840)

MONDAY, Oct. 7.

This afternoon, almost the first time in which the two interpreters Covey and Pratt have not been engaged with special reference to the trial to take place in November, one of the captives named Grabeau, was requested to give a narrative of himself since leaving Africa, for publication in the papers. The interpreters, who are considerably exhausted by the examinations which have already taken place, only gave the substance of what he said, without going into details, and it was not thought advisable to press the matter. Grabeau first gave an account of the passage from Africa to Havana. On board the vessel there was a large number of men, but the women and children were far the most numerous. They were fastened together in couples by the wrists and legs, and kept in that situation day and night. Here Grabeau and another of the Africans named Kimbo, lay down upon the floor, to show the painful position in which they were obliged to sleep. By day it was no better. The space between decks was so small,—according to their account not exceeding four feet,—that they were obliged, if they attempted to stand, to keep a crouching posture. The decks, fore and aft, were crowded to overflowing. They suffered (Grabeau said) terribly. They had rice enough to eat, but had very little to drink. If they left any of the rice that was given to them uneaten, either from sickness or any other cause, they were whipped. It was a common thing for them to be forced to eat so much as to vomit. Many of the men, women, and children died on the passage.

They were landed by night at a small village near Havana. Soon several white men came to buy them, and among them was the one claiming to be their master, whom they call Pipi, said to be a Spanish nick-name for Jose. Pipi, or Ruiz, selected such as he liked, and made them stand in a row. He then felt of each of them in every part of the body; made them open their mouths to see if their teeth were sound, and carried the examination to a degree of minuteness of which only a slave dealer would be guilty.

When they were separated from their companions who had come with them from Africa, there was weeping among the women and children, but Grabeau did not weep, "because he is a man." Kimbo, who sat by, said that he also shed no tears—but he thought of his home in Africa, and of friends left there whom he should never see again.

The men bought by Ruiz were taken on foot through Havana in the night, and put on board a vessel. During the night they were kept in irons, placed about the hands, feet and neck. They were treated during the day in a somewhat milder manner, though all the irons were never taken off at once. Their allowance of food was very scant, and of water still more so. They were very hungry, and suffered much in the hot days and nights from thirst. In addition to this there was much whipping, and the cook told them that when they reached land they would all be eaten. This "made their hearts burn." To avoid being eaten, and to escape the bad treatment they experienced, they rose upon the crew with the design of returning to Africa.

Such is the substance of Grabeau's story, confirmed by Kimbo, who was present most of the time. He says he likes the people of this country, because, to use his own expression, "they are good people—they believe in God, and there is no slavery here."

The story of Grabeau was then read and interpreted to Cingue, while a number of the other Africans were standing about, and confirmed by all of them in every particular. When the part relating to the crowded state of the vessel from Africa to Havana was read, Cingue added that there was scarcely room enough to sit or lie down. Another showed the marks of the irons on his wrists, which must at the time have been terribly lacerated. On their separation at Havana, Cingue remarked that almost all of them were in tears, and himself among the rest, "because they had come from the same country, and were now to part forever." To the question, how it was possible for the Africans, when chained in the manner he described, to rise upon the crew, he replied that the chain which connected the iron collars about their necks was fastened at the end by a padlock, and that this was first broken, and afterwards the other irons. Their object, he said, in the affray, was to make themselves free. He then requested it to be added to the above, that "if he tells a lie, God sees him by day and by night."

Herman Melville

Herman Melville (1819–1891) was never strictly speaking a journalist, but his years of service as a sailor and whale-man lent his early novels documentary authenticity. In White-Jacket*—written immediately before* Moby-Dick*—Melville took that documentary authority a step further, calling for reform of the U.S. Navy's brutal punishment system with precise accounts drawn from his own research and observation. Placing hair-raising factual polemic at the center of a fictionalized yarn,* White-Jacket *is a direct ancestor of twentieth-century muckraking novels such as* The Jungle *and* The Grapes of Wrath. *Like Upton Sinclair and John Steinbeck, Melville hoped his novel would prove an effective vehicle for making visible the abuses endured by a profoundly exploited population otherwise unknown to his readers.*

FLOGGING THROUGH THE FLEET

From *White-Jacket,* 1850

The flogging of an old man like Ushant, most landsmen will probably regard with abhorrence. But though, from peculiar circumstances, his case occasioned a good deal of indignation among the people of the Neversink, yet, upon its own proper grounds, they did not denounce it. Man-of-war's-men are so habituated to what landsmen would deem excessive cruelties, that they are almost reconciled to inferior severities.

And here, though the subject of punishment in the Navy has been canvassed in previous chapters, and though the thing is every way a most unpleasant and grievous one to enlarge upon, and though I painfully nerve myself to it while I write, a feeling of duty compels me to enter upon a branch of the subject till now undiscussed. I would not be like the man, who, seeing an outcast perishing by the road-side, turned about to his friend, saying, "Let us cross the way; my soul so sickens at this sight, that I can not endure it."

There are certain enormities in this man-of-war world that often secure impunity by their very excessiveness. Some ignorant people will refrain from permanently removing the cause of a deadly malaria, for fear of the temporary spread of its offensiveness. Let us not be of such.

The more repugnant and repelling, the greater the evil. Leaving our women and children behind, let us freely enter this Golgotha.

Years ago there was a punishment inflicted in the English, and I believe in the American Navy, called *keel-hauling*—a phrase still employed by man-of-war's-men when they would express some signal vengeance upon a personal foe. The practice still remains in the French national marine though it is by no means resorted to so frequently as in times past. It consists of attaching tackles to the two extremities of the main-yard, and passing the rope under the ship's bottom. To one end of this rope the culprit is secured; his own shipmates are then made to run him up and down, first on this side, then on that—now scraping the ship's hull under water—anon, hoisted, stunned and breathless, into the air.

But though this barbarity is now abolished from the English and American navies, there still remains another practice which, if any thing, is even worse than *keel-hauling.* This remnant of the Middle Ages is known in the Navy as *"flogging through the fleet."* It is never inflicted except by authority of a court-martial upon some trespasser deemed guilty of a flagrant offence. Never, that I know of, has it been inflicted by an American man-of-war on the home station. The reason, probably, is, that the officers well know that such a spectacle would raise a mob in any American sea-port.

By XLI. of the Articles of War, a court-martial shall not, "for any one offence not capital," inflict a punishment beyond one hundred lashes. In cases "not capital" this law may be, and has been, quoted in judicial justification of the infliction of more than one hundred lashes. Indeed, it would cover a thousand. Thus: One act of a sailor may be construed into the commission of ten different transgressions, for each of which he may be legally condemned to a hundred lashes, to be inflicted without intermission. It will be perceived, that in any case deemed "capital," a sailor, under the above Article, may legally be flogged to the death.

But neither by the Articles of War, nor by any other enactment of Congress, is there any direct warrant for the extraordinary cruelty of the mode in which punishment is inflicted, in cases of flogging through the fleet. But as in numerous other instances, the incidental aggravations of this penalty are indirectly covered by other clauses in the Articles of War; one of which authorizes the authorities of a ship—in certain indefinite cases—to correct the guilty "*according to the usages of the sea-service.*"

One of these "usages" is the following:

All hands being called "to witness punishment" in the ship to which the culprit belongs, the sentence of the court-martial condemning him is read, when, with the usual solemnities, a portion of the punishment is inflicted. In order that it shall not lose in severity by the slightest exhaustion in the arm of the executioner, a fresh boatswain's mate is called out at every dozen.

As the leading idea is to strike terror into the beholders, the greatest number of lashes is inflicted on board the culprit's own ship, in order to render him the more shocking spectacle to the crews of the other vessels.

The first infliction being concluded, the culprit's shirt is thrown over him, he is put into a boat—the Rogue's March being played meanwhile—and rowed to the next ship of the squadron. All hands of that ship are then called to man the rigging, and another portion of the punishment is inflicted by the boatswain's mates of that ship. The bloody shirt is again thrown over the seaman; and thus he is carried through the fleet or squadron till the whole sentence is inflicted.

In other cases, the launch—the largest of the boats—is rigged with a platform (like a headsman's scaffold), upon which halberds, something like those used in the English army, are erected. They consist of two stout poles, planted upright. Upon the platform stand a Lieutenant, a Surgeon, a Master-at-arms, and the executioners with their "cats." They are rowed through the fleet, stopping at each ship, till the whole sentence is inflicted, as before.

In some cases, the attending surgeon has professionally interfered before the last lash has been given, alleging that immediate death must ensue if the remainder should be administered without a respite. But instead of humanely remitting the remaining lashes, in a case like this, the man is generally consigned to his cot for ten or twelve days; and when the surgeon officially reports him capable of undergoing the rest of the sentence, it is forthwith inflicted. Shylock must have his pound of flesh.

To say, that after being flogged through the fleet, the prisoner's back is sometimes puffed up like a pillow; or to say that in other cases it looks as if burned black before a roasting fire; or to say that you may track him through the squadron by the blood on the bulwarks of every ship, would only be saying what many seamen have seen.

Several weeks, sometimes whole months, elapse before the sailor is sufficiently recovered to resume his duties. During the greater part of that interval he lies in the sick-bay, groaning out his days and nights; and unless he has the hide and constitution of a rhinoceros, he never is the man he was before, but, broken and shattered to the marrow of his bones, sinks into death before his time. Instances have occurred where he has expired the day after the punishment. No wonder that the Englishman, Dr. Granville—himself once a surgeon in the Navy—declares, in his work on Russia, that the barbarian "knout" itself is not a greater torture to undergo than the Navy cat-o'-nine-tails.

Some years ago a fire broke out near the powder magazine in an American national ship, one of a squadron at anchor in the Bay of Naples. The utmost alarm prevailed. A cry went fore and aft that the ship was about to blow up. One of the seamen sprang overboard in affright. At length the fire was got under, and the man was picked up. He was tried before a court-martial, found guilty of cowardice, and condemned to be flogged through the fleet. In due time the squadron made sail for Algiers, and in that harbor, once haunted by pirates, the punishment was inflicted—the Bay of Naples, though washing the shores of an absolute king, not being deemed a fit place for such an exhibition of American naval law.

While the Neversink was in the Pacific, an American sailor, who had deposited a vote for General Harrison for President of the United States, was flogged through the fleet.

Henry Adams

In 1869 the Wall Street tycoons Jay Gould and Jim Fisk sought to corner the national market on gold in order to finance expansion of the Erie Railway, which they had gained control of in a shareholder coup a year earlier. The result was a market panic.

Henry Adams (1838–1918) found the events, in his words, "startling—astounding—terrifying." Heir to one of the most famous names in American politics, he had chosen instead a career in literature, eventually leaving a prolific legacy: biographies, essays, a definitive history of the Jefferson and Madison administrations, and his own autobiography. In the machinations of Gould and Fisk, in their alliance with legislatures and courts controlled by New York's corrupt Tammany Hall, Adams saw an immense threat to democracy. "The corporation is in its nature a threat against the popular institutions which are spreading so rapidly over the whole world," he wrote. Together with his brother Charles Francis Adams, Jr., Henry Adams set out to tell the inside story—observing Congress, mastering the intricacies of Wall Street, interviewing Jim Fisk and other key players, and finally producing a small masterpiece of explanatory journalism on a nationwide corporate scandal.

FROM CHAPTERS OF ERIE

1872

It was the morning of Thursday, the 3d; Gould and Fisk went to Broad Street together, but as usual Gould was silent and secret, while Fisk was noisy and communicative. There was now a complete separation in their movements. Gould acted entirely through his own firm of Smith, Gould, & Martin, while Fisk operated principally through his old partner, Belden. One of Smith's principal brokers testifies:—

> 'Fisk never could do business with Smith, Gould, & Martin very comfortably. They would not do business for him. It was a very uncertain thing of course where Fisk might be. He is an erratic sort of genius. I don't think anybody would want to follow him

> very long. I am satisfied that Smith, Gould, & Martin controlled their own gold, and were ready to do as they pleased with it without consulting Fisk. I do not think there was any general agreement. . . . None of us who knew him cared to do business with him. I would not have taken an order from him nor had anything to do with him.' Belden was considered a very low fellow. 'I never had anything to do with him or his party,' said one broker employed by Gould. 'They were men I had a perfect detestation of; they were no company for me. I should not have spoken to them at all under any ordinary circumstances.' Another says, 'Belden is a man in whom I never had any confidence in any way. For months before that, I would not have taken him for a gold transaction.'

And yet Belden bought millions upon millions of gold. He himself says he had bought twenty millions by this Thursday evening, and this without capital or credit except that of his brokers. Meanwhile Gould, on reaching the city, had at once given secret orders to sell. From the moment he left Corbin, he had but one idea, which was to get rid of his gold as quietly as possible. "I purchased merely enough to make believe I was a bull," says Gould. This double process continued all that afternoon. Fisk's wild purchases carried the price up to 144, and the panic in the street became more and more serious as the bears realized the extremity of their danger. No one can tell how much gold which did not exist they had contracted to deliver or pay the difference in price. One of the clique brokers swears that on this Thursday evening the street had sold the clique one hundred and eighteen millions of gold, and every rise of one per cent on this sum implied a loss of more than £200,000 to the bears. Naturally the terror was extreme, for half Broad Street and thousands of speculators would have been ruined if compelled to settle gold at 150 which they had sold at 140. It need scarcely be said that by this time nothing more was heard in regard to philanthropic theories of benefit to the Western farmer.

Mr. Gould's feelings can easily be imagined. He knew that Fisk's reckless management would bring the government upon his shoulders, and he knew that unless he could sell his gold before the order came from Washington he would be a ruined man. He knew, too, that Fisk's contracts must inevitably be repudiated. This Thursday evening he sat at his desk in the Erie offices at the opera-house, while Fisk and Fisk's brokers chattered about him.

> I was transacting my railway business. I had my own views about the market, and my own fish to fry. I was all alone, so to speak, in what I did, and I did not let any of those people know exactly how I stood. I got no ideas from anything that was said there. I had been selling gold from 35 up all the time, and I did not know till the next morning that there would probably come an order about twelve o'clock to sell gold.

He had not told Fisk a word in regard to Corbin's retreat, nor his own orders to sell.

When the next day came, Gould and Fisk went together to Broad Street, and took possession of the private back office of a principal broker, "without asking the privilege of doing so," as the broker observes in his evidence. The first news brought to Gould was a disaster. The government had sent three men from Washington to examine the bank which Gould owned, and the bank sent word to Mr. Gould that it feared to certify for him as usual, and was itself in danger of a panic, caused by the presence of officers, which created distrust of the bank. It barely managed to save itself. Gould took the information silently, and his firm redoubled sales of gold. His partner, Smith, gave the orders to one broker after another,—"Sell ten millions!" "The order was given as quick as a flash, and away he went," says one of these men. "I sold only eight millions." "Sell, sell, sell! do nothing but sell!—only don't sell to Fisk's brokers," were the orders which Smith himself acknowledges. In the gold-room Fisk's brokers were shouting their rising bids, and the packed crowd grew frantic with terror and rage as each successive rise showed their increasing losses. The wide streets outside were thronged with excited people; the telegraph offices were overwhelmed with messages ordering sales or purchases of gold or stocks; and the whole nation was watching eagerly to see what the result of this convulsion was to be. All trade was stopped, and even the President felt that it was time to raise his hand. No one who has not seen the New York gold-room can understand the spectacle it presented; now a perfect pandemonium, now silent as the grave. Fisk, in his dark back office across the street, with his coat off, swaggered up and down, "a big cane in his hand," and called himself the Napoleon of Wall Street. He really believed that he directed the movement, and while the street outside imagined that he and Gould were one family, and that his purchases were made for the clique, Gould was silently flinging away his gold at any price he could get for it.

Whether Fisk really expected to carry out his contract, and force the bears to settle, or not, is doubtful; but the evidence seems to show that he was in earnest, and felt sure of success. His orders were unlimited. "Put it up to 150," was one which he sent to the gold-room. Gold rose to 150. At length the bid was made—"160 for any part of five millions," and no one any longer dared take it. "161 for five millions,"—"162 for five millions." No answer was made, and the offer was repeated,—"162 for any part of five millions." A voice replied, "Sold one million at 62." The bubble suddenly burst, and within fifteen minutes, amid an excitement without parallel even in the wildest excitements of the war, the clique brokers were literally swept away, and left struggling by themselves, bidding still 160 for gold in millions which no one would any longer take their word for; while the premium sank rapidly to 135. A moment later the telegraph brought from Washington the government order to sell, and the result was no longer possible to dispute. Mr. Fisk had gone too far, while Mr. Gould had secretly weakened the ground under his feet.

Gould, however, was saved. His fifty millions were sold; and although no one yet knows what his gains or losses may have been, his firm was now able to meet its contracts and protect its brokers. Fisk was in a very different situation. So soon as it became evident that his brokers would be unable to carry out their contracts, every one who had sold gold to them turned in wrath to Fisk's office. Fortunately for him it was protected by armed men whom he had brought with him from his castle of Erie; but nevertheless the excitement was so great that both Mr. Fisk and Mr. Gould thought it best to retire as rapidly as possible by a back entrance leading into another street, and to seek the protection of the opera-house. There nothing but an army could disturb them; no civil mandate was likely to be served without their permission within these walls, and few men would care to face Fisk's ruffians in order to force an entrance.

The subsequent winding up of this famous conspiracy may be stated in few words. But no account could possibly be complete which failed to reproduce in full the story of Mr. Fisk's last interview with Mr. Corbin, as told by Fisk himself.

> I went down to the neighborhood of Wall Street, Friday morning, and the history of that morning you know. When I got back to our office, you can imagine I was in no enviable state of mind, and the moment I got up street that afternoon I started right round to old Corbin's to rake him out. I went into the room, and sent word that Mr. Fisk wanted to see him in the dining-room. I was too mad to say anything civil, and when he came into the room, said I, 'You damned old scoundrel, do you know what you have done here, you and your people?' He began to wring his hands, and, 'Oh!' he says, 'this is a horrible position. Are you ruined?' I said I didn't know whether I was or not; and I asked him again if he knew what had happened? He had been crying, and said he had just heard; that he had been sure everything was all right; but that something had occurred entirely different from what he had anticipated. Said I, 'That don't amount to anything; we know that gold ought not to be at 31, and that it would not be but for such performances as you have had this last week; you know damned well it would not if you had not failed.' I knew that somebody had run a saw

> right into us, and said I, 'This whole damned thing has turned out just as I told you it would.' I considered the whole party a pack of cowards, and I expected that when we came to clear our hands they would sock it right into us. I said to him, 'I don't know whether you have lied or not, and I don't know what ought to be done with you.' He was on the other side of the table, weeping and wailing, and I was gnashing my teeth. 'Now,' he says, 'you must quiet yourself.' I told him I didn't want to be quiet. I had no desire to ever be quiet again, and probably never should be quiet again. He says, 'But, my dear sir, you will lose your reason.' Says I, 'Speyers [a broker employed by him that day] has already lost his reason; reason has gone out of everybody but me.' I continued, 'Now what are you going to do? You have got us into this thing, and what are you going to do to get out of it?' He says, 'I don't know. I will go and get my wife.' I said, 'Get her down here!' The soft talk was all over. He went up stairs and they returned, tottling into the room, looking older than Stephen Hopkins. His wife and he both looked like death. He was tottling just like that. [Illustrated by a trembling movement of his body.] I have never seen him from that day to this.

This is sworn evidence before a committee of Congress; and its humor is perhaps the more conspicuous, because there is every reason to believe that there is not a word of truth in the story from beginning to end. No such interview ever occurred, except in the unconfined apartments of Mr. Fisk's imagination. His own previous statements make it certain that he was not at Corbin's house at all that day, and that Corbin did come to the Erie offices that evening, and again the next morning. Corbin himself denies the truth of the account without limitation; and adds, that when he entered the Erie offices the next morning Fisk was there. "I asked him how Mr. Gould felt after the great calamity of the day before." He remarked, "O, he has no courage at all. He has sunk right down. There is nothing left of him but a heap of clothes and a pair of eyes." The internal evidence of truth in this anecdote would support Mr. Corbin against the world.[3]

In regard to Mr. Gould, Fisk's graphic description was probably again inaccurate. Undoubtedly the noise and scandal of the moment were extremely unpleasant to this silent and impenetrable intriguer. The city was in a ferment, and the whole country pointing at him with wrath.

3 Mr. Fisk to the Editor of the Sun:—

Erie Railway Company, Comptroller's Office,

NEW YORK, October 4, 1869.

TO THE EDITOR OF THE SUN.

Dear Sir,—. . . Mr. Corbin has constantly associated with me; . . . *he spent more than an hour with me in the Erie Railway Office on the afternoon of Saturday, September 25th, the day after the gold panic.* . . . I enclose you a few affidavits which will give you further information concerning this matter.

I remain your obedient servant,

JAMES FISK, JR.

Affidavit of Charles W. Pollard.

"State of New York, City and County of New York, ss.

"C. W. Pollard, being duly sworn, says: 'I have frequently been the bearer of messages between Mr. James Fisk, Jr., and Mr. Abel R. Corbin, brother-in-law of President Grant. . . . Mr. Corbin called on me at the Erie building on Thursday, 23d September, 1869, telling me he came to see how Messrs. Fisk and Gould were getting along. . . . He called again on Friday, the following day, at about noon; appeared to be greatly excited and said he feared *we* should lose a great deal of money. The following morning, Saturday, September 25, Mr. Fisk told me to take his carriage and call upon Mr. Corbin and say to him that he and Mr. Gould would like to see him (Corbin) at their office. I called and saw Mr. Corbin. He remarked upon greeting me: "How does Mr. Fisk bear his losses?" and added, "*It is terrible for us.*" He then asked me to bring Mr. Fisk up to his house immediately, as he was indisposed, and did not feel able to go down to his (Fisk's) office. I went after Mr. Fisk, who returned immediately with me to Mr. Corbin's residence, but shortly after came out with Mr. Corbin, who accompanied him to Mr. Fisk's office, where he was closeted with him and Mr. Gould for about two hours. . . .' "

There are obvious inconsistencies among these different accounts, which it is useless to attempt to explain. The fact of Saturday's interview appears, however, to be beyond dispute.

The machinery of the gold exchange had broken down, and he alone could extricate the business community from the pressing danger of a general panic. He had saved himself, it is true; but in a manner which could not have been to his taste. Yet his course from this point must have been almost self-evident to his mind, and there is no reason to suppose that he hesitated.

His own contracts were all fulfilled. Fisk's contracts, all except one, in respect to which the broker was able to compel a settlement, were repudiated. Gould probably suggested to Fisk that it was better to let Belden fail, and to settle a handsome fortune on him, than to sacrifice something more than £1,000,000 in sustaining him. Fisk therefore threw Belden over, and swore that he had acted only under Belden's order; in support of which statement he produced a paper to the following effect:—

> September 24.
>
> DEAR SIR,—I hereby authorize you to order the purchase and sale of gold on my account during this day to the extent you may deem advisable, and to report the same to me as early as possible. It is to be understood that the profits of such order are to belong entirely to me, and I will, of course, bear any losses resulting.
>
> Yours,
>
> WILLIAM BELDEN.
>
> JAMES FISK JR.

This document was not produced in the original, and certainly never existed. Belden himself could not be induced to acknowledge the order; and no one would have believed him if he had done so. Meanwhile the matter is before the national courts, and Fisk may probably be held to his contracts: but it will be far more difficult to execute judgment upon him, or to discover his assets.

One of the first acts of the Erie gentlemen after the crisis was to summon their lawyers, and set in action their judicial powers. The object was to prevent the panic-stricken brokers from using legal process to force settlements, and so render the entanglement inextricable. Messrs. Field and Shearman came, and instantly prepared a considerable number of injunctions, which were sent to their judges, signed at once, and immediately served. Gould then was able to dictate the terms of settlement; and after a week of complete paralysis, Broad Street began at last to show signs of returning life. As a legal curiosity, one of these documents, issued three months after the crisis, may be reproduced, in order to show the powers wielded by the Erie managers:—

> SUPREME COURT.
> H. N. SMITH, JAY GOULD, H. H. MARTIN,
> and J. B. BACH, Plaintiffs,
> against
> JOHN BONNER and ARTHUR L. SEWELL,
>
> } Injunction by order
>
> Defendants,
> It appearing satisfactorily to me by the complaint duly verified by the plaintiffs that sufficient grounds for an order of injunction exist, I do hereby order and enjoin. . . . That the defendants, John Bonner and Arthur L. Sewell, their agents, attorneys, and servants, refrain from pressing their pretended claims against the plaintiffs, or either of them, before the Arbitration Committee of the New York Stock Exchange, or from taking any proceedings thereon, or in relation thereto, except in this action.
> GEORGE G. BARNARD, J. S. C.
> NEW YORK, December 29, 1869.

Mr. Bonner had practically been robbed with violence by Mr. Gould, and instead of his being able to bring the robber into court as the criminal, the robber brought him into court as criminal, and the judge forbade him to appear in any other character. Of all Mr. Field's distinguished legal reforms and philanthropic projects, this injunction is beyond a doubt the most brilliant and the most successful.[4]

The fate of the conspirators was not severe. Mr. Corbin went to

4 These remarks on Mr. Field's professional conduct as counsel of the Erie Railway have excited a somewhat intemperate controversy, and Mr. Field's partisans in the press have made against the authors of the "Chapters of Erie" a charge which certainly has the merit of even exaggerated modesty on the part of the New York bench and bar, namely, that these writers "have indelicately interfered in a matter alien to them in every way"; the administration of justice in New York being, in this point of view, a matter in which Mr. Field and the Erie Railway are alone concerned. Mr. Field himself has published a letter in the *Westminster Review* for April, 1871, in which, after the general assertion that the passages in the "New York Gold Conspiracy" which relate to him "cover about as much untruth as could be crowded into so many lines," he proceeds to make the following corrections:

First, he denies, what was never suggested, that he was in any way a party to the origin or progress of the Gold Conspiracy; until (secondly) he was consulted on the 28th of September; when (thirdly) he gave an opinion as to the powers of the members of the Gold and Stock Exchanges. Fourthly, he denies that he has relations of any sort with any judge in New York, or any power over these judges, other than such as English counsel have in respect to English judges. Fifthly, he asserts that out of twenty-eight injunctions growing out of the gold transactions, his partners obtained only ten, and only one of these ten, the one quoted above, from Justice Barnard. Sixthly, that this injunction was proper to be sought and granted. Seventhly, that Mr. Bonner was not himself the person who had been "robbed with violence," but the assignee of the parties.

On the other hand it does not appear that Mr. Field denies that the injunction as quoted is genuine, or that he is responsible for it, or that it did, as asserted, shut the defendants out of the courts as well as out of the Gold Exchange Arbitration Committee, or that it compelled them to appear only as defendants in a case where they were the injured parties.

In regard to the power which Mr. Field, whether as a private individual or as Erie counsel, has exercised over the New York bench, his modest denial is hardly calculated to serve as a final answer. And in regard to Mr. Bonner, the fact of his being principal or representative scarcely affects the character of Mr. Field's injunction. Finally, so far as the text is concerned, after allowing full weight to all Mr. Field's corrections, the public can decide for itself how many untruths it contains. The subject has, however, ceased to be one of consequence even to Mr. Field since the subsequent violent controversy which arose in March, 1871, in regard to other points of Mr. Field's professional conduct, and in another month after his letter was written he would perhaps have thought the comments of the *Westminster Review* so comparatively trifling in importance as not to deserve his attention.

Washington, where he was snubbed by the President, and at once disappeared from public view, only coming to light again before the Congressional Committee. General Butterfield, whose share in the transaction is least understood, was permitted to resign his office without an investigation. Speculation for the next six months was at an end. Every person involved in the affair seemed to have lost money, and dozens of brokers were swept from the street. But Mr. Jay Gould and Mr. James Fisk, Jr., continued to reign over Erie, and no one can say that their power or their credit was sensibly diminished by a shock which for the time prostrated all the interests of the country.

Nevertheless it is safe to predict that sooner or later the last traces of the disturbing influence of war and paper money will disappear in America, as they have sooner or later disappeared in every other country which has passed through the same evils. The result of this convulsion itself has been in the main good. It indicates the approaching end of a troubled time. Messrs. Gould and Fisk will at last be obliged to yield to the force of moral and economical laws. The Erie Railway will be rescued, and its history will perhaps rival that of the great speculative manias of the last century. The United States will restore a sound basis to its currency, and will learn to deal with the political reforms it requires. Yet though the regular process of development may be depended upon, in its ordinary and established course, to purge American society of the worst agents of an exceptionally corrupt time, there is in the history of this Erie corporation one matter in regard to which modern society everywhere is directly interested. For the first time since the creation of these enormous corporate bodies, one of them has shown its power for mischief, and has proved itself able to override and trample on law, custom, decency, and every restraint known to society, without scruple, and as yet without check. The belief is common in America that the day is at hand when corporations far greater than the Erie—swaying power such as has never in the world's history been trusted in the hands of mere private citizens, controlled by single men like Vanderbilt, or by combinations of men like Fisk, Gould, and Lane, after having created a system of quiet but irresistible corruption—will ultimately succeed in directing government itself. Under the American form of society, there is now no authority capable of effective resistance. The national government, in order to deal with the corporations, must assume powers refused to it by its fundamental law, and even then is always exposed to the chance of forming an absolute central government which sooner or later is likely to fall into the very hands it is struggling to escape, and thus destroy the limits of its power only in order to make corruption omnipotent. Nor is this danger confined to America alone. The corporation is in its nature a threat against the popular institutions which are spreading so rapidly over the whole world. Wherever there is a popular and limited government this difficulty will be found in its path, and unless some satisfactory solution of the problem can be reached, popular institutions may yet find their very existence endangered.

THE New York Times

In 1860 William March Tweed, a three-hundred-pound firefighter-turned-politician, engineered his own election as chairman of the New York City Democratic Party and as leader of its social club, Tammany Hall. New York was changing and Tweed understood it: through a combination of patronage jobs for his loyalists, assistance to the immigrant poor, and massive public-works building projects that kicked back millions to the Tammany coffers and his own pockets, Boss Tweed built the nation's most potent political machine.

In 1871 two disgruntled low-level city bureaucrats brought Tammany's account ledgers for public-works projects—notably a new courthouse begun in 1861—to the New York Times, *then a Republican paper edited by Louis J. Jennings. It remains one of the great whistle-blower exposés. Carpenters and contractors who happened to be Tammany operatives were paid hundreds of thousands of dollars for a few days' work; stone was purchased from quarries* *partly owned by Tweed himself; a thermometer was purchased from a Tammany ally for $7,500.*

The Times' *exposé convinced a reform-minded Democratic legislator and former Tammany ally, Samuel Tilden, to pursue an independent investigation of the Tweed Ring, which in turn helped propel him first to the New York governorship and then the 1876 Democratic presidential nomination. Tweed was indicted and tried three times, and died in prison in 1878. Tammany's continuing influence would be dissected again a generation later by Lincoln Steffens—who, unlike the* Times, *focused on businesses and other constituencies with a direct stake in the machine's persistence.*

MORE RING VILLAINY
GIGANTIC FRAUDS IN THE RENTAL OF ARMORIES

1871

EXORBITANT PRICES GIVEN FOR REGIMENTAL HEAD-QUARTERS—STABLE-LOFTS AT A PREMIUM—THOUSANDS OF DOLLARS PAID FOR BARE WALLS AND UNOCCUPIED ROOMS—OVER EIGHTY PER CENT. OF THE MONEY STOLEN

Reliable and incontrovertible evidence of numerous gigantic frauds on the part of the rulers of this City has been given to the public form time to time in these columns. Few, if any, of the frauds, however, which have been thus exposed will be found to be of greater magnitude or of a more shameful character than those which are presented in this article. The facts which are narrated are obtained from what we consider a good and trustworthy source, and the figures which help to explain them are transcribed literally from books in the Controller's office. If Controller Connolly can prove them to be inaccurate he is heartily welcome to do so.

The National Guard of this State was organized for the protection of our citizens, but under the baneful influence of the Ring it is made, as far as regards the First Division, an engine of political power, and a source of pecuniary profit to the soulless vampires who now control this City.

Nominally, about three-quarters of a million of dollars is annually appropriated for the armories and drill-rooms of the First Division, but this sum forms only a small percentage of the amount actually paid out every year, ostensibly for "rents and repairs," but in fact to be divided among the thieves of the Ring and the miserable tools who perform their dirty work. Conspicuous among the latter class is Jas. H. Ingersoll, who is a partner of William M. Tweed in the chair business, and President of an Arms Company, (virtually owned by Tweed,) the arms of which the Ring are now trying to foist on the National Guard. He is also one of the New Court-House Commissioners, and the confidential agent of "Boss" Tweed in many of the schemes in which the latter is engaged. Ingersoll was formerly a member of the Seventh Regiment, and an intimate acquaintance of Major Joseph B. Young, the Clerk to the Board of Supervisors, when Tweed was President of that immaculate body. He early developed a talent for manipulating jobs, and so commended himself to the favor of Tweed that the latter selected him to look after his (Tweed's) interests in the division of the spoils accruing from the rental and fitting up of armories. Nor was Tweed mistaken in his man. What had previously been but a bungling, imperfect system was soon reduced to a science, the most elaborate and comprehensive in its details. Buildings that had long remained unoccupied were selected in all parts of the City, without any regard to their adaptability for armory purposes, or any reference to the convenience of the troops that were intended to occupy them. Many of the old armories had been handsomely fitted up, but under the new order of things the substantial black-walnut and oak arm-racks, and the stout serviceable chairs, tables and desks, gave place to more pretentious but less substantial furniture and fixtures.

The renting and fitting up of the armories of the First Division National Guard is now under the absolute control of Ingersoll. He has his runners to find out where there is an empty loft, and to ascertain the best terms that can be made with the party desiring to rent it. When rented he locks it up, takes the keys, and keeps it unoccupied just as long as it suits him, charging the City rent for it all the time. Thus several armories that were rented in May, 1870, have remained unoccupied until May, 1871, while others that were rented at the same time, and still others that were vacated by regiments being moved or disbanded, are yet unoccupied.

During the year 1869, with the exception of the Eighty-fourth, there were no changes made in the location of the different regiments, and but little repairs were attempted, and yet, within thirty days, commencing March 12, 1870, more than Half a Million Dollars were paid out of the City Treasury for "repairs on armories and drill-rooms." The checks representing this amount were drawn in favor of Ingersoll & Watson, A. J. Garvey, Keyser & Co., (John H. Keyser,) and George S. & James L. Miller; but as they were all returned from the bank bearing the indorsement of James H. Ingersoll, the public will scarcely fail to properly estimate the justice of the claims, or to divine the channel into which the various amounts was directed. But as Mr. Controller Connolly keeps these checks and vouchers, and the books in which they are recorded, securely under lock and key, we will not dwell longer on that branch of the subject at present, but will proceed to describe the different premises that are now rented by the Ring for the use of the National Guard.

The armory of the Sixth Regiment, Col. Sterry commanding, is located on the top floor of Tammany Hall, on Fourteenth-street, and consists of a room of about 100 feet square, which is broken by a semi-circular row of fifteen pillars, practically reducing the size of the room, for drill purposes, to 100x40 feet. The officers' room and the company meeting-rooms are on the next floor below, and consist of the five or six small rooms that were used by Jarrett & Palmer for offices and lumber-rooms during their occupancy of the Tammany Theatre. The entire portion of the building that is used for military purposes could not be let for any legitimate business for $3,000 a year, but the municipal Ring pays Henry Vanderwater, the Treasurer of the Tammany Society, the snug little sum of $36,000 per year. The lease of this place was made in the Spring of 1870, and the City has since been paying rent for it, although it was not until the Spring of 1871 that the Sixth moved into it. Previous to the latter period the Sixth occupied an armory over Centre Market, but as this was City property nothing could be made of it by the Ring, and on the regiment leaving it, Ingersoll and his men when in and ripped out everything in the shape of furniture and fixtures that was on the premises.

The Twelfth Regiment have their armory at the corner of Broadway and Thirty-fourth-street. It consists of a hall that was formerly known as the "Everett Assembly Rooms." It has a frontage on Broadway of about 35 feet, and extends along Thirty-fourth-street the full depth of the lot, about 125 feet. In addition to this there are the company meeting-rooms, five in number, a reception-room, a room for the Board of Officers, and the armorer's quarters. The property belongs to Peter B. Sweeny and Hugh Smith, and would let probably for from $3,000 to $4,000 a year, but the incorruptible Mr. Sweeny does not hesitate to take $15,000 for it from the tax-payers of the City. But this is not all. Adjoining this armory, and forming an L on Thirty-third-street, is a portion of the same property that is occupied by the Washington Grey Troop. At the head of the stairs of the two-story building No. 55 West Thirty-third street is the entrance to a squad-room 30 by 33 feet; on the left of this are three small rooms, fronting on the street, which are used as a reception-room, an officers' room and a meeting-room for the troop, respectively. By crossing the squad-room diagonally from the entrance another flight of stairs is reached, leading into what was originally the yards in rear of the stores on the Broadway side of the premises, but which, by running up four fragile walls and roofing them over, has been transformed into a room 45 by 55 feet in extent. This is supposed to be the drill-room of the troop, but as the troop can only muster about thirty men on the most important occasion, they concluded that they did not want the room, and have let it to Hlasko, the dancing-master. These premises could scarcely be made available for any business purpose, and would not rent for more than $1,500 for a year, but the Ring pays $15,000 for them, making $30,000 a year for premises that, at the most liberal estimate, could not be let for $6,000. The leases on this property were taken by the Ring, in the Spring of 1870, for five years, but it is only about two months since Ingersoll placed them in a condition fit for occupancy, so that a year's rent has been virtually thrown away.

For many years the Eighth Regiment have had their armory over Centre Market, where it still remains. During the Spring of 1870, when Ingersoll was seeking every pretext which would enable him to rent additional premises, the Eighth was promised a new armory, and its commanding officer, Col. Scott, was requested to send in his application. In due time the top floor over Shephard & Palmer's stables, corner of Ninth-Avenue and Twenty-seventh-street, was selected, and the regiment were notified to move in. They occupied the building for one evening, found it utterly unsuited to their wants—there being neither company meeting-rooms nor rooms for the officers, and no gas in the place—and were compelled to return to their old and more comfortable quarters over Centre Market. The Ninth-avenue loft is owned by the proprietors of the Twenty-third-street and Ninth-avenue line of stages, who occupy the three lower floors themselves, and let the top floor to the Ring at $18,000 per annum. The loft was rented in the Spring of 1870, and still remains unoccupied, although a semi-military company, which is not a part of the National Guard, has been permitted to use it for the last three or four months.

$16,500 FOR A STABLE LOFT.

Since the organization of the First Regiment of Infantry its armory has been on the northwest corner of Broadway and Fourth-Street, the City paying $10,000 a year rent. Nearly a year ago the command was moved into the armory formerly occupied by the Seventy-first Regiment, at No. 118 West Thirty-second-street. These premises are controlled by Ryerson, Brown & Davis, the lower part being occupied as livery stables. It is well known that the ammonia generated in the stables is most injurious to arms, equipments and clothing, and that the effluvia arising therefrom are often so offensive as to render the upper part of these buildings unfit for human occupancy. But, notwithstanding these objections, no less than eight of these places have been selected for armories, all at enormous rents. The rooms over Ryerson's & Brown's stables are no exception to the rule. They could not be made available for any ordinary business, and would scarcely rent for $2,000 per annum, yet the Ring pays Sixteen Thousand Five Hundred Dollars for them, and Two Thousand Five Hundred to the same parties for two wretched rooms at No. 71 University-place, although the latter have not been occupied for two or three years.

The armory of the Ninth Regiment is over a stable on Twenty-sixth-street, between Seventh and Eighth avenues. The rooms occupy considerable space, but as no insurance could be obtained they could not be let for ordinary business purposes. For these lofts the Ring charges the City a yearly rent of Twenty-Four Thousand Dollars.

When the Thirty-seventh were consolidated with the Seventy-first, the latter regiment moved into the armory previously occupied by the former, at the junction of Broadway, Sixth-avenue and Thirty-fifth-street. These rooms are well located, well lighted and ventilated, and under favorable auspices, might let for $3,000 or $4,000 per annum but the Ring charges the City a yearly rent of Twenty-three Thousand Dollars.

The armory of the Seventy-ninth regiment is located in the fifth story of a building on the corner of Greene and Houston streets. The distance to be traversed through dark, dingy halls, and up dirty stairs, and the wretched accommodations that meets them on arriving at the top of the building, has effectually disgusted many of the members, and has well-nigh broken up an organization that has a war-record second to no regiment in the service of the State. It is doubtful if this loft could be let for any purpose for $1,000 a year, but the Ring, with characteristic liberality, charges the City a yearly rent of Eight Thousand Dollars.

The Ninety-sixth Regiment is in the last stages of dissolution, being unable to parade more than 150 men. The armory of the regiment is located in the Germania Assembly Rooms, on the Bowery, and is the same that they occupied seven years ago, when the regiment could parade 600 active members. The building was controlled at one time by Earnest O. Bernet, a former Lieutenant-Colonel of the regiment, and he rented the armory to the City at $3,000 a year, retaining $2,000 himself, and paying $1,000 to a member of the Supervisor's Ring. Subsequently Bernet sold out to the Koch Brothers, but said nothing about the arrangement with the Ring, and when a demand was made on John

Koch by the Ring thief for his share of the spoils, Koch very properly refused to recognize his claims or countenance the fraud in any way. At a later period, the Koch Brothers sold out to G. W. Sauer, the present proprietor, and on the expiration of the lease he had it renewed at a yearly rent of Five Thousand Dollars—admitting, however, that only about half of that amount was to accrue to him. The lease has still three years to run, but notwithstanding this, and the fact that the regiment is likely to be disbanded, the Ring has taken a new armory for the Ninety-sixth, at a yearly rent of Fourteen Thousand Dollars. This new armory is on the corner of Broadway and Fourth-street, and was formerly occupied by the First Infantry. As soon as the First Regiment moved out, James H. Ingersoll, accompanied by a furniture-dealer named Conrad Boller, of No. 116 Wooster-street, and several laborers, went into the rooms and literally gutted them of everything movable. Furniture, carpets, desks, arm-racks, gas-fixtures—even to the water-closets—everything was ripped up and carried off, and the rooms are now a perfect wreck, to which we would invite the attention of all skeptical readers. This was done notwithstanding the fact that these rooms had been fitted up only a short time before, at an expense of several thousand dollars. The rooms are utterly unsuited to the purpose for which they have been rented, and probably would not bring, in a legitimate way, over $3,000 a year. The building is controlled by the Howe Sewing-machine Company, but Mr. Levi Stockwell, who is the representative man of the Company, rents the lofts from the Company, (at, it is believed, about $3,000 per annum,) and sub-lets them to the Ring at $14,000.

The Eighty-fourth Regiment has the armory that was formerly occupied by the Twelfth Regiment, at the south-east corner of Broadway and Fourth-street. The rooms are on the top floor, and were formerly let to the Twelfth at $3,000 per year. The Ring could make nothing out of this arrangement, and accordingly refused to pay the agents, Messrs. Cruikshank, of No. 55 Broadway. The latter sued for their money and finally compromised, but refused to let the rooms to the Ring for another term. Ingersoll was equal to the emergency. He called in one of his partners, Frank Sterry, and the latter leased the floor for (as near as can be ascertained) $3,000 a year, and then let it to the Ring at Eleven Thousand. Frank Sterry is colonel of the Sixth Regiment, (which occupies Tammany Hall at a yearly rent of $36,000,) and is now a candidate for the position of Brigadier-General.

The fifth Regiment has its armory in a rear room on the second story of a lager-beer saloon, in a wretched neighborhood in Hester-street, between Mott and Mulberry streets. The building is owned by Joseph Hielenbrand, (who formerly kept the saloon,) and the part of it that is used for an armory could not be made available for any purpose except for meeting-rooms for societies or ward clubs during the Winter, and would not net the owner $1,000 a year. Yet, for these premises, the Ring charges the City a yearly rent of $10,000—a larger sum than the entire block would let for. The Third Cavalry Regiment has had its armory at Nos. 37 and 37½ Bowery for several years, for which the City has been paying a yearly rent of $4,500; while the First Cavalry Regiment had its armory over a stable corner of Seventh-avenue and Forty-seventh-street, for which $5,000 has been paid. A year ago the First Regiment ceased to occupy their armory, although the lease had two years to run, and the accommodating J.H. Ingersoll tendered them the use of the same rooms that were (and are) occupied by the Third Regiment at a yearly rent of $9,000, thus charging the City Thirteen Thousand Five Hundred Dollars. Nor is this all: Carl Klein keeps a lager-beer saloon in the Bowery, and commands what is called a "separate-troop" of cavalry—formerly a battery in the First Regiment Artillery. Before the latter organization was disbanded the entire regiment found ample accommodations in the City Arsenal, corner of White and Elm streets. But now that the regiment has been broken up and that there remains only three batteries and one troop of cavalry, (less than half the strength of the regiment,) they must needs have separate armories. One of Ingersoll's runners found that two upper floors over the private stable of Mr. A. B. Darling, of the Fifth-avenue Hotel, were vacant, and Ingersoll accordingly laid his plans for another haul. He rented these two floors for something like $4,000 a year, and turned them over to the City at Seventeen Thousand per Year. As Ingersoll & Watson were already receiving $5,000 a year for an imaginary armory in Chrystie-street, (which will be described further on) it was not desirable to use the firm name a second time for a similar purpose, and Ingersoll therefore called in a lawyer named A. T. Compton, of No. 41 Pinestreet, in whose name the lease to the City stands. Ingersoll, however, receives and receipts for the rent. The lofts for which the City is paying this $17,000 per annum are located at No. 108 West Twenty-fourth-street. The first and second floors are occupied as stables. The third floor consists of eight small rooms, four of which are dark, and the top floor is supposed to be the drill-room, and is 40 by 80 feet. These rooms were rented in the Spring of 1870, and Ingersoll has received the rent for them, but up to the present time they *have never been occupied for an hour,* and it was only within the last week that any attempt was made to furnish the officers' rooms.

In addition to this, Ingersoll & Watson have been drawing Five Thousand Dollars a year for an indefinite period for an armory that never had any existence. It is described as being at No. 53 Chrystie-street, but the most diligent inquiry through the building and in the neighborhood has failed to elicit the fact that any part of the premises has ever been used for military purposes. The building is in a wretched neighborhood, in rear of Ingersoll & Watson's store, at No. 71 Bowery. The upper floors are let to different parties, and are all occupied; the store and basement have been unoccupied since the 1st of May, up to which time they were occupied by a tobacco manufactory—so that the pretext that any part of the building has ever been used as an armory is glaringly false and fraudulent.

The Ninety-fifth Regiment had its armory over a stable at No. 609 Sixth-avenue, two doors above Thirty-sixth-street. The regiment had scarcely moved in when the order was issued to disband it, and for some time the armory remained unoccupied. Then the Fourth Regiment was moved in, but about two years ago that regiment was disbanded, and since then the armory has remained unoccupied. Ingersoll pursued the same course in regard to this armory that he has in the case of the First, Sixth, and other regiments—he went in and literally stripped the place of everything he could carry off, and the City is now paying Eight thousand dollars a year for the bare walls.

The Second Regiment had its armory corner of Hall-place and Seventh-street, for which the City paid $5,000—just five times its value. The regiment was disbanded about two years ago, and the armory remained unoccupied for a considerable time, until finally the Fifty-fifth Regiment was removed form its armory, No. 19 Avenue A, and that Armory, for which the City paid $3,500 per year, remained unoccupied. There is another unoccupied armory over a stable corner of Twenty-sixth-street and Fourth-avenue. The lease of this armory was carried through the Board of Supervisors by Brooke Postley, late Brigadier-General of the defunct Cavalry Brigade. While Gen. Postley was in command of his brigade he had two sons of William M. Tweed on his staff, and through his intimacy with them he obtained a foothold as a skirmisher for the Ring. The loft that was rented for an armory might let for $1,000 per year if it were not over a stable. The City agreed to pay $4,000 a year for it, and the owner of the building agreed to let Postley draw every alternate quarter's rent until the sum of *five thousand dollars* should have been paid. Postley drew the $5,000 from the Comptroller's Office, but not content with this, he claimed interest on the amount from the time the contract was made until the payment of the last installment, and notified the Controller not to pay the owner of the property. On the 1st of last May, the latter had to engage the services of Lawyer Hull, of No. 140 Broadway, and finally had to compromise with Postley before he could draw his money. Postley has engineered several other jobs through the Board of Supervisors, the best authenticated being the lease of a riding-school at Nos. 11 and 13 West Thirteenth-street. This was formerly occupied as a riding-school by Col. Dickel, and Postley got the Ring to rent it, ostensibly as a head-quarters for his brigade, but in fact to be used as a private stable and riding-school. The premises were not worth $2,000 a year, but the Ring agreed to pay $6,000, and Dickel gave Postley a year's rent for his services.

All the arrangements had been made by the Ring to commence a profitable campaign this year, but they had only rented lofts in two buildings when it leaked out that their operations were about to be ventilated. The first of these lofts is on the corner of Broadway and Fourth-street, and the second includes the two upper floors of Bryant's Minstrel building, on Twenty-third-street. These rooms are utterly unfit for even a company, the lower one being broken up, and divided by a series of iron stanchions which support an immense beam upon which the upper floor rests. The upper floor resembles a rude platform more than a properly constructed loft, but neither floor has either partition or door separating it from the stairs—they are mere open lofts, fit only for stable lofts or storage, but the Ring charges the city Seven Thousand Five Hundred Dollars a year for them. They are not yet occupied.

The following is a recapitulation of the amounts paid as rent for the armories now occupied, compared with what *should* be paid:

	Yearly Rent.	Worth.
Top floor of Tammany Hall, (6th Regiment)	$36,000	$4,000
Everett Rooms, Broadway and 34th-st., (12th Regiment)	15,000	4,000
Part of same premises on 33d-st., (Washington Grey Troop)	15,000	1,500
Lofts over stable, 26th-st., near 7th-av., (9th Regiment)	24,000	10,000
Lofts over stable, No. 118 West 32d-st., (1st Infantry)	16,500	2,000
Floor over lager-beer saloon, Hester-st., (5th Regiment)	10,000	1,000
Floor corner Broadway and 35th-st., (71st Regiment)	23,000	4,000
Rooms at Nos. 37 and 37½ Bowery, (1st and 3d Cavalry)	13,500	4,500
Top floor south-east corner Broadway and 4th-st., (84th Regiment)	11,000	3,000

Rooms corner 7th-st. and Hall-place, (55th Regiment)	5,000	1,000
Rooms corner Delancey and Chrystie sts., (11th Regiment)	4,000	4,000
Armory of 22d Regiment, 14th-st.	4,600	4,600
Rear rooms in Germania Hall, Bowery, (96th Regiment)	5,000	2,000
Top loft corner Greene and Houston sts., (79th Regiment)	8,000	1,000
Total	$190,600	$46,600

(The Seventh, Eighth and Sixty-ninth Regiments have their armories over markets and pay no rent, the markets being City property.)

UNOCCUPIED ARMORIES FOR WHICH RENT IS PAID.

	Yearly rent.
Top loft over stable, No. 281 Ninth-avenue	$18,000
Lofts north-west corner Broadway and Fourth-street	14,000
Lofts over stable, No. 108 West Twenty-fourth-street	17,000
Two small rooms, No. 71 University-place	2,500
Loft over stable, corner Fourth-avenue and Twenty-fifth-street	4,000
Floor over lager-beer saloon, Avenue A	3,500
Loft over stable, No. 619 Sixth-avenue	8,000
Loft over stable, corner Forty-seventh-street and Seventh-avenue	5,000
Riding-school, No. 11 West Thirteenth-street	6,000
Two upper floors in Bryant's Minstrel Hall, Twenty-third-street	7,500
Total	$85,500

(In addition to the above, the armories formerly occupied by the Sixth and Seventy-first Regiments, over Centre Market, are unoccupied.)

Besides this, the yearly rent collected by James H. Ingersoll, for an armory alleged to be at No. 53 Christy-street, but which never had any existence, is $5,000. The grand total amount, then, drawn from the City Treasury by the Ring as rent for occupied and unoccupied armories, is $281,100, being an expenditure of just $234,500 more than what should be honestly paid.

Another fact, and then we are done for the present. Tweed and Ingersoll are now having a building erected on the south side of Twenty-third-street, between Seventh and Eighth avenues, the upper part of which, when finished, is to be divided into armories, (the Eight Regiment has already been promised an armory in the building,) to be leased to the City at not less than Seventy-Five Thousand Dollars a year, and the aggregate cost of armories for fourteen regiments and two separate troops of cavalry will then reach the enormous sum of Three Hundred and Fifty-six Thousand One Hundred Dollars.

Who are responsible for these frauds? First, Mayor Hall and Controller Connolly, who pass upon these claims and sign checks for their payment—knowing them to be fraudulent. Second, William M. Tweed and Peter B. Sweeny, who pocket their share of the proceeds—knowing it to have been fraudulently obtained. Third, James H. Ingersoll, Joseph B. Young, Clerk to the Board of Supervisors, and Stephen C. Lynes, Jr., the present County Auditor, whose agency in these matters is as palpable as it is shameful.

John Swinton

Abolitionist, labor-union champion, and one of the most thoughtful newspaper editors of his era, John Swinton (1829–1901) was born in Scotland, trained as a typesetter in Canada, and learned his newspapering in Lawrence, Kansas, amid the Freesoil debates. In a long career Swinton covered Abraham Lincoln's 1860 campaign, interviewed and corresponded with Karl Marx, and befriended Eugene V. Debs. Editorial director of the New York Times *during the Civil War and later managing editor of the* New York Sun, *he became disillusioned with commercial daily reporting and the influence of publishers—"There is no such thing, at this date of the world's history, in America, as an independent press," he told the New York Press Club in 1880. In 1884, Swinton founded his own weekly,* John Swinton's Paper. *Swinton's weekly incorporated dispatches on wages and working conditions from labor activists around the country with his own in-depth reports.*

THE NEW SLAVE TRADE

From *John Swinton's Paper,* January 6, 1884

[Inside a slave market in New York City]

This city is the headquarters of the new slave trade, although the barracoons have not yet been erected along the water front. Here are managed the operations of the contractors who import to this country gangs of contract-immigrants bound to service and labor wherever they may be sent, under the orders of corporations and capitalists—in mines, in mills, in railroad building, along the Southern levees, in tunneling, in factory work, and in common labor of every kind. An unlimited supply of them can be found in Hungary, Italy and elsewhere, and the demand for them by the contractors is limited only by the circumstances of the times. They can be procured for wages upon which American workers cannot live, and they live in their gangs after a fashion in which no class of American workingmen ought to be allowed to live. The contract-immigrant slave trade, which has been begun and is now carried on here, will undoubtedly reach gigantic proportions if means be not taken to put an end to it. It will influence all the industries of the country, affect the condition of American society, establish among us a class more slavish than we have ever had, result in the further cutting of wages, and lead to still harder times for the great body of working people, putting them more than ever at the mercy of the great corporations, manufacturers and capitalists, who are now absorbing the wealth and strength of the country.

The other day a reporter of this paper undertook to look into the operations of the traffickers in human flesh in this city. He ascertained that there were not a few of them doing business on a large scale in a quiet way; and he found that their quarters are in the lower part of the city, some of them not more than a stone's throw from the office of this paper. They are all engaged in the "banking business" at the same time that they are making ventures in the slave traffic. Through them you can procure gangs of Italian or Hungarian lazzaroni, from ten to two hundred to five thousand, in lots to suit contractors, under contracts that most of the poor creatures appear to be willing to keep.

Inside a slave market in New York City:

"Can I have a few minutes' talk with you?"

The question was addressed to a man about sixty years of age, with full gray beard, a bulging nose, spectacled eyes, which peered sharply from under shaggy eyebrows; a skull cap ornamented the top of his head and added to the impression that it was the veritable Shylock of Venice—the bloody bondholder.

The outside had not been inviting. A small basement window, adorned with a wire screen; a signboard with the words "Banca Italiana" and "Notaro Pubblico"in one of our public streets. A place that almost everyone passed without noticing—grimy, forlorn. On entering, the interior presented no greater attractions than the exterior: a number of newly-arrived immigrants, male and female, lounging around the dingy office; a glass screen on one side, with pigeon holes at intervals and an opening at the centre. In front of this opening was the individual to whom we addressed our query:

"Can I have a few minutes' talk with you?"

Looking at us sharply, we were ushered into a dark back room, where everything bespoke penury, and where the dust of ages covered the rickety furniture.

We stated our business: An iron company desired to obtain two hundred Italian laborers for its mines, and we wanted to know whether he could procure them, and if so, on what terms.

"Certainly," replied the slave-trader, "any number. I have brought over *fourteen thousand* men. Having been in the business twenty years, I know just what is wanted. I do this for love of my poor countrymen. I do not make anything out of them, and I want to be sure they will be well treated, because if they were not they would make complaints that would injure my business."

We asked him about the particulars of his business: the cost of bringing them out; if the company advanced their fare; whether it would be reimbursed; and whether binding contracts could be made with them for any length of time. He then repeated that he had brought out from Italy to this country *fourteen thousand Italian laborers under contract, six thousand* of whom had returned to Italy. He had agents in Naples, and had $80,000 deposited in the Bank of Naples. He had to furnish guarantee bonds for $100 for each individual, but that was all a matter of form.

His son had just gone over to Naples to attend to his business there. For the Pennsylvania mines it would be necessary to have large men, strong and broad-shouldered.

Here the old man called "Pietro." A clerk made his appearance—a stoutly-built young fellow. "That" continued Shylock, "is from the part of the country we get our men. Not in Naples, they are small, but in the hill country around."

His men went out to their village to procure them. They would sign contracts for any length of time. Of course the American company would have to advance their passage money over here.

"No trouble about that. Let us have particulars."

"Well, then, the passage from Naples to New York will be $26; and the fare from the places where they live will be from ten to twenty miles away, $0 to $4; from there will be the making of the papers, which will cost $2. We have all the machinery in Naples for doing this. Then you will have to give them some money to spend while they are waiting for the vessel to start. Ten *lira,* about $2, will be enough. The fare from New York to destination is, you say, $4. So that will make in all $87, and six per cent interest. In sending them from New York, my men go to a railroad company and hire a car, or any number of cars, and it only costs $50 or $75 for each car, thus saving $2.50 or $3 on each passenger, which goes to the importing company. You will not be taking anything from the immigrant; he would have to pay $4 for his fare if he went alone. It's quite honest. Of course the cars are old ones, but then they know no better, and it is only for a day or so. On the sea, we contract for cheap steerage prices."

"Now, how much do you want for this job?"

"Oh, that will depend on the circumstances. It may be $3 or $4 apiece."

"How about wages here?"

"I have furnished men at $1 a day; but they usually get $1.25, and sometimes, when the work is very hard, $1.50."

"How is the company reimbursed?"

"The men will sign a contract to repay the money advanced, with interest at six per cent, at any rate the company desires."

"How would $4 a month do?"

"Capital! Those would be liberal terms. They would jump at that."

"Have you heard," we asked, "that a great many Hungrians, under contract, are being sent into Pennsylvania?"

"Yes, but they are not as good as Italians. The poor Italians are like sheep. You can do anything with them. The Hungarians are slyer."

It was evident that the slave-trader did not want to lose the contract of bringing over a gang of his contract-countrymen; but he found, after all, as we stood in his office, that he would have to get hold of another customer before he could make any money out of that branch of his business.

As already told, we found other offices or slave-markets of the same kind in that vicinity, with signs concealing their true character, and only giving information that they were "banks."

Last June a friend of ours was employed by the Hudson River Iron and Ore Company, in Lielithgow, near Livingston Station, Columbia County, this State. They had a large number of Hungarian laborers working in their mines at $1 a day. The pay day was monthly, and fifteen days were always kept in hand. Every month the poor fellows made a great outcry about their wages, claiming that they had been defrauded. They were huddled together in shanties, and lived on rye bread and potatoes, and saw but little rest. These people have invariably been brought here to fill the places of working-men already in service, to flood the market, and thus to depress wages.

In further prosecuting our researches on this subject, we found difficulty. No one in the city seemed to know anything about the manner in which these contract-bondmen are obtained. We made a tour of the shipping offices to see what could be found out. We visited the offices of Messrs. Henderson Bros., agents for steamers plying between this port and and Glasgow, London, Liverpool, and Mediterranean ports. A member of the firm stated that they had no positive knowlege of contract-immigrants being brought to this country; that he had never seen a contract; and that no complaints had been made to them. Applications were sometimes made at their office in this city for steerage passage tickets in quantities of forty and fifty at a time, but they made no inquiries as to whom they were for. He believed there were a number of men in the city who had agents in Italy, and procured laborers for those who needed them. One of these men had a contract some time ago to furnish the Street Cleaning Bureau with a hundred men a month. He could not say whether that contract was still in force.

Messrs. Oetrichs and Co., agents for the North German Lloyds, do the largest passenger business of any of the Transatlantic lines. Their manager said that he had received many applications for German men and women, usually in small gangs, but sometimes for two or three hundred at a time. They were wanted for cotton and other mills, and iron mines and factories. The company could not undertake to procure laborers, having as much as they could attend to in their transportation. He had two applications last year, one for 200 women for a cotton mill in New England, the name of which he had forgotten.

Mr. Kunhardt of the Hamburg Line ridiculed the subject; it was all nonsense, this outcry of contract labor; he didn't know anything about it, and didn't believe it was done. (Perhaps Mr. Kunhardt could have told more if he wanted to do so.)

We spoke on the subject to Superintendent Jackson of Castle Garden, who said he had no doubt that the system of making contracts with laborers in Europe was carried on to a great extent by corporations in this country, who have their agents abroad. He could not tell about it positively; but large numbers arrive bound for the same place, and they were met on their arrival by someone who took them in charge.

NELLIE BLY

By the late nineteenth century, the competition for readers among big-city newspapers encouraged the emergence of reporters as celebrities in their own right. One of the most flamboyant and inventive was Nellie Bly (1867–1922), the pseudonym of Elizabeth Cochrane. Born in Pennsylvania in a family of fifteen children raised by a widowed mother, Bly moved to Pittsburgh to work at age sixteen. In 1885 she wrote a furious letter to the Pittsburgh Post Dispatch *responding to an article arguing that women were fit only for housework. The letter so impressed editor George Madden that he commissioned her to write on the lives of working women, and soon took her on as a full-time reporter.*

In Pittsburgh and later at Joseph Pulitzer's New York World, *Bly pioneered the art of undercover reporting—working in a factory to document child labor, hiring herself out to a corps de ballet, and feigning mental illness to gain admission to the Blackwell's Island asylum, the subject of the following excerpt from her book* Ten Days in a Madhouse. *An intrepid foreign correspondent as well, Bly was thrown out of Mexico for reporting on political corruption and covered the eastern front of World War I. In 1889 she set out to break the fictional travel record set by Phileas Fogg in* Around the World in Eighty Days, *and her success—she shaved a week off Fogg's circumnavigation time—made her the subject of a popular song, her image printed on playing cards. In 1895 she married millionaire industrialist Robert Seaman, and upon his death introduced model health care programs and other reforms to his factories.*

CHOKING AND BEATING PATIENTS

From *Ten Days in a Madhouse,* 1887

Miss Tillie Mayard suffered greatly from cold. One morning she sat on the bench next to me and was livid with the cold. Her limbs shook and her teeth chattered. I spoke to the three attendants who sat with coats on at the table in the center of the floor.

"It is cruel to lock people up and then freeze them," I said. They replied she had on as much as any of the rest, and she would get no more. Just then Miss Mayard took a fit and every patient looked frightened. Miss Neville caught her in her arms and held her, although the nurses roughly said:

"Let her fall on the floor and it will teach her a lesson." Miss Neville told them what she thought of their actions, and then I got orders to make my appearance in the office.

Just as I reached there Superintendent Dent came to the door and I told him how we were suffering from the cold, and of Miss Mayard's condition. Doubtless, I spoke incoherently, for I told of the state of the food, the treatment of the nurses and their refusal to give more clothing, the condition of Miss Mayard, and the nurses telling us, because the asylum was a public institution, we could not expect even kindness. Assuring him that I needed no medical aid, I told him to go to Miss Mayard. He did so. From Miss Neville and other patients I learned what transpired. Miss Mayard was still in the fit, and he caught her roughly between the eyebrows or thereabouts, and pinched until her face was crimson from the rush of blood to the head, and her senses returned. All day afterward she suffered from terrible headache, and from that on she grew worse.

Insane? Yes, insane; and as I watched the insanity slowly creep over the mind that had appeared to be all right I secretly cursed the doctors, the nurses and all public institutions. Some one may say that she was insane at some time previous to her consignment to the asylum. Then if she were, was this the proper place to send a woman just convalescing, to be given cold baths, deprived of sufficient clothing and fed with horrible food?

On this morning I had a long conversation with Dr. Ingram, the assistant superintendent of the asylum. I found that he was kind to the helpless beings in his charge. I began my old complaint of the cold, and he called Miss Grady to the office and ordered more clothing given the patients. Miss Grady said if I made a practice of telling it would be a serious thing for me, she warned me in time.

Many visitors looking for missing girls came to see me. Miss Grady yelled in the door from the hall one day:

"Nellie Brown, you're wanted."

I went to the sitting-room at the end of the hall, and there sat a gentleman who had known me intimately for years. I saw by the sudden blanching of his face and his inability to speak that the sight of me was wholly unexpected and had shocked him terribly. In an instant I determined, if he betrayed me as Nellie Bly, to say I had never seen him before. However, I had one card to play and I risked it. With Miss Grady within touching distance I whispered hurriedly to him, in language more expressive than elegant:

"Don't give me away."

I knew by the expression of his eye that he understood, so I said to Miss Grady:

"I do not know this man."

"Do you know her?" asked Miss Grady.

"No; this is not the young lady I came in search of," he replied, in a strained voice.

"If you do not know her you cannot stay here," she said, and she took him to the door. All at once a fear struck me that he would think I had been sent there through some mistake and would tell my friends and make an effort to have me released. So I waited until Miss Grady had the door unlocked. I knew that she would have to lock it before she could leave, and the time required to do so would give me opportunity to speak, so I called:

"One moment, senor." He returned to me and I asked aloud:

"Do you speak Spanish, senor?" and then whispered, "It's all right. I'm after an item. Keep still." "No," he said, with a peculiar emphasis, which I knew meant that he would keep my secret.

People in the world can never imagine the length of days to those in asylums. They seemed never ending, and we welcomed any event that might give us something to think about as well as talk of. There is nothing to read, and the only bit of talk that never wears out is conjuring up delicate food that they will get as soon as they get out. Anxiously the hour was watched for when the boat arrived to see if there were any new unfortunates to be added to our ranks. When they came and were ushered into the sitting-room, the patients would express sympathy to one another for them and were anxious to show them little marks of attention. Hall 6 was the receiving hall, so that was how we saw all newcomers.

Soon after my advent a girl called Urena Little-Page was brought in. She was, as she had been born, silly, and her tender spot was, as with many sensible women, her age. She claimed eighteen, and would grow very angry if told to the contrary. The nurses were not long in finding this out, and then they teased her.

"Urena," said Miss Grady, "the doctors say that you are thirty-three instead of eighteen," and the other nurses laughed. They kept up this until the simple creature began to yell and cry, saying she wanted to go home and that everybody treated her badly. After they had gotten all the amusement out of her they wanted and she was crying, they began to scold and tell her to keep quiet. She grew more hysterical every moment until they pounced upon her and slapped her face and knocked her head in a lively fashion. This made the poor creature cry the more, and so they choked her. Yes, actually choked her. Then they dragged her out to the closet, and I heard her terrified cries hush into smothered ones. After several hours' absence she returned to the sitting-room, and I plainly saw the marks of their fingers on her throat for the entire day.

This punishment seemed to awaken their desire to administer more. They returned to the sitting-room and caught hold of an old gray-haired woman whom I have heard addressed both as Mrs. Grady and Mrs. O'Keefe. She was insane, and she talked almost continually to herself and to those near her. She never spoke very loud, and at the time I speak of was sitting harmlessly chattering to herself. They grabbed her, and my heart ached as she cried:

"For God sake, ladies, don't let them beat me."

"Shut up, you hussy!" said Miss Grady as she caught the woman by her gray hair and dragged her shrieking and pleading from the room. She was also taken to the closet, and her cries grew lower and lower, and then ceased.

The nurses returned to the room and Miss Grady remarked that she had "settled the old fool for awhile." I told some of the physicians of the occurrence, but they did not pay any attention to it.

One of the characters in Hall 6 was Matilda, a little old German woman, who, I believe, went insane over the loss of money. She was small, and had a pretty pink complexion. She was not much trouble, except at times. She would take spells, when she would talk into the steam-heaters or get up on a chair and talk out of the windows. In these conversations she railed at the lawyers who had taken her property. The nurses seemed to find a great deal of amusement in teasing the harmless old soul. One day I sat beside Miss Grady and Miss Grupe, and heard them tell her perfectly vile things to call Miss McCarten. After telling her to say these things they would send her to the other nurse, but Matilda proved that she, even in her state, had more sense than they.

"I cannot tell you. It is private," was all she would say. I saw Miss Grady, on a pretense of whispering to her, spit in her ear. Matilda quietly wiped her ear and said nothing.

Jacob Riis

In 1877, Jacob Riis (1849–1914), a Danish immigrant and son of a schoolteacher, found work as a police reporter for the New York Tribune. *Police headquarters was in the heart of the Lower East Side tenement district. Riis was shocked by the overcrowding, degradation, and filth of a neighborhood where thirty-seven thousand tenements housed a population of more than one million. "I am satisfied from my own observation," he wrote in the* Tribune, *"that hundreds of men, women and children are every day slowly starving to death in the tenements." With notebook and a bulky flash camera, Riis haunted the Lower East Side's worst districts, finally publishing* How the Other Half Lives *in 1890, combining minute observation with careful statistical documentation of how slumlords herded immigrants into airless railroad flats, charging exorbitant rents sure to produce further overcrowding.*

Riis bore virulent prejudices against the Irish, Italian and Jewish immigrants whom he chronicled: "The swarthy Italian immigrant has his redeeming traits." "Thrift is the watchword of Jewtown, as of its people the world over." A moralist rather than a political radical, he believed that better housing would save "the other half" from their own degraded inclinations.

Yet the range and depth of Riis's investigation into poverty has rarely been equaled in popular media; his photos, like Roman Vishniac's images of 1930s Europe, still provide a searing record of a vanished world; and How the Other Half Lives *provoked a host of reforms in New York housing codes that remain in force today.*

PAUPERISM IN THE TENEMENTS

From *How the Other Half Lives*, 1890

1. The reader who has followed with me the fate of the Other Half thus far, may not experience much of a shock at being told that in eight years 135,595 families in New York were registered as asking or receiving charity. Perhaps, however, the intelligence will rouse him that for five years past one person in every ten who died in this city was buried in the Potter's Field. These facts tell a terrible story. The first means that in a population of a million and a half, very nearly, if not quite, half a million

persons were driven, or chose, to beg for food, or to accept it in charity at some period of the eight years, if not during the whole of it. There is no mistake about these figures. They are drawn from the records of the Charity Organization Society, and represent the time during which it has been in existence. It is not even pretended that the record is complete. To be well within the limits, the Society's statisticians allow only three and a half to the family, instead of the four and a half that are accepted as the standard of calculations which deal with New York's population as a whole. They estimate upon the basis of their everyday experience that, allowing for those who have died, moved away, or become for the time being at least self-supporting, eighty-five per cent. of the registry are still within, or lingering upon, the borders of dependence. Precisely how the case stands with this great horde of the indigent is shown by a classification of 5,169 cases that were investigated by the Society in one year. This was the way it turned out: 327 worthy of continuous relief, or 6.4 per cent.; 1,269 worthy of temporary relief, or 24.4 per cent.; 2,698 in need of work, rather than relief, or 52.2 per cent.; 875 unworthy of relief, or 17 per cent.

2. That is, nearly six and a half per cent. of all were utterly helpless—orphans, cripples, or the very aged; nearly one-fourth needed just a lift to start them on the road of independence, or of permanent pauperism, according to the wisdom with which the lever was applied. More than half were destitute because they had no work and were unable to find any, and one-sixth were frauds, professional beggars, training their children to follow in their footsteps—a veritable "tribe of Ishmael," tightening its grip on society as the years pass, until society shall summon up pluck to say with Paul, "if any man will not work neither shall he eat," and stick to it. It is worthy of note that almost precisely the same results followed a similar investigation in Boston. There were a few more helpless cases of the sort true charity accounts it a gain to care for, but the proportion of a given lot that was crippled for want of work, or unworthy, was exactly the same as in this city. The bankrupt in hope, in courage, in purse, and in purpose, are not peculiar to New York. They

are found the world over, but we have our full share. If further proof were wanted, it is found in the prevalence of pauper burials. The Potter's Field stands ever for utter, hopeless surrender. The last the poor will let go, however miserable their lot in life, is the hope of a decent burial. But for the five years ending with 1888 the average of burials in the Potter's Field has been 10.03 per cent. of all. In 1889 it was 9.64. In that year the proportion to the total mortality of those who died in hospitals, institutions, and in the Almshouse was as 1 in 5.

3. The 135,595 families inhabited no fewer than 31,000 different tenements. I say tenements advisedly, though the society calls them buildings, because at least ninety-nine per cent. were found in the big barracks, the rest in shanties scattered here and there, and now and then a fraud or an exceptional case of distress in a dwelling-house of better class. Here, undoubtedly, allowance must be made for the constant moving about of those who live on charity, which enables one active beggar to blacklist a dozen houses in the year. Still the great mass of the tenements are shown to be harboring alms-seekers. They might almost as safely harbor the small-pox. That scourge is not more contagious than the alms-seeker's complaint. There are houses that have been corrupted through and through by this pestilence, until their very atmosphere breathes beggary. More than a hundred and twenty pauper families have been reported from time to time as living in one such tenement.

4. The truth is that pauperism grows in the tenements as naturally as weeds in a garden lot. A moral distemper, like crime, it finds there its most fertile soil. All the surroundings of tenement-house life favor its growth, and where once it has taken root it is harder to dislodge than the most virulent of physical diseases. The thief is infinitely easier to deal with than the pauper, because the very fact of his being a thief presupposes some bottom to the man. Granted that it is bad, there is still something, a possible handle by which to catch him. To the pauper there is none. He is as hopeless as his own poverty. I speak of the pauper, not of the honestly poor. There is a sharp line between the two; but athwart it stands the tenement,

all the time blurring and blotting it out. "It all comes down to character in the end," was the verdict of a philanthropist whose life has been spent wrestling with this weary problem. And so it comes down to the tenement, the destroyer of individuality and character everywhere. "In nine years," said a wise and charitable physician, sadly, to me, "I have known of but a single case of permanent improvement in a poor tenement family." I have known of some, whose experience, extending over an even longer stretch, was little better.

5. The beggar follows the "tough's" rule of life that the world owes him a living, but his scheme of collecting it stops short of violence. He has not the pluck to rob even a drunken man. His highest flights take in at most an unguarded clothes-line, or a little child sent to buy bread or beer with the pennies he clutches tightly as he skips along. Even then he prefers to attain his end by stratagem rather than by force, though occasionally, when the coast is clear, he rises to the height of the bully. The ways he finds of "collecting" under the cloak of undeserved poverty are numberless, and often reflect credit on the man's ingenuity, if not on the man himself. I remember the shock with which my first experience with his kind—her kind, rather, in this case: the beggar was a woman—came home to me. On my way to and from the office I had been giving charity regularly, as I fondly believed, to an old woman who sat in Chatham Square with a baby done up in a bundle of rags, moaning piteously in sunshine and rain, "Please, help the poor." It was the baby I pitied and thought I was doing my little to help, until one night I was just in time to rescue it from rolling out of her lap, and found the bundle I had been wasting my pennies upon just rags and nothing more, and the old hag dead drunk. Since then I have encountered bogus babies, borrowed babies, and drugged babies in the streets, and fought shy of them all. Most of them, I am glad to say, have been banished from the street since; but they are still occasionally to be found. It was only last winter that the officers of the Society for the Prevention of Cruelty to Children arrested an Italian woman who was begging along Madison Avenue with a poor little wreck of a girl, whose rags and pinched face

were calculated to tug hard at the purse-strings of a miser. Over five dollars in nickels and pennies were taken from the woman's pockets, and when her story of poverty and hunger was investigated at the family's home in a Baxter Street tenement, bank-books turned up that showed the Masonis to be regular pauper capitalists, able to draw their check for three thousand dollars, had they been so disposed. The woman was fined $250, a worse punishment undoubtedly than to have sent her to prison for the rest of her natural life. Her class has, unhappily, representatives in New York that have not yet been brought to grief.

6. Nothing short of making street begging a crime has availed to clear our city of this pest to an appreciable extent. By how much of an effort this result has been accomplished may be gleaned from the fact that the Charity Organization Society alone, in five years, caused the taking up of 2,594 street beggars, and the arrest and conviction of 1,474 persistent offenders. Last year it dealt with 612 perambulating mendicants. The police report only 19 arrests for begging during the year 1889, but the real facts of the case are found under the heading "vagrancy." In all, 2,633 persons were charged with this offence, 947 of them women. A goodly proportion of these latter came from the low groggeries of the Tenth Ward, where a peculiar variety of the female tramp-beggar is at home, the "scrub." The scrub is one degree perhaps above the average pauper in this, that she is willing to work at least one day in the week, generally the Jewish Sabbath. The orthodox Jew can do no work of any sort from Friday evening till sunset on Saturday, and this interim the scrub fills out in Ludlow Street. The pittance she receives for this vicarious sacrifice of herself upon the altar of the ancient faith buys her rum for at least two days of the week at one of the neighborhood "morgues." She lives through the other four by begging. There are distilleries in Jewtown, or just across its borders, that depend almost wholly on her custom. Recently, when one in Hester Street was raided because the neighbors had complained of the boisterous hilarity of the hags over their beer, thirty-two aged "scrubs" were marched off to the station-house.

7. It is curious to find preconceived notions quite upset in a review of the nationalities that go to make up this squad of street beggars. The Irish head the list with fifteen per cent., and the native American is only a little way behind with twelve per cent., while the Italian, who in his own country turns beggary into a fine art, has less than two per cent. Eight per cent. were Germans. The relative prevalence of the races in our population does not account for this showing. Various causes operate, no doubt, to produce it. Chief among them is, I think, the tenement itself. It has no power to corrupt the Italian, who comes here in almost every instance to work—no beggar would ever emigrate from anywhere unless forced to do so. He is distinctly on its lowest level from the start. With the Irishman the case is different. The tenement, especially its lowest type, appears to possess a peculiar affinity for the worse nature of the Celt, to whose best and strongest instincts it does violence, and soonest and most thoroughly corrupts him. The "native" twelve per cent. represent the result of this process, the hereditary beggar of the second or third generation in the slums.

8. The blind beggar alone is winked at in New York's streets, because the authorities do not know what else to do with him. There is no provision for him anywhere after he is old enough to strike out for himself. The annual pittance of thirty or forty dollars which he receives from the city serves to keep his landlord in good humor; for the rest his misfortune and his thin disguise of selling pencils on the street corners must provide. Until the city affords him some systematic way of earning his living by work (as Philadelphia has done, for instance) to banish him from the street would be tantamount to sentencing him to death by starvation. So he possesses it in peace, that is, if he is blind in good earnest, and begs without "encumbrance." Professional mendicancy does not hesitate to make use of the greatest of human afflictions as a pretence for enlisting the sympathy upon which it thrives. Many New Yorkers will remember the French schoolmaster who was "blinded by a shell at the siege of Paris," but miraculously recovered his sight when arrested and deprived of his children by the officers of Mr. Gerry's society. When last heard of

he kept a "museum" in Hartford, and acted the overseer with financial success. His sign with its pitiful tale, that was a familiar sight in our streets for years and earned for him the capital upon which he started his business, might have found a place among the curiosities exhibited there, had it not been kept in a different sort of museum here as a memento of his rascality. There was another of his tribe, a woman, who begged for years with a deformed child in her arms, which she was found to have hired at an almshouse in Genoa for fifteen francs a month. It was a good investment, for she proved to be possessed of a comfortable fortune. Some time before that, the Society for the Prevention of Cruelty to Children, that found her out, had broken up the dreadful padrone system, a real slave trade in Italian children, who were bought of poor parents across the sea and made to beg their way on foot through France to the port whence they were shipped to this city, to be beaten and starved here by their cruel masters and sent out to beg, often after merciless mutilation to make them "take" better with a pitying public.

9. But, after all, the tenement offers a better chance of fraud on impulsive but thoughtless charity, than all the wretchedness of the street, and with fewer risks. To the tender-hearted and unwary it is, in itself, the strongest plea for help. When such a cry goes up as was heard recently from a Mott Street den, where the family of a "sick" husband, a despairing mother, and half a dozen children in rags and dirt were destitute of the "first necessities of life," it is not to be wondered at that a stream of gold comes pouring in to relieve. It happens too often, as in that case, that a little critical inquiry or reference to the "black list" of the Charity Organization Society, justly dreaded only by the frauds, discovers the "sickness" to stand for laziness, and the destitution to be the family's stock in trade; and the community receives a shock that for once is downright wholesome, if it imposes a check on an undiscriminating charity that is worse than none at all.

10. The case referred to furnished an apt illustration of how thoroughly corrupting pauperism is in such a setting. The tenement woke up early to the gold mine that was being worked under its roof, and before the

day was three hours old the stream of callers who responded to the newspaper appeal found the alley blocked by a couple of "toughs," who exacted toll of a silver quarter from each tearful sympathizer with the misery in the attic.

11. A volume might be written about the tricks of the professional beggar, and the uses to which he turns the tenement in his trade. The Boston "widow" whose husband turned up alive and well after she had buried him seventeen times with tears and lamentation, and made the public pay for the weekly funerals, is not without representatives in New York. The "gentleman tramp" is a familiar type from our streets, and the "once respectable Methodist" who patronized all the revivals in town with his profitable story of repentance, only to fall from grace into the saloon door nearest the church after the service was over, merely transferred the scene of his operations from the tenement to the church as the proper setting for his specialty. There is enough of real suffering in the homes of the poor to make one wish that there were some effective way of enforcing Paul's plan of starving the drones into the paths of self-support: no work, nothing to eat.

12. The message came from one of the Health Department's summer doctors, last July, to the King's Daughters' Tenement-house Committee, that a family with a sick child was absolutely famishing in an uptown tenement. The address was not given. The doctor had forgotten to write it down, and before he could be found and a visitor sent to the house the baby was dead, and the mother had gone mad. The nurse found the father, who was an honest laborer long out of work, packing the little corpse in an orange-box partly filled with straw, that he might take it to the Morgue for pauper burial. There was absolutely not a crust to eat in the house, and the other children were crying for food. The great immediate need in that case, as in more than half of all according to the record, was work and living wages. Alms do not meet the emergency at all. They frequently aggravate it, degrading and pauperizing where true help should aim at raising the sufferer to self-respect and self-dependence. The experience of the Charity Organization Society in raising, in eight years, 4,500 families out of the rut of pauperism into proud, if modest,

independence, without alms, but by a system of "friendly visitation," and the work of the Society for Improving the Condition of the Poor and kindred organizations along the same line, shows what can be done by well-directed effort. It is estimated that New York spends in public and private charity every year a round $8,000,000. A small part of this sum intelligently invested in a great labor bureau, that would bring the seeker of work and the one with work to give together under auspices offering some degree of mutual security, would certainly repay the amount of the investment in the saving of much capital now worse than wasted, and would be prolific of the best results. The ultimate and greatest need, however, the real remedy, is to remove the cause—the tenement that was built for "a class of whom nothing was expected," and which has come fully up to the expectation. Tenement-house reform holds the key to the problem of pauperism in the city. We can never get rid of either the tenement or the pauper. The two will always exist together in New York. But by reforming the one, we can do more toward exterminating the other than can be done by all other means together that have yet been invented, or ever will be.

IDA B. WELLS

Born into slavery in Mississippi, Ida B. Wells (1862–1931) began teaching school at the age of fourteen. In 1884 she moved to Memphis, continuing to teach while attending Fisk University, but she lost her contract after writing newspaper articles criticizing limited educational opportunities for African-Americans. Instead she turned to journalism full-time, investing her savings in The Memphis Free Speech and Light. *In 1891, three Memphis friends, all black business leaders, were lynched. Wells responded with a series of scathing articles and editorials on the pervasive use of lynch law to enforce Jim Crow. While on a speaking tour her newspaper's offices in Memphis were burned and sacked, and Wells decided not to return. She joined the staff of the* New York Age, *continuing her systematic documentation of the lynching epidemic.*

In 1895 Wells published A Red Record, *from which this selection is excerpted. In its exhaustive survey of lynchings, Wells's work anticipates modern human-rights investigation, and the kind of statistical analysis now familiar from computer-assisted reporting.*

The same year, Wells married Chicago newspaper publisher Ferdinand Barnett. A leader in women's suffrage as well as the anti-lynching campaign, she founded the Negro Fellowship League and remained an active desegregationist until her death.

LYNCHING OF INNOCENT MEN (LYNCHED ON ACCOUNT OF RELATIONSHIP)

From *A Red Record,* 1897

If no other reason appealed to the sober sense of the American people to check the growth of Lynch Law, the absolute unreliability and recklessness of the mob in inflicting punishment for crimes done, should do so. Several instances of this spirit have occurred in the year past. In Louisiana, near New Orleans, in July, 1893, Roselius Julian, a colored man, shot and killed a white judge, named Victor Estopinal. The cause of the shooting has never been definitely ascertained. It is claimed that the Negro resented an insult to his wife, and the killing of the white man was an act of a Negro (who dared) to defend his home. The judge was killed in the court house, and Julian, heavily armed, made his escape to the swamps near the city. He has never been apprehended, nor has any information ever been gleaned as to his whereabouts. A mob determined to secure the fugitive murderer and burn him alive. The swamps were hunted through and through in vain, when, being unable to wreak their revenge upon the murderer, the mob turned its attention to his unfortunate relatives. Dispatches from New Orleans, dated September 19, 1893, described the affair as follows: "Posses were immediately organized and the surrounding country was scoured, but the search was fruitless so far as the real criminal was concerned. The mother, three brothers and two sisters of the Negro were arrested yesterday at the Black Ridge in the rear of the city by the police and taken to the little jail on Judge Estopinal's place about Southport, because of the belief that they were succoring the fugitive. "About 11 o'clock twenty-five men, some armed with rifles and shotguns, came up to the jail. They unlocked the door and held a conference among themselves as to what they should do. Some were in favor of hanging the five, while others insisted that only two of the brothers should be strung up. This was finally agreed to, and the two doomed Negroes were hurried to a pasture one hundred yards distant, and there asked to take their last chance of saving their lives by making a confession, but the Negroes made no reply. They were then told to kneel down and pray. One did so, the other remained standing, but both prayed fervently. The taller Negro was then hoisted up. The shorter Negro stood gazing at the horrible death of his brother without flinching. Five minutes later he was also hanged. The mob decided to take the remaining brother out to Camp Parapet and hang him there. The other two were to be taken out and flogged, with an order to get out of the parish in less than half an hour. The third brother, Paul, was taken out to the camp, which is about a mile distant in the interior, and there he was hanged to a tree."

Another young man, who was in no way related to Julian, who perhaps did not even know the man and who was entirely innocent of any offense in connection therewith, was murdered by the same mob. The same paper says: "During the search for Julian on Saturday one branch of the posse visited the house of a Negro family in the neighborhood of Camp Parapet, and failing to find the object of their search, tried to induce John Willis, a young Negro, to disclose the whereabouts of Julian. He refused to do so, or could not do so, and was kicked to death by the gang."

An Indiana Case.

Almost equal to the ferocity of the mob which killed the three brothers, Julian and the unoffending, John Willis, because of the murder of Judge Estopinal, was the action of a mob near Vincennes, Ind. In this case a wealthy colored man, named Allen Butler, who was well known in the community, and enjoyed the confidence and respect of the entire country, was made the victim of a mob and hung because his son had become unduly intimate with a white girl who was a servant around his house. There was no pretense that the facts were otherwise than as here stated. The woman lived at Butler's house as a servant, and she and Butler's son fell in love with each other, and later it was found that the girl was in a delicate condition. It was claimed, but with how much truth no one has ever been able to tell, that the father had procured an abortion, or himself had operated on the girl, and that she had left the house to go back to her home. It was never claimed that the father was in any way responsible for the action of his son, but the authorities procured the arrest of both father and son, and at the preliminary examination the father gave bail to appear before the Grand Jury when it should convene. On the same night, however, the mob took the matter in hand and with the intention of hanging the son. It assembled, while the boy, who had been unable to give bail, was lodged in jail at Lawrenceville. As it was impossible to reach Lawrenceville and hang the son, the leaders of the mob concluded they would go to Butler's house and hang him. Butler was found at his home, taken out by the mob and hung to a tree. This was in the law-abiding state of Indiana, which furnished the United States its last president and which claims all the honor, pride and glory of Northern civilization. None of the leaders of the mob were apprehended, and no steps whatever were taken to bring the murderers to justice.

KILLED FOR HIS STEPFATHER'S CRIME.

An account has been given of the cremation of Henry Smith, at Paris, Texas, for the murder of the infant child of a man named Vince. It would appear that human ferocity was not sated when it vented itself upon a human being by burning his eyes out, by thrusting a red hot iron down his throat, and then by burning his body to ashes. Henry Smith, the victim of these savage orgies, was beyond all the power of torture, but a few miles outside of Paris, some members of the community concluded that it would be proper to kill a stepson named William Butler as a partial penalty for the original crime. This young man, against whom no word has ever been said, and who was in fact an orderly, peaceable boy, had been watched with the severest scrutiny by members of the mob who believed he knew something of the whereabouts of Smith. He declared from the very first that he did not know where his stepfather was, which statement was well proven to be a fact after the discovery of Smith in Arkansas, whence he had fled through swamps and woods and unfrequented places. Yet Butler was apprehended, placed under arrest, and on the night of February 6th, taken out on Hickory Creek, five miles southeast of Paris, and hung for his stepfather's crime. After his body was suspended in the air, the mob fired it with bullets.

LYNCHED BECAUSE THE JURY ACQUITTED HIM.

The entire system of the judiciary of this country is in the hands of white people. To this add the fact of the inherent prejudice against colored people, and it will be clearly seen that a white jury is certain to find a Negro prisoner guilty if there is the least evidence to warrant such a finding.

Meredith Lewis was arrested in Roseland, La., in July of last year. A white jury found him not guilty of the crime of murder wherewith he stood charged. This did not suit the mob. A few nights after the verdict was rendered, and he declared to be innocent, a mob gathered in his vicinity and went to his house. He was called, and suspecting nothing, went outside. He was seized and hurried off to a convenient spot and hanged by the neck until he was dead for the murder of a woman of which the jury had said he was innocent.

LYNCHED AS A SCAPEGOAT.

Wednesday, July 5th, about 10 o'clock in the morning, a terrible crime was committed within four miles of Wickliffe, Ky. Two girls, Mary and Ruby Ray, were found murdered a short distance from their home. The news of this terrible cowardly murder of two helpless young girls spread like wild fire, and searching parties scoured the territory surrounding Wickliffe and Bardwell. Two of the searching party, the Clark brothers, saw a man enter the Dupoyster cornfield; they got their guns and fired at the fleeing figure, but without effect; he got away, but they said he was a white man or nearly so. The search continued all day without effect, save the arrest of two or three strange Negroes. A bloodhound was brought from the penitentiary and put on the trail which he followed from the scene of the murder to the river and into the boat of a fisherman named Gordon. Gordon stated that he had ferried one man and only one across the river about half past six the evening of July 6th; that his passenger sat in front of him, and he was a white man or a very bright mulatto, who could not be told from a white man. The bloodhound was put across the river in the boat, and he struck a trail again at Bird's Point on the Missouri side, ran about three hundred yards to the cottage of a white farmer named Grant and there lay down refusing to go further.

Thursday morning a brakesman on a freight train going out of Sikeston, Mo., discovered a Negro stealing a ride; he ordered him off and had hot words which terminated in a fight. The brakesman had the Negro arrested. When arrested, between 11 and 12 o'clock, he had on a dark woolen shirt, light pants and coat, and no vest. He had twelve dollars in paper, two silver dollars and ninety-five cents in change; he had also four rings in his pockets, a knife and razor which were rusted and stained. The Sikeston authorities immediately jumped to the conclusion that this man was the murderer for whom the Kentuckians across the river were searching. They telegraphed to Bardwell that their prisoner had on no coat, but wore a blue vest and pants which would perhaps correspond with the coat found at the scene of the murder, and that the names of the murdered girls were in the rings found in his possession.

As soon as this news was received, the sheriffs of Ballard and Carlisle counties and a posse of thirty well armed and determined Kentuckians, who had pledged their word the prisoner should be taken back to the scene of the supposed crime, to be executed there if proved to be the guilty man, chartered a train and at nine o'clock Thursday night started for Sikeston. Arriving there two hours later, the sheriff at Sikeston, who had no warrant for the prisoner's arrest and detention, delivered him into the hands of the mob without authority for so doing, and accompanied them to Bird's Point. The prisoner gave his name as Miner, his home at Springfield, and said he had never been in Kentucky in his life, but the sheriff turned him over to the mob to be taken to Wickliffe, that Frank Gordon, the fisherman, who had put a man across the river might identify him.

In other words, the protection of the law was withdrawn from C. J. Miner, and he was given to a mob by this sheriff at Sikeston, who knew that the prisoner's life depended on one man's word. After an altercation with the train men, who wanted another $50 for taking the train back to Bird's Point, the crowd arrived there at three o'clock, Friday morning. Here was anchored "The Three States," a ferry boat plying between Wickliffe, Ky., Cairo, Ill., and Bird's Point, Mo. This boat left Cairo at twelve o'clock, Thursday, with nearly three hundred of Cairo's best citizens and thirty kegs of beer on board. This was consumed while the crowd and the bloodhound waited for the prisoner.

When the prisoner was on board "The Three States" the dog was turned loose, and after moving aimlessly around, followed the crowd to where Miner sat handcuffed and there he stopped. The crowd closed in on the pair and insisted that the brute had identified him because of that action. When the boat reached Wickliffe, Gordon, the fisherman, was called on to say whether the prisoner was the man he ferried over the river the day of the murder.

The sheriff of Ballard county informed him sternly that if the prisoner was not the man, he (the fisherman) would be held responsible as knowing who the guilty man was. Gordon stated before, that the man he ferried across was a white man or a bright colored man; Miner was a dark brown skinned man, with kinky hair, "neither yellow nor black," says the *Cairo Evening Telegram* of Friday, July 7th. The fisherman went up to Miner from behind, looked at him without speaking for fully five minutes, then slowly said, "Yes, that's the man I crossed over." This was about six o'clock, Friday morning, and the crowd wished to hang Miner then and there. But Mr. Ray, the father of the girls, insisted that he be taken to Bardwell, the county seat of Ballard, and twelve miles inland. He said he thought a white man committed the crime, and that he was not satisfied that was the man. They took him to Bardwell and at ten o'clock, this same excited, unauthorized mob undertook to determine Miner's guilt. One of the Clark brothers who shot at a fleeing man in the Dupoyster cornfield, said the prisoner was the same man; the other said he was not, but the testimony of the first was accepted. A colored woman who had said she gave breakfast to a colored man clad in a blue flannel suit the morning of the murder, said positively that she had never seen Miner before. The gold rings found in his possession had no names in them, as had been asserted, and Mr. Ray said they did not belong to his daughters. Meantime a funeral pyre for the purpose of burning Miner to death had been erected in the center of the village. While the crowd swayed by passion was clamoring that he be burnt, Miner stepped forward and made the following statement: "My name is C. J. Miner. I am from Springfield, Ill.; my wife lives at 716 N. 2d Street. I am here among you today, looked upon as one of the most brutal men before the people. I stand here surrounded by men who are excited, men who are not willing to let the law take its course, and as far as the crime is concerned, I have committed no crime, and certainly no crime gross enough to deprive me of my life and liberty to walk upon the green earth."

A telegram was sent to the chief of the police at Springfield, Ill., asking if one C. J. Miner lived there. An answer in the negative was returned. A few hours after, it was ascertained that a man named Miner, and his wife, did live at the number the prisoner gave in his speech, but the information came to Bardwell too late to do the prisoner any good. Miner was taken to jail, every stitch of clothing literally torn from his body and examined again. On the lower left side of the bosom of his shirt was found a dark reddish spot about the size of a dime. Miner said it was paint which he had gotten on him at Jefferson Barracks. This spot was only on the right side, and could not be seen from the under side at all, thus showing it had not gone through the cloth as blood or any liquid substance would do.

Chief-of-police Mahaney, of Cairo, Ill., was with the prisoner, and he took his knife and scraped at the spot, particles of which came off in his hand. Miner told them to take his clothes to any expert, and if the spot was shown to be blood, they might do anything they wished with him. They took his clothes away and were gone some time. After a while they were brought back and thrown into the cell without a word. It is needless to say that if the spot had been found to be blood, that fact would have been announced, and the shirt retained as evidence. Meanwhile numbers of rough, drunken men crowded into the cell and tried to force a confession of the deed from the prisoner's lips. He refused to talk save to reiterate his innocence. To Mr. Mahaney, who talked seriously and kindly to him, telling him the mob meant to burn and torture him at three o'clock, Miner said: "Burning and torture here lasts but a little while, but if I die with a lie on my soul, I shall be tortured forever. I am innocent." For more than three hours, all sorts of pressure in the way of threats, abuse and urging, was brought to bear to force him to confess to the murder and thus justify the mob in its deed of murder. Miner remained firm, but as the hour drew near, and the crowd became more impatient, he asked for a priest. As none could be procured, he then asked for a Methodist minister, who came, prayed with the doomed man, baptized him and exhorted Miner to confess. To keep up the flagging spirits of the dense crowd around the jail, the rumor went out more than once, that Miner had confessed. But the solemn assurance of the minister, chief-of-police, and leading editor who were with Miner all along is that this rumor is absolutely false.

At three o'clock the mob rushed to the jail to secure the prisoner. Mr. Ray had changed his mind about the promised burning; he was still in doubt as to the prisoner's guilt. He again addressed the crowd to that effect, urging them not to burn Miner, and the mob heeded him so far, that they compromised on hanging instead of burning, which was agreed to by Mr. Ray. There was a loud yell, and a rush was made for the prisoner. He was stripped naked, his clothing literally torn from his body, and his shirt was tied around his loins. Someone declared the rope was "a white man's death," and a log-chain, nearly a hundred feet in length, weighing over one hundred pounds, was placed round Miner's neck and body, and he was led and dragged through the streets of the village in that condition followed by thousands of people. He fainted from exhaustion several times, but was supported to the platform where they first intended burning him.

The chain was hooked around his neck, a man climbed the telegraph pole and the other end of the chain was passed up to him and made fast to the cross-arm. Others brought a long forked stick which Miner was made to straddle. By this means he was raised several feet from the ground and then let fall. The first fall broke his neck, but he was raised in this way and let fall a second time. Numberless shots were fired into the dangling body, for most of that crowd were heavily armed, and had been drinking all day. Miner's body hung thus exposed from three to five o'clock, during which time, several photographs of him as he hung dangling at the end of the chain were taken, and his toes and fingers were cut off. His body was taken down, placed on the platform, the torch applied, and in a few moments there was nothing left of C. J. Miner save a few bones and ashes. Thus perished another of the many victims of Lynch Law, but it is the honest and sober belief of many who witnessed the scene that an innocent man has been barbarously and shockingly put to death in the glare of the 19th century civilization, by those who profess to believe in Christianity, law and order.

II.

MUCKRAKERS AND THE ERA OF REFORM: 1900–1920

Lincoln Steffens

To call Lincoln Steffens (1866–1936) one of the founders of the muckraking movement would be like describing Martin Luther King as organizer of the Montgomery Bus Boycott: factually true, but nowhere near enough. Journalist, publisher, socialist, observer of revolutions in Mexico and Russia, novelist, and autobiographer, Steffens was a critical bridge between nineteenth-century reform and twentieth-century radicalism.

Born in San Francisco, Steffens began his career as a New York police reporter, anti-Tammany columnist, and protégé of Jacob Riis. In 1903 Steffens was recruited by S.S. McClure as managing editor for his magazine, but he had little taste for life behind the desk. Instead, McClure sent him on the road to investigate political corruption in municipalities nationwide, a series eventually published in book form as The Shame of the Cities. *The first installment, reprinted here, appeared in* McClure's *in the same issue as Ida Tarbell's Standard Oil chronicle and an article by Ray Stannard Baker on trade-union corruption. That number of* McClure's *is generally credited with launching muckraking in mass-market magazines.*

Following the collapse of the muckraking movement, Steffens went through several evolutions—from cynical newsman to Christian reformer to an enthusiastic acolyte of the Russian Revolution, remaining a defender of Stalin up until his death. He was also mentor to a generation of writers transcending any narrow political definition (he even appears in one of Ezra Pound's "Cantos"). Steffens's autobiography, published in 1931, won acclaim as, in the words of critic Newton Arvin, "the extended epitaph of a whole generation, a whole social movement, a whole class."

But his principal legacy is as a journalist. Combining information already on the record with his own inquiries, Steffens brought to reporting all the aspirations of literature: his exposés are alive with precisely drawn characters, individual motivation, a sense of place, and high-velocity storytelling. Before Steffens, urban-reform reporting focused narrowly on corrupt acts of office. Steffens connected the dots, showing the bargains between political machines and corporate interest.

The Shame of Minneapolis: The Rescue and Redemption of a City that Was Sold Out

From *McClure's Magazine,* 1903

Whenever anything extraordinary is done in American municipal politics, whether for good or for evil, you can trace it almost invariably to one man. The people do not do it. Neither do the "gangs," "combines," or political parties. These are but instruments by which bosses (not leaders; we Americans are not led, but driven) rule the people, and commonly sell them out. But there are at least two forms of the autocracy which has supplanted the democracy here as it has everywhere it has been tried. One is that of the organized majority by which, as in Tammany Hall in New York and the Republican machine in Philadelphia, the boss has normal control of more than half the voters. The other is that of the adroitly managed minority. The "good people" are herded into parties and stupefied with convictions and a name, Republican or Democrat; while the "bad people" are so organized or interested by the boss that he can wield their votes to enforce terms with party managers and decide elections. St. Louis is a conspicuous example of this form. Minneapolis is another. Colonel Ed. Butler is the unscrupulous opportunist who handled the non-partisan minority which turned St. Louis into a "boodle town." In Minneapolis "Doc" Ames was the man.

Minneapolis is a New England town on the upper Mississippi. The metropolis of the Northwest, it is the metropolis also of Norway and Sweden in America. Indeed, it is the second largest Scandinavian city in the world. But Yankees, straight from Down East, settled the town, and their New England spirit predominates. They had Bayard Taylor lecture there in the early days of the settlement; they made it the seat of the University of Minnesota. Yet even now, when the town has grown to a population of more than 200,000, you feel that there is something Western about it too—a Yankee with a small Puritan head, an open prairie heart, and a great, big Scandinavian body. The Roundhead takes the Swede and Norwegian bone out into the woods, and they cut lumber by forests, or they go out on the prairies and raise wheat and mill it into fleet-cargoes of flour. They work hard, they make money, they are sober, satisfied, busy with their own affairs. There isn't much time for public business. Taken together, Miles, Hans, and Ole are very American. Miles insists upon strict laws, Ole and Hans want one or two Scandinavians on their ticket. These things granted, they go off on raft or reaper, leaving whoso will to enforce the laws and run the city.

The people who were left to govern the city hated above all things strict laws. They were the loafers, saloon keepers, gamblers, criminals, and the thriftless poor of all nationalities. Resenting the sobriety of a staid, industrious community, and having no Irish to boss them, they delighted to follow the jovial pioneer doctor, Albert Alonzo Ames. He was the "good fellow"—a genial, generous reprobate. Devery, Tweed, and many more have exposed in vain this amiable type. "Doc" Ames, tall, straight, and cheerful, attracted men, and they gave him votes for his smiles. He stood for license. There was nothing of the Puritan about him. His father, the sturdy old pioneer, Dr. Alfred Elisha Ames, had a strong strain of it in him, but he moved on with his family of six sons from Garden Prairie, Ill., to Fort Snelling reservation, in 1851, before Minneapolis was founded, and young Albert Alonzo, who then was ten years old, grew up free, easy, and tolerant. He was sent to school, then to college in Chicago, and he returned home a doctor of medicine before he was twenty-one. As the town waxed soberer and richer, "Doc" grew gayer and more and more generous. Skilful as a surgeon, devoted as a physician, and as a man kindly, he increased his practice till he was the best-loved man in the community. He was especially good to the poor. Anybody could summon "Doc" Ames at any hour to any distance. He went, and he gave not only his professional service, but sympathy, and often charity. "Richer men than you will pay your bill," he told the destitute. So there was a basis for his "good-fellowship." There always is; these good fellows are not frauds—not in the beginning.

But there is another side to them sometimes. Ames was sunshine not to the sick and destitute only. To the vicious and the depraved also he was a comfort. If a man was a hard drinker, the good Doctor cheered him with another drink; if he had stolen something, the Doctor helped to get him off. He was naturally vain; popularity developed his love of approbation. His loose life brought disapproval only from the good people, so gradually the Doctor came to enjoy best the society of the barroom and the streets. This society, flattered in turn, worshipped the good Doctor, and, active in politics always, put its physician into the arena.

Had he been wise, or even shrewd, he might have made himself a real power. But he wasn't calculating, only light and frivolous, so he did not organize his forces and run men for office. He sought office himself from the start, and he got most of the small places he wanted by changing his party to seize the opportunity. His floating minority, added to the regular partisan vote, was sufficient ordinarily for his useless victories. As time went on he rose from smaller offices to be a Republican mayor, then twice at intervals to be a Democratic mayor. He was a candidate once for Congress; he stood for governor once on a sort of Populist-Democrat ticket. Ames could not get anything outside of his own town, and after his third term as mayor it was thought he was out of politics altogether. He was getting old, and he was getting worse.

Like many a "good fellow" with hosts of miscellaneous friends down town to whom he was devoted, the good Doctor neglected his own family. From neglect he went on openly to separation from his wife and a second establishment. The climax came not long before the election of 1900. His wife was dying, and his daughter wrote to her father a note saying that her mother wished to see and forgive him. The messenger found him in a saloon. The Doctor read the note, laid it on the bar, and scribbled across it a sentence incredibly obscene. His wife died. The outraged family would not have the father at the funeral, but he appeared, not at the house, but in a carriage on the street. He sat across the way, with his feet up and a cigar in his mouth, till the funeral moved; then he circled around, crossing it and meeting it, and making altogether a scene which might well close any man's career.

It didn't end his. The people had just secured the passage of a new primary law to establish direct popular government. There were to be no more nominations by convention. The voters were to ballot for their party candidates. By a slip of some sort, the laws did not specify that Republicans only should vote for Republican candidates, and only Democrats for Democratic candidates. Any voter could vote at either primary. Ames, in disrepute with his own party, the Democratic, bade his followers vote for his nomination for mayor on the Republican ticket. They all voted; not all the Republicans did. He was nominated. Nomination is far from election, and you would say that the trick would not help him. But that was a Presidential year, so the people of Minneapolis had to vote for Ames, the Republican candidate for Mayor. Besides, Ames said he was going to reform; that he was getting old, and wanted to close his career with a good administration. The effective argument, however, was that, since McKinley had to be elected to save the country, Ames must be supported for Mayor of Minneapolis. Why? The great American people cannot be trusted to scratch a ticket.

Well, Minneapolis got its old mayor back, and he was reformed. Up to this time Ames had not been very venal personally. He was a "spender," not a "grafter," and he was guilty of corruption chiefly by proxy; he took the honors and left the spoils to his followers. His administrations were no worse than the worst. Now, however, he set out upon a career of corruption which for deliberateness, invention, and avarice has never been equalled. It was as if he had made up his mind that he had been careless long enough, and meant to enrich his last years. He began early.

Immediately upon his election, before he took office (on January 7th), he organized a cabinet and laid plans to turn the city over to outlaws who were to work under police direction for the profit of his administration. He chose for chief his brother, Colonel Fred W. Ames, who had recently returned under a cloud from service in the Philippines. The Colonel had commanded a Minnesota regiment out there till he proved a coward under fire; he escaped court-martial only on the understanding that he should resign on reaching San Francisco, whither he was immediately shipped. This he did not do, and his brother's influence at Washington saved him to be mustered out with the regiment. But he was a weak vessel for chief of police, and the mayor picked for chief of detectives an abler man, who was to direct the more difficult operations. This was Norman W. King, a former gambler, who knew the criminals needed in the business ahead. King was to invite to Minneapolis thieves, confidence men, pickpockets, and gamblers, and release some that were in the local jail. They were to be organized into groups, according to their profession, and detectives were assigned to assist and direct them. The head of the gambling syndicate was to have charge of the gambling, making the terms and collecting the "graft," just as King and a Captain Hill were to collect from the thieves. The collector for women of the town was to be Irwin A. Gardner, a medical student in the Doctor's office, who was made a special policeman for the purpose. These men looked over the force, selected those men who could be trusted, charged them a price for their retention, and marked for dimissal 107 men out of 225, the 107 being the best policemen in the department from the point of view of the citizens who afterward reorganized the force. John Fitchette, better known as "Coffee John," a Virginian (who served on the Jeff Davis jury), the keeper of a notorious coffee-house, was to be a captain of police, with no duties except to sell places on the police force.

And they did these things that they planned—all and more. The administration opened with the revolution on the police force. They liberated the thieves in the local jail, and made known to the Under World generally that "things were doing" in Minneapolis. The incoming swindlers reported to King or his staff for instructions, and went to work, turning the "swag" over to the detectives in charge. Gambling went on openly, and disorderly houses multiplied under the fostering care of Gardner, the medical student. But all this was not enough. Ames dared to break openly into the municipal system of vice protection.

There was such a thing. Minneapolis, strict in its laws, forbade vices which are inevitable, then regularly permitted them under certain conditions. Legal limits, called "patrol lines," were prescribed, within which saloons might be opened. These ran along the river front, out through part of the business section, with long arms reaching into the Scandinavian quarters, north and south. Gambling also was confined, but more narrowly. And there were limits, also arbitrary, but not always identical with those for gambling, within which the social evil was allowed. But the novel feature of this scheme was that disorderly houses were practically licensed by the city, the women appearing before the clerk of the Municipal Court each month to pay a "fine" of $100. Unable at first to get this "graft," Ames's man Gardner persuaded women to start houses, apartments, and, of all things, candy stores, which sold sweets to children and tobacco to the "lumber Jacks" in front, while a nefarious traffic was carried on in the rear. But they paid Ames, not the city, and that was all the reform administration cared about.

The revenue from all these sources must have been enormous. It only whetted the avarice of the mayor and his Cabinet. They let gambling privileges without restriction to location or "squareness"; the syndicate could cheat and rob as it would. Peddlers and pawnbrokers, formerly licensed by the city, bought permits now instead from "Gardner's father," A. L. Gardner, who was the mayor's agent in this field. Some two hundred slot machines were installed in various parts of the town, with owner's agent and mayor's agent watching and collecting from them enough to pay the mayor $15,000 a year as his share. Auction frauds were instituted. Opium joints and unlicensed saloons, called "blind pigs," were protected. Gardner even had a police baseball team, for whose games tickets were sold to people who had to buy them. But the women were the easiest "graft." They were compelled to buy illustrated biographies of the city officials; they had to give presents of money, jewelry, and gold stars to police officers. But the money they still paid direct to the city in fines, some $35,000 a year, fretted the mayor, and at last he reached for it. He came out with a declaration, in his old character as friend of the oppressed, that $100 a month was too much for these women to pay. They should be required to pay the city fine only once in two months. This puzzled the town till it became generally known that Gardner collected the other month for the mayor. The final outrage in this department, however, was an order of the mayor for the periodic visits to disorderly houses, by the city's physicians, at from $5 to $20 per visit. The two physicians he appointed called when they willed, and more and more frequently, till toward the end the calls became a pure formality, with the collections as the one and only object. In a general way all this business was known. It did not arouse the citizens, but it did attract criminals, and more and more thieves and swindlers came hurrying to Minneapolis. Some of them saw the police, and made terms. Some were seen by the police and invited to go to work. There was room for all. This astonishing fact that the government of a city asked criminals to rob the people is fully established. The police and the criminals have confessed it separately. Their statements agree in detail. Detective Norbeck made the arrangement, and introduced the swindlers to Gardner, who, over King's head, took the money from them. Here is the story "Billy" Edwards, a "big mitt" man, told under oath of his reception in Minneapolis:

"I had been out to the coast, and hadn't seen Norbeck for some time. After I returned I boarded a Minneapolis car one evening to go down to South Minneapolis to visit a friend. Norbeck and Detective DeLaittre were on the car. When Norbeck saw me he came up and shook hands, and said, 'Hullo, Billy, how goes it?' I said, 'Not very well.' Then he says, 'Things have changed since you went away. Me and Gardner are the whole thing now. Before you left they thought I didn't know anything, but I turned a few tricks, and now I'm It.' 'I'm glad of that, Chris,' I said. He says, 'I've got great things for you. I'm going to fix up a joint for you.' 'That's good,' I said, 'but I don't believe you can do it.' 'Oh, yes, I can,' he replied. 'I'm It now—Gardner and me.' 'Well, if you can do it,' says I, 'there's money in it.' 'How much can you pay?' he asked. 'Oh, $150 or $200 a week,' says I. 'That settles it,' he said; 'I'll take you down to see Gardner, and we'll fix it up.' Then he made an appointment to meet me the next night, and we went down to Gardner's house together."

There Gardner talked business in general, showed his drawer full of bills, and jokingly asked how Edwards would like to have them. Edwards says:

"I said, 'That looks pretty good to me,' and Gardner told us that he had 'collected' the money from the women he had on his staff, and that he was going to pay it over to the 'old man' when he got back from his hunting trip next morning. Afterward he told me that the mayor had been much pleased with our $500, and that he said everything was all right, and for us to go ahead."

"Link" Crossman, another confidence man who was with Edwards, said that Gardner demanded $1,000 at first, but compromised on $500 for the mayor, $50 for Gardner, and $50 for Norbeck. To the chief, Fred Ames, they gave tips now and then of $25 or $50. "The first week we ran," said Crossman, "I gave Fred $15. Norbeck took me down there. We shook hands, and I handed him an envelope with $15. He pulled out a list of steerers we had sent him, and said he wanted to go over them with me. He asked where the joint was located. At another time I slipped $25 into his hand as he was standing in the hallway of City Hall." But these smaller payments, after the first "opening, $500," are all down on the pages of the "big mitt" ledger. This notorious book, which was kept by Charlie Howard, one of the "big mitt" men, was much talked of at the subsequent trials, but was kept hidden to await the trial of the mayor himself.

The "big mitt" game was swindling by means of a stacked hand at stud poker. "Steerers" and "boosters" met "suckers" on the street, at hotels, and railway stations, won their confidence, and led them to the "joint." Usually the "sucker" was called, by the amount of his loss, "the $102 man" or "the $35 man." Roman Meix alone had the distinction among all the Minneapolis victims of going by his own name. Having lost $775, he became known for his persistent complainings. But they all "kicked" some. To Norbeck at the street door was assigned the duty of hearing their complaints, and "throwing a scare into them." "Oh, so you've been gambling," he would say. "Have you got a license? Well, then, you better get right out of this town." Sometimes he accompanied them to the station and saw them off. If they were not to be put off thus, he directed them to the chief of police. Fred Ames tried to wear them out by keeping them waiting in the anteroom. If they outlasted him, he saw them and frightened them with threats of all sorts of trouble for gambling without a license. Meix wanted to have payment on his check stopped. Ames, who had been a bank clerk, told him so, and then had the effrontery to say that payment on such a check could not be stopped.

Burglaries were common. How many the police planned may never be known. Charles F. Brackett and Fred Malone, police captains and detectives, were active, and one well-established crime of theirs is the robbery of the Pabst Brewing Company office. They persuaded two men, one an employee, to learn the combination of the safe, open and clean it out one night, while the two officers stood guard outside.

The excesses of the municipal administration became so notorious that some of the members of it remonstrated with the others, and certain county officers were genuinely alarmed. No restraint followed their warnings. Sheriff Megaarden, no Puritan himself, felt constrained to interfere, and he made some arrests of gamblers. The Ames people turned upon him in a fury; they accused him of making overcharges in his accounts with the county for fees, and laying the evidence before Governor Van Sant, they had Megaarden removed from office. Ames offered bribes to two county commissioners to appoint Gardner sheriff, so as to be sure of no more trouble in that quarter. This move failed, but the lesson taught Megaarden served to clear the atmosphere, and the spoliation went on as recklessly as ever. It became impossible.

Even lawlessness must be regulated. Dr. Ames, never an organizer, attempted no control, and his followers began to quarrel among themselves. They deceived one another; they robbed the thieves; they robbed Ames himself. His brother became dissatisfied with his share of the spoils, and formed cabals with captains who plotted against the administration and set up disorderly houses, "panel games," and all sorts of "grafts" of their own. The one man loyal to the mayor was Gardner, and Fred Ames, Captain King, and their pals, plotted the fall of the favorite. Now anybody could get anything from the Doctor, if he could have him alone. The Fred Ames clique chose a time when the mayor was at West Baden; they filled him with suspicion of Gardner and the fear of exposure, and induced him to let a creature named "Reddy" Cohen, instead of Gardner, do the collecting, and pay over all the moneys, not directly, but through Fred. Gardner made a touching appeal. "I have been honest. I have paid you all," he said to the mayor. "Fred and the rest will rob you." This was true, but it was of no avail.

Fred Ames was in charge at last, and he himself went about giving notice of the change. Three detectives were with him when he visited the women, and here is the women's story, in the words of one, as it was told again and again in court: "Colonel Ames came in with the detectives. He stepped into a side room and asked me if I had been paying Gardner. I told him I had, and he told me not to pay no more, but to come to his office later, and he would let me know what to do. I went to the City Hall in about three weeks, after Cohen had called and said he was 'the party.' I asked the chief if it was all right to pay Cohen, and he said it was."

The new arrangement did not work so smoothly as the old. Cohen was an oppressive collector, and Fred Ames, appealed to, was weak and lenient. He had no sure hold on the force. His captains, free of Gardner, were undermining the chief. They increased their private operations. Some of the detectives began to drink hard and neglect their work. Norbeck so worried the "big mitt" men by staying away from the joint, that they complained to Fred about him. The chief rebuked Norbeck, and he promised to "do better," but thereafter he was paid, not by the week, but by piece work—so much for each "trimmed sucker" that he ran out of town. Protected swindlers were arrested for operating in the street by "Coffee John's" new policemen who took the places of the negligent detectives. Fred let the indignant prisoners go when they were brought before him, but the arrests were annoying, inconvenient, and disturbed business. The whole system became so demoralized that every man was for himself. There was not left even the traditional honor among thieves.

It was at this juncture, in April, 1902, that the grand jury for the summer term was drawn. An ordinary body of unselected citizens, it received no special instructions from the bench; the county prosecutor offered it only routine work to do. But there was a man among them who was a fighter—the foreman, Hovey C. Clarke. He was of an old New England family. Coming to Minneapolis when a young man, seventeen years before, he had fought for employment, fought with his employers for position, fought with his employees, the lumber-Jacks, for command, fought for his company against competitors; and he had won always, till now he had the habit of command, the impatient, imperious manner of the master, and the assurance of success which begets it. He did not want to be a grand juryman, he did not want to be a foreman; but since he was both, he wanted to accomplish something.

Why not rip up the Ames gang? Heads shook, hands went up; it was useless to try. The discouragement fired Clarke. That was just what he would do, he said, and he took stock of his jury. Two or three were men with backbone; that he knew, and he quickly had them with him. The rest were all sorts of men. Mr. Clarke won over each man to himself, and interested them all. Then he called for the county prosecutor. The prosecutor was a politician; he knew the Ames crowd; they were too powerful to attack.

"You are excused," said the foreman.

There was a scene; the prosecutor knew his rights.

"Do you think, Mr. Clarke," he cried, "that you can run the grand jury and my office, too?"

"Yes," said Clarke, "I will run your office if I want to; and I want to. You're excused."

Mr. Clarke does not talk much about his doings last summer; he isn't the talking sort. But he does say that all he did was to apply simple business methods to his problem. In action, however, these turned out to be the most approved police methods. He hired a lot of local detectives who, he knew, would talk about what they were doing, and thus would be watched by the police. Having thus thrown a false scent, he hired some other detectives whom nobody knew about. This was expensive; so were many of the other things he did; but he was bound to win, so he paid the price, drawing freely on his own and his colleagues' pockets. (The total cost to the county for a long summer's work by this grand jury was $259.) With his detectives out, he himself went to the jail to get tips from the inside, from criminals who, being there, must have grievances. He made the acquaintance of the jailor, Captain Alexander, and Alexander was a friend of Sheriff Megaarden. Yes, he had some men there who were "sore" and might want to get even.

Now two of these were "big mitt" men who had worked for Gardner. One was "Billy" Edwards, the other "Cheerful Charlie" Howard. I heard too many explanations of their plight to choose any one; this general account will cover the ground: In the Ames mêlée, either by mistake, neglect, or for spite growing out of the network of conflicting interests and gangs, they were arrested, arraigned, not before Fred Ames, but a judge, and held in bail too high for them to furnish. They had paid for an unexpired period of protection, yet could get neither protection nor bail. They were forgotten. "We got the double cross all right," they said, and they bled with their grievance; but squeal, no, sir!—that was "another deal."

But Mr. Clarke had their story, and he was bound to force them to tell it under oath on the stand. If they did, Gardner and Norbeck would be indicted, tried, and probably convicted. In themselves, these men were of no great importance; but they were the key to the situation, and a way up to the mayor. It was worth trying. Mr. Clarke went into the jail with Messrs. Lester Elwood and Willard J. Hield, grand jurors on whom he relied most for delicate work. They stood by while the foreman talked. And the foreman's way of talking was to smile, swear, threaten, and cajole. "Billy" Edwards told me afterwards that he and Howard were finally persuaded to turn state's evidence, because they believed that Mr. Clarke was the kind of a man to keep his promises and fulfil his threats. "We," he said, meaning criminals generally, "are always stacking up against juries and lawyers who want us to holler. We don't, because we see they ain't wise, and won't get there. They're quitters; they can be pulled off. Clarke has a hard eye. I know men. It's my business to size 'em up, and I took him for a winner, and I played in with him against that whole big bunch of easy things that was running things on the bum." The grand jury was ready at the end of three weeks of hard work to find bills. A prosecutor was needed. The public prosecutor was being ignored, but his first assistant and friend, Al. J. Smith, was taken in hand by Mr. Clarke. Smith hesitated; he knew better even than the foreman the power and resources of the Ames gang. But he came to believe in Mr. Clarke, just as Edwards had; he was sure the foreman would win; so he went over to his side, and, having once decided, he led the open fighting, and, alone in court, won cases against men who had the best lawyers in the State to defend them. His court record is extraordinary. Moreover, he took over the negotiations with criminals for evidence, Messrs. Clarke, Hield, Elwood, and the other jurors providing means and moral support. These were needed. Bribes were offered to Smith; he was threatened; he was called a fool. But so was Clarke, to whom $28,000 was offered to quit, and for whose slaughter a slugger was hired to come from Chicago. What startled the jury most, however, was the character of the citizens who were sent to them to dissuade them from their course. No reform I ever studied has failed to bring out this phenomenon of virtuous cowardice, the baseness of the decent citizen.

Nothing stopped this jury, however. They had courage. They indicted Gardner, Norbeck, Fred Ames, and many lesser persons. But the gang had courage, too, and raised a defence fund to fight Clarke. Mayor Ames was defiant. Once, when Mr. Clarke called at the City Hall, the mayor met and challenged him. The mayor's heelers were all about him, but Clarke faced him.

"Yes, Doc Ames, I'm after you," he said. "I've been in this town for seventeen years, and all that time you've been a moral leper. I hear you were rotten during the ten years before that. Now I'm going to put you where all contagious things are put—where you cannot contaminate anybody else."

The trial of Gardner came on. Efforts had been made to persuade him to surrender the mayor, but the young man was paid $15,000 "to stand pat," and he went to trial and conviction silent. Other trials followed fast—Norbeck's, Fred Ames's, Chief of Detectives King's. Witnesses who were out of the State were needed, and true testimony from women. There was no county money for extradition, so the grand jurors paid these costs also. They had Meix followed from Michigan down to Mexico and back to Idaho, where they got him, and he was presented in court one day at the trial of Norbeck, who had "steered" him out of town. Norbeck thought Meix was a thousand miles away, and had been bold before. At the sight of him in court he started to his feet, and that night ran away. The jury spent more money in his pursuit, and they caught him. He confessed, but his evidence was not accepted. He was sentenced to three years in state's prison. Men caved all around, but the women were firm, and the first trial of Fred Ames failed. To break the women's faith in the ring, Mayor Ames was indicted for offering the bribe to have Gardner made sheriff—a genuine, but not the best case against him. It brought the women down to the truth, and Fred Ames, retried, was convicted and sentenced to six and a half years in state's prison. King was tried for accessory to felony (helping in the theft of a diamond, which he afterward stole from the thieves), and sentenced to three and a half years in prison. And still the indictments came, with trials following fast. Al. Smith resigned with the consent and thanks of the grand jury; his chief, who was to run for the same office again, wanted to try the rest of the cases, and he did very well.

All men were now on the side of law and order. The panic among the "grafters" was laughable, in spite of its hideous significance. Two heads of departments against whom nothing had been shown suddenly ran away, and thus suggested to the grand jury an inquiry which revealed another source of "graft," in the sale of supplies to public institutions and the diversion of great quantities of provisions to the private residences of the mayor and other officials. Mayor Ames, under indictment and heavy bonds for extortion, conspiracy, and bribe-offering, left the State on a night train; a gentleman who knew him by sight saw him sitting up at eleven o'clock in the smoking-room of the sleeping-car, an unlighted cigar in his mouth, his face ashen and drawn, and at six o'clock the next morning he still was sitting there, his cigar still unlighted. He went to West Baden, a health resort in Indiana, a sick and broken man, aging years in a month. The city was without a mayor, the ring was without a leader; cliques ruled, and they pictured one another hanging about the grand-jury room begging leave to turn state's evidence. Tom Brown, the mayor's secretary, was in the mayor's chair; across the hall sat Fred Ames, the chief of police, balancing Brown's light weight. Both were busy forming cliques within the ring. Brown had on his side Coffee John and Police Captain Hill. Ames had Captain "Norm" King (though he had been convicted and had resigned), Captain Krumweide, and Ernest Wheelock, the chief's secretary. Alderman D. Percy Jones, the president of the council, an honorable man, should have taken the chair, but he was in the East; so this unstable equilibrium was all the city had by way of a government.

Then Fred Ames disappeared. The Tom Brown clique had full sway, and took over the police department. This was a shock to everybody, to none more than to the King clique, which joined in the search for Ames. An alderman, Fred M. Powers, who was to run for mayor on the Republican ticket, took charge of the mayor's office, but he was not sure of his authority or clear as to his policy. The grand jury was the real power behind him, and the foreman was telegraphing for Alderman Jones. Meanwhile the cliques were making appeals to Mayor Ames, in West Baden, and each side that saw him received authority to do its will. The Coffee John clique, denied admission to the grand-jury room, turned to Alderman Powers, and were beginning to feel secure, when they heard that Fred Ames was coming back. They rushed around, and obtained an assurance from the exiled mayor that Fred was returning only to resign. Fred—now under conviction—returned, but he did not resign; supported by his friends, he took charge again of the police force. Coffee John besought Alderman Powers to remove the chief, and when the acting mayor proved himself too timid, Coffee John, Tom Brown, and Captain Hill laid a deep plot. They would ask Mayor Ames to remove his brother. This they felt sure they could persuade the "old man" to do. The difficulty was to keep him from changing his mind when the other side should reach his ear. They hit upon a bold expedient. They would urge the "old man" to remove Fred, and then resign himself, so that he could not undo the deed that they wanted done. Coffee John and Captain Hill slipped out of town one night; they reached West Baden on one train and they left for home on the next, with a demand for Fred's resignation in one hand and the mayor's own in the other. Fred Ames did resign, and though the mayor's resignation was laid aside for a while, to avoid the expense of a special election, all looked well for Coffee John and his clique. They had Fred out, and Alderman Powers was to make them great. But Mr. Powers wobbled. No doubt the grand jury spoke to him. At any rate he turned most unexpectedly on both cliques together. He turned out Tom Brown, but he turned out also Coffee John, and he did not make their man chief of police, but another of some one else's selection. A number of resignations was the result, and these the acting mayor accepted, making a clearing of astonished rascals which was very gratifying to the grand jury and to the nervous citizens of Minneapolis.

But the town was not yet easy. The grand jury, which was the actual head of the government, was about to be discharged, and, besides, their work was destructive. A constructive force was now needed, and Alderman Jones was pelted with telegrams from home bidding him hurry back. He did hurry, and when he arrived, the situation was instantly in control. The grand jury prepared to report, for the city had a mind and a will of its own once more. The criminals found it out last.

Percy Jones, as his friends call him, is of the second generation of his family in Minneapolis. His father started him well-to-do, and he went on from where he was started. College graduate and business man, he has a conscience which, however, he has brains enough to question. He is not the fighter, but the slow, sure executive. As an alderman he is the result of a movement begun several years ago by some young men who were convinced by an exposure of a corrupt municipal council that they should go into politics. A few did go in; Jones was one of these few.

The acting mayor was confronted at once with all the hardest problems of municipal government. Vice rose right up to tempt or to fight him. He studied the situation deliberately, and by and by began to settle it point by point, slowly but finally, against all sorts of opposition. One of his first acts was to remove all the proved rascals on the force, putting in their places men who had been removed by Mayor Ames. Another important step was the appointment of a church deacon and personal friend to be chief of police, this on the theory that he wanted at the head of his police a man who could have no sympathy with crime, a man whom he could implicitly trust. Disorderly houses, forbidden by law, were permitted, but only within certain patrol lines, and they were to pay nothing, in either blackmail or "fines." The number and the standing and the point of view of the "good people" who opposed this order was a lesson to Mr. Jones in practical government. One very prominent citizen and church member threatened him for driving women out of two flats owned by him; the rent was the surest means of "support for his wife and children." Mr. Jones enforced his order.

Other interests—saloon keepers, brewers, etc.—gave him trouble enough, but all these were trifles in comparison with his experience with the gamblers. They represented organized crime, and they asked for a hearing. Mr. Jones gave them some six weeks for negotiations. They proposed a solution. They said that if he would let them (a syndicate) open four gambling places down town, they would see that no others ran in any part of the city. Mr. Jones pondered and shook his head, drawing them on. They went away, and came back with a better promise. Though they were not the associates of criminals, they knew that class and their plans. No honest police force, unaided, could deal with crime. Thieves would soon be at work again, and what could Mr. Jones do against them with a police force headed by a church deacon? The gamblers offered to control the criminals for the city.

Mr. Jones, deeply interested, declared he did not believe there was any danger of fresh crimes. The gamblers smiled and went away. By an odd coincidence there happened just after that what the papers called "an epidemic of crime." They were petty thefts, but they occupied the mind of the acting mayor. He wondered at their opportuneness. He wondered how the news of them got out.

The gamblers soon reappeared. Hadn't they told Mr. Jones crime would soon be prevalent in town again? They had, indeed, but the mayor was unmoved; "porch climbers" could not frighten him. But this was only the beginning, the gamblers said: the larger crimes would come next. And they went away again. Sure enough, the large crimes came. One, two, three burglaries of jewelry in the houses of well-known people occurred; then there was a fourth, and the fourth was in the house of a relative of the acting mayor. He was seriously amused. The papers had the news promptly, and not from the police.

The gamblers called again. If they could have the exclusive control of gambling in Minneapolis, they would do all that they had promised before, and, if any large burglaries occurred, they would undertake to recover the "swag," and sometimes catch the thief. Mr. Jones was sceptical of their ability to do all this. The gamblers offered to prove it. How? They would get back for Mr. Jones the jewelry recently reported stolen from four houses in town. Mr. Jones expressed a curiosity to see this done, and the gamblers went away. After a few days the stolen jewelry, parcel by parcel, began to return; with all due police-criminal mystery it was delivered to the chief of police.

When the gamblers called again, they found the acting mayor ready to give his decision on their propositions. It was this: There should be no gambling, with police connivance, in the city of Minneapolis during his term of office.

Mr. Jones told me that if he had before him a long term, he certainly would reconsider this answer. He believed he would decide again as he had already, but he would at least give studious reflection to the question—Can a city be governed without any alliance with crime? It was an open question. He had closed it only for the four months of his emergency administration. Minneapolis should be clean and sweet for a little while at least, and the new administration should begin with a clear deck.

IDA TARBELL

Hired by S.S. McClure in 1894 to produce a serial biography of Napoleon for forty dollars per week, Ida Tarbell (1857–1944) was by the turn of the twentieth century already a popular author who had followed her Napoleon series with a successful biography of Abraham Lincoln. In 1902, at McClure's urging, she turned her biographer's skills to John D. Rockefeller and the Standard Oil Company. Ferreting out court documents, interviewing financiers and executives, she produced one of the touchstones of business journalism. The History of the Standard Oil Company *led to antitrust reforms and government action against Standard Oil itself. It also was a road map for future journalists looking to public records for revelations of corporate crime.*

Later in life, Tarbell turned sharply to the right. She opposed women's suffrage, wrote enthusiastically of "scientific" assembly lines, and published admiring biographies of executives of U.S. Steel and General Electric.

THE OIL WAR OF 1872

From *The History of Standard Oil*, 1903

For several days an uneasy rumor had been running up and down the Oil Regions. Freight rates were going up. Now an advance in a man's freight bill may ruin his business; more, it may mean the ruin of a region. Rumor said that the new rate meant just this; that is, that it more than covered the margin of profit in any branch of the oil business. There was another feature to the report; the railroads were not going to apply the proposed tariffs to everybody. They had agreed to give to a company unheard of until now—the South Improvement Company—a special rate considerably lower than the new open rate. It was only a rumor and many people discredited it. *Why* should the railroads ruin the Oil Regions to build up a company of outsiders?

The Uprising in the Oil Regions

On the morning of February 26, 1872, the oil men read in their morning papers that the rise which had been threatening had come; moreover, that all members of the South Improvement Company were exempt from the advance. At the news all Oildom rushed into the streets. Nobody waited to find out his neighbor's opinion. On every lip there was but one word, and that was "conspiracy." In the vernacular of the region, it was evident that "a torpedo was filling for that scheme."

In twenty-four hours after the announcement of the increase in freight rates a mass meeting of three thousand excited, gesticulating oil men was gathered in the Opera House at Titusville. Producers, brokers, refiners, drillers, pumpers were in the crowd. Their temper was shown by the mottoes on the banners which they carried: "Down with the conspirators"—"No compromise"—"Don't give up the ship!" Three days later, as large a meeting was held at Oil City, its temper more warlike if possible; and so it went. They organized a Petroleum Producers' Union, pledged themselves to reduce their production by starting no new wells for sixty days and by shutting down on Sundays, to sell no oil to any person known to be in the South

Improvement Company, but to support the Creek refiners and those elsewhere who had refused to go into the combination, to boycott the offending railroads, and to build lines which they would own and control themselves. They sent a committee to the Legislature asking that the charter of the South Improvement Company be repealed, and another to Congress demanding an investigation of the whole business on the ground that it was an interference with trade. They ordered that a history of the conspiracy, giving the names of the conspirators and the designs of the company, should be prepared, and 30,000 copies sent to "judges of all courts, Senators of the United States, members of Congress and of State Legislatures, and to all railroad men and prominent business men of the country, *to the end that enemies of the freedom of trade may be known and shunned by all honest men.*"

They prepared a petition ninety-three feet long, praying for a free pipe-line bill, something which they had long wanted, but which, so far, the Pennsylvania Railroad had prevented their getting, and sent it by a committee to the Legislature; and for days they kept a thousand men ready to march on Harrisburg at a moment's notice if the Legislature showed signs of refusing their demands. In short, for weeks the whole body of oil men abandoned regular business and surged from town to town intent on destroying the "Monster," the "Forty Thieves," the "Great Anaconda," as they called the mysterious South Improvement Company. Curiously enough, it was chiefly against the combination which had secured the discrimination from the railroads—not the railroads which had granted it—that their fury was directed. They expected nothing but robbery from the railroads, they said. They were used to that; but they would not endure it from men in their own business.

FIGHTING IN THE DARK

When they began the fight, the mass of the oil men knew nothing more of the South Improvement Company than its name and the fact that it had secured from the railroads advantages in rates which were bound to ruin all independent refiners of oil and to put all producers at its mercy. Their tempers were not improved by the discovery that it was a secret organization, and had been at work under their very eyes for some weeks without their knowing it. At the first public meeting this fact came out, leading refiners of the Region relating their experience with the "Anaconda." According to one of these gentlemen, Mr. J. D. Archbold—the same who afterward became vice-president of the Standard Oil Company, which office he now holds—he and his partners had heard of the scheme some months before. Alarmed by the rumor, a committee of independent refiners had attempt to investigate, but could learn nothing until they had given a promise not to reveal what was told them. When convinced that a company had been formed actually strong enough to force or persuade the railroads to give to it special rates and refuse them to all persons outside, Mr. Archbold said that he and his colleagues had gone to the railway kings to remonstrate, but all to no effect. The South Improvement Company by some means had convinced the railroads that they owned the Oil Regions, producers and refiners both, and that hereafter no oil of any account would be shipped except as they shipped it. Mr. Archbold and his partners had been asked to join the company, but had refused, declaring that the whole business was iniquitous, that they would fight it to the end, and that in their fight they would have the backing of the oil men, as a whole. They excused their silence up to this time by citing the pledge[1] exacted from them before they were informed of the extent and nature of the South Improvement Company.

THE "DERRICK'S" BLACKLIST

Naturally the burning question throughout the Oil Region, convinced as it was of the iniquity of the scheme, was: who are the conspirators? Whether the gentlemen concerned regarded themselves in the light of "conspirators" or not, they seem from the first to have realized that it would be discreet not to be identified publicly with the scheme, and to have allowed one name alone to appear in all signed negotiations. This was the name of the president, Peter H. Watson. However anxious the

1 Two forms of these pledges were published at the time. See *McClure's Magazine* for December, 1902.

members of the South Improvement Company were that Mr. Watson should combine the honors of president with the trials of scapegoat, it was impossible to keep their names concealed. The *Oil City Derrick,* at that time one of the most vigorous, witty, and daring newspapers in the country, began a blacklist at the head of its editorial columns the day after the raise in freights was announced, and it kept it there until it was believed complete. It stood finally as follows:

THE BLACK LIST.
P. H. WATSON, PRES., S. I. CO.
Charles Lockhart,
W. P. Logan,
R. S. Waring,
A. W. Bostwick,
W. C. Warden,
John Rockefeller,
Amasa Stone.
These seven are given as the Directors of the Southern Improvement Company. They are refiners or merchants of petroleum
Atlantic & Gt. Western Railway.
L. S. &. M. S. Railway.
Philadelphia & Eric Railway.
Pennsylvania Central Railway.
New York Central Railway.
Erie Railway.
Behold "The Anaconda" in all his hideous deformity!

This list was not exact,[2] but it was enough to go on, and the oil blockade, to which the Petroleum Producers' Union had pledged itself, was now enforced against the firms listed, and as far as possible against the railroads.

2 See *McClure's Magazine* for December, 1902, for stockholders of the South Improvement Company, and list of railroads signing contracts with the Company.

All of these refineries had their buyers on the Creek, and although several of the buyers were young men generally liked for their personal and business qualities, no mercy was shown them. They were refused oil by everybody, though they offered from seventy-five cents to a dollar more than the market price. They were ordered at one meeting "to desist from their nefarious business or leave the Oil Region," and when they declined they were invited to resign from the Oil Exchanges of which they were members. So strictly, indeed, was the blockade enforced that in Cleveland the refineries were closed and meetings for the relief of the workmen were held. In spite of the excitement there was little vandalism, the only violence at the opening of the war being at Franklin, where a quantity of the oil belonging to Mr. Watson was run on the ground.

THE OIL MEN ASK LEADING QUESTIONS

The sudden uprising of the Oil Regions against the South Improvement Company did not alarm its members at first. The excitement would die out, they told one another. All that they needed to do was to keep quiet, and stay out of the oil country. But the excitement did not die out. Indeed, with every day it became more intense and more widespread. When Mr. Watson's tanks were tapped he began to protest in letters to a friend, F. W. Mitchell, a prominent banker and oil man of Franklin. The company was misunderstood, he complained. "Have a committee of leading producers appointed," he wrote, and "we will show that the contracts with the railroad are as favorable to the producing as to other interests; that the much-denounced rebate will enhance the price of oil at the wells, and that our entire plan in operation and effect will promote every legitimate American interest in the oil trade." Mr. Mitchell urged Mr. Watson to come openly to the Oil Regions and meet the producers as a body. A mass meeting was never a "deliberative body," Mr. Watson replied, but if a few of the leading oil men would go to Albany or New York, or any place favorable to calm investigation and deliberation, and therefore outside of the atmosphere of excitement which enveloped the Oil Country, he would see them. These letters were read to the producers, and a motion to appoint a committee was made. It was received with protests and jeers. Mr. Watson was afraid to come to the Oil Regions, they said. The letters were not addressed to the association, they were private—an insult to the body. "We are lowering our dignity to treat with this man Watson," declared one man. "He is free to come to these meetings if he wants to." "What is there to negotiate about?" asked another. "To open a negotiation is to concede that we are wrong. Can we go halves with these middle men in their swindle?" "He has set a trap for us," declared another. "We cannot treat with him without guilt," and the motion was voted down.

The stopping of the oil supply finally forced the South Improvement Company to recognize the Producers' Union officially, by asking that a committee of the body be appointed to confer with them, on a compromise. The producers sent back a pertinent answer. They believed the South Improvement Company meant to monopolize the oil business. If that was so they could not consider a compromise with it. If they were wrong, they would be glad to be enlightened, and they asked for information. First: the charter under which the South Improvement Company was organized. Second: the articles of association. Third: the officers' names. Fourth: the contracts with the railroads and who signed them. Fifth: the general plan of management.

Until we know these things, the oil men declared, we can no more negotiate with you than we could sit down to negotiate with a burglar as to his privileges in our house.

An Omnibus Charter

The Producers' Union did not get the information they asked from the company at that time, but it was not long before they did, and much more, too. The committee which they had appointed to write a history of the South Improvement Company reported on March 20th, and in April the Congressional Committee appointed at the insistence of the oil men made its investigation. The former report was published broadcast, and is readily accessible to-day. The Congressional investigation was not published officially, and no trace of its work can now be found in Washington, but while it was going on, reports were made in the newspapers of the Oil Regions, and at its close the Producers' Union published in Lancaster, Pennsylvania, a pamphlet called the "Rise and Fall of the South Improvement Company," which contains the full testimony taken by the committee. This pamphlet is rare, the writer never having been able to find a copy save in three or four private collections. The most important part of it is the testimony of Peter H. Watson, the president, and W. G. Warden, the secretary of the South Improvement Company. It was in these documents that the oil men found full justification for the war they were carrying on and for the losses they had caused themselves and others. Nothing, indeed, could have been more damaging to a corporation than the publication of the charter of the South Improvement Company. As its president told the Congressional Investigating Committee, when he was under examination, "this charter was a sort of clothes-horse to hang a scheme upon." As a matter of fact, it was a clothes-horse big enough to hang the earth upon. It granted powers practically unlimited. There really was no exaggeration in the summary of its powers made and scattered broadcast by the irate oil men in their "History of the South Improvement Company":

> The Southern Improvement Company can own, contract or operate any work, business or traffic (save only banking); may hold and transfer any kind of property, real or personal; hold and operate on any leased property (oil territory, for instance); make any kind of contract; deal in stocks, securities, and funds; loan its credit; guarantee any one's paper; manipulate any industry; may seize upon the lands of other parties for railroading or *any other purpose*; may absorb the improvements, property or franchises of any other company, *ad infinitum*; may fix the fares, tolls or freights to be charged on lines of transit operated by it, or on any business it gives to *any other company* or line, without limit.
>
> Its capital stock can be expanded or "watered" at liberty; it can change its name and location at pleasure; can go anywhere and do almost anything. It is not a Pennsylvania corporation, only; it can, so far as these enactments are valid, or are confirmed by other Legislatures, operate in any State or Territory; its directors must be only citizens of the United States—not

> necessarily of Pennsylvania. It is responsible to no one; its stockholders are only liable to the amount of their stock in it; its directors, when wielding all the princely powers of the corporation, are also responsible only to the amount of their stock in it; it may control the business of the continent and hold and transfer millions of property and yet be rotten to the core. It is responsible to no one; makes no reports of its acts or financial condition; its records and deliberations are secret; its capital illimitable; its object unknown. It can be here to-day, to-morrow away. Its domain is the whole country; its business everything. Now it is petroleum it grasps and monopolizes; next year it may be iron, coal, cotton, or breadstuffs. They are landsmen granted perpetual letters of marque to prey upon all commerce everywhere.

When the course of this charter through the Pennsylvania Legislature came to be traced, it was found to be devious and uncertain. The company had been incorporated in 1870, and vested with all the "powers, privileges, duties, and obligations" of two earlier companies—the Continental Improvement Company and the Pennsylvania Company, both of which were children of that interesting body known as the "Tom Scott Legislature." The act incorporating the company was never published, the name of the member introducing it was never known, and no votes on it are recorded. The origin of the South Improvement Company has always remained in darkness. It was one of thirteen "improvement" companies chartered in Pennsylvania at about the same time, and enjoying the same commercial *carte blanche.*

AMAZING CONTRACTS WITH THE RAILROADS

Bad as the charter was in appearance, the oil men found that the contracts which the new company had made with the railroads were worse. These contracts advanced the rates of freight from the Oil Regions over 100 per cent., but it was not the railroad that got the greater part of this advance; it was the South Improvement Company. Not only did it ship its own oil at fully a dollar a barrel cheaper on an average than anybody else could, but it received fully a dollar a barrel "rake-off" on every barrel its competitors shipped. It was computed and admitted by the members of the company who appeared before the investigating committee of Congress that this discrimination would have turned over to them fully $6,000,000 annually on the carrying trade. It is hardly to be wondered at that when the oil men had before them the full text of these contracts they refused absolutely to accept the repeated assertions of the members of the South Improvement Company that their scheme was intended only for "the good of the oil business." The committee of Congress could not be persuaded to believe it either. "Your success meant the destruction of every refiner who refused for any reason to join your company, or whom you did not care to have in, and it put the producers entirely in your power. It would make a monopoly such as no set of men are fit to handle," the chairman of the committee declared. Mr. Warden, the secretary of the company, protested again and again that they meant to take in all the refiners, though he had to admit that the contracts with the railroads were not made on this condition. Mr. Watson affirmed and reaffirmed before the committee that it was the intention of the company to take care of the producers. "It was an essential part of this contract that the producers should join it," he declared. But no such condition was embodied in the contract. It was verbal only, and, besides, it had never been submitted to the producers themselves in any form until after the trouble in the Oil Region began. The committee, like the oil men, insisted that under the circumstances no such verbal understanding was to be trusted.

No part of the testimony before the committee made a worse impression than that showing that one of the chief objects of the combination was to put up the price of refined oil. "Under your arrangement," said the chairman, "the public would have been put to an additional expense of $7,500,000 a year." "What public?" said Mr. Warden. "They would have had to pay it in Europe." "But to keep up the price abroad you would have to keep up the price at home," said the chairman. Mr. Warden conceded the point: "You could not get a better price for that exported without having a better price here." Thirty-two cents a gallon was the ideal price they had in view, though refined had not sold for that since 1869, the average price in 1870 being 26 ⅜ and in 1871 24 ¼. The average price of crude in 1870 was $3.90 a barrel; in 1871, $4.40. The Congressional Committee claimed that any combination formed for the purpose of putting up the price of an article of general consumption was an injury to the public, but the members of the company would not admit it as such. Everybody in the business should make more money, they argued; the profits were too small—the consumer ought to be willing to pay more.

Popular Sympathy for the Oil Regions

It did not take the full exposition of the objects of the South Improvement Company, brought out by the Congressional Investigating Committee, with the publication of charters and contracts, to convince the country at large that the Oil Regions were right in their opposition. From the first the sympathy of the press and the people were with the oil men. It was evident to everybody that if the railroads had made the contracts as charged (and it daily became more evident they had done so), nothing but an absolute monopoly of the whole oil business by this combination could result. It was robbery, cried the newspapers all over the land. "Under the thin guise of assisting in the development of oil refining in Pittsburg and Cleveland," said the New York *Tribune,* "this corporation has simply laid its hand upon the throat of the oil traffic with a demand to 'stand and deliver.' " And if this could be done in the oil business, what was to prevent its being done in any other industry? Why should not a company be formed to control wheat or beef or iron or steel, as well as oil? If the railroads would do this for one company, why not for another? The South Improvement Company, men agreed, was a menace to the free trade of the country. If the oil men yielded now, all industries must suffer from their weakness. The railroads must be taught a lesson as well as would-be monopolists.

Reinforcements from New York

The oil men had no thought of yielding. With every day of the war their backbones grew stiffer. The men were calmer, too, for their resistance had found a moral ground which seemed impregnable to them, and arguments against the South Improvement Company now took the place of denunciations. The country so buzzed with discussion on the duties of the railroads, that reporters sent from the Eastern newspapers commented on it. Nothing was commoner, indeed, on the trains which ran the length of the region, and were its real forums, than to hear a man explaining that the railways derived their existence and power from the people, that their charters were contracts with the people, that a fundamental provision of these contracts was that there should be no discriminating in favor of one person or one town, that such a discrimination was a violation of charter, that therefore the South Improvement Company was founded on fraud, and the courts must dissolve it if the railways did not abandon it.

They now met the very plausible reasons given by the members of the company for their combination more intelligently than at first. There were grave abuses in the business, they admitted; there was too great refining capacity; but this they argued was a natural development in a new business whose growth had been extraordinary and whose limits were by no means defined. Time and experience would regulate it. Give the refiners open and regular freights, with no favors to any one, and the stronger and better equipped would live, the others die—but give all a chance. In fact, time and energy would regulate all the evils of which they complained if there was fair play.

The oil men were not only encouraged by public opinion and by getting their minds clear on the merits of their case; they were upheld by repeated proofs of aid from all sides; even the women of the region were asking what they could do, and offering to wear their "black velvet bonnets" all summer if necessary. Solid support came from the independent refiners and shippers in other parts of the country, who were offering to stand in with them in their contest. New York was already one of the chief refining centers of the country, and the South Improvement Company had left it entirely out of its combination. As incensed as the Creek itself, the New York interests formed an association, and about the middle of March sent a committee of three, with H. H. Rogers of Charles Pratt & Company at its head, to Oil City, to consult with the Producers'

Union. Their arrival in the Oil Regions was a matter of great satisfaction. What made the oil men most exultant, however, was their growing belief that the railroads—the crux of the whole scheme—were weakening.

THE RAILROADS BACK DOWN

However fair the great scheme may have appeared to the railroad kings in the privacy of the council chamber, it began to look dark as soon as it was dragged into the open, and signs of a scuttle soon appeared. General G. B. McClellan, president of the Atlantic and Great Western, sent to the very first mass meeting this telegram:

> NEW YORK, *February* 27, 1872.
>
> Neither the Atlantic and Great Western, or any of its officers, are interested in the South Improvement Company. Of course, the policy of the road is to accommodate the petroleum interest.
>
> G. B. MCCLELLAN.

A great applause was started, only to be stopped by the hisses of a group whose spokesman read the following:

> Contract with South Improvement Company signed by Geo. B. McClellan, president, for the Atlantic and Great Western Railroad. I only signed it after it was signed by all the other parties.
>
> JAY GOULD.

The railroads tried in various ways to appease the oil men. They did not enforce the new rates. They had signed the contracts, they declared, only after the South Improvement Company had assured them that all the refineries and producers were to be taken in. Indeed, they seem to have realized within a fortnight that the scheme was doomed, and to have been quite ready to meet cordially a committee of oil men which went east to demand that the railroads revoke their contracts with the South Improvement Company. This committee, which was composed of twelve persons, three of them being the New York representatives already mentioned, began its work by an interview with Colonel Scott at the Colonial Hotel in Philadelphia. With evident pride the committee wrote back to the Producers' Union that: "Mr. Scott, differing in this respect from the railroad representatives whom we afterwards met, notified us that he would call upon us at our hotel." An interesting account of their interview was given to the Hepburn Committee in 1879 by Mr. W. T. Scheide, one of the number:

> We saw Mr. Scott on the 18th of March, 1872, in Philadelphia, and he said to us that he was very much surprised to hear of this agitation in the Oil Regions; that the object of the railroads in making this contract with the South Improvement Company was to obtain an evener to pool the freight—pool the oil freights among the different roads; that they had been cutting each other on oil freights for a number of years, and had not made any money out of it, although it was a freight they should have made money from; that they had endeavored to make an arrangement among themselves, but had always failed; he said that they supposed that the gentlemen representing the South Improvement Company represented the petroleum trade, but as he was now convinced they did not, he would be very glad to make an arrangement with this committee, who undoubtedly did represent the petroleum trade; the committee told him that they could not make any such contract; that they had no legal authority to do so; he said that could be easily fixed, because the Legislature was then in session, and by going to Harrisburg a charter could be obtained in a very few days; the committee still said that they would not agree to any such arrangement, that they did not think the South Improvement Company's contract was a good one, and they were instructed to have it broken, and so they did not feel that they could accept a similar one, even if they had the power.

Leaving Colonel Scott, the committee went on to New York, where they stayed for about a week, closely watched by the newspapers, all of which treated the "Oil War" as a national affair. Various conferences were held, leading up to a final all-important one on March 25th, at the Erie offices. Horace Clark, president of the Lake Shore and Michigan Southern Railroad, was chairman of this meeting, and, according to H. H. Rogers's testimony before the Hepburn Committee, in 1879, there were present, besides the oil men, Colonel Scott, General McClellan, Director Diven, William H. Vanderbilt, Mr. Stebbins, and George Hall.

MR. ROCKEFELLER TO THE RESCUE

The meeting had not been long in session before Mr. Watson, president of the South Improvement Company, and Mr. John D. Rockefeller, presented themselves for admission. Up to this time Mr. Rockefeller had kept well out of sight in the affair. He had given no interviews, offered no explanations. He had allowed the president of the company to wrestle with the excitement in his own way, but things were now in such critical shape that he came forward in a last attempt to save the organization by which he had been able to concentrate in his own hands the refining interests of Cleveland. With Mr. Watson, he knocked for admission to the council going on in the Erie offices. The oil men flatly refused to let them in. A dramatic scene followed, Mr. Clark, the chairman, protesting in agitated tones against shutting out his "lifelong friend, Watson." The oil men were obdurate. They would have nothing to do with anybody concerned with the South Improvement Company. So determined were they that although Mr. Watson came in, he was obliged at once to withdraw. A *Times* reporter who witnessed the little scene between the two supporters of the tottering company after its president was turned out of the meeting remarks sympathetically that Mr. Rockefeller soon went away, "looking pretty blue."

The acquiescence of the "railroad kings" in the refusal of the oil men to recognize representatives of the South Improvement Company was followed by an unwilling promise to break the contracts with the company. A strong effort was made to persuade the independents to make the same contracts on condition that they shipped as much oil, but they would not hear of it. They demanded open rates, with no rebates to any one. The Vanderbilts particularly stuck for this arrangement, but were finally obliged to consent to revoke the contracts and to make a new one embodying the views of the Oil Regions. The contract finally signed at this meeting by H. F. Clark for the Lake Shore Road, O. H. P. Archer for the Erie, W. H. Vanderbilt for the Central, George B. McClellan for the Atlantic and Great Western, and Thomas A. Scott for the Pennsylvania, agreed that all shipping of oil should be made on "a basis of perfect equality to all shippers, producers, and refiners, and that no rebates, drawbacks, or other arrangements of any character shall be made or allowed that will give any party the slightest difference in rates or discriminations of any character whatever."

The same rate was put on refined oil from Cleveland, Pittsburg, and the Creek, to eastern shipping points; that is, Mr. Rockefeller could send his oil from Cleveland to New York at $1.50 per barrel; so could his associates in Pittsburg, and this was what it cost the refiner on the Creek; but the latter had this advantage: he was at the wells. Mr. Rockefeller and his Pittsburg allies were miles away, and it cost them, by the new contract, fifty cents to get a barrel of crude to their works. The Oil Regions meant that geographical position should count. Unless there was some way to get around this contract, it looked at that moment very much as if Mr. Rockefeller had bought a white elephant when he swept up the refineries of Cleveland.

GRANT ON MONOPOLIES

This contract was the first effective thrust into the great bubble. Others followed in quick succession. On the 28th, the railroads officially annulled their contracts with the company. About the same time the Pennsylvania legislature repealed the charter. On March 30th, the committee of oil men sent to Washington to be present during the Congressional investigation, now about to begin, spent an hour with President Grant. They wired home that on their departure he said: "Gentlemen, I have noticed the progress of monopolies, and have long been convinced that the National Government would have to interfere and protect the people against them." The President and the members of Congress of both parties continued to show the greatest interest in the investigation, and there was little or no dissent from the final judgment of the committee, given early in May, that the South Improvement Company was the "most gigantic and daring conspiracy" a free country had ever seen. This decision finished the work. The "monster" was slain, the Oil Regions proclaimed exultantly.

The Standard Again Buys Oil

And now came the question; what should they do about the blockade established against the members of the South Improvement Company? The railroads they had forgiven; should they forgive the members of the South Improvement Company? This question came up immediately on the repeal of the charter. The first severe test to which their temper was put was early in April, when a firm of Oil City brokers sold some 20,000 barrels of oil to the Standard Oil Company. The moment the sale was noised a perfect uproar burst forth. Indignant telegrams came from every direction condemning the brokers. "Betrayal," "infamy," "mercenary achievement," "the most unkindest cut of all," was the gist of them. From New York, Porter and Archbold telegraphed annulling all their contracts with the guilty brokers. The Oil Exchange passed votes of censure, and the Producers' Union turned them out. A few days later it was learned that a dealer on the Creek was preparing to ship 5,000 barrels to the same firm. A mob gathered about the cars and refused to let them leave. It was only by stationing a strong guard that the destruction of the oil was prevented.

But something had to be done. The cooler heads argued that the blockade, which had lasted now forty days, and from which the Region had, of course, suffered enormous loss, should be entirely lifted. The objects for which it had been established had been accomplished—that is, the South Improvement Company had been destroyed;—now let free trade be established. If anybody wanted to sell to "conspirators," it was his look-out. A long and excited meeting of men from the entire oil country was held at Oil City to discuss the question. At this meeting telegrams to the president of the Petroleum Producers' Union, Captain William Hasson, from officials of the railroads were read, declaring that the contracts with the South Improvement Company were canceled. Also the following from the Standard Oil Company was read:

> CLEVELAND, OHIO, *April* 8, 1872.
>
> *To Captain William Hasson:* In answer to your telegram, this company holds no contract with the railroad companies or any of them, or with the South Improvement Company. The contracts between the South Improvement Company and the railroads have been canceled, and I am informed you have been so advised by telegram. I state unqualifiedly that reports circulated in the Oil Region and elsewhere, that this company, or any member of it, threatened to depress oil, are false.
>
> JOHN D. ROCKEFELLER, *President.*

It was finally decided that "inasmuch as the South Improvement Company contracts were annulled, and the Pennsylvania Legislature had taken pains to safeguard the interests of the trade, and Congress was moving on the same line, after the 15th trade should be free to all." This resolution put an official end to the "oil war."

But no number of resolutions could wipe out the memory of the forty days of terrible excitement and loss which the region had suffered. No triumph could stifle the suspicion and the bitterness which had been sown broadcast through the region. Every particle of independent manhood in these men whose very life was independent action had been outraged. Their sense of fair play, the saving force of the region in the days before law and order had been established, had been violated. These were things which could not be forgotten. There henceforth could be no trust in those who had devised a scheme which, the producers believed, was intended to rob them of their business.

THE SOUTH IMPROVEMENT COMPANY *ALIAS* THE STANDARD OIL COMPANY

It was inevitable that under the pressure of their indignation and resentment some person or persons should be fixed upon as responsible, and should be hated accordingly. Before the lifting of the embargo this responsibility had been fixed. It was the Standard Oil Company of Cleveland, so the Oil Regions decided, which was at the bottom of the business, and the "Mephistopheles of the Cleveland Company," as they put it, was John D. Rockefeller. Even the Cleveland *Herald* acknowledged this popular judgment. "Whether justly or unjustly," the editor wrote, "Cleveland has the odium of having originated the scheme." This opinion gained ground as the days passed. The activity of the president of the Standard in New York, in trying to save the contracts with the railroads, and his constant appearance with Mr. Watson, and the fact brought out by the Congressional investigation that a larger block of the South Improvement Company's stock was owned in the Standard than in any other firm, strengthened the belief. But what did more than anything else to fix the conviction was what they had learned of the career of the Standard Oil Company in Cleveland. Before the oil war the company had been known simply as one of several successful firms in that city. It drove close bargains, but it paid promptly, and was considered a desirable customer. Now the Oil Regions learned for the first time of the sudden and phenomenal expansion of the company. Where there had been at the beginning of 1872 twenty-six refining firms in Cleveland, there were but six left. In three months before and during the oil war the Standard had absorbed twenty plants. It was generally charged by the Cleveland refiners that Mr. Rockefeller had used the South Improvement scheme to persuade or compel his rivals to sell to him. "Why," cried the oil men, "the Standard Oil Company has done already in Cleveland what the South Improvement Company set out to do for the whole country, and it has done it by the same means."

By the time the blockade was raised, another unhappy conviction was fixed on the Oil Regions—the Standard Oil Company meant to carry out the plans of the exploded South Improvement Company. The promoters of the scheme were partly responsible for the report. Under the smart of their defeat they talked rather more freely than their policy of silence justified, and their remarks were quoted widely. Mr. Rockefeller was reported in the "Derrick" to have said to a prominent oil man of Oil City that the South Improvement Company could work under the charter of the Standard Oil Company, and to have predicted that in less than two months the gentleman would be glad to join him. The newspapers made much of the following similar story reported by a New York correspondent:

> A prominent Cleveland member of what was the South Improvement Company had said within two days: The business *now* will be done by the Standard Oil Company. We have a rate of freight by water from Cleveland to New York at 70 cents. No man in the trade shall make a dollar this year. We purpose so manipulating the market as to run the price of crude on the Creek as low as two and a half. We mean to show the world that the South Improvement Company was organized for business and means business in spite of opposition. The same thing has been said in substance by the leading Philadelphia member.

"The trade here regards the Standard Oil Company as simply taking the place of the South Improvement Company and as being ready at any moment to make the same attempt to control the trade as its progenitors did," said the *New York Bulletin* about the middle of April. And the *Cleveland Herald* discussed the situation under the heading, "South Improvement Company *alias* Standard Oil Company." The effect of these reports in the Oil Regions was most disastrous. Their open war became a kind of guerrilla opposition. Those who sold oil to the Standard were ostracized, and its president was openly scorned.

Mr. Rockefeller Begins All Over Again

If Mr. Rockefeller had been an ordinary man the outburst of popular contempt and suspicion which suddenly poured on his head would have thwarted and crushed him. But he was no ordinary man. He had the powerful imagination to see what might be done with the oil business if it could be centered in his hands—the intelligence to analyze the problem into its elements and to find the key to control. He had the essential element to all great achievement, a steadfastness to a purpose once conceived which nothing can crush. The Oil Regions might rage, call him a conspirator and those who sold him oil traitors; the railroads might withdraw their contracts and the legislature annul his charter; undisturbed and unresting he kept at his great purpose. Even if his nature had not been such as to forbid him to abandon an enterprise in which he saw promise of vast profits, even if he had not had a mind which, stopped by a wall, burrows under or creeps around, he would nevertheless have been forced to desperate efforts to save his business. He had increased his refining capacity in Cleveland to 10,000 barrels on the strength of the South Improvement Company contracts. These contracts were annulled, and in their place was one signed by officials of all the oil-shipping roads refusing rebates to everybody. His geographical position was such that it cost him under these new contracts 50 cents more to get oil from the wells to New York than it did his rivals on the Creek. What could he do?

MR. ROCKEFELLER GETS A REBATE

He got a rebate. In spite of the binding nature of the contracts signed in New York on March 25th by representatives of all the railroads, before the middle of April the Standard Oil Company was shipping oil eastward from Cleveland for $1.25—this by the sworn testimony of Mr. H. M. Flagler before a commission of the Ohio State Legislature, in March, 1879. How much less a rate than $1.25 Mr. Rockefeller had before the end of April the writer does not know. Of course the rate was secret, and he probably understood now, as he had not two months before, how essential it was that he keep it secret. His task was more difficult now, for he had an enemy active, clamorous, contemptuous, whose suspicions had reached that acute point where they could believe nothing but evil of him—the producers and independents of the Oil Regions. It was utterly impossible that he should ever silence this enemy, for their points of view were diametrically opposed.

They believed in independent effort—every man for himself and fair play for all. They wanted competition, loved open fight. They considered that all business should be done openly—that the railways were bound as public carriers to give equal rates—that any combination which favored one firm or one locality at the expense of another was unjust and illegal.

Mr. Rockefeller's Opinions and Character

Mr. Rockefeller's point of view was different. He believed that the "good of all" was in a combination which would control the business as the South Improvement Company proposed to control it. Such a combination would end at once all the abuses the business suffered. As rebates and special rates were essential to this control, he favored them. Of course Mr. Rockefeller knew that the railroad was a public carrier, and that its charter forbade discrimination. But he knew that the railroads did not pretend to obey the laws governing them, that they regularly granted special rates and rebates to those who had large amounts of freight. That is, you could bargain with the railroads as you could with a man carrying on a strictly private business depending in no way on a public franchise. Moreover, Mr. Rockefeller knew that if he did not get rebates somebody else would; that they were for the wariest, the shrewdest, the most persistent. If somebody was to get rebates, why not he? This point of view was no uncommon one. Many men held it and felt a sort of scorn, as practical men always do for theorists, when it was contended that the shipper was as wrong in taking rates as the railroads in granting them.

Thus, on one hand there was an exaggerated sense of personal independence, on the other a firm belief in combination; on one hand a determination to root out the vicious system of rebates practised by the railway, on the other a determination to keep it alive and profit by it. Those theories which the body of oil men held as vital and fundamental Mr. Rockefeller and his associates either did not comprehend or were deaf to. This lack of comprehension by many men of what seems to other men to be the most obvious principles of justice is not rare. Many men who are widely known as good, share it. Mr. Rockefeller was "good." There was no more faithful Baptist in Cleveland than he. Every enterprise of that church he had supported liberally from his youth. He gave to its poor. He visited its sick. He wept with its suffering. Moreover, he gave unostentatiously to many outside charities of whose worthiness he was satisfied. He was simple and frugal in his habits. He never went to the theater, never drank wine. He was a devoted husband, and he gave much time to the training of his children, seeking to develop in them his own habits of economy and of charity. Yet he was willing to strain every nerve to obtain for himself special and illegal privileges from the railroads which were bound to ruin every man in the oil business not sharing them with him. Religious emotion and sentiments of charity, propriety and self-denial seem to have taken the place in him of notions of justice and regard for the rights of others.

Unhampered, then, by any ethical consideration, undismayed by the clamor of the Oil Regions, believing firmly as ever that relief for the disorders in the oil business lay in combining and controlling the entire refining interest, this man of vast patience and foresight took up his work. The day after the newspapers of the Oil Regions printed the report of the Congressional Committee on Commerce denouncing the South Improvement Company as "one of the most gigantic and dangerous conspiracies ever attempted," and declaring that if it had not been checked in time it "would have resulted in the absorption and arbitrary control of trade in all the great interests of the country,"[3] Mr. Rockefeller and several other members of the South Improvement Company appeared in the Oil Regions. They had come, they explained, to present a new plan of cooperation, and to show the oil men that it was to their interest to go into it. Whether they would be able to obtain by persuasion what they had failed to obtain by assault was now an interesting uncertainty.

3 The report of the Committee of Congress which investigated the South Improvement Company was not made until May 7, over a month after the organization was destroyed by the canceling of the contracts with the railroads.

Upton Sinclair

A secular socialist, Upton Sinclair (1878–1978) had already published a long shelf of pulp novels and historical fiction when in 1904 the editor of the radical popular weekly Appeal to Reason *urged him to take twentieth-century "wage slaves" as his subject. Sinclair found a job in Chicago's stockyards, living among its slaughterhouse workers for seven weeks. The working conditions and catastrophically low wages, the horrifically unsanitary meatpacking procedures, the crooked managers, all were poured in documentary fashion into* The Jungle, *serialized in the* Appeal *and published by Doubleday in 1906. Loosely draped in a plot concerning a Lithuanian immigrant family, Sinclair's essentially journalistic depiction of the meat-packing industry had sensational impact, leading directly to passage of the Pure Food and Drug Act and the Meat Inspection Act. In the following article from* Everybody's Magazine, *he rebuts attacks from meatpacking executives by detailing his work methods and sourcing.*

Sinclair was never an elegant writer, but he remained a prolific and vigorous critic of American capitalism, publishing a long string of socially conscious novels as well as nonfiction studies of the press, American education, and profiteering by churches, among other subjects. In 1930 he ran for the Democratic nomination for governor of California on an antipoverty platform, securing 44 percent of the vote.

The Condemned-Meat Industry: A Reply to Mr. J. Ogden Armour

From *Everybody's Magazine*, 1908

Editor's note—*J. Ogden Armour has at last been smoked out of the sullen retirement in which the Beef Trust bosses have kept themselves since the fires of public indignation against them were lighted by Charles E. Russell's powerful series on the Beef Trust in this magazine. Mr. Armour, in an article in the* Saturday Evening Post, *makes the flat-footed assertion that the Government inspection of the Beef Trust slaughter-houses is an impregnable wall protecting the public from impure meat, and that not an atom of diseased meat finds its way into the products of the Armours.* EVERYBODY'S *having lighted the fire, feels impelled to discuss this statement. Mr. Russell is in the Orient working out for us his notable series "Soldiers of the Common Good." Mr. Upton Sinclair, the author of the* The Jungle *(a terrific statement of Packingtown conditions, which we commend to our readers aside from its political conclusions), is preparing for us a similar review of labor conditions in other industries. In collecting data for* The Jungle, *Mr. Sinclair studied the meat industry for two years, including much time spent in the Chicago stock-yards as a workman; he is the best equipped outside authority on stock-yard conditions. We have asked Mr. Sinclair to suspend work on his new series in order to confront Mr. Armour in Mr. Russell's place. His answer is startling, and yet convincing. "Soldiers of the Common Good" will be resumed in our June number.*

In the course of his recent defense of the Beef Trust, Mr. J. Ogden Armour writes as follows:

> Government inspection is another important feature of the packers' business. To the general public, the meat-eating public, it ought to appeal as one of the *most important* features of any and all business in the whole country. It is the wall that stands between the meat-eating public and the sale of diseased meat. This Government inspection alone, if there were no other business or economic reasons, would be an all-sufficient reason for the existence of the packing and dressed-meat business on a mammoth scale. It should, if understood, make the general public a partisan supporter of the large packers.
>
> Strangely enough, in view of its vital importance, this Government inspection has been the subject of almost endless misrepresentation—of *ignorantly or maliciously false statements.* The public has been told that meat animals and carcasses condemned as diseased are afterward secretly made use of by the

> packers and sold to the public for food in the form of both dressed meats and canned meats. Right here I desire to brand such statements as absolutely false as applied to the business of Armour & Co. I believe they are equally false as to all establishments in this country that are classed as packing-houses. I repeat: "In Armour & Co.'s business *not one atom of any condemned animal or carcass finds its way directly or indirectly, from any source, into any food product or food ingredient."*

This denial is positive and all-inclusive. It comes from a man of immense wealth, occupying a position of enormous responsibility, and having a considerable standing in the community. It is a denial of acts which, if really committed, would be atrocious and abominable crimes; and, accordingly, ninety-nine per cent. of the people who read it, and who possess no information about the matter, accept it as final and conclusive. A man who proposes to controvert it must set out with all the convictions of his readers against him.

A year or so ago, when I was familiar with Packingtown, and with the methods employed in Mr. Armour's factories, but not with the conditions in his office, I should have been inclined to say that Mr. Armour was mistaken; I should have said that it was the Valentines and the Connors and the Arthur Meekers of his establishment who did the things which are regularly done; and that he, Mr. Armour, in making his denial to the public, was simply ignorant of the real truth. Now, however, I know that such is not the case; for I know that Mr. Armour is the master at Armour & Co.'s, and that he knows everything that goes on there. I know that he gets up and stands at his telephone every morning at seven o'clock, and fixes the prices which are to be paid for live stock throughout the markets of the United States on that day; I know this from men who have stood at the other end of the telephone when he did it. I know that in the consultations which take place concerning the business of Armour & Co., he is deferred to by all as the head and leader; I know this from men who attend these consultations. I know that he has his finger upon every detail of the packing-house business; and therefore—using italics, in accordance with Mr. Armour's own example—I know that *in the statements quoted above, Mr. Armour willfully and deliberately states what he absolutely and positively knows to be falsehoods.*

I have had to face Mr. Armour, and his power, and his prestige, and his respectability, so often that I am now grown used to it. I had to face it, for instance, when I went out to find a publisher for my book; I know that several declined to print it, because they believed Mr. Armour, and did not believe me.

The firm which at present publishes it sent out to a man in Chicago, asking for an impartial opinion about the book, and in reply received a twenty-eight-page typewritten report, purporting to be the result of an impartial investigation, and branding *The Jungle* as a tissue of falsehoods, and as a malicious attempt to inflict gratuitous injury on the great and philanthropic house of Armour & Co.

Fortunately, however, I was in a position to show the falsity of some of these statements, and I then suggested to the publishers the only plan by which they could assure themselves of the truth of my book, which was that they themselves should send out a man, of whose intelligence and integrity they were absolutely sure, who should make a thorough and first-hand investigation, and report to them the results. They adopted this suggestion; and in order that they might feel absolutely certain, they selected their own attorney, a gentleman intimately known to the members of the firm. The firm was Doubleday, Page & Co.; and the lawyer was Mr. Thomas H. McKee, of 111 Broadway, New York. He went to Chicago, met some of my witnesses, and made some private investigations of his own; and I will now quote one paragraph from the formal report which he transmitted over his signature to the firm which had sent him out:

> With a special conductor, Mr. B. J. Mullaney, provided for me by Mr. Urion, attorney for Armour interests, I went through the Armour plant again. Mullaney introduced me to T. J. Conners, manager, who called Mr. Hull, superintendent of beef plant, and said to him: 'I have just told Mr. McKee that we have nothing here to conceal, and that he can see anything he wants, and can

stay as long as he likes. Please see that my promise is made good.' I expressed my desire to investigate two points: first, the system of inspection; second, the by-product food industry.

I saw six hogs hung in line which had been condemned. *A truck loaded with chopped-up condemned hogs was, in my presence (I followed it), placed in one of the tanks from which lard comes.* I asked particularly about this, and the inspector, together with Mr. Hull, stated that lard and fertilizer would be the product from that tank. The tanks are in a long room. The east side is lined with tanks for manufacture of lard and fertilizer; the west side with tanks whose product is grease and fertilizer. The grease is for soap, lubricator, etc. Here is a clear infraction of the law, because it requires that such condemned meat be mixed with sufficient offal to destroy it as food. Of the six condemned hogs referred to, two were afflicted with cholera, the skin being red as blood and the legs scabbed; three were marked 'tubercular,' though they appeared normal to a layman; the sixth had an ulcer in its side which was apparent. Two men were engaged in chopping up hogs from this line. The truck-load prepared while I stood there was deposited in a lard tank. I asked particularly about the line of demarcation between the carcasses used for lard and carcasses used for grease. No explanation was given either by the inspector or by my conductor. 'It all depends upon how bad he is,' was the answer. I gathered the impression, however, that not very many carcasses were placed in grease tanks.

I have no comments to make on the above narrative, except to refer the reader to the law, Department of Agriculture Rules, June 27, 1904, Article IX; and then to quote once more the italicized statement from Mr. Armour's article: "*Not one atom of any condemned animal or carcass finds its way, directly or indirectly, from any source, into any food product or food ingredient.*"

Mr. Armour speaks of "ignorantly or maliciously false statements"; just what he imagines to be the cause of the malice in my case, he has not stated. I can only say that I went out to Chicago without the slightest idea of any of the things which I was to discover in Mr. Armour's establishment. I selected

Packingtown because I wished to give a picture of working-class life in a modern, highly concentrated industry, and because I knew that Packingtown was a place where modern commercial forces had full and unrestricted sway. I lived among the stock-yards people for many weeks, making the most minute and painstaking examination into every detail of their lives, as well as of the packing-house methods. I shall never forget my emotions on my very first evening in the yards, when I sat in the kitchen of one of Mr. Armour's cattle-butchers, an old Lithuanian working man, who had spent twenty-five years of his life in Packingtown. He had been one of Tom Carey's "Indians" in his early days; he had been naturalized when only two months in America, and had voted seven times at a recent election. He was intimately familiar with every detail of Mr. Armour's business—as familiar, I dare say, as Mr. Armour himself—and when he was fairly started at telling me what he had seen and done, my hair began to rise on end. He told me that meat which had been condemned as unfit for food, and had been dropped into tanks to be rendered into fertilizer, was taken out at the bottom of the tanks, and canned or cut up for sausage. He told me that he had done this with his own hands; he told me that his brother-in-law, who worked in another of the big packing-houses, had done it quite recently; and still I could not believe him—it *could* not be true! I took the story to the head of the University Settlement in the stock-yards, and asked her what she thought about it. She said: "Mr. Sinclair, I have lived thirteen years in this neighborhood, and during that time scarcely a week passes that some one does not tell me some such story; but I can't believe them—they *can't* be true! Will your man, or his brother-in-law, or other men that know of it, make an affidavit to it?" I took the question to the grizzled old cattle-butcher, and he laughed. "Sure," he said, "I'll make an affidavit to it—on one condition." "What is that?" I asked. "Simply that the lady will go under bond to give me a job for the balance of my life."

I count in my memory five men who worked in the yards who told me that they had positive knowledge of this practice; but my efforts to see it with my own eyes were unavailing. I got into many places in the big packing-houses and I saw sights of filth and horror such as I hope never to see again; but even disguised as a working man, and in company with men who were intimately known in the establishments, I was unable to get past the "spotters" and watchmen who guard those particular doors that I wished to pass. I tried it until I was known at all the places, and then I had to give it up; and so I came away—and in mentioning this matter in my book, because I had not seen it myself, I told of it as a thing which my hero did not see, but which he heard as a rumor from other people. And then only the other day I came upon positive evidence of this crime—*and in Mr. Armour's own establishment!*

At the time of the embalmed-beef scandal, at the conclusion of the Spanish War, when the whole country was convulsed with fury over the revelations made by soldiers and officers (including General Miles and President Roosevelt) concerning the quality of meat which Armour & Co. had furnished to the troops, and concerning the death-rate which it had caused, the enormity of the "condemned-meat industry" became suddenly clear to one man who had formally supervised it. Mr. Thomas F. Dolan, then residing in Boston, had, up to a short time previous, been a superintendent at Armour & Co.'s, and one of Mr. Philip D. Armour's most capable and trusted men. He had letters, written in a familiar tone, showing that Mr. Armour was of the opinion that he, Mr. Dolan, could kill more cattle for him in a given time than any other man he ever had; he had a jeweled pin presented to him by Mr. Armour, and a gold watch with Mr. Armour's name in it. When he read of the death-rate in the army, he made an affidavit concerning the things which were done in the establishment of Armour & Co., and this affidavit he took to the New York *Journal*, which published it on March 4, 1899. Here are some extracts from it:

> For ten years I was employed by Philip D. Armour, the great Chicago beef packer and canner. I rose from a common beef skinner to the station of superintendent of the beef-killing gang, with 500 men directly under me. . . .
>
> There were many ways of getting around the inspectors—so many, in fact, that not more than two or three cattle out of one thousand were condemned. I know exactly what I am writing of

in this connection, as my particular instructions from Mr. W. E. Pierce, superintendent of the beef houses for Armour & Co., were very explicit and definite.

Whenever a beef got past the yard inspectors with a case of lumpy jaw and came into the slaughter-house or the "killing-bed," I was authorized by Mr. Pierce to take his head off, thus removing the evidences of lumpy jaw, and after casting the smitten portion in the tank where refuse goes, to send the rest of the carcass on its way to market.

In cases where tuberculosis became evident to the men who were skinning the cattle it was their duty, on instructions from Mr. Pierce, communicated to them through me, at once to remove the tubercles and cast them into a trap-door provided for that purpose.

I have seen as much as forty pounds of flesh afflicted with gangrene cut from the carcass of a beef, in order that the rest of the animal might be utilized in trade.

One of the most important regulations of the Bureau of Animal Industry is that no cows in calf are to be placed on the market. Out of a slaughter of 2,000 cows, or a day's killing, perhaps one-half are with calves. My instructions from Mr. Pierce were to dispose of the calves by hiding them until night, or until the inspectors left off duty. The little carcasses were then brought from all over the packing-house and skinned by boys, who received two cents for removing each pelt. The pelts were sold for fifty cents each to kid-glove manufacturers. This occurs every night at Mr. Armour's concern at Chicago, or after each killing of cows.

I now propose to state here exactly what I myself have witnessed in Philip D. Armour's packing-house with cattle that have been condemned by the Government inspectors.

A workman, one Nicholas Newson during my time, informs the inspector that the tanks are prepared for the reception of the condemned cattle and that his presence is required to see the beef cast into the steam-tank. Mr. Inspector proceeds at once to the place indicated, and the condemned cattle, having been brought up to the tank-room on trucks, are forthwith cast into the hissing steam-boilers and disappear. That is to say, they disappear so far as the inspector is concerned. He cranes his neck slightly, nods his head approvingly, and walks away.

But the condemned steer does not stay in the tank any longer than the time required for his remains to drop through the boiler down to the floor below, where he is caught on a truck and hauled back again to the cutting-room. The bottom of the tank was open, and the steer passed through the aperture.

I have witnessed the farce many times. I have seen the beef dropped into the vat in which a steam-pipe was exhausting with a great noise so that the thud of the beef striking the truck below could not be heard, and in a short time I have witnessed Nicholas bringing it back to be prepared for the market.

I have even marked beef with my knife so as to distinguish it, and watched it return to the point where it started. . . .

Of all the evils of the stock-yards, the canning department is perhaps the worst. It is there that the cattle from all parts of the United States are prepared for canning. No matter how scrawny or debilitated canners are, they must go the route of their brothers and arrive ultimately at the great boiling vats, where they are steamed until they are reasonably tender. Bundles of gristle and bone melt into pulpy masses and are stirred up for the canning department.

I have seen cattle come into Armour's stock-yard so weak and exhausted that they expired in the corrals, where they lay for an hour or two, dead, until they were afterward hauled in, skinned, and put on the market for beef or into the canning department for cans.

It was the custom to make a pretense of killing in such cases. The coagulated blood in their veins was too sluggish to flow, and instead of getting five gallons of blood, which is the amount commonly taken from a healthy steer, a mere dark-red clot would form at the wound.

In other words, the Armour establishment was selling carrion.

There are hundreds of other men in the employ of Mr. Armour who could verify every line I have written. They have known of these things ever since packing has been an industry. But I do not ask them to come to the front in this matter. I stand on my oath, word for word, sentence for sentence, and statement for statement.

I write this story of my own free will and volition, and no one is responsible for it but myself. It is the product of ten years of experience. It is the truth, the whole truth, and nothing but the truth, so help me God.

Thomas F. Dolan

Sworn to and subscribed before me this first day of March, 1899.

Orville P. Derby
Notary Public, Kings County, N.Y.
Certificate filed in New York County.

You read all that, and you say: "It is a Hearst story. It is one of the romances of the yellow journals. It was made up by a man who is engaged in stirring up class hatred, and in selling extra editions of his newspapers. The thing is probably a fake from beginning to end." Very well, suppose we grant it; that is nothing whatever to the point. The essential thing is an entirely different thing from the truth of the story—it is that the story was *published*; and that it was published in a newspaper whose proprietor owns property, and can be reached by the courts. It was a definite and explicit charge concerning certain things which Mr. Armour has "branded," over his own signature, as "absolutely false"; and now the one question of any importance is:

What did Mr. Armour do about it?

Did he have Mr. Thomas F. Dolan arrested for criminal libel; did he bring a suit for a million dollars libel against Mr. William R. Hearst; did he defy his accusers to produce their evidence and prove the atrocious crimes with which they had charged him? *No, he did not do any of these things!* What he did, I happen to know from a man who was present in Mr. Armour's office when he did it, and who advised and urged Mr. Armour strongly *not* to do it; what he did, upon his own decision, was to send an agent to Boston with five new, crisp one-thousand-dollar bills, to offer to Mr. Dolan, provided that he would make another affidavit declaring that his former statements were false, and that he had been paid a large sum of money by the New York *Journal* to make them!

The man whom Mr. Armour sent is now in an insane asylum at Peoria, Ill.; his name is Gilligan. He went to Mr. Dolan and offered him, not merely the five new, crisp one-thousand-dollar bills, but also a trip to Europe, with expenses for himself and family paid for three years, provided that he would make oath to a falsehood, and then take the next steamer. Mr. Dolan referred the matter to the newspaper people, who agreed with him that he could make quite as good use of the $5,000 as could Mr. Armour, and so Mr. Dolan took the five new, crisp one-thousand-dollar bills and deposited them in bank, to be held in trust for the education of his children; and that afternoon Mr. Gilligan, on his way back to report his triumph to his employer, was confronted with a copy of the New York *Evening Journal*, of March 16, 1899, containing the whole affidavit and the whole story, under the caption (in letters which it would take a good part of this magazine page to reproduce):

ARMOUR PAYS $5,000 FOR A GOLD BRICK IN BOSTON!

This is a pretty story. It falls in so beautifully with the letter recently made public by President Roosevelt, describing how Mr. Armour's attorneys had been bribing newspaper reporters to misrepresent the evidence at the Government prosecutions in Chicago. It also falls in beautifully with Mr. Armour's statement concerning the endless blackmail to which a packer would be liable who undertook to profit by the "condemned-meat industry." As a matter of fact, any one who knows anything at all about Mr. Armour's affairs knows that his life is made miserable by blackmailers. Scarcely an employee of any responsibility leaves Armour & Co., who fails to take with him some incriminating documents, and then come back and sell them to Mr. Armour at fancy prices. I wish I were at liberty to tell some of the stories which I know about such things. Only last week an intimate friend of mine was conversing with a man who had gotten an immense sum from Mr. Armour; that I do not name the man and the exact figure is simply because Mr. Armour might buy him again, and thus close an important source of information.

But not all the persons who have information about the practises of the Chicago packers are blackmailers. Some of them are honest and public-spirited men. One of these is Dr. William K. Jaques, of 4316 Greenwood Avenue, Chicago, a physician of large practise in the city, a professor of bacteriology in the Illinois State University, and bacteriologist in charge of the city inspection of meat during the years 1902-3. Dr. Jaques was a competent and conscientious official, who conceived it to be his duty to protect the people of the United States from eating diseased and tainted meat. He found that the carcasses of steers which had been condemned for tuberculosis, actinomycosis, lumpy jaw, and gangrene, and which were supposed to be "locked up in bond" (until they could be deposited in tanks and rendered into fertilizer), were left upon open platforms and carted away at night to be sold in Chicago for human food. He found also that the bodies of hogs which had been smothered or killed in transit were dumped out upon the platforms and left until a convenient time, and then loaded into box-cars, shipped to a place called Globe, in Indiana, and made into a fancy grade of lard. In his efforts to prevent these practises Dr. Jaques armed his inspectors with bicycle pumps, and ordered them to inject kerosene into all meat which they condemned. As a result of this Dr. Jaques was removed for "insubordination"; shortly afterward the entire city bureau of inspection was abolished.

Mr. Armour makes a great deal of the inspection of his meat by the Federal Government, and after describing in detail how the work of inspection is done, he adds: "This Government inspection thus becomes an important adjunct of the packer's business from two view-points. It puts the stamp of legitimacy and honesty upon the packer's product, and so is to him a necessity; to the public it is an *insurance* against the selling of diseased meats." This is a statement which the packers make continuously; it is hard for a man who knows the truth to read them and preserve his temper. What *is* the truth about this Federal inspection? To put it into one sentence—again following Mr. Armour's example by using italics—it is this: *That the Federal inspection of meat was, historically, established at the packers' request; that it is maintained and paid for by the people of the United States for the benefit of the packers; that men wearing the blue uniforms and brass buttons of the United States service are employed for the purpose of certifying to the nations of the civilized world that all the diseased and tainted meat which happens to come into existence in the United States of America is carefully sifted out and consumed by the American people.*

This is a strong statement; and yet I might go even farther. I might say this also: *that the laws regulating the inspection of meat were written by the packers, and written by the packers for the express purpose of making this whole condemned-meat industry impossible of prevention.* The Federal inspectors have power to condemn meat, but they have no power to destroy it. This power is delegated, under the law, to the representatives of "the State or municipality in which it is found." I cannot do better, upon this whole point, than to quote a letter written to me last January by Dr. Jaques, who is an unimpeachable authority upon this subject:

> The condemnation of diseased meat is a State function and it is delegated to the city of Chicago in its charter. The city ordinance empowers the Commissioner of Health to perform this duty. Federal inspectors *do* condemn and destroy meat, but they have no legal right to do this. Their instructions as to separating and tagging of diseased meat ends with "to be disposed of according to the laws and ordinances of the State and municipality in which it is found." This throws it into the hands of the city inspectors, and they are the only ones who can legally destroy it. The Federal inspectors admit this, and claim that their condemnations are made under the threat of withdrawing the inspection if not allowed to do so.
>
> *Foreign countries refused our meat and the packers appealed to our Government. It was finally arranged that Germany would accept American meat if our Government would guarantee its*

> *quality; to this end Federal inspection was instituted at the packing-houses.* The Federal inspector comes to the packer to inspect his meat for export, and at his bidding. He is under the packer's influence continually, and if not satisfactory to the packer will lose his place. His instructions make it easy for him by saying that the diseased meat is "to be disposed of according to the laws and ordinances of the State and municipality in which it is found." The city inspectors are the usual grade of employees, on duty during City Hall hours, from 9 until 5. The Civic Federation employed a detective to watch three of these, and found that most of their time was spent in saloons. There were only four of them at the yards. They were under a head of department at the City Hall, who got his position for strenuous activity in the last campaign. The packers' contribution made this same duty pleasant.
>
> Just to show how the packers have their hands on the situation I have only to say that the first of this month Dr. Biehn, my successor, was withdrawn from this work and the stock-yards inspection placed under "Fish" Murray, a protégé of the stock-yards alderman, Cary. Murray was fish inspector under me and laughed at my efforts to make him do something to earn his salary. To my knowledge, he never condemned a pound of fish nor did a day's work in the fourteen months that I was his chief. The Health Department now issues a statement that the condition is remedied, and that Chicago is no longer a dumping-ground for bad meat. The truth is that the mayor is already fixing up his fences for reelection.

I quote this at length in order that the reader may realize in all its hideous detail the exact significance of that innocent-looking little provision in our national laws that meat which is condemned as unfit for food shall be disposed of "according to the laws and ordinances of the State or municipality in which it is found." If anything further is necessary to convince him of the truth of my statement that these laws were written by the packers, and in order to make the "condemned-meat industry" impossible of prevention, let him consider these two sentences—as bald and explicit as sentences can be:

"Rules and Regulations for the Inspection of Live Stock and their Products; United States Department of Agriculture, Bureau of Animal Industries, Order No. 125, Section 25: 'A microscopic examination for trichinosis shall be made of all swine products exported to countries requiring such examination. *No microscopic examination will be made of hogs slaughtered for interstate trade, but this examination shall be confined to those intended for the export trade.*'" Since one and one-half per cent. of all the hogs slaughtered in Chicago are found to be infected with trichinosis, it follows that the American people eat not only their own one and one-half per cent., but also the one and one-half per cent. of the share of Europe!

Mr. Armour dilates at length upon the fact that the Federal inspectors are appointed by the Government, and that they are all trained veterinarians. It is a pity that he did not go into detail, and state how many of them there are and how much work they have to do. When I was in Packingtown I met Mr. Adolphe Smith, an English specialist who had been sent out as correspondent of the London *Lancet,* the leading medical paper of Great Britain. Mr. Smith had made a lifelong study of the subject of slaughter-houses; for the past fourteen years he had been inspecting for the *Lancet* the abattoirs of every country in the civilized world; and in the articles which he wrote for the *Lancet* (January 7, 14, 21, 28, 1905) he denounced the conditions which he found in Chicago as unspeakable and abominable, worthy of the Dark Ages. Among the things which he censured most severely were the insufficiency of the Government inspection force, the ridiculously inadequate pay of the inspectors, and the disgraceful lack of consideration with which they were treated. "At the Chicago stock-yards," he wrote, "I could not but feel scandalized and humiliated when I saw the foul and abominable premises in which the representatives of science, the representatives of the United States of America, the representatives of the majesty of law, condescended to work daily in the accomplishment of their mission. . . . It is a very good thing that inspectors are appointed by the authorities at Washington, but it would be better still if they were first sent to Berlin to learn not only how a slaughter-house ought to be managed and constructed, but to observe how those who have the honor of being entrusted with a public duty are more respected than business men, however rich."

Some time after Dr. Jaques left his position a brief account of his experiences crept into print, and a Chicago newspaper interviewed him and misquoted him; he offered a statement of what he had really said, which the newspaper—the same one to which I have referred previously in this article—refused to print. The following is a brief extract from that statement:

> My education as a physician teaches me that disease follows the same law whether in animals or human beings. An accurate post mortem requires close inspection of all the internal organs together with the use of the microscope, before a physician can say there is no disease present. How many post mortems could the most expert physician make in a day? Ten would be a big day's work; fifty would tax the endurance of the most strenuous. It is reported that 150,000 animals have been received at the Union Stock-yards in a single day. How many animal pathologists are employed by the Government who are capable of making a reliable post mortem and saying that an animal is not diseased? In round numbers, say there are fifty—a few more or less, for the sake of illustration, are not material. Say there are only fifty thousand animals killed a day at the stock-yards. This would be a thousand to each inspector, a hundred an hour, nearly two a minute. What is such inspection as that worth? It is true, there is some inspection that is well done; it is that which is done for the sharp eyes of the foreigner.
>
> Inspection to be effective should include the entire twenty-four hours. Federal inspection is probably effective in daylight. City inspectors work during City Hall hours. The railroads and express companies bring animals into the city every hour of the day. When the chief inspector has access to every room in the packing-houses and knows what is done there every hour in the twenty-four; when his army of inspectors know the disposition of the meat brought into the city by more than thirty railroads; when he knows the destination and use of the refuse which the meat and liver wagons gather after nightfall from Fulton Market, South Water Street, and other markets; when he knows the meat that comes to the city by wagon and other ways; then in my estimation, he can give

> something like an accurate estimation of the amount of diseased, putrid meat that is converted into food in Chicago. Until he has this information, he must confess to the ignorance of which he accuses others. No one has this information. There are a hundred streets and avenues by which diseased meat can enter the city and be put on sale in the markets. The public has made no effort to find out, and it is left to the men who deal in this merchandise to dump what they please into the stomachs of the blissfully ignorant public. Neither do any of us know how much disease and suffering this food causes. The diagnosis of the best physicians is so often turned down at the post-mortem table that the actual results of diseased food are difficult to ascertain.

Owing to the agitation created in Chicago by the revelations of the London *Lancet,* the city inspection bureau, which had been restored by Mayor Dunne, went to work really to enforce the law. The results are set forth in the city bulletins. During the week ending September, 1905, the city inspectors condemned at the Chicago stock-yards 173,769 pounds of meat; *and during the corresponding week of the previous year they had condemned only 2,002 pounds!* By October 28th six new meat inspectors had been appointed, and they destroyed in one week 496 animals, weighing 145,345 pounds. The Federal Government employs in the packing-houses of the entire country a total of 411 inspectors; and during the year 1904 these inspectors condemned 19,097 carcasses, an average of 367 per week, or less than one per week for each inspector. During one week, as we have seen, the eight or nine new appointees of the city of Chicago condemned 496 animals, or an average of *over fifty for each inspector!* The 411 Government inspectors *passed* a total of 104,203,753 carcasses; and assuming that each inspector was on duty eight hours a day for 300 days, he examined and certified to the good condition of 105 animals an hour, or nearly two a minute—a calculation for the entire country, which gives about the same result as that of Dr. Jaques for the inspection in Chicago. In the bulletin of the Chicago Board of Health for September 23, 1905, we are told what happened in the stock-yards when the city inspection so suddenly woke up:

> Among these animals were six cattle that had been passed by the Government inspectors. Two cattle were found last week by the Department inspectors that had been passed by the Government inspectors after the evidences of tuberculosis had been trimmed out. The city inspectors destroyed these cattle. The Government inspectors refused to allow the city meat inspectors to remove glands and other organs suspected of being diseased, for the purpose of microscopic examination by the laboratory bacteriologists.

At the close of the Spanish War there was held a court of inquiry which took testimony that shed a flood of light upon packing-house methods. I quote a few facts which were brought out dealing with this question of the efficiency of the Federal inspection, concerning which Mr. Armour boasts so boldly. In the course of the *The Jungle* I describe how "downers," that is, cattle which have been injured or killed in transit, are slaughtered at night, and how the big packing-houses have special elevators upon which to lift them to the "killing-beds." Dr. George Lytle, an assistant inspector, on duty at Swift's and Armour's, testified that he left the packing-house at about half past five in the afternoon; that he went on at seven o'clock the next morning; and that during the thirteen or fourteen hours between he was not there, nor was any one else connected with the bureau there, and that the room was not "secured or locked or fastened in any way." Dr. Lytle also admitted that the inspectors had no authority to prevent the use of chemicals in the preserving of meat. There was brought into evidence a letter from Dr. D. E. Salmon, chief of the Bureau of Animal Industry in Washington, which letter stated explicitly that "the inspection of live animals and meat products by this bureau is made before and at the time of slaughter to determine the disease, or announce an unwholesome condition of the animal or meat at that time. The stamps which are affixed to the packages are simply to indicate that an inspection as stated above has been made, and is no guarantee that the meat has been properly cured and packed."

Let the reader realize the full significance of this fact, and the light which it throws upon the system of inspection upon which Mr. Armour congratulates the American people. In a pamphlet put out by the Kentucky State Food Control Department occurs the following paragraph:

> This [Government] stamp was intended by Congress to show that the animal has been passed by the veterinary inspector as fit for slaughter, and the carcass as fit for packing, having in mind the physiological wholesomeness only. But the public has been educated by continuous advertisement to believe that this unqualified "*Meat Inspection Stamp*" guarantees the product against all forms of unwholesomeness and adulteration, when the facts are, meats bearing this stamp often contain antiseptics, aniline dyes, and such other adulterations as the packer may find profitable, thereby making this unqualified stamp of the Federal Government on of the grossest forms of food misbranding.

In the course of the testimony before the court, the chief men of Armour & Co. admitted that the "canned roast beef" which they furnished to our soldiers during the Spanish War had first been boiled to make "extracts"; and we see that the Federal inspection is powerless to prevent that. I have charged, and I charge here again, that the so-called "potted ham" and "deviled ham" sold by Armour & Co, consists of the old dry waste ends of smoked beef, ground up with potato skins, with the hard cartilaginous gullets of beef, and with the udders of cows, dyed to prevent their showing white. And the Federal inspection has no power to prevent *that!* The Federal inspection has no power to say whether or not any measures shall be taken to see that poisoned rats are not ground up in the sausage meat, as man after man in the yards told me that he had seen; it has no power to prevent the "doctoring" of spoiled hams with all sorts of chemicals; to prevent the preserving of sausage with borax and salicylic acid, and the dyeing of it to save the time and expense incidental to smoking! It has no power to prevent the adulteration of sausages with "potato flour," the by-product of the manufacture of potato-alcohol; or to prevent the adulteration of lard with beef fat, tallow and lard stearin, paraffin and cottonseed oil. Does Mr. Armour deny that all these things which I have named are done in his establishment? If he does deny it, I will refer him to the Tenth Biennial Report of the Minnesota State Dairy and Food Commissioner, in which, on page 173, the "Shield Leaf Lard" of Armour & Co. is officially branded as "illegal"; and again, on page 175, the "Lard," and on page 176, the "Vegetol," and on page 182, the "Shield Lard" are described in the same way. What has Mr. Armour to say to that? Mr. Armour advertises extensively his "Veribest" brands of potted meats. In the Bulletin of the Dairy and Food Division of the Pennsylvania Department of Agriculture, for November 15, 1905, I find that Armour & Co.'s "Veribest" potted ham is declared, as a result of analyses by the State chemist, to be "preserved." What has Mr. Armour to say to that? Similarly his "Frankfurter Sausage," purchased in open market in Altoona, Pa., was found to be "preserved"; similarly his "Minced Ham," purchased in Greenburg and in Pittsburg, and his potted ham, purchased in Lancaster. In the Kentucky pamphlet previously quoted are some cases reported to the courts in September and October, 1905, and among them are Mr. Armour's "Star Sausage" and "Oleo-margarine," both preserved with "boric acid." In Bulletin No. 63 of the North Dakota Agricultural College, I find the following among the meats labeled "illegal," as containing either borax or sulphites: Armour's "Sliced Star Brand" of dried beef, Armour's "White Label Brand" of sliced dried beef, Armour's "Gold Brand" breakfast bacon, Armour's bologna sausage, and again Armour's "Gold Brand" breakfast bacon. The report continues: "The question is asked as to the amount of these preservatives present in meats. In ham, dried beef, and like cured products we have found from five to fifteen grains of boric acid per pound of meat. In sausages, bolognas, hamburger steak, etc., we have found from twenty grains to fifty grains of boric acid per pound." In the Bulletin of the North Carolina State Board of Agriculture for December, 1904, I find the "Oxford Smoked" chipped beef of Armour & Co. containing salicylic acid, and the "Shield Brand" dried chipped beef of the Armour Canning Company, containing salicylic acid. In the Fifteenth Annual Report of the Ohio Dairy and Food Commissioner, I find the pork and sausage from Armour & Co. analyzed as preserved with borax and adulterated with starch. In the Monthly Bulletin of the Indiana State Board of Health for November, 1905, I find three different brands of Armour & Co.'s sausage containing borax, also one brand of "Leberwurst." According to the New York *Health Journal* "borax and boric acid have been proven by French investigators to cause deterioration of the blood-corpuscles on continued use, so that now in that country it is no longer permitted to be mixed with butter as a preservative." Dr. Wiley, the Government chemist, made a practical test of them upon his "poison-squad," and after two years of exhaustive experiment he made a report summarized in the press as follows:

> The results obtained from the experiments show that even in doses not exceeding a half gram (7 ½ grains) a day, boric acid and borax as preservatives are prejudicial to health when consumed for a long time. The safe rule is to exclude these preservatives from food for general consumption. When mixed with food they are absorbed into the circulation from the intestinal canal. If continued for a long time in quantities not exceeding a half-grain per day they cause occasional periods of loss of appetite, bad feelings, fulness in the head, and distress in the stomach. If given in larger and increasing doses, these symptoms are more rapidly developed and accentuated with a slight clouding of the mental processes. When increased to three grams a day the doses sometimes cause nausea and vomiting.

In the Fourteenth Annual Report of the Ohio Dairy and Food Commissioner, page 110, Mr. Armour's "Berlin Ham" is branded as colored with aniline dye; a discovery which the reader will not fail to connect with my statement concerning the grinding up and dyeing of the udders of cows and the gullets of beef! At an exhibition given before the National Association of Stewards at Philadelphia a few weeks ago, three dogs were shown which had been fed on colored foods, and had lost flesh and become weak. After a fifteen days' diet of artificially colored foods, a St. Bernard dog lost thirty-two pounds. One of these dogs was scarcely able to stagger across the stage, and the Philadelphia Society for the Prevention of Cruelty to Animals was asked to stop the experiments!

Writing in a magazine of large circulation and influence, and having the floor all to himself, Mr. Armour spoke serenely and boastfully of the quality of his meat products, and challenged the world to impeach his integrity, but when he was brought into court charged with *crime* by the commonwealth of Pennsylvania, he spoke in a different tone, and to a different purport; he said "guilty." He pleaded this to a criminal indictment for selling "preserved" minced ham in Greenburg, and paid the fine of $50 and costs. He pleaded guilty again in Shenandoah, Pa., on June 16, 1905, to the criminal charge of selling adulterated "blockweirst"; and again he paid the fine of $50 and costs. Why should Mr. Armour be let off with fines which are of less consequence to him than the price of a postage stamp to you or me, instead of going to jail like other convicted criminals who do not happen to be millionaires?

III.

FACTORIES, FIELDS, AND FASCISTS: INVESTIGATIVE JOURNALISM'S FORGOTTEN DECADES, 1920–1960

Vera Connolly

"I don't see any value in exposing a public evil unless you have some remedy to offer," Vera Connolly (1888–1964) once wrote. The child of an Army captain whose postings carried the family from a California Indian reservation to Southeast Asia, Connolly wrote her first articles for the New York Sun *in 1917. By the twenties she had found a niche in women's magazines such as* Good Housekeeping *and in 1937 helped found* Woman's Day.

If Connolly had begun her career a decade earlier, she would have been recognized as a peer of the muckrakers. Instead, she is nearly forgotten. Connolly shared the muckrakers' progressive social reform agenda, their reportorial tenacity and depth, their dedication to narrative writing. She broke fresh ground, departing from the muckrakers' focus on corrupt politicians for unsparing stories on social institutions gone awry: juvenile jails, education, marriage. Not a liberal in the contemporary sense—she believed so strongly in the responsibility of the individual that she opposed Roosevelt's New Deal—she was nonetheless a social feminist, motivated by an unbending sense of moral justice.

Connolly's most powerful and influential work was a series of three long articles for Good Housekeeping *on conditions at Indian reservations—a subject virtually invisible in the press of her day. She spent a year on research in New Mexico, Arizona, Colorado, Washington, and Wisconsin, cultivating sources at the Bureau of Indian Affairs and poring over statistics. "Cry of a Broken People," the first article in her series, appeared in February 1929. The series led to congressional hearings and the resignation of the BIA commissioner.*

The Cry of a Broken People: A Story of Injustice and Cruelty that Is as Terrible as It Is True

From *Good Housekeeping,* 1929

The solemnity of that roomful! Never shall I forget it!

It was in the Indian pueblo of Taos, New Mexico, in July, 1928. A Council of grave import was being held for us by the head men of the tribe.

All around the bare, whitewashed walls ran a narrow seat. On this we sat, tense and waiting; a few palefaces in a long line of silent, dignified Indian men.

In a corner by the fireplace stood a table with a small lamp. Beside this sat the Indian "Governor" of the pueblo: a man of majestic stillness, with a hawk face and quietly folded arms. He wore a shirt of faded red that glowed softly in the lamp-light. His hair hung forward over his shoulders in two braids twisted with colored strands. Near him, crouching on the floor, respectful, silent, was the Indian interpreter.

In a rear room huddled the women and young girls. They had greeted us, when we arrived, with the gracious gestures of an ancient race. Then, soft-voiced, charming in their vivid shawls, they had quietly withdrawn. The Council is not for Indian women.

The room, after that, had commenced rapidly to fill with sober-faced Indian men. Like Arabs they had come slipping in, swathed in their white cotton blankets, and had taken their seats solemnly around the wall. Now every inch of the encircling seat was occupied. And the doorway was filled with shrouded figures, beyond whom, on the moonlit desert without, we could faintly discern a throng of other still forms.

The seated men had thrown off their white blankets, and the room glowed with the soft colors of their shirts, faded blue, sage green, pale vermilion. Some wore turquoise earrings, and a few had about their necks strings of old Indian jewelry: wampum, coral, and silver beads—in some cases the owner's sole wealth. For though self-supporting and of regal dignity, these were poor Indians.

Presently the Governor raised his hand. The Council began.

He first addressed the Indians, speaking in the native tongue. He told them that we—their white visitors—had heard, in New York City, that all was not well with the Indian people, wards of our nation. We had come out to the West to learn if these rumors of misery and injustice were true.

When he had finished speaking, the interpreter repeated the words to us in English. And again a sober silence fell. Outside, on the moonlit rooftops, an Indian drum sounded softly, then a low, minor chanting began and drifted in at the doorway.

Suddenly, one by one, the Indians commenced to speak. They spoke heatedly, rapidly, with gestures. Yet their passion was so restrained that no voice ever rose above a tense monotone. Each addressed the Governor, who in turn asked the interpreter to translate for us.

It was a passionate plea for just one thing—better treatment of Indian children in the government boarding schools. The other wrongs the race may have suffered in the past at our hands—loss of lands, water rights, and personal freedom—obviously signified nothing in their eyes compared to the sufferings of the 27,000 Indian children in the government boarding schools today.

These children, it was explained to us, are taken forcibly from their mothers' arms, as early as six years of age in some Indian communities, and sent away to distant boarding schools to stay till eighteen. There they are underfed, roughly treated, and required to work half of every day at hard industrial labor, in the fields or in the laundry, in addition to the half-day of school.

It was a story of frightened, lonely, hungry, exhausted childhood they told. Of children poorly housed in crowded dormitories, with so little protection against disease that infections rage through the schools. Of children cruelly overworked. Of children so underfed that they snatch like famished little animals at plates of bread. Of children struck and thrown into the school "jails" for infringement of minor rules.

And these statements coincided with the rumors that had caused the Editor of *Good Housekeeping* to send me West, to the Indians themselves, to ascertain the facts.

The Governor told of visiting one of these schools himself in May, 1928, and finding the food not only insufficient in quantity, but of the wrong kind for growing children forced to do hard work.

The Children Are Hungry

Another Indian, Alvino Lujan, described his visit to the Santa Fé School in 1928.

"I sat down to supper with the little boys," he said, "and when the bread arrived, the boys grabbed all of it, yet were still hungry. No more was served them. I asked for some bread for myself and was given two thin slices. But when it came, the little boy beside me kept staring so at my bread—he was so pitiful—I turned my head away. When I looked around again, my bread was gone.

"At breakfast the same thing happened. The boys snatched the bread as though half starved. I went to San Idlefonso pueblo and asked some bread from the Indians and took it to the hungry boys at the school. All this is wrong! Those children work very hard! The night I slept there one boy was awakened at midnight to go out and work on some machinery."

A third Indian—Juan Archuleta—declared that the main meal at noon, when he visited the Santa Fé School in 1927, consisted of "gravy, a kind of tea just like water, and some bread and sirup." And "The boys did not have enough of this," he added. "They left the table hungry."

Antonio Mirabal, the interpreter—a man with a fine, thoughtful face—told with quiet compassion of his visit to the Albuquerque School in March, 1927. "Breakfast was oatmeal with sirup, bread and coffee. The boys rushed for it. There was not nearly enough. So I ate nothing. I wanted them to have it all."

When the men had finally ceased speaking, some of the boys, home on vacation, told timidly of their treatment in the schools. Again it was a tale of loneliness, overwork, undernourishment, and brutal discipline. How tragic, thought the writer, for this cruelty to be inflicted on the boys and girls of a race noted for its love of children! One may wander all day about an Indian pueblo, up and down the ladders, in and out of the quaint, many-storied house, and never see a child struck or hear a harsh word spoken to it. Indian women, if one of their number scolds a child, derisively call her "white woman." Firm discipline of childhood, yes. That is to be found in the Indian household. But it is not the rule of fist and boot.

"The disciplinarian closed the door," said Fernando Romero, a schoolboy, in describing the punishment meted to him at the Santa Fé boarding school because of a misunderstanding over the washing of some shirts, "and grabbed hold of my neck and tried to choke me. Then he struck my mouth, and it began to bleed. Then he grabbed me again and knocked my head against the door and told me to go back to work. I couldn't eat for two days, my mouth was so swollen."

Other boys told me of the cruel jails at the schools; of little boys of twelve forced to dig ditches and do other work too hard for them; of boys hit in the face for coming late to work; of the terrible food—usually oatmeal, sirup, bread, and coffee for breakfast; gravy and bread, potatoes and tea for dinner; and beans and bread and tea for supper. And never, never enough!

Leaving the Council room the writer slipped back for a word with the shy girls in the rear part of the house. They told a similar story, describing the long, exhausting hours in sewing-room and laundry before the school day began. Girls were roughly punished, too: sometimes struck, sometimes made to kneel on the floor in the hall all night for being late to work.

Several girls had tubercular coughs.

"They never sick till they go away to boarding school," said a woman, with quiet despair, in broken English.

I recalled then some of the statements in the official reports I had recently seen—that the Indian boarding schools are overcrowded, unsanitary, and foul with two diseases—tuberculosis, a gift of the white race to the Indian people, and trachoma, an eye disease closely connected with malnutrition.

I had read that often healthy children were brought to these schools and, after being subjected to years of hunger, unkindness, overwork, and infection, sent home dying of tuberculosis or half-blind with trachoma, to infect their helpless families and communities.

Could these things be? In the United States of America?

THEIR HOPE IS IN US

I returned to the Council room. The meeting was over; and we departed, promising to tell white Americans—parents themselves—what the Indian child is suffering in the boarding schools. And promising to make a plea that day schools on the reservations be substituted for these distant boarding schools.

When we passed out the door, the white-robed, Arab-like forms fell back respectfully, and we walked between them across the plaza, upon which the centuries-old houses look down, to our waiting automobile.

As we drove away over the moonlit desert-plateau, we looked back at the Sacred Mountain, with ancient Taos pueblo crouching at its foot. From the roof tops there still reached us faintly the chanting of the singers. It was buoyant, confident singing! It was a Song of Good Hope, explained one who was with us—a hope that the Council meeting had not been in vain.

In the weeks that followed, the writer of this article visited many groups of Indians, not only in New Mexico, but in Arizona, Colorado, Oregon, Washington, and Wisconsin. In all these states, and in California, she also studied every official report she was able to obtain. Besides, she interviewed prominent white men and women who for years have been quietly battling for the Indian people.

Partly as a result of her own fleeting observations, but chiefly through her interviews and study of authentic reports, among them the one submitted a year ago by the Institute for Government Research after a fifteen months' investigation made at the request of the Secretary of the Interior—the writer found abundant verification of all that had been claimed in the Taos Council regarding the boarding schools. And she also discovered that this wrong being done the Indian people is one of many!

Gaunt poverty is apparent on almost all reservations today. And so is hunger. And so is contagious disease. And so is complete subjugation of person and property. Although all Indians today are citizens, made such in recognition of their voluntary service during the World War, the Indian Bureau—which for seventy years has had despotic control over the Indian—pronounces 225,000 of them "incompetent." This Bureau regards its acts as not subject to court review.

To quote from Congressman James A. Frear, of Wisconsin, in a recent issue of *Plain Talk*:

"The Indian Bureau holds itself above the law and, in the disposition of property belonging to 'incompetent' Indians, considers that its acts are not reviewable by the courts. This arbitrary stand makes it impossible for the 225,000 'incompetent' Indians to prevent the wholesale wasting of their property. More than $90,000,000 in cash and securities and more than $1,600,000,000 in land and personal property belonging to Indians are under the exclusive control of the Indian Bureau, while the owners of the property are denied any voice in its disposal and often refused any share of the proceeds. As an inevitable consequence, the property of the Indians has literally been looted to the extent of millions of dollars."

SLAVERY STILL EXISTS

The American Indian can not sell his own lands. He can not worship in his own way. He can not rear his own children. If he leaves the reservation without permission, he can be tried by a "judge" appointed by the Agent and thrown into jail for any length term in ball and chain. For him there is no jury trial unless he has been specifically charged with one of eight major crimes named in Federal law; in the latter case he may demand and get trial in the Federal Courts, though the Bureau controls his money for hiring attorneys and his choice of attorneys. For all other cases, for crimes and misdemeanors named or unnamed in law, or for simple disagreements with Bureau officials, the Indian may be, and is, arrested without warrant, imprisoned without (a) trial in any court of record, (b) advice of counsel, (c) right to be confronted by accuser or to compel attendance of witnesses, or (d) any right of court review. The Indian Agent carries out the whole process, or an "Indian Judge" appointed by the Agent and paid $11 a month carries it out. THERE IS NO LIMIT IN ANY LAW OF CONGRESS TO THE AMOUNT OF FINE OR LENGTH OF IMPRISONMENT.

Virtual slaves, in a land where slavery was abolished years ago, victims of horrible diseases the whites have brought but will not bother to cure, deprived of the children they have borne, hungry and in despair, thousands of our Indian citizens present a spectacle that touches the heart.

"If Harriet Beecher Stowe were here," said Congressman Frear before a Senate Committee, on his return from a 4,500-mile trip at his own, expense to twenty reservations, "she could write a story far worse than anything that ever appeared in *Uncle Tom's Cabin.*

The writer of this article found that the information she was obtaining was of three sorts—personal wrongs, maladministration of property, and suggestions as to a solution of the Indian problem. She has therefore prepared three articles, one devoted to each of these phases.

This first article will deal with the personal wrongs.

The maltreatment of the Indian child has already been touched upon, and will be referred to again later in this article.

Next, there is the dire poverty of the Indians. For most of them are poor, bitterly poor. A few tribes have discovered oil on their arid lands, and the sudden wealth of these has created the public impression that all Indians today are prospering. This is a mistake. Most of them are extremely poor. Some are starving.

Next to the threat of starvation, our greatest crime against the Indians today is our gross neglect of their health. This is of tragic importance. Not only is a lovable, picturesque race dying of contagious diseases we have bestowed on it—the Indian death-rate increased 62 percent from 1921 through 1925—but in dying the Indians are unconsciously wreaking on us, their white conquerors, a grim revenge for our century and a half of cruelty and neglect. For today many Indian settlements threaten to become dangerous sources of infection, from which contagious diseases will spread to the surrounding white communities.

Such is the sober warning sounded in the Institute Report. It is the statement of all recent investigators. And it is my earnest warning, fleeting as were my glimpses, in six states, of Indian life.

At Walpi, an ancient sky-town of crazy, picturesque stone houses flung up in wild beauty against the heavens atop a mesa, or rock island, rising sheer from the Arizona desert, I saw a gifted people so afflicted with a virulent skin disease (impetigo) that some faces were literally covered with scabs. It is here that the famous Snake Dance is held, to which tourists flock from all over the world. The danger to the white race is obvious! And so is the needlessness of the situation! We are told in the Reference Handbook of the Medical Sciences that treatment of impetigo is simple and effective. It consists of "removal of the crusts by soaking in olive oil . . . after which an application of a five to ten percent ointment of ammoniated mercury completes the healing in a few days." Why were those Indians not receiving this treatment?

At Zuni, in the home of the pueblos' Governor, while I listened to a story of contaminated drinking water, dysentery, and a reservation doctor who would not pay visits to sick Indians, I saw a young mother anxiously looking down into the face of the terribly sick baby in her arms. The child was covered with a scabby disease.

At Hotavilla, an Indian pueblo on the Arizona desert, I stopped to witness a ceremonial dance in the plaza. It was a colorful scene. The partly naked men dancers were painted and hung with green sprigs and animal skins; their heads were encased in grotesque masks; they carried gourd rattles which they shook as they danced. On the roof tops sat the Indian women, one blaze of color in mantas, kerchiefs, and shawls. And thronging the narrow street were white tourists under vivid parasols. Yet within ten feet of me, in that crowd of Indians, I observed four women and five children in advanced stages of trachoma. This village is a favorite haunt of tourists.

TUBERCULOSIS RAGES UNCHECKED

As for tuberculosis—it was appallingly in evidence in all Indian settlements I visited, especially on the Bad River Indian Reservation in Wisconsin. Even on the blazing Arizona desert it seemed, to me, to be raging. Figures prove that my impression was correct, as the tuberculosis death-rate among Arizona Indians is seventeen times the general rate for the country as a whole. This is partly due to the children returning from the boarding schools, infected, and giving tuberculosis to the adults.

Statistics show that the medical service provided by the Indian Bureau is hopelessly inadequate in virtually all Indian communities. In some settlements there is none at all. As a result, 21 percent of all Indians, or more than 60,000, have trachoma. And the average Indian death-rate in the country as a whole is 2 1/4 times that of the general population.

At Pine Ridge, South Dakota, an investigator recently discovered two physicians serving 7,800 Indians scattered over 2,400 square miles. In the western Navajo jurisdiction one serves 8,000 Indians scattered over 5,000 square miles. At Soboba in southern California, Dr. Allan F. Gillihan, who was making a survey for the State Board of Health, found one doctor serving 1,500 Indians, his territory extending 100 miles to the east of the hospital and 25 miles to the west and south. Dr. Gillihan had previously surveyed conditions in northeastern California. He offered the following conclusions regarding the California Indians:

> "1. That the ill treatment of the Indians during the past 70 years has resulted in reducing the population from over 100,000 to about 17,300 . . .
>
> "2. That the Indians are now living a hand-to-mouth existence.
> (a) In houses not fit to live in.
> (b) Upon land that is useless.
> (c) Without water.
>
> "3. That they are not receiving an education worthy of the name.
>
> "4. That a great deal of sickness exists among them, and they are receiving absolutely no care.
>
> "5. That they are not receiving any advice, assistance, or encouragement in their business dealings with the outside world or in the personal side of their lives or in the lives and health of their families."

At Odanah, Wisconsin, on the Bad River Reservation, the writer talked to a number of Chippewa Indians and to two white missionaries. All declared health conditions on the Reservation unspeakably bad.

"According to government statistics," said W. H. Thompson, the Methodist missionary, "over 60 percent on this Reservation have venereal disease. Tuberculosis is rife here as well. I've been here four years, and eighty percent of my funerals have been over tuberculosis victims. No effort is made to check these diseases. WE HAVE NO DOCTOR. WE HAVE NO HOSPITAL. Conditions are pitiable!"

And Rev. E. Wheeler, a noted missionary and lifelong friend of the Chippewas, had this to say of the Bad River Reservation:

"Things are seriously, horribly wrong here. The Reservation seems wide open to liquor and prostitution. Venereal disease is rampant."

MEDICAL SERVICE IS IMPERATIVE

Sometimes it is claimed that a good medical service would be wasted on the Indians, that they would not make use of it. Congressman Frear quotes as follows Dr. Frances Sage Bradley, director of the State Division of Child Welfare, Montana. She is speaking of the Blackfeet Indians:

"Pathetic and hopeless is the physical condition of young children and the eagerness of the mothers for help. We have held what we call children's conferences on various reservations, and men and women have sledded their children thirty-five and forty miles in snow on a level with their roofs, with the thermometer fourteen below zero, to find out how to cure rickets, trachoma, tuberculosis . . . I want to state that nothing but a prompt, vigorous, baby-saving campaign can prevent the extermination of the Blackfeet."

If we wonder at this high mortality rate among the Blackfeet, perhaps we can find the explanation of it in the testimony given in 1927 before the Senate Indian Affairs Committee by William Madison, who had just returned from the Fort Peck, Blackfeet, and Flathead Reservations in Montana.

He tells of old Indians living in tents in the bitter cold, with no food but the flesh of horses found on the town dump or killed by passing trains. He describes one old woman who was refused food and help by the Agent, the latter telling her to drown out gophers for meat to eat. He cites the case of a woman whose child died eight days after birth, and who, while the child was still in the coffin, and with the thermometer at 30 degrees below zero, was ordered with her husband to vacate the house, the exposure making her a hopeless invalid.

Hunger? Sickness? Maltreatment? They are to be found, apparently, in some form, from the Canadian border to the Pima Reservation in Arizona!

At Riverside, California, the writer interviewed the gallant, silver-haired white woman, Mrs. Stella M. Atwood, who is gratefully called "Mother" today by Indians all over the United States. It was Mrs. Atwood who, in 1921, at the Salt Lake Convention of the General Federation of Women's Clubs, informed the clubwomen of America of the tragic plight of the Indian people. She was assisted in her plea by Mrs.

Gertrude Bonnin, a beautiful and cultivated Indian woman. And so eloquently did the two plead that there was created the Indian Welfare Division of the General Federation, with Mrs. Atwood at its head.

The torch Mrs. Atwood lighted was caught up by John Collier, already a student of the subject, and a publicist, and thrust up before the public gaze. For over seven years these two pioneers have fought—Mrs. Atwood with the clubwomen of America as a mighty force behind her, John Collier as Executive Secretary of the American Indian Defense Association. They have fought in season and out, at home and abroad, in Congress, among the Indians, among the whites. And they have blocked some of the most vicious legislation of recent years designed to rob the Indians.

An epitome of courage, strength, and motherly kindness—of all that is best in womanhood—Mrs. Atwood sat facing the writer, in Riverside, last August, telling of pitiable conditions among the Indians today.

"The health service," she declared, "is atrocious! Indian Reservation doctors are, for the most part, derelicts. I found four doctors who were dope fiends the first month I was in this work, nearly eight years ago."

Many of the doctors, she went on to say, while not dope fiends or liquor addicts, are callously indifferent. Frequently they refuse flatly to respond to a summons. She cited an instance. A doctor on the Navajo Reservation in 1927 refused point-blank to drive forty miles at night, with some white people who had come for him, to attend a Navajo woman dying of hemorrhages after childbirth.

FOOD FOR THIS STARVING PEOPLE

"But the first, the crying need of our Indians today," Mrs. Atwood exclaimed, and tears sprang suddenly her eyes, "is food! Simply enough food to satisfy the pangs of semi-starvation! About five years ago I was invited out to Arizona, to Sacaton, where the Indians and whites were celebrating San Carlos Day. The Agent—there are kind subordinate officials in the Indian Service, as well as the other sort—was giving the Indians a feast that day, consisting of frijoles, beef, coffee, and bread.

"I walked with him to the place where the food was. And when I saw the Indians coming out with hungry, eager faces and trembling hands, I exclaimed, "Why, these Indians are famished." He said, "Yes, this is the only full meal they'll get during the year." These were the Pima Indians, gentlemen and gentlewomen. Their proud boast is that they have never shed a drop of paleface blood. In the early days they always succored the whites, taking them into their homes, when dying of thirst, and nursing them to health.

"These Indians were starving because the whites had taken their water from them on the upper reaches of the Gila River. The government had built a storage dam but had failed to put any laterals down to the Indian land. So for three successive years the Pimas had planted their crops and seen them wither and die. It was all wicked injustice! They are such fine farmers that when they could get even a little water, they took all the sweepstakes in prizes in state and county fairs."

But we are digressing! This article has to do only with personal, not property wrongs. Just a word more about cruelty to adults, then we will consider again, briefly, the plight of the little Indian child.

Chain-and-ball treatment for both sexes—in one case an Indian woman was put in a one-room jail with three men; semi-starvation; the giving of spoiled food to helpless old Indians as "rations"; the refusal of Reservation doctors to attend women dying in childbirth; permitted bootlegging and moral evils: these cruelties to the Indian race were reported in almost all sections I visited.

Mrs. Gertrude Bonnin—Zitkala-Sa, President of the National Council of American Indians, a descendant of Sitting Bull, and one of the most cultivated women of her race, made the following statement to me:

> During my visit this summer to various reservations, I saw, at one place, Indians bathing the corpse of a man. They cried aloud so hopelessly that I wept with them. The body of the dead did not have a bit of flesh on it. It was just skin and bones. He had starved to death. He had had no food and no proper medical care. I saw hungry Indians everywhere I went.
>
> Then, too, there is increasing immorality and drunkenness, due to slack supervision, on all reservations.

Now—one last word about the children! The writer is convinced that if the white children of this country, whose beloved outdoor clubs are based on Indian woodcraft and Indian folklore, could know of the treatment the little Indian child is receiving, there would be a modern Children's Crusade. Perhaps, when the facts are told, there will be a crusade of American white mothers in behalf of the Indian child, our ward.

Think what is required, in an average American family, to feed a white child one day. Then listen to this, taken from page 327 of the Institute report, regarding the Indian boarding schools:

"The average allowance for food per capita is approximately eleven cents a day. . . . At Rice School (San Carlos Apache Reservation, Arizona) . . . the average amount spent for food was nine cents a day. The dietary was examined . . . and it was obvious that the children were not receiving an adequate amount of food of the very limited variety supplied. Malnutrition was evident. They were indolent, and when they had the chance to play, they merely sat about on the ground, showing no exuberance of healthy youth."

Exuberance? In an Indian boarding school?

Labor Is Enforced in School

I visited a number of these prison-like schools. Everywhere, I found extensive provisions for child-labor. Provisions for play were almost lacking. In two schools I was shown "recreation rooms." Both were gloomy, musty-smelling basement rooms. And this on the desert where sunlight and space are cheap! But the rooms showed no signs of use. Indian boarding-school children evidently have neither the time nor the vitality for play.

"The labor of children as carried on in Indian boarding schools," the Report tells us farther on, "would, it is believed, constitute a violation of child-labor laws in most states."

And the Report goes on to tell us:

> The laundry is an important feature of every government school. It is one of the chief sources of labor for the pupils. . . . The space allotted to the laundry is often small. At one large school

> this fact is capitalized. The Superintendent reported that he can get much more work out of the children if he keeps large piles of laundry before them. An inspection of the plant verified his statement. A number of small children were literally hidden behind great piles of wet laundry in a greatly overcrowded room, filled with steam . . .

Finally: "The prevalence of tuberculosis in boarding schools is alarming," the Report informs us on page 206.

There is not room here to tell of half the horrors in these schools where our little Indian wards spend their lives from six to eighteen, virtually as prisoners, though they have committed no offense except that of being Indians instead of whites.

One investigator last year found 30 children sleeping two in a bed, in single beds, at one school. And at a school in Arizona the writer saw one dormitory which contained 18 beds and only two small outside windows. Bathing and sanitary facilities are usually of the very worst, and epidemics sweep the schools.

Dr. B. O. Thrasher, formerly the doctor at the Fort Apache Indian School, describes as follows the condition of the little Indian children being "civilized" hundreds of miles from their mothers' arms:

> Many of these small boys came to the clinics with their hair filled with nits. Some with crusted sores on their heads from lice. Many with clothing many sizes too large for them. Clothing of some stiff with dirt. Stockings tied up with pieces of string. Some were found using segments of automobile tubes as garters. These little boys were being criminally neglected . . . in their dormitory.

In the Towoac School, in Colorado, the cook discovered that the dried fruit was full of worms. The attention of the school principal was called to the situation; but he told her that when the water boiled it would sterilize the worms, and it would not hurt the children to eat them. She was made to serve this food, and also to cook and serve maggoty meat.

More light has been shed on this Towoac School by the former matron, who loved the children and was loved by them. The flour—she declares—which was stored in the basement, was infested with mice, rats, and weevils. In addition, when the floors above were scrubbed, the dirty water would drip down on the flour. Finally she ordered all the flour removed. The school principal, hearing of this, declared that the flour was all right, in proof of which he thrust his hand into a sack. When he withdrew his hand, it contained a number of small mice as well as flour. Yet he ordered a portion of the flour used for the children. The remainder was put in storage and given to the poor and old Indians.

The children, this former matron declares, were lice-infested and pitifully underclad. Only cheap canvas shoes were provided, gingham dresses, and no petticoats, and only the thinnest of underwear. All were underfed. The food actually "smelled." There was much sickness, and the children received no care. She sent one very sick little girl to the hospital, but the doctor twice returned her, refusing to have her there.

The boarding schools! Everywhere the writer went among the Indians, she heard the pitiful plea:

"We don't want boarding schools, away off; our children come home sick: we want day schools here."

And the bitter complaint from the children: "We work too hard. They don't give us enough to eat."

On the Colorado plain, near Ignacio, the Utes—in gorgeous bead and feather regalia, for it happened to be the last day of a four day Sun Dance—gathered around the writer and told their troubles. The elders complained of injustice, of lack of medical care, of cruel neglect of aged Indians. The shy young people, home on vacation, told of harsh punishments in the distant boarding schools.

School Discipline Is Cruel

And as the writer continued to move about among Indians and whites, in half a dozen states, she heard more and more of the cruel discipline at the Indian boarding schools.

"I have seen Indian boys chained to their beds at night for punishment," Construction Engineer Russell of Flagstaff, Arizona, has declared. "I have seen them thrown into cellars under the building which the superintendent called a jail. I have seen their shoes taken from them and they forced to walk through the snow to the barn to help milk. I have seen them whipped with a hemp rope, also a water hose, and forced to do servants' work for employees and superintendent without compensation, under the guise of industrial education."

W. Carson Ryan, Jr., Professor of Education, Swarthmore College—one of the Institute investigators—found these conditions, on his trip to Wahpeton, North Dakota:

"School supplies right down to rock bottom—not sure whether they can hold out, and superintendent may have to keep youngsters alive out of his own pocket. Rations consist of bread and mush. This and other schools in the Dakotas and Minnesota make one wonder if Dakota is not the Siberia of the Indian Service.

"The superintendent showed me a dungeon in the basement previously used for girls—up to his coming two years ago. 'I never locked up any Indian child yet, and I don't intend to begin,' he said. The dungeon is 18 by 8, absolutely dark. Girls told the superintendent of two or three of them sleeping there on mattresses and rats crawling over them at night. Their food was bread and water. Brick walls showed where the girls had worked holes through and escaped."

Finally, Mrs. Bonnin made to the writer the following statement in regard to the Oglala School in South Dakota:

> Conquering Bear's two boys were in Ogala boarding school, and they ran away to Corn Creek, about forty miles away. Policeman Jumping Eagle and the disciplinarian went after them and brought them back and gave them a severe beating. They were about 12 and 14 years at the time. Their heads were shaved, though it was winter. One of the boys had a ball and chain locked onto his leg and was locked to the bed at night. My informant saw this herself. The boys were in the jail above

> her room. They were in a dirty, filthy place, with a bucket to be used as toilet.
>
> She said it hurt her so to see all these things, such as this little boy carrying the ball when marching to meals, that she could not eat. The boy even went to school with the ball and chain on, and it bothered the other children. Many requests were made to the principal to have the disciplinarian take the chain off, but days went by before this was actually done.

And Mrs. Bonnin related this incident:

> A district school teacher, still in the Indian Service, hitched twelve little boys together and plowed an acre of ground. When a boy lagged behind, because of exhaustion, he was prodded with a sharp stick. The father of one of the boys told me this during my visit last summer.

WHO IS RESPONSIBLE?

What of the Indian Bureau—the Indians' "guardian"—while these things are taking place? Are these frightful conditions never reported to the Indian Commissioner and Assistant Commissioner?

I am informed they are. That every now and then some Bureau employee, placing loyalty to humanity above loyalty to superintendent or other petty superior, reports conditions directly to Indian Commissioner Burke.

For example: Dr. S. S. Warren, at the Leupp Boarding School on the Navajo Reservation, made such an appeal, in desperation, during an epidemic, in 1925, to save the lives of little Navajo children. First, however, he notified the local Superintendent of the epidemic, as follows:

"We have approximately 100 cases of measles; and seven cases of pneumonia. Having just gone through an epidemic of influenza, our nursing force of teachers and two nurses are worn out and unfit for duty."

For a time he made these appeals daily to the reservation Superintendent, urging the desperate need of more nurses and medical assistance. He did not get either. Finally, as a last measure with children dying all about him needlessly, he wired directly to Indian Commissioner Burke, on April 29th, in these words:

> We have had an epidemic of measles and influenza since March 17th. Four deaths and typhus suspect in hospital now. Dormitories and hospitals foul with contagion. No sanitary measures have been taken in conformity with public health and state laws to clean up. Children being bedded in and occupying quarters used for the sick to the future detriment of health.

Doctor Warren obtained no aid. Six months later the following rebuke was sent him:

> In the Indian Service all matters of importance should be carried out through the superintendent as administrative officer. If you will inform the superintendent in writing as to what you believe should be done . . . your responsibility ceases. All such matters are checked up on sooner or later and should the superintendent fail in his duty, he must take the consequences.

Checked up on sooner or later? Ah, no doubt.

But the dying little Navajos had not been able to wait. They had gone on the long trail to hunting grounds which, we hope, were happier than those.

Edwin M. Stanton, Secretary of War in Lincoln's cabinet, said, in 1864, when Bishop Whipple of Minnesota was in Washington on behalf of the Sioux Indians:

> What does Bishop Whipple want. If he has come here to tell us of the corruption of our Indian system, and the dishonesty of Indian

agents, tell him that we know it. *But the Government never reforms an evil until the people demand it. Tell him that when he reaches the heart of the American people, the Indians will be saved.*

DREW PEARSON

Drew Pearson (1897–1969) probably survived more libel suits, and made more enemies in high places, than any Washington reporter in history. General Douglas MacArthur, Congressman Adam Clayton Powell, Senator Joe McCarthy, and a host of others, spanning the administrations of Herbert Hoover through LBJ, all found their ethical lapses dragged into the spotlight in Pearson's column.

Drew Pearson came to Washington as a diplomatic correspondent for the Baltimore Sun. *But what distinguished his reporting from his very first book,* Washington Merry-Go-Round *(co-written with Robert Allen), was a steadfast refusal to take for granted the culture of political and financial back-scratching among elected officials, lobbyists, and business leaders. Pearson's technique and his subject were one in the same: he simply declared as his beat the gifts, business dealings, and favors that other Washington reporters cynically called business as usual.*

Pearson was raised a Quaker, and retained a deep affinity for civil liberties and skepticism of the military. Often working with collaborators and ghostwriters, Pearson was never a literary journalist, but his writing always had precision and bite. His books—on Congress, the Supreme Court, and foreign policy—are snapshots of American power brokers mid-century, illuminated by the unforgiving glare of his reportorial flash.

THE MAN WHO STAYED TOO LONG

From *Washington Merry-Go-Round,* 1931

Andrew William Mellon will go down in history as the man who did not know when to quit.

For eight years be dominated the national capital. For eight years his word was law with every banker throughout the land. For eight years Presidents served under him. So powerful was his influence, so great his prestige that he told them what to do and his judgment was final.

In Congress his name was spoken in hushed tones. By the press he was referred to only with profound obeisance. When he rewrote the taxation system of the United States, the entire nation echoed his praise. When he relieved the wealthy of their taxes, when he took billions out of the Treasury in the form of tax refunds and returned them to already over-prosperous corporations, only a handful of Senators raised their voices against him.

His awesome presence squelched a damning senatorial investigation whose report later disclosed that he and his corporations had been the biggest gainers through tax refunds. When another Senate Committee, examining the Continental Corporation phase of the Teapot Dome oil lease scandal, asked him to explain a secret $25,000 contribution to the Harding campaign deficit, even so stern a prosecutor as Senator Thomas J. Walsh of Montana treated him with gentleness and deference.

Small, emaciated, shy, giving the impression of being timid, but always surrounded by an army of assistants and servitors, Andrew Mellon became a figure of might and power. To his simply furnished office in the barred and guarded Treasury Building, politicians, social leaders, diplomats and the barons of big business came to bow before him.

For eight years he was reverenced in high places. For eight years his wisdom was hailed as sublime. For eight years his views were acclaimed as enduring philosophy, his achievements labeled historic. Far and wide he was heralded as Great.

He was King Andrew, the Mighty, ruler of the taxes, the surpluses, the finances, the prosperity of the United States. He was the monarch who sat on an intangible throne of prestige more powerful than that in the White House. He wielded a golden scepter of colossal wealth. His sway was all-powerful.

But to-day, like so many monarchs, who, having failed to gauge the pulse of popular rebellion against their rule, King Andrew is no more.

Gone are his magic surpluses. Gone are his promises of tax reduction. Gone are the hallowed days of prosperity. Gone is the time when the White House accepted his word as law.

Fame, throne, specter, halo, all have been torn from him.

They disappeared the day Herbert Hoover persuaded him to remain in office. For Herbert Hoover he had neither regard nor affection. But he had listened to the adulation of the multitude. He had heard his name on the lips of the people. He liked it. And he stayed on.

So now he speaks when it suits the White House, and he says what the White House wants him to say. If the White House wants an announcement that there will be no deficit, Mr. Mellon announces that there will be no deficit. If the White House says there is to be continued tax reduction, Mr. Mellon reverses his original statement and says there is to be continued tax reduction.

And behind Mr. Mellon's back the world titters.

Calvin Coolidge, a lesser but wiser man, refused to tempt fate. But King Andrew could not tear himself away. He stayed to maintain the prestige of another fictitious character, and they both went down together.

Had King Andrew, in the fullness of his glory, retired on March 4, 1929, he would be doubly revered to-day. In retrospect, his era of golden surpluses, contrasted with the present dismal days of Treasury deficits, would have made him appear more than ever the legendary hero he had been hailed.

Press and magnate would have sighed for him and recalled his financial wizardry. His successor, even had he been the mighty Alexander Hamilton himself, would have received the blame. King Andrew's scepter would have been put aside but his glory would have gone marching on.

Every month since March 4, 1929, King Andrew has sunk in public esteem. His calculations and estimates have been mocked and derided.

His tax policies have been denounced and condemned. The Senate has flaunted him and the House of Representatives has booed his name.

In the closing session of the Seventy-first Congress as the House prepared to enact the increased soldier bonus over the protests of the White House and Treasury, Representative Treadway of Massachusetts arose on behalf of Mr. Mellon to make a last appeal against the bill.

"The greatest Secretary of the Treasury since Alexander Hamilton," Congressman Treadway boomed, confident that this, at least, would get across.

The House leaned back and roared in derision.

King Andrew had stayed too long.

Andrew W. Mellon became the third or fourth richest man in the United States chiefly through a series of fortuitous circumstances over which he had little control. Of course, Mr. Mellon did nothing to stem the tide of fate which carried him on to wealth and power, and, in fact, materially aided it. But Mellon was born rich, and would have been a millionaire to-day had he done nothing more energetic than spend his life on the front porch of a nursing home.

His father migrated to the United States from County Tyrone North Ireland, early in the last century, landed at Baltimore, went overland to Pittsburgh and having the usual Irish aptitude for politics, became Judge of the Court of Common Pleas of Allegheny County. The position was one conducive to both prestige and wealth, and eventually Thomas Mellon retired to establish the private banking firm of T. Mellon and Sons, later to be known as the Mellon National Bank.

Andrew Mellon is fond of telling the story of how as a boy he sat under the Judge's bench, where no one but his father could see him, and listened to cases being tried in Court. On one of these occasions news came that Lee had surrendered at Appomattox. Such an uproar followed that Thomas Mellon adjourned court, and the crowd having piled into the streets, the Judge and his son left the court room together, Thomas Mellon stopping on the way to wind the clock.

From his father Andrew Mellon inherited a certain business shrewdness, an aptitude for juggling figures, and a large portion of his private fortune, plus a precise and orderly process of thought such as that which prompted him to wind clocks in moments of great stress.

Long before his father's death, however, Andrew Mellon had come to play an important part in the latter's bank. Early in their teens, young Mellon and his brothers—Richard and James—had been taken into the bank and given the responsibility of passing upon loans.

Like any common parasite, the Mellon fortune was built on the back of Pittsburgh industry—steel, coal, glass and power companies. The bank took slight risks and got a three-fifths interest in most of the business. The *entrepreneur* got two-fifths. As he prospered, the Mellons prospered.

Thus the Mellons loaned to one Henry C. Frick, then a clerk in the Overholt Distillery, the sum of $20,000. Frick had the vision of building ovens at Connellsville, Pennsylvania, to turn coal into coke. The Mellon bank took a mortgage on the plant and an interest in the business. It loaned Frick an additional $40,000 and then another $50,000. And as Mr. Frick, later head of the Carnegie Steel Corporation, increased the profits, so also increased the profits of the Mellon family.

The work of the young Mellon brothers in passing on loans took them out into the industrial field. It was their job to spend several weeks studying the factory which applied for the loan, making a survey of its production, its markets and its balance sheets. Young Andrew showed unusual ability at this, and at the age of 25 he was practically in charge of his father's bank. Five years later, Thomas Mellon retired, leaving Andrew in control of his entire estate.

Mellon's banking career was not one of great genius. It was conservative and sound, but without initiative. The two exceptions to this were when he broke Standard Oil in Pennsylvania by building a rival pipe line from the western oil region to the Delaware River, and when he foresaw the great use to which aluminum was going to be put and cornered the bauxite deposits of the United States.

Aside from this, however, Mellon millions have come from the process of advancing the money and reaping the profits from the initiative of others; and through this, Mellon influence has reached its tentacles into steel, linseed oil, railways, water power, construction, plate glass, traction, locomotives, insurance, shipping, engines, bridges, motor trucks, steel cars and gun carriages.

As a banker, Andrew Mellon was relatively unknown outside of Pittsburgh. He lived a secluded, sheltered life, surrounded by friends and relatives. Up until the time he came to Washington, not only had he never been interviewed by the press, but he quailed before the thought of such sordid contact with the every-day world. Despite this he knew something about politics, in fact had built up the powerful Mellon machine which occasionally defeated the Vare organization for the control of Pennsylvania patronage.

How this rather shrinking individual happened to land in the very middle of the Washington political maelstrom is something which never has been satisfactorily explained. It appears, however, that Mellon, timid as he was, modest as he pretended to be when it came to the political limelight, had begun to get a little tired of the monotonous routine of walking back and forth between his home, his club and his bank, had begun to be bored with donating money to hospitals, with buying rare portraits, and with seeing everything he touched turn to gold. He yearned for new worlds to conquer. So it was not mere accident that found him at the top of the list of heavy contributors to the $7,000,000 Republican campaign fund raised by men who expected to realize far more than six percent on their investment by putting Warren G. Harding in the White House.

Andrew Mellon was one of the first to cash in on his investment. As Secretary of the Treasury he later paid himself a tax refund of $400,000, the largest awarded to any single individual.

The first time Andrew Mellon came to Washington, then a boy of 16, the Washington Monument was not yet completed. It had been built up to the point where the marble now ends, and young Andrew had the distinction of climbing up the scaffolding of the monument that far.

Mellon did not visit the White House on his first trip to Washington.

In fact, he did not visit the White House at all until the day he entered it as a member in the ill-fated Cabinet of President Harding. Since then he has been going in and out of the White House, always by the rear entrance, like the swinging to and fro of a saloon door.

With these frequent goings and comings he became the mystery man of the Coolidge Administration, about whom was built up a myth—the myth that placed in his hand the scepter of power, and that made him King Andrew, the Mighty, the monarch who stayed too long.

While still a member of the Coolidge Cabinet there was no man in public life who so captured the public's imagination. Much of the basis for this Mellon myth rested upon his personality. A thin, half-frightened individual, Mr. Mellon looks so esthetic, so almost spiritual, that the natural impulse of the press and even of congressional investigating committees was to protect him.

When he first came to Washington, he made so pathetic an appearance that his under-secretary always stood at his side at press conferences and bore the brunt of the questioning from congressional committees.

Now, Mr. Mellon has become much more assured and confident. He has an air of composure and detachment—the worn, fragile face of a poet and dreamer. If one did not know that he was among the half-dozen richest men in the world, the expression of his face almost could be compared with the aloofness and spiritual composure on that of Mahatma Gandhi.

Mellon's fingers are long and tapering like those of an artist, and in them he nervously twists a cigar, the size of a cigarette. The fingers do not belie Mr. Mellon's character, for his art collection, although not large, is exceptionally rare, and reveals the soul of an artist.

Nor do Mr. Mellon's fine features belie his character. Through it runs the quality of instinctive courtesy combined with loyalty, decision and generosity, all of which endear him to his friends and contribute materially to the Mellon myth.

The myth, however, extends far beyond the small circle of friends who have the privilege of personally knowing some of Mr. Mellon's admirable qualities. In fact the myth, as far as the general public is concerned, rests solely upon three factors:

First, Mr. Mellon has established himself as the great sorcerer who waved his wand and brought taxes tumbling from their war-time peak to almost nothing.

Second, Mr. Mellon is the wonder-worker who entered the Treasury, then, "running amuck under wasteful and ignorant Democrats," balanced the budget, and out of his magic hat began pulling surpluses.

Finally, Mr. Mellon is the stern realist who made the dilatory war debtors of Europe reach down in their jeans and cough up the billions they had been owing Uncle Sam.

The net total of all these illusions in the public mind created the super-illusion that Andrew William Mellon was the crafty old wonder-worker to whom the public was really indebted for eight years of so-called Coolidge prosperity.

To what extent Mr. Mellon actually was responsible for turning Treasury deficits into surpluses, he is his own best witness. The credit given him for this has been the result of the clever publicity promoters of the Republican National Committee, for he himself repeatedly has said that he was merely carrying out the sound policies worked out for the reduction of public expenditure after the war by his Democratic predecessors, Carter Glass and David F. Houston.

Mr. Mellon was lucky enough to take over the Treasury when it was the easiest and most popular job any man had held in a generation. All he had to do was sit still and watch the sinking fund reduce the public debt. With this reduction he could bring about a simultaneous reduction in taxes—and get all the credit for it.

War-time expenditures would have been reduced no matter who was Secretary of the Treasury. When a nation is paying out billions of dollars to feed an army of 5,000,000 men, to buy tons of ammunition and to build fleets of ships, and when that expenditure suddenly becomes unnecessary, it requires no particular genius to bring about Treasury surpluses and tax reduction.

One of the first things Mr. Mellon did to endear him in the hearts of his banking colleagues was to refund the public debt. A total of $7,000,000,000 was due to be repaid or refunded within two years, and for every percent of reduction in interest rates, American taxpayers would save $70,000,000 annually. Interest rates had dropped after the War, and Mr. Mellon, taking advantage of this drop, was able to save them this much and more.

He was hailed as a wonder-worker.

Compared with the refunding operations of the Treasury after the Civil War, however, his was no miracle at all. At that time Benjamin H. Bristow, faced with comparatively as heavy a debt, refunded it with a reduction just as great as that achieved by Mellon, despite the fact that he was in the middle of the post–Civil War financial panic with interest rates much higher than those after the World War.

Mr. Mellon and his miracle deserved the sober praise extended by the Journal of Commerce—"a good Secretary of the Treasury, faithful, businesslike and efficient"—and that was about all.

The Mellon settlement of the Allied War debts was easy. Europe not only could not repay the United States what she owed for carrying on the war to end war but she needed to borrow more money with which to build up her shattered industries, construct new fleets, and maintain armies even larger than those which were ready to be mobilized when the bomb struck the Archduke Franz Ferdinand at Sarajevo in 1914.

The State Department, however, ruled that this new money could not be borrowed until the old debts had been settled. One by one, therefore, and very reluctantly, the Allies sent their delegations to Washington to receive the terms Mr. Mellon was willing to give them. On their way home, they stopped in New York and borrowed from Wall Street more than enough to pay Mr. Mellon—as Calvin Coolidge so eloquently testified in his 1928 Armistice Day speech. Mr. Mellon's debt-funding operation, therefore, merely consisted of shifting the burden of the war debts from the Federal Treasury to the American buyer of European bonds.

Mr. Mellon's idea of tax reduction was first conceived by a New York bank and worked out by that very capable individual, Parker Gilbert. The great contribution which the Secretary of the Treasury gave to the plan was publicity. On every possible and conceivable occasion he hammered home the idea that tax reduction would release funds for investment and bring about prosperity. The idea got across big. Every small business concern, every bank, every newspaper in the country rallied behind it.

Only the elder La Follette and the Democrats stood out against him. Still remembering the war days when the country had been taught to believe that wealth should bear a greater sacrifice than the poor, they blocked the Mellon move to reduce the tax on large incomes from forty to only twenty-five percent. But later, when La Follette, the chief obstructionist, died, the Democrats yielded to popular pressure and permitted a reduction down even to twenty percent.

By this cut, Mr. Mellon, chief sponsor of the reduction, lopped about $1,500,000 off his own income tax.

All this, of course, was lost in the general paean of praise and prosperity which followed Mr. Mellon's so-called master stroke. The oil scandals were forgotten. The machinations of the Ohio Gang, the trivialities of Calvin Coolidge, the petty politics of Warren Harding—all were obscured in the rejoicing over tax reduction. That tax reduction was inevitable, was just as certain as the fact that the War had ended. And in the face of the tax-reduction "wizardry" of Andrew W. Mellon, no scandal conceivable by the hand of man could have prevented the reelection of Calvin Coolidge in 1924.

Mr. Mellon is a man of such great personal magnetism, such apparent sincerity that it is difficult to reconcile these with two qualities of character which, the record of his life shows must exist. One is vindictiveness, which Mr. Mellon has given vent to so bitterly, both in the treatment of his wife and in his case against Senator Couzens. The other is carelessness in accepting large favors, both for himself and his firms, from the Federal Government.

His record in the latter respect is astonishing and with men of less standing would be called dishonesty.

Mr. Mellon, of course, is a good enough executive not to fret himself about every tax refund made by his Department, and therefore it is only fair to absolve him from any knowledge regarding the action of his subordinates in illegally refunding to the Mellon banks the sum of $91,472, supposedly for surplus taxes which the Democrats had collected in 1917. However, it does seem that after this refund became a public incident, Mr. Mellon might at least have protected his old friend and senatorial office boy, David Aiken Reed.

As it turned out, Senator Reed, whose law firm protects Mr. Mellon in Pittsburgh, and who considers it his duty to extend that protection also to Washington, immediately rushed to Mr. Mellon's support on the floor of the United States Senate. He said that the sum of $91,472 could not be returned to the Treasury since the case was now definitely closed; following which the Treasury inconsiderately acknowledged Mr. Mellon's critics to be right and David Aiken Reed to be wrong.

Mr. Mellon also may have been completely ignorant of the action of his subordinates in refunding taxes to various firms which the Mellon family owns, but the record is not one of which the other great Secretary of the Treasury, Alexander Hamilton, would be proud. More than one million dollars was refunded to each of forty organizations and people, among them the Gulf Oil Company, the Aluminum Company and its subsidiaries, and the Standard Steel Car Company, all three largely owned and completely controlled by Mr. Mellon.

It may also be true, but it is scarcely conceivable, that Mr. Mellon was ignorant of the favoritism shown to certain newspapers which supported the Administration. He may not have known, for instance, that whereas the excess profits tax for forty-five representative newspapers was about twenty percent, some of them who had stood by the Grand Old Party had theirs scaled down to around two percent. He may not have known also that William Randolph Hearst's Star Publishing Company, a staunch supporter of the Administration, got reductions in tax liabilities for three years totaling $1,737,007.

It seems incredible, however, that Mr. Mellon was able to maintain the same convenient ignorance regarding some of the moves Congress and Coolidge made on behalf of his own interests.

Mr. Mellon's aluminum company has a monopoly control of

aluminum production, and the Republican-written Fordney McCumber Tariff made its hold on the domestic market doubly certain by increasing the duties on aluminum 250 percent. Shortly after this, the Tariff Commission pointed out that the duty on linseed oil of about 25 cents a gallon was too high and recommended that it be decreased. Mr. Mellon owns two of the eight large linseed crushers in the United States, and President Coolidge, not ignorant of this fact, pigeon-holed the Commission's report. The tariff on linseed oil never was reduced.

Most of these items in the record of King Andrew, the Mighty, would be gathering dust in the archives of the Treasury Department had it not been for Senator Jim Couzens of Michigan. Single-handed except for the support of a handful of Progressives, Senator Couzens forced an investigation of the Mellon myth.

The Democrats, frequently more servile to wealth than their Republican confrères—because they so seldom come in contact with it—stood on the side-lines. They did not even give platonic support. Mr. Mellon was too rich, had too powerful support from wealthy newspapers and was too popular with the banking interests because of his tax reduction.

Besides, even a Democratic Senator must frequently appeal to the Bureau of Internal Revenue on behalf of some wealthy constituent in order to get his taxes reduced, and if you have been a critic of the Secretary of the Treasury, who heads the Bureau, your chances of tax reduction are slim.

"Give me control of the Internal Revenue Bureau and I will run the politics of the whole darn country," Senator Couzens once said.

And so he fought alone.

Frank Kent tells the story of how both Mellon and Senator Couzens were invited to dine at the White House through the mistake of a social secretary. For several hours Mrs. Coolidge suffered exquisite agonies. However, when Mr. Mellon, always the perfect gentleman, arrived, he saw Senator and Mrs. Couzens across the room, and took his daughter Ailsa over to meet them.

If this story is true, Mr. Mellon has the ability to draw a line of demarcation between social and political hates which he has not evidenced in many other things and for which few people have given him credit. Bankers who have opposed Mr. Mellon in business have discovered to their regret that he was a good hater.

Senator Couzens also discovered this when Mellon started a counterattack on him by reopening an old suit in which the Treasury demanded a $10,000,000 additional tax payment on the sale of Couzens' stock in the Ford Motor Company—a suit which Couzens won and which made King Andrew look ridiculous.

The most vindictive chapter of Mr. Mellon's life, however, is that dealing with his marriage.

Nora McMullen was the grand-daughter of old Peter Guinness, famous as the manufacturer of Ireland's best-advertised stout. It was not Mr. Mellon's ownership of the Overholt Distillery which brought them together, as is sometimes supposed, but a tourist party which visited the United States in 1897. The party was entertained at the Mellon home in Pittsburgh, and Miss McMullen was a member. She was vivacious, rosy-cheeked and twenty years old. Mellon was forty-five. He fell in love. He visited her again in England, wooed her ardently and after three years of persuasion, she consented.

They were married in 1900, and went back to live in Mellon's palatial Pittsburgh residence in an atmosphere of iron, steel and hard work as foreign to the green moors of England and Ireland as anything ever could be.

The cards were stacked against a happy marriage from the start. Mellon slid back into the groove into which he had fitted as a hard-working bachelor for forty-eight years. He had the same friends, the same long office hours, the same devotion to his work. To Nora McMullen Mellon all this was new and difficult. She was homesick from the first and it was only natural that she should make repeated trips to her family in Hertfordshire and in Ireland. These visits became longer and longer, until nine years after their marriage it became known that the Mellons both sought a divorce.

The story of the divorce proceedings is not one which the Greatest Secretary of the Treasury since Alexander Hamilton likes to contemplate. Perhaps realizing this, he was successful at the time in keeping the story out of all except one newspaper. However, the record in an Allegheny County Court, in the State capital at Harrisburg and in the files of the Philadelphia *North American* tells the story—and it is one which involves detectives, kidnapping, dictaphones, and a special law passed by the Pennsylvania Legislature.

The Mellons had two children, Paul and Ailsa, now Mrs. David K. E. Bruce, daughter-in-law of the former Senator Bruce of Maryland. The fight largely centered around their custody.

In 1909, according to the *North American,* Mrs. Mellon entered suit for divorce against her husband, "making serious charges." He objected to answering the charges in open court and consented to a separation agreement by which Mrs. Mellon received an allowance of $60,000 annually, and the custody of the children for seven months a year. She returned to her old home in Hertfordshire.

Mellon, however, according to the *North American,* resented this bargain and got Senator Boise Penrose, then political dictator of Pennsylvania, to pass a bill through the State Legislature, later known as the Scott Divorce Law, giving judges the right to deny women the right of trial by jury in divorce cases. The bill was passed "under cover" and was repealed after the Mellon divorce fight was settled, so that scarcely any one knows of its one-time existence even to this day.

Assured that his name and standing as Pittsburgh's foremost banker would not be besmirched by sordid scandal, Mellon sued for divorce not on the charge of desertion as previously agreed with Mrs. Mellon, but on the charge of infidelity. He charged his wife with misconduct at different times and different places with Alfred George Curphey, an Englishman she had known ever since childhood.

Meanwhile, Mellon had hired detectives to shadow his wife at her home in England. Detectives also scoured Europe for evidence. One of them was Gaston B. Means, later famous as a Department of Justice operative during the Harding scandals and as the author of "The Strange

Death of President Harding." Another detective, Barney Devlin, Pittsburgh ex–saloon keeper, "after many weeks of shadowing, went insane," according to the *North American.* That paper, reporting Mrs. Mellon's efforts to keep her children, said:

"She held on to them until hired thugs entered her home, and after beating her and a friend, took the little ones away to a home provided by the banker."

Mrs. Mellon, determined not to relinquish her children, returned to the United States. All the power of the Mellon millions, all the influence of one of the most ruthless political machines which ever dominated any state, was pitted against her. Mellon even had induced the District Attorney of Allegheny County to go to Europe to help the fight against his wife. When Curphey, charged with illicit relations with Mrs. Mellon, arrived in New York to help her fight the case, he and his friend Captain Kirkbride were arrested on Mellon's orders. Governor Dix of New York, however, refused to honor the Pennsylvania extradition papers.

What Mrs. Mellon faced was a situation wherein she had been publicly accused of infidelity, and wherein she could be forced, under the special law passed by Boise Penrose, to answer those charges in secret. The chances of clearing herself seemed hopeless. However, she demanded a trial not before a master but before a jury in order that the world might know the truth.

At first it looked as if Mrs. Mellon's nerve would force a decision in her favor. Despite the law, October, 1911, was set for a jury trial. Mellon influence overruled this, however, and the Pittsburgh courts appeared inclined to grant Mellon's plea for a secret trial.

The dispute dragged on. Several things happened which dampened Mellon's ardor and made him fear that publicity would besmirch his name, despite the precautions he had taken. One was a powerful argument made by Judge James Gay Gordon of Philadelphia who appeared before a court in Pittsburgh and challenged the constitutionality of the Scott Divorce Act. Another was an incident staged by the reporter of the *North American* who took Mrs. Mellon out to her former home in an effort to see her children. He carried a photographer along, with the idea of getting a "sob" picture of the weeping children clinging to their mother. As Mrs. Mellon got out of her car in front of the Mellon mansion, however, detectives hustled her back into it and manhandled the reporter and photographer. The children barely got a glimpse of their mother.

Mr. Mellon had been prepared for any emergencies but apparently the fight was wearing on his nerves. He finally consented to sue his wife on the grounds of desertion, each of them getting the children for six months of the year. John P. Hunter, Master in the case, filed his report in an Allegheny County Court on May 25, 1912, and the decree was granted on July 3 of the same year.

Mrs. Mellon has always received the devotion and affection of her two children. They have visited her religiously every year and, according to their friends, have made several attempts to bring about a reconciliation.

Mr. Mellon, however, seems never to have forgiven his wife. There is only one thing he likes less than being referred to as the country's third richest man, and that is any allusion to his wife or his divorce. When a Washington newspaper, reporting that Paul Mellon had purchased a large Virginian estate on which his mother would live, alluded to the possibility of a reconciliation, Mr. Mellon expressed his disapproval and disgust in no uncertain terms.

When Andrew Mellon first arrived in Washington he was disappointed and began methodically marking off the months on his calendar. He looked forward to the forty-eighth month, when he would be finished. To-day he could have marked off one hundred and twenty months had he not given up the practice after the twenty-fourth. The reason he gave it up was because he suddenly discovered he liked Washington.

Some people attribute Mr. Mellon's desire to linger on to an ambition to be Secretary of the Treasury longer than any other man. Already he has achieved that record with the possible exception of Albert Gallatin, also a Pennsylvanian, who at the end of the last century served for twelve years. During two of those, however, Gallatin was abroad on a diplomatic mission and Congress declared his cabinet office vacant, thus giving him a net service of ten years which is identical with Mellon's.

Longevity of service, however, is not Mr. Mellon's reason for lingering on. The truth is that despite the criticism and abuse that have been heaped upon his head, Mr. Mellon tremendously enjoys his job. As a private citizen he had become prodigiously bored with seeing everything he touched turn to gold. Having made more money than any but two or three other men in the world, it was no sacrifice for him to quit making more of it. In Pittsburgh be was relatively unknown. In Washington he has been all-powerful. His name was the on the lips of every one.

So he has stayed. He has even changed his age in order that he may appear to be more youthful, so that in *Who's Who* from 1918 to 1921 he has listed himself as born in 1852; from 1921 to 1929, as born in1854; while in *Who's Who* for 1930–31 he puts himself down as born in 1855. Thus in the past thirteen years he has aged by only ten!

And during this time Mr. Mellon has been a reasonably efficient Secretary of the Treasury. Considering his reputation as a rival of Alexander Hamilton, his estimates for national revenue have been amazingly wide of the mark—never within $100,000,000 of being right and $1,132,000,000 off in 1923. But he has had the rich man's usual facility for handling large sums without being staggered at their size. He has kept politics consistently out of his Department, refusing, when he first came in, to discharge competent Democrats merely because they were Democrats, and forcing Harding to fire Elmer Dover, whom the Ohio Gang had first put over on him as an Assistant Secretary of the Treasury.

He has worked hard. He has had little time for his few diversions—walking, riding, and golf. He is to be found at his office promptly at nine and he remains there until six or seven. He walks to his office in all kinds of weather and is so methodical that he has figured his total ten-year mileage between the Treasury and his apartment as equal to walking from Washington to San Francisco and halfway back again. He also has estimated that the walk takes him twenty-one minutes if he is not in a hurry or nineteen if he is. On those rare occasions when he takes a taxicab he sometimes has been known to find himself without a cent and has held the driver waiting while be went inside to borrow money from his secretary.

So Mr. Mellon, in one way or another, has come to be looked upon as a saintly and wealthy old gentleman who has dedicated the last remaining years of his life to the public's welfare—first to building up prosperity, and now to salvaging it.

And in the Mellon myth, badly punctured in places as it now is, two facts still remain completely unexposed and unappreciated. One is the fact that Mr. Mellon's tax reduction led to the orgy of speculation which in turn caused the recent crash. The other is the fact that Mr. Mellon, having been repeatedly warned of the impending crash before it fell reverberating around his ears, did nothing to prepare the public for a gradual dénouement.

To Calvin Coolidge is given credit for beguiling the people into believing that stock market values could be pyramided indefinitely and for leading them up to the brink of the crash. But Calvin Coolidge would no more have gone counter to Mr. Mellon's advice than a faithful Mohammedan would have ignored the teachings of the Prophet. He was the mere mouthpiece for Mr. Mellon's bull-market optimism.

Two years before the crash came, experts of the Federal Reserve Board, charged with keeping sound the financial structure of the country, warned that the inflated stock market could not last and urged that the public be told to ease out while the easing was good. Time after time when the Federal Reserve Board, the American Bankers Association, and various business journals announced that speculation had gone far beyond the point of safety, Mr. Mellon either himself or through his White House spokesman, Mr. Coolidge, issued statements contradicting them. He assured the public that all was well and that it could continue buying on margin with impunity and with profit.

When, because of a Federal Reserve Board warning on June 5, 1928, the stock market broke badly, Mr. Mellon, ex officio head of the Board, issued a statement that the break was without significance. When, on

January 6, 1929, the Federal Reserve Board issued another formal warning against the increased use of credit for stock market purposes, Mr. Mellon three days later "explained informally" that this was not intended to "bring about a sudden slump in stocks."

And why not?

Mr. Mellon and his family had made a net profit of $300,000,000 from the increased stock values of Gulf Oil and the Aluminum Company alone. Perhaps he believed that the stocks of these companies had sufficient earnings really to merit this increase. Perhaps he believed that the public was entitled to share in their enhanced value. Other men, however, who had reason to know something about the corporations which they headed, announced that stocks were much too high, and they made those announcements a year before the crash, which left the myth of Coolidge–Mellon prosperity nothing but a mass of smoking ruins.

Mr. Mellon's failure, however, goes far deeper than a mere failure to warn. Not only had he breathed new life into the great stock market bubble every time it showed signs of deflation, but it was he who started the bubble in the first place.

It was Mr. Mellon who advocated the reduction of income taxes in the higher brackets. It was Mr. Mellon who on every conceivable occasion preached the doctrine that this reduction would release funds which would create business prosperity.

It did. The wealthy became more wealthy. They bought more yachts, more country estates, built more golf clubs. But there is a limit even to that which a wealthy man can spend. He can use only one yacht, one country house and not more than three or four golf courses. It was impossible, for instance, for Mr. Mellon to spend on himself alone all of the $1,500,000 he received in reduced taxes; so like every one else, he put it in the stock market.

Meanwhile those not blessed with as much wealth or with as much proportionate tax reduction were expected to buy the products which industry, spurred on by the stock market, was turning out in greater and greater volume. And they did—up to a point.

Encouraged by national advertising to the tune of a billion dollars a year, they bought all that an over-taxed system of installment buying would permit—until their buying power was exhausted.

But since Mr. Mellon's new plan of tax reduction had served to divert money from the pockets of the poor to the pockets of the rich, and thence to the stock market, the saturation point—even under the installment plan—very soon was reached. After which . . . the deluge!

Facts percolate to the public mind almost as slowly as mountains rise or oceans fall—but nevertheless they do percolate.

The days when Mellon, the Mighty, was viewed as "a sacred personality of whom it is sacrilege to speak save with the most reverent admiration" are now gone.

Gone also are the days when it was considered a "national calamity" if Andrew W. Mellon should leave the Cabinet.

For King Andrew, the Great, ruler of the taxes, the surpluses, the finances, the prosperity of the United States, is now looked upon as the man who stayed too long.

Carey McWilliams

It was Earl Warren, newly elected governor of California, who in 1943 gave Carey McWilliams (1905–1980) a full-time career in journalism—by firing him from a top job in the state immigration and housing bureaucracy. McWilliams's offense had been to write a book denouncing the wartime internment of Japanese-Americans.

Attorney, activist, scholar of American culture, McWilliams in the 1930s had grown increasingly preoccupied with racism, particularly against Mexicans and Japanese immigrants in California, where he had lived all his life. In Factories in the Field *(1939) he enriches an investigative history of the rise of industrial agriculture with the tools of sociology and ethnography. In 1945 he joined* The Nation *as West Coast correspondent, eventually serving as editorial director and finally editor from 1955–1975, spanning cold war witch-hunts, the civil rights movement, and Vietnam.*

THE RISE OF FARM FASCISM

From *Factories in the Field*, 1939

Following the great wave of strikes which swept California in 1933, the farmers of the State began to form new organizations with which to combat the instinctive struggle of the State's 250,000 agricultural workers to achieve unionization. Farmers have never lacked organization in California; in fact, they have long set the pace for organizational activities among American farmers. They were pioneers in the field of co-operative marketing. Today every crop is organized through a series of co-operative organizations, many of which are institutions of great power and wealth. For a great many years these organized farm groups have held the balance of political power in the State through their control of the State Senate. Holding a veto power on all State legislation, they have dictated to governors and defied the will of the people of the entire State. In addition to co-operative marketing organizations, the canning and packing houses have long been organized into powerful trade associations and, in 1926, the Western Growers Protective Association was formed, for the purpose of consolidating various smaller organizations of shippers and growers in the State. Shortly after the 1933 trouble, in February, 1934, American Institutions, Inc., was organized in California by Mr. Guernsey Frazer, a prominent American Legion official, for the purpose of selling the large shipper-growers a high-pressure pro-Fascism legislative program. This attempt to impose Fascism from the outside, so to speak, was not successful, but by 1934, the large growers themselves recognized the necessity of organizing for the primary purpose of fighting labor organization. The organization which they effected, Associated Farmers of California, Inc., which today has membership in California of 40,000, has played an important role in the social history of the West. Inasmuch as it is the first organization of its type to appear in the United States, and as it has many points of similarity with organizations of a like character in Nazi Germany,[1] it warrants careful scrutiny.

1. "FROM APATHY TO ACTION"

In 1933 the California Farm Bureau Federation and the State Chamber of Commerce appointed a joint committee to study farm-labor conditions in the State. At the conclusion of this survey the farmers of Imperial Valley—"the Cradle of Vigilantism"—formed a voluntary association known as Associated Farmers, "pledged to help one another in case of emergency. They agreed to co-operate to harvest crops in case of strikes and to offer their services to the local sheriff immediately as special deputies in the event of disorders arising out of picketing and sabotage." As soon as this group was organized, the State Farm Bureau and the State Chamber of Commerce each designated a representative to go from county to county "explaining the Associated Farmers idea to local Farm Bureaus, businessmen, and peace officers." Within one year, twenty-six counties had formed associated farmer groups, and, on May 7, 1934, a convention was held in Fresno for the purpose of creating a Statewide organization. I have a stenographic report of this organization meeting. It was presided over by S. Parker Frisselle (Mr.

1 See "The Fascist Threat to Democracy," by Robert A. Brady, *Science and Society*, Vol. II, No. 2.

Frisselle was the first president and served for two years; his successor, and the present president, is Colonel Walter E. Garrison), who stated that the finances for the organization would unquestionably have to come from the banks and utility companies. The initial funds were, in fact, raised by Mr. Earl Fisher, of the Pacific Gas & Electric Company, and Mr. Leonard Wood, of the California Packing Company. At this meeting, it was decided that farmers should "front" the organization, although the utility companies and banks would exercise ultimate control.

Today the Associated Farmers have their headquarters in San Francisco and branch offices in practically every county of the State.[2] Each farmer is supposed to pay one dollar a year, as membership dues, and an additional dollar for each thousand dollars a year spent in wages. In some counties, dues are levied on the basis of so many cents per ton of fruit and vegetables harvested. Every member pledges himself, "in case of trouble," to report at the local sheriff's office. "Under agreement with the local sheriffs, no volunteer farmer will be asked to carry a gun or throw a gas bomb, even if he is deputized. He is armed with a pick handle about twenty inches long. A good many of the Associated Farmers would prefer fire-arms. But they have been overruled by cooler heads who say that in the heat of defending their homes by invading strike pickets, the embittered farmers might use their guns too effectively and turn public opinion against the organization." The "idea" back of these mobilizations, according to Mr. Taylor, "is to muster a show of force when required." How effectively some of the mobilizations have been organized may be indicated by the fact that in the Salinas strike, 1,500 men were mobilized for deputy duty in less than a day; in the Stockton strike, 2,200 deputies were mobilized in a few hours and in Imperial Valley 1,200 deputies were recently mobilized on a few minutes' notice. When one realizes that approximately 50 per cent of the farm lands in Central and Northern California are controlled by

2 See "The Right to Harvest," by Frank J. Taylor, *The Country Gentleman,* October, 1937.

one institution—the Bank of America—the irony of these "embittered" farmers defending their "homes" against strikers becomes apparent.

An efficient espionage system is maintained by the Associated Farmers. In 1935, I inspected the "confidential" files of the organization in San Francisco. At that time, they had a card-index file on "dangerous radicals" containing approximately one thousand names, alphabetically arranged, with front- and side-view photographs of each individual including notations of arrests, strike activities, affiliations and so forth. Each reference contained a number which referred to a corresponding identification record in the archives of the State Bureau of Criminal Identification. Sets of this file have been distributed to over a hundred peace officers in the State and lists have been sent to members of the association. Local offices or branches of the Associated Farmers maintain elaborate records of a similar nature, including a "check-up" system whereby workers with a reputation for independence may be readily identified and rousted out of the locality. The State Bureau of Criminal Identification, the State Highway Patrol, and local law enforcement agencies work in the closest co-operation with agents of the association; in a sense, the association may be said to direct the activities of these public agencies. The State Bureau of Criminal Identification had its private investigators sleuthing for the Tagus Ranch in the San Joaquin Valley and it employed, at one time or another, the various stool pigeons upon whose testimony the Sacramento criminal-syndicalism prosecution was based.

In addition to its espionage activities, the Associated Farmers maintain a carefully organized propaganda department. Regular bulletins, heavily larded with "anti-Communist" information, are sent to the members; special articles are reprinted and distributed throughout the State; and a steady flow of statements and releases are supplied to the press. In recent years, the association has begun to dabble in a more ambitious type of propaganda. One of its spokesmen, Mr. John Phillips, a State Senator, recently visited Europe. Upon his return, Mr. Phillips published a series of articles in the *California Cultivator* (February 1 and 15, 1936) on his travels. One article was devoted to Mr. Philips' impressions of the Nazis (he was in Nuremberg when the party was in session). Mr. Phillips particularly noticed the new type of German citizenship—the *Reichsburger*—under which "you simply say that anybody who agrees with you is a citizen of the first class, and anybody who does not agree with you is a non-voting citizen." His admiration for Hitler is boundless: "I would like to tell you how the personality of Hitler impressed me and how I feel that he has a greater personal appeal, a greater personal influence on his people than many of the nations realize." "Hitler," he said in a speech on January 18, 1938, "has done more for democracy than any man before him." Some years ago, Frances Perkins, Secretary of Labor, issued a statement repudiating a circular that the Associated Farmers had distributed in which they had attempted to make out, by reference to a faked marriage license, that she was a Jewess. Throughout California in 1936 and 1937, the Associated Farmers sponsored and organized meetings for the Reverend Martin Luther Thomas, of Los Angeles, who heads a "Christian American Crusade," and who is a notorious anti-Semite and Red-baiter. As a result of Mr. Thomas's harangues, the authorities in Riverside County employed a special detective, at a salary of $1,800 a year, to spy on the "subversive activities" of school children in the Riverside public schools. Mr. Phillips, who is frequently teamed with the Rev. Mr. Thomas at anti-Communist meetings sponsored by the Associated Farmers, was, for a time, holding a county office in Riverside County, designated as "labor coordinator." More recently the Associated Farmers have sponsored Samuel J. Hume, of the California Crusaders, who has spoken throughout the State inveighing against labor organization.

Shortly after its formation, the Associated Farmers launched a campaign, in the rural counties, for the enactment of the anti-picketing and so-called "emergency-disaster" ordinances. Anti-picketing ordinances have, as a consequence, been enacted in practically every rural county. The alleged justification for the "emergency-disaster" ordinances, which provide for a mobilization of all the forces of the community in case of a "major disaster," was the earthquake which occurred in Southern California in March, 1933. Today practically every county in the State, and most of the cities and towns, have such ordinances in effect. There is nothing in the wording of most of these ordinances to prevent their use in case of a "strike," which, in the eyes of the farmers during harvest, is certainly a "major disaster." The ordinances provide, in elaborate detail, for the formation of a kind of "crisis," or extra-legal governmental machinery, which is to come into existence, with broad powers, upon the declaration by the appropriate executive officer in the community that a state of emergency exists. The purpose back of the campaign for the enactment of these ordinances has been clearly indicated. For example, on December 18, 1936, the county counsel in Los Angeles was instructed to draft legislation which "would permit counties to spend funds for erecting concentration camps for use during major disasters." Thus the governmental apparatus for a kind of constitutional Fascism actually exists in California today.

It would be suggested, of course, that I am exaggerating the importance of these ordinances and misstating the purpose for which they were enacted. But other evidence exists which points to the real intention back of these measures. Concentration camps are to be found in California today. I described, in some detail, such a camp in an article that appeared in *The Nation* (July 24, 1935). It is located a few miles outside of Salinas, California. Here a stockade has been constructed which is admittedly intended for use as a concentration camp. When local workers inquired of the shipper-growers why such a curious construction had been established, they were told that it was built "to hold strikers, but of course we won't put white men in it, just Filipinos." A similar stockade at one time existed at the farm factory of the Balfour-Guthrie Company (a large British-owned concern) at Brentwood, California. During a strike at this farm in 1935, "a substantial fence surmounted by plenty of barbed wire" was built about the workers' camp, with "the entrance guarded night and day." When questioned about this camp, the growers protested that "agitators continually refer to it as a stockade, a cattle corral, or a prison, and its inhabitants as slaves or prisoners." Mr. P. S. Bancroft, president of the Contra Costa unit of the Associated Farmers, in defending the camp, said that "obviously the fence and guard were there to keep the lawless element out, not to keep the contented workmen in." When the striking workers in the Imperial Valley set up a camp and strike headquarters in 1934, however, the camp was raided by local police, because, to quote from the *Shipper-Grower Magazine* (March, 1934), "it was a concentration camp in which the workers were being kept against their wishes." The burning question, therefore, would seem to be: When is a concentration camp not a concentration camp? At the Tagus Ranch, in 1934,[3] a huge moat was constructed around an orchard in order "to protect the properties," with armed guards stationed at the entrance and with a machine gun mounted on a truck. "All roads leading to the ranch with the exception of the main entrance where guards are stationed, are blocked by barbed wire and flooded with water by dikes. Fifty old employees report nightly to the ranch manager regarding the conduct of employees under suspicion."

There is much similar evidence, all tending to show that the great farm factories of California take on the appearance of fortified camps under military surveillance whenever a strike is threatened.

Throughout the year 1934 the Associated Farmers stimulated many "trial mobilizations." On July 23, 1934, Sheriff O. W. Toland at Gridley announced that a "trial mobilization" of American Legion men and special deputies had come off perfectly: "All Legionnaires were at the hall in ten minutes and in forty-five minutes the entire assembly was present." Many Legion Posts throughout the State practised similar mobilizations which were timed to coincide with organizational activity among agricultural workers. From Merced, on July 14, 1934, came word that the California Lands, Inc. (Bank of America) and the California Packing Company had demanded forty extra deputy sheriffs, "equipped sufficiently to cope with violence." From Hanford, July 16, 1934, came the report that county officials had organized an Anti-Communist League "to co-operate with county officers in case of emergencies." Most of this vigilante recruiting has been done by elected officials, sheriffs and district attorneys, and peace officers. For example, in 1934 Sheriff Howard Durley, according to the *Fillmore Herald,* "prepared to organize a county-wide vigilante group for the purpose of handling emergencies.

3 See United Press stories for July 9 and July 21, 1934.

Approximately 200 special deputies were sworn in, chosen from prepared lists, and these will be organized into smaller units of ten men each in all sections of the county." I could quote an abundance of similar evidence.

In the following year, 1935, the strategy was carried a point further, when the growers began to order "preventive" arrests. On December 30, 1935, the Sheriff of Imperial Valley (where 4,000 gun permits had been issued in the summer), at the opening of the winter harvest season, "launched a valley-wide roundup of professional agitators, Communists and suspects *to avert a possible strike* among lettuce workers." Commenting upon this move, the *Los Angeles Times* stated editorially: "Professional agitators who are busily engaged in fomenting new labor trouble in the Imperial Valley winter lettuce will find the authorities ready for them. Sheriff Ware and his deputies have *the jump on them this time,*" i.e., arrests were made before a strike could be called and in advance of the season.

Needless to say, the Associated Farmers have a powerful legislative lobby in Sacramento and an elaborate legislative program. In general, they have sponsored the enactment of laws restricting labor's right to organize on the avowed theory that such legislation "would help cut down the cost of labor"; the incorporation of all labor unions; laws prohibiting sympathetic strikes; measures designed to prevent the unionization of governmental and utility-company employees; provisions limiting the right of strikers to relief; and a number of other measures, such as laws making it illegal to interfere with the delivery of food or medical supplies, outlawing the Communist Party and prohibiting all picketing. At present, the farm groups are fighting strenuously against a proposal for a unicameral legislative body in California, for, under the present system, they actually hold a legislative veto through their control of the State Senate. Until this hold is broken, democratic processes cannot function.

George Seldes

George Seldes (1890–1995) called his autobiography Witness to a Century*—an understatement. Seldes covered World War I and the Spanish civil war, interviewed Lenin, Hindenburg, and Trotsky, employed a then-unknown Benito Mussolini as a stringer, and was forced to flee Stalin's Soviet Union and fascist Italy (where his erstwhile stringer sent black-shirted thugs to kill him). "Tell the truth and run" became his standard advice to young reporters.*

Seldes's greatest fame, though, came as a pioneering reporter and critic on the press itself, as well as on domestic fascism and big business profiteering. In book after book in the 1930s, Seldes documented how publishers were aligned with powerful industrial interests, undermining independent reporting and censoring the news. In 1940 Seldes launched what he called "A weekly antidote for falsehood in the daily press," the newsletter In Fact, *which ran for ten years.*

Decades before The Insider, *Seldes reported on how tobacco companies suppressed studies on the hazards of cigarettes. This dispatch from* In Fact *is quintessential Seldes: combining careful reading of the neglected scientific record with precise analysis of the media's dependence on tobacco advertising.*

THE SUPPRESSED TOBACCO STORY

From *In Fact*, January 13, 1941

Tobacco Shortens Life

Smoking shortens life. Between the ages of 30 and 60, 61 percent more heavy smokers die than non-smokers. A human being's span of life is impaired in direct proportion to the amount of tobacco he uses, but the impairment among even light smokers is "measurable and significant."

The facts for the foregoing statements come from Johns Hopkins University, department of biology. They constitute one of the most important and incidentally one of the most sensational stories in recent American history, but there is not a newspaper or magazine in America (outside scientific journals) which has published all the facts.

The mention by Secretary Ickes of the suppression of this story resulted in one of the major scandals of American journalism. Many prominent newspapers which had suppressed the story published false statements and refused to print corrections.

Here are the facts.

"MAKE USERS' FLESH CREEP"

For generations there have been arguments about tobacco. Moralists preached against cigarets. Scientists differed. But in February 1938 Dr. Raymond Pearl, head biologist, Johns Hopkins, gave the New York Academy of Medicine the scientific result of a study of the life histories of some 7,000 Johns Hopkins cases which, for newspapers, should have constituted a story "to scare the life out of tobacco manufacturers and make the tobacco users' flesh creep," as *Time* commented (March,1938).

The Associated Press, United Press and special correspondents of New York papers heard Dr. Pearl tell the story. But a paragraph or two buried under less important matter, in one or two papers was all the great free press of America cared to make known to its readers, the consumers of 200,000,000,000 cigarets a year.

Science News Letter (March 12, 1938, p. 163) had this to say:

> Scientists can tell you whether or not groups of men are marked for early death.
>
> They can do this while these men are still in good health, years before the first appearance of any signs of the disease that will eventually kill them.
>
> The studies which make this possible were reported publicly for the first time by Dr. Raymond Pearl. . . .
>
> Tobacco smokers do not live as long as nonsmokers. This conclusion was based on life tables for the number, out of 100,000 non-smoking men, 100,000 moderate smokers (men) and 100,000 heavy smokers (men) who were still alive at each age level after 30 years. At age 60, for example, 66,564 of the 100.000 non-smokers were still living, 61,911

of the moderate smokers were living, and 46.226 of the 100,000 heavy smokers were still living. . . .

The studies show that smoking is associated with a definite impairment of longevity. This impairment is proportional to the habitual amount of tobacco usage by smoking, being great for heavy smokers and less for moderate smokers, but even in the latter, sufficient to be measurable and significant.

61 PERCENT EXCESS DEATHS

Writing in La Follette's *Progressive* (no advertising taken) Francis A. Porter popularized Dr. Pearl's tables as follows:

Deaths from age 30 to 60 among:

	per 100,000	per 100
1. Non-smokers	3,436	33
2. Moderate	38,089	38
3. Heavy	53,774	54

Percentage of excess deaths:

1. Moderate smokers	14 per cent
2. Heavy smokers	61 per cent

ALCOHOL VERSUS TOBACCO

Writing on the subject of longevity in *Scientific Monthly* (May 1938) Dr. Pearl said of the use of alcohol:

> The problem of the effect of such usage upon longevity has excited violent and unreasoning prejudice on the part of large numbers of people. They contend that alcohol always and everywhere shortens the life of its users. There is much evidence, experimental, statistical and actuarial, that this is not a universally valid generalization.

Dr. Pearl had previously studied the use of alcohol. He now

concluded: "Moderate drinking does not significantly shorten life when compared with total abstention from alcohol, while heavy drinking does seriously diminish the length of life." This too would have been a big story for any newspaper which had the courage to publish anything about such matters.

Of tobacco, Dr. Pearl explains how he picked his 7,000 cases, and concludes:

> These are not large numbers from an actuarial point of view, but are sufficient to be probably indicative of the trends that would be shown by more ample material. Naturally the men included in the observation were an unselected lot except as to their tobacco habits. That is to say they were taken at random and then sorted into categories relative to tobacco usage.

The result of the study is summed up in Dr. Pearl's life and death table, which follows:

> Death rate (1000 q.), at 5-year intervals, starting at age 30; % (a) non-users of tobacco; (b) moderate smokers who did not chew tobacco or take snuff; (c) heavy smokers who did not chew tobacco or take snuff.

Age	Non-Users	Moderate Smokers	Heavy Smokers
30	08.18	07.86	16.89
35	08.78	09.63	21.27
40	10.01	11.89	23.91
45	12.04	14.80	25.69
50	15.16	18.61	27.49
65	19.82	23.67	30.09
60	26.73	30.49	34.29
65	36.88	39.83	41.20
Age	Non-Users	Moderate Smokers	Heavy Smokers

70	51.69	52.84	52.72
75	73.02	71.28	72.33
80	103.22	97.95	100.44
85	142.78	136.50	139.48
90	197.49	190.23	193.68
95	273.2	265.10	268.90

The net result is obvious. In this group of nearly 7,000 men, the smoking of tobacco was associated definitely with an impairment of life duration and the amount or degree of this impairment increased as the habitual amount of smoking increased. The contrast between the life tables relative to the implied effect upon longevity of moderate smoking on the one hand and the moderate use of alcoholic beverages on the other hand is very striking. The moderate smokers in this material are definitely shorter lived than the total abstainers from tobacco; the moderate drinkers are not significantly worse or better off in respect of longevity than the total abstainers from alcohol. Heavy indulgence in either tobacco or alcohol is associated with a very poor life table, but the life table for heavy smokers is definitely worse than that for heavy drinkers.

OTHER SCIENTIFIC EVIDENCE

In 1927 the present editor of *In Fact,* then representing the *Chicago Tribune* in Berlin, went to Prof. Dr. Johann Plesch, head of the medical school of the University of Berlin, for treatment of malaria. Dr. Plesch suggested cutting down on tobacco. He himself was not an anti-nicotine fanatic, but he was an authority; he had written a heavy tome on the subject. He named arsenic, prussic acid, other deadly poisons as present in tobacco, and laid down this law: inasmuch as all tobaccos contain poisons, the continued use of certain kinds of cigarets is dangerous. To escape danger to one's health, the tobacco user must continually change the kind of tobacco he uses, so that the minute amounts of poisons they contain may not affect him. This does not mean switching from Camels to Old Golds, from Chesterfields to Luckies, as these contain exactly the same tobaccos and same poisons; it means switching from American tobacco to Turkish or to Greek or South African.

This story was sent to the *Chicago Tribune* and its newspaper syndicate, but if any paper in America used it, it escaped the eye of the clipping bureaus.

Doctors still argue whether or not smoking is a cause of heart disease. Dr. Frederick Arthur Willius of the Mayo Clinic says it is. With two assistants he studied several thousand cases and concluded that there was three times as much heart disease among 569 smokers aged 40 to 59 as among that many nonsmokers.

Dr. Edwin E. Barksdale warns people allergic to arsenic to stop smoking. Farmers spray tobacco plants with arsenate of lead to kill horn worms and apparently there is no way to remove the poison from the leaves.

RADIO ALSO SUPPRESSES

Some years ago Lucky Strike's slogan was "Reach for a Lucky instead of a sweet," an appeal to women who wanted to reduce. Authorized by the New York medical association, Dr. Benjamin Jablons prepared a speech in which appeared the lines: "Excessive use of tobacco to kill the appetite is a double-edged sword, for nicotine poisoning and starvation both leave dire results in their train." This statement was censored by the radio stations and press.

HOW TO SAVE YOUR LIFE

Medical authorities differ as to what constitutes heavy, medium and light smoking. Readers should consult their doctors. It is now scientifically established that smoking involves taking into the system not only nicotine and arsenic, but ammonia, pyridine and pyridine derivatives, cyanides and sulpho-cyanides. One authority holds that "it is not the nicotine . . . but something much more subtle or poisonous that causes the unfortunate results. Whatever it is, and this is as yet unknown, it is contained in the protein which results from the burning of the cigarets" (*Commonweal,* April 9, 1937).

Most doctors believe that 40 cigarets a day mean heavy smoking, but the most important disclosure by Dr. Pearl was that even light smoking shortens life.

TOBACCO SHORTENS LIFE (PART 2)

No publication in America, outside of scientific journals, told the whole story of how tobacco shortens human life, as detailed in the last issue of *In Fact.* (In brief: Dr. Pearl, biologist at Johns Hopkins, published documented findings from 7,000 cases proving that between the ages of 30 and 60, 61 per cent more heavy smokers die than non-smokers, and that the impairment to longevity among light smokers is "measurable and significant.")

In New York the *Herald Tribune, Sun, News, Mirror, Post,* and *Journal-American* suppressed this story, although the Associated Press, United Press and Hearst's International News sent it out, and although science reporters turned in stories. The *Times* and *World-Telegram* buried a few lines, omitting Pearl's frightening death tables.

Then, after having suppressed the story, the same newspapers attacked Secretary of the Interior Ickes because he intimated that "the press" suppressed the story without qualifying his statement by adding that a mere 98 or 99 per cent of the press suppressed it.

Here follows the evidence of the venality of the press as regards tobacco—an industry which pays the press $50,000,000 a year.

VENAL METROPOLITAN PRESS

The American press bears other grudges against Ickes, who is the hatchet man of the Administration when it comes to newspapers. Editors and publishers let loose a terrific campaign in which not one of Mr. Ickes' main arguments was answered.

The *Herald Tribune*'s editorial, headed "Mr. Ickes Stumbles," said that "he was guilty of more misstatements and misrepresentations of fact than we have been led to expect from even a spokesman of the Administration." Mr. Ickes had also said that the *Herald Tribune* refused an ad for *Lords of the Press.* Continued the *Herald Tribune* editorial: "No advertisement of this book was ever refused by the *Herald Tribune.*" This is a falsehood. Photostats of the proofsheets of the censored ad set up by the *Herald Tribune* appeared in the labor press throughout the U.S.

The Federated Press, serving the labor press (which is not venal, and which gets precious little cigaret advertising) reported that the *Herald Tribune* not only suppressed the tobacco story but claimed it never saw it. FP said: "Wilbur Forest, executive editor (said) his paper had been scooped on the tobacco story."

Asked how an Associated Press member could be scooped on an AP story, he explained that the *Herald Tribune* does not get the AP local service. This excuse was punctured by AP executives, who insisted that the story went not only to the *Herald Tribune* but also to other NY papers that failed to print a line. Here is the private FP report of January 20, 1938:

"Talked with X of AP (he did not want his name used) and he put the finger on Forrest. After I got it straight that the *Herald Tribune* did receive the story, I told X that they denied it. He stuck to his story, even called back to say that Howard Blakeslee, science editor, had personally covered the Pearl story."

BIG MONEY IN CIGARETS

Six cigaret companies grossed $200,000,000 in 1937 (SEC report). A combined profit after all charges of $83,000,000 that year was reported by the Census of American Listed Corporations (April 5, 1939).

The major companies spent as high as $50,000,000 a year on advertising, notably:

Company	Best-Known Brand	1937	1939
Reynolds	Camels	$15,422,744	$9,296,470
Liggett & Myers	Chesterfield	14,822,120	8,926,148
Lorillard	Old Gold	9,714,286	1,722,663

American Tobacco	Lucky Strike	7,441,554	5,002,056

The newspapers, Editor & Publisher, *Saturday Evening Post,* all say that advertising has nothing to do with editorial policy. The facts are:

1. The cigaret companies spend up to $50,000,000 a year.
2. News inimical to tobacco is not published.
3. 99 percent of the American press suppresses government fraud orders against advertisers.

Lowell L. Leake and PM

In 1940, Ralph Ingersoll—who had created Fortune *magazine for Henry Luce—convinced department-store magnate Marshall Field to back a bold new venture: a daily New York newspaper without advertising.* PM *failed after eight years, but it was one of the great experiments in journalism, marked by a liberal editorial policy and by innovations in both reporting and design; Ingersoll, I. F. Stone would recall years later, "taught us all new ways to write." For consistent attention to investigative reporting,* PM *was without peer in its day, its targets ranging from war profiteering to public education funding. The paper's most consistent subject was domestic fascism, which its reporters traced from boardrooms to religious pulpits to street corner gangs.*

This story, by reporter Lowell L. Leake, is a notable example of PM*'s willingness to go further than most daily newspapers in pointing out lines of accountability in high places. Leake's examination of U.S. companies' collaboration with Hitler's Germany anticipates by nearly twenty years the first serious postwar scholarship on corporate involvement with the Nazi regime.*

Hitler Gets Millions for War Chest Through Links with American Firms

Purchases from Standard Oil of New Jersey and Sterling Products Aid Nazis by Indirect Route

From *PM*, 1941

Americans have poured millions into Germany's war chest through purchases from the Standard Oil Co. of New Jersey, in which the Rockefeller family holds a large interest, and the Sterling Products Co., Inc., the largest drug and medical goods advertiser in the U.S.A.

The millions have gone to Hitler as cash payments or credits to the I. G. Farben Industries, which is the German dye trust; the General Aniline and Film Corp., in which Edsel B. Ford is a director, and the I.G. Swiss Chemie, a Swiss holding company controlled by Farben.

Government hearings, financial records and reports from credit-rating organizations reveal an amazing story of dual ownerships, interlocking dictatorships, stock trading, and patent and royalty payments among these major companies and their hundreds of subsidiaries.

Most of these activities are perfectly legal. However, some activities are now under grand jury investigation.

The plain fact is that Adolf Hitler has used and is using American citizens and American laws to advance the Nazi cause in this hemisphere and in the Old World. Thus is fulfilled the boast of Hitler's Propaganda Minister, Paul Joseph Goebbels, that Americans would help Hitler win the Americas.

HOW IT IS DONE

The amazing highlights in the story of how this is done:

- The three great German-Swiss holding companies collected more than $1,000,000 in dividends ALONE from the Standard Oil Co. of New Jersey in just one year, 1939. Dividends since then have been greater.
- These three companies were I.G. Farben, of which the Ford Motor Co. of Germany is a part; Swiss Chemie, controlled by I.G. Farben and itself once or now the holder of 388,000 shares of Standard of New Jersey stock; and General Aniline and Film, controlled by Farben and itself a holder of 203,053 shares of Standard of New Jersey stock. Standard has issued 27,000,000 shares of stock. Standard's annual sales are almost $1,000,000,000.
- General Aniline, which changed its name from American I.G. just after the war started, holds 20 per cent of the stock of a Standard Oil of New Jersey subsidiary. This was the Standard I.G. Co., which within the last few months also has changed its name—to Standard Catalytic Co. The letters "I.G." have become a liability. The letters stand for *Internationale Gesellschaft,* or International Corporation.
- General Aniline is controlled by I.G. Farben or I.G. Swiss Chemie or by other corporations, some of them small holding

companies, which in turn are controlled by I.G. Farben. Farben guarantees General Aniline bonds and interest.

- General Aniline owns 37,880 out of 1,700,000 shares of Sterling Products, Inc., which ranked ninth in total advertising in U.S. newspapers, magazines and radio in 1939. Sterling thus is not only one of America's most powerful advertisers, but it is tops in its own field.

PARTNERSHIP

- General Aniline and Sterling are 50-50 partners in two American drug companies, Winthrop and Alba. Through these, General Aniline gets not only huge dividends, amounts not publicized, but huge royalties on such items as Bayer products sold in the Western Hemisphere. Some of these royalties run as high as 75 per cent.
- General Aniline owned a half interest in the American Magnesium Corp. The Mellons' Aluminum Co. of America owns the other half. This magnesium interest is involved in anti-trust law indictments returned this spring. General Aniline sold its magnesium interest just before the indictments were returned.
- General Aniline also owned or owns 5,500 shares in Du Pont, 10,000 shares in Standard Oil of California, 22,299 shares in Mission Corp. (another oil holding company) and 5,900 shares in Standard Oil of Indiana.
- General Aniline dividends from Sterling Products and these other miscellaneous stocks totaled more than $215,000 in 1939 ALONE. These are in addition to dividends from the highly profitable half interests in Alba, American Magnesium and Winthrop, from whom General Aniline collected not only dividends but huge royalties.

DROP IN THE BUCKET

- The known dividend payments to the Nazi-controlled holding companies are only a drop in the bucket. Other smaller Farben-controlled or Chemie-controlled corporations in occupied lands own smaller blocks of stock in the American companies. Officials of all these Nazi-controlled corporations have individual holdings of stock which also draw dividends. And, of course, there are the royalty payments, amounts unknown but high.

- Among important transactions adding to the Nazi war chest are several mentioned during SEC hearings in 1938. They involved options, or sale agreements. In one, General Aniline bought 200,000 shares of Standard of New Jersey at $23 a share under the market, a profit of $4,500,000. In another a Nazi-controlled group got 146,000 shares at little more than one-third their market value, $18.50 a share under the market. This was a profit of $2,701,000.
- This same hearing developed the fact that Nazi-controlled investments of cash or credit in General Aniline, once known as American I.G., totaled about $30,000,000. American investments totaled about $30,000,000. The Nazi-controlled vote, however, was 3,400,000, against only 250,000 American votes. The capital set-up of the Nazi-American corporations thus has been manipulated in a perfectly legal manner to use American capital, under the control of Nazi votes.
- This financial crazy quilt has played an ironical trick on the Rockefeller family. It has a huge stake in Standard of New Jersey, which, like Sterling Products, has developed highly profitable business in Latin America and Great Britain. Nazi stockholders share the profits, and Hitler can use them for direct purchase of war material, or for propaganda in North or South America. Nelson Rockefeller, son of John D., is a leader in the U.S. group successfully advancing commercial and cultural relations with Latin America. Its job is to off-set Nazi propaganda. Thus in an indirect manner some of the money earned by Rockefeller interests works against the Rockefeller family wishes.

The jigsaw financial picture of these corporations is no more amazing than stories of some persons directing the corporations.

These stories of individuals highlight the record:

Walter C. Teagle

Mr. Teagle is chairman of the board, Standard Oil Co. of New Jersey, and a power in the 260 or more subsidiaries. He also is a $1-a-year man at Washington, engaged in various defense activities, and a director of the Federal Reserve Bank.

He became a stockholder, debenture holder and director of American I.G. (now General Aniline) back in 1929 and for 10 years remained a director. He admitted in a 1938 SEC hearing that he did not know "the real owners" of the Class A and B stocks which were the voting stocks of American I.G. Asked if he tried to find out, he replied "No, sir." He added that it was a "safe assumption" to say they were controlled by "European interests."

It was also developed during the hearing that American I.G. held 9 per cent of the I.G. Chemie stock, and the I.G. Chemie held 11 per cent of American I.G. Also, I.G. Chemie bought through a third party additional stock in American I.G., sometimes above, and sometimes below the market. Mr. Teagle didn't explain that. And he did not know who controlled I.G. Chemie.

It also was developed that a Swiss corporation formed by a Swiss lawyer and his clerk and capitalized at about $20,000 held more than a third of the voting shares of the American I.G., valued in the millions. The Swiss corporation was traced to German interests. A few days ago, Kurt Rieth, once Nazi Minister and advance man to Australia and otherwise active in Nazi economic and propaganda agencies, was arrested here charged with falsifying passport statements, and he is now held at Ellis Island.

He had said that he was a personal friend of Mr. Teagle. Mr. Teagle told the *Herald Tribune*: "You can't make my denial of any knowledge of him or of ever having known or seen him too emphatic."

Mr. Teagle had said he had been told by the FBI weeks earlier that Rieth was using his name. What Mr. Teagle did to stop this practice was not made known. He may have acted through the Department of Justice.

At any rate, it developed that Rieth was interested in buying for about 25 cents on the dollar Standard Oil interests in a Hungarian subsidiary which the Nazis already had under control. The speculation was that this was a good-will gesture, intended to "soften up" American business men so they would feel grateful for a chance to do business with the Nazis.

It was revealed that Standard of New Jersey would not be opposed to receiving some cash for a subsidiary already lost.

Mr. Teagle's situation is that of hundreds of business men who years ago made German business alliances to make money for their stockholders. They now find those alliances working against the interests of America and Britain.

E. I. McClintock

He is an official of Sterling Products, Inc., and an officer and director of many of its subsidiaries. Among them are the Bayer Co. and the Sterling Products Export Co.

He was an employee of the Alien Property Custodian's office during the World War. After Sterling subsidiaries obtained valuable German Bayer patents from that office, he became an officer of Sterling.

He is a director of Winthrop Drug, which is half owned by the German-controlled General Aniline and Film Corporation.

W. E. Weiss

Aggressive small-city druggist who made good. He came from Canton, Ohio, and got started on his way up in Wheeling, West Virginia.

He is chairman of the board of Sterling Products, Inc. He is a director and officer in many of the 40 or more subsidiaries, including Winthrop and Bayer and several foreign corporations. He is a director of General Aniline and Film Corp.

J. E. Crane

Director of Standard I.G. and many subsidiaries of Standard Oil of New Jersey.

W. E. Currie

Director of Standard I.G. and several Standard of New Jersey subsidiaries.

E. Schwarz

Naturalized American, German-born, former director of I.G. Farben. Now director of General Aniline and Film.

Karl Milde

German-born American, long an official and employee of General Aniline and Film.

F. A. Howard

A sort of liaison man between Farben and Standard of New Jersey. He is vice-president of Standard of New Jersey, president of Standard Development Co. and Standard I.G. (now Standard Catalytic). Standard Development and its subsidiaries and affiliates promote the use of Farben patents, such as those covering synthetic gas and synthetic rubber. These companies hold exclusive rights to those Farben patents outside Germany.

D. A. Schmitz

Naturalized American born in Germany. Director-general of Aniline and Film Corp. and American Magnesium Corp.

E. M. Clark

Director-general of Aniline and Film, Standard I.G., Ethyl Gasoline Corp. and Agfa-Ansco, and a former vice-president of Standard of New Jersey.

Edsel B. Ford
Director of Ford Motor Co., Ford Motor Co., Ltd., Ford Motor Co. of Canada, Ltd., Ford Motor Co. Exports, Inc., General Aniline and Film Corp.

E. V. Murpheree
Director of Standard I.G. and several Standard of New Jersey subsidiaries.

William H. Vom Rath
German-born American, son of the late Walther vom Rath, who was once vice-chairman of the I.G. Farben board. He is a former employe of I.G. Farben, now a director of General Aniline and Film.

Rudolf Hutz
German-born American, former employee of I.G. Farben now a director of General Aniline and Film.

Dr. Felix Iselin
Swiss subject, officer of I.G. Chemie, which has large stock interest in Standard of New Jersey and General Aniline and Film.

Herman Schmitz
German citizen, member of the board of management of I.G. Farben, and president of I.G. Chemie, Swiss holding company whose dividends are guaranteed by I.G. Farben.

JOHN BARTLOW MARTIN

"Most journalists make a living by interviewing the great," John Bartlow Martin once said. "I made mine by interviewing the humble—what the Spaniards call los de abajo, *those from below."*

Martin's subjects ranged from the neglected history of his native Indiana to racketeering by Teamsters leader Jimmy Hoffa. His stories are marked by an astute interviewer's ear, depth of research, and exceptional narrative craft, which Martin attributed to early work for detective magazines. In 1948, Harper's *sent him to cover a devastating mine accident in Illinois. The 18,500 words that resulted–almost an entire issue of the magazine—earned comparison to John Hersey's* Hiroshima, *and led to the downfall of Governor Dwight Green.*

In 1952 Martin went to work for Illinois governor Adlai Stevenson, beginning a new career as a speechwriter and advanceman for Stevenson, John F. Kennedy and Robert Kennedy, and FCC chairman Newt Minow. He served as President Kennedy's ambassador to the Dominican Republic, and was a key adviser to RFK's 1968 presidential campaign. After Robert Kennedy's assassination he returned to journalism as an influential teacher at Northwestern University's Medill School.

THE BLAST IN CENTRALIA NO. 5: A MINE DISASTER NO ONE STOPPED

From *Harper's* Magazine, March 1948

One afternoon about a year ago William E. Rowekamp and a few other coal miners, their day's work done, were sitting around underground at the bottom of the shaft of the Centralia No. 5 mine, waiting for time to go "on top" and home, when all at once a foul cloud of coal smoke and powder smoke billowed from the mouth of the Main South Entry, the main tunnel leading southward into the mine workings. An ex-GI asked, "What is it, Uncle Bill?" Rowekamp, an old coal miner and an officer of the local union, knew the lad was nervous so he said only, "It could be several things." But Rowekamp knew what it was—an explosion. Somewhere far back in the catacomb of entries and crosscuts and rooms, somewhere among the fifteen-odd miles of active tunnels or the hundred-odd miles of abandoned workings, an explosion had occurred, and this cloud of smoke was the backwash of the tornado of flame and blast. Rowekamp had no way of knowing it then but one hundred and eleven men were dead or dying.

Quickly Rowekamp and the others went up in the cage. On the surface all was calm. The sky was gray, the day was bleak and raw with a strong wind blowing. They grew chilled. Uncertain what they ought to do, Rowekamp and another man did what they did at this hour each day: went to the washhouse to bathe and change into their street clothes. Word came that they were wanted back at the tipple.

The Superintendent, H. C. Niermann, the top company official on hand, had put in phone calls for the State Mine Inspector and for state mine rescue teams at other Illinois towns. Nobody knew how bad the explosion was. A sick miner who had just come from underground said he had been walking toward the shaft bottom along the First West Entry when a roaring, smoky wind hit him from behind, and to keep from falling he had begun to run, and he had run all the way to the shaft bottom. Others working near the shaft bottom also had escaped. But more than a hundred men were still below, nearly all of them far back in the mine, and, ominously, nothing had been heard from them.

Superintendent Niermann and several others descended the 540 feet to the bottom. They got aboard a motor, a small electric locomotive used to pull cars of coal, and rode about 1,200 feet south to the intersection of the First West Entry, where the airshaft and fan were located. Here the chunky underground boss, Mine Manager William H. Brown, told them the explosion's great force had knocked out the electric power and reversed the fan; in remedying this Brown had collapsed. Cliff Copple and John Lorenzini, having hauled him to safety, now had gone on down the Main South Entry to look for Cliff Copple's brother. They had not returned. To rescue them Superintendent Niermann sent Rowekamp and two others. Rowekamp, a man of fifty-eight with high cheek bones and thinning hair, headed their motor slowly down Main South through dust and smoke. After a half mile Rowekamp said he saw a light. One of the others said,

"Uncle Bill, you are just seeing things," but Rowekamp recalled later, "We got closer and we saw it was a man—Brother Lorenzini." Lorenzini, a wiry, agile little man, now was staggering around in the tunnel, flailing his arms, crazed with gas and smoke. Where was his buddy, Cliff Copple? They went a little farther. One of them was getting sick from the fumes. They found water and washed their faces. They reached a place where the roof comes down low. The smoke was billowing through thick. Copple must be beyond. But they would have to crawl; they needed more men and equipment. So they took Lorenzini to the shaft bottom. (Copple died.)

Superintendent Niermann, Mine Manager Brown, and some other men, exploring the First West Entry, had found the pumper, a man of seventy-one. They thought fresh air might revive him but it didn't. They went on. More than a mile back along the First West they found 20 men, 16 dead and four living. The dead were lying on the fireclay floor of the entry as though asleep; gas, not violence, had killed them. The four living were like wild men. One of the rescuers knew that his own father was somewhere back in the mine but they dared go no farther: the corridors were full of gas, the doors and stoppings were scarred by violence—beyond lay the actual area of explosion.

This ended impromptu rescue work. The State Mine Inspector, Driscoll O. Scanlan, took over. It was now 9:00 P.M. on March 25, 1947, five and a half hours after the blast. Thirty-one had come out alive, 17 were known dead. What of the 94 others? This was the question that lay on the minds of those in the crowd all that night and during the succeeding days and nights.

Already the crowd had gathered. Cars clogged the short, black rock road from the highway to the mine, cars bearing curious spectators and relatives and friends of the men entombed. State troopers and deputy sheriffs and the prosecuting attorney came, and officials from the company, the Federal Bureau of Mines, the Illinois Department of Mines and Minerals. Ambulances arrived, and doctors and nurses and Red Cross workers and soldiers with stretchers from Scott Field. Mine rescue teams came, and a federal rescue unit, experts burdened with masks and oxygen tanks and other awkward paraphernalia of disaster.

By now the word had spread all over Centralia, and to other towns and settlements. Centralia is a quiet town on the Illinois prairie, its streets are deserted by nine o'clock, but on this night cars raced late through the streets on terrible errands. Lights burned night-long in the homes of the miners. In a tiny house near a coal mine shaft close by sat a big woman, Mrs. Joe Bryant, surrounded by eight of her children, by relatives and friends, waiting for news of her husband and her first-born son, both trapped; she waited all night, her son's wife with her, both of them pregnant, but there was no news. Some of the miners' women went to the mine. They pressed against the ropes and wires that police had strung to keep them back from the shaft. A bitter, freezing wind was blowing coal dust through the air, and not long after dark it started to rain, a cold winter rain that presently turned to snow, and the hundreds of churning feet and wheels soon whipped the snow and rain and earth into a sticky, gray-tan mud.

When they became too cold the women went to the washhouse, a dim-lit, moist, barnlike building. Here each morning their men donned their working clothes, and now their men's street clothes were hanging from racks by chains and pulleys, so that the washhouse looked like a vast laundry. Each woman—many were widows already, though they refused to believe it—found, without words or prearrangement, her husband's clothes and sat down under them to wait. (This was one place he would surely come if they brought him out alive.) Now and then a rescue worker, exhausted and half-sick with fumes, would come in for coffee or whiskey, and when the door opened the women would look up; but the rescuer would only shake his head, and the women would look back down at the damp concrete floor. Outside, the hoisting machinery would rumble and the cables sway taut and the cage would come up, sometimes with only the rescuers, sometimes with a stretcher; and sometimes nobody could hold back the crowd. Off in the distance the sky glowed red above the Illinois Central shops, and, closer by, the mine buildings loomed black against the sky; but to the east, beyond the lighted taverns, there was nothing but the dark Illinois plains.

II

One hundred and eleven men were killed in that explosion. Killed needlessly, for almost everybody concerned had known for months, even years, that the mine was dangerous. Yet nobody had done anything effective about it. Why not? Let us examine the background of the explosion. Let us study the mine and the miners, Joe Bryant and Bill Rowekamp and some others, and also the numerous people who might have saved the miners' lives but did not. The miners had appealed in various directions for help but got none, not from their state government nor their federal government nor their employer nor their own union. (In threading the maze of officialdom we must bear in mind the four agencies in authority: The State of Illinois, the United States Government, the Centralia Coal Company, and the United Mine Workers of America, that is, the UMWA of John L. Lewis.) Let us seek to fix responsibility for the disaster. This will raise the broader question: What is the matter with the coal industry? But first let us glance at the men at the bottom of the heap, the miners, and at their town.

Centralia lies 65 miles east of St. Louis, south of the fat farmland of Illinois, a town of 16,000 with another 4,000 in adjacent towns. The Illinois Central built Centralia, and named it, and it is still a railroad town—all but 900 of its 2,800 workingmen work for the railroads. On Saturday noon a Diesel honks desolately in the wide yards, and down the main street, Broadway, walks a tall railroader in a blue peaked cap. He is stopping in at Walgreen's for lunch; he steps into line at the cafeteria rail alongside clerks and merchants. Centralia is a farm town, too, and on the street a block away a thin farm woman in a flowered dress is arguing with her gaunt husband, who is carrying bundles. Outside Centralia the gray-brown clay of the flatlands is planted to wheat, but the rolling hills are covered with orchards: peaches are the thing. Some farmers have earned enough money off them to build homes in town, the cool large houses where lucky Midwest farmers end their days rocking on the L-shaped porch. Downtown the young men in khakis and wide-brimmed hats are Texans, come to work in the new oil fields. In

1938 a fever swept Centralia; today the derricks are thick in the countryside, and in the backyards in town along quiet tree-arched streets squat little pumps chug efficiently away.

But Illinois ranks third among the states in coal production and though today only two mines remain at Centralia, employing but 500 where once there were jobs for 1,000, the mines are still a part of the town, and so are the miners. "Miners are just like anybody else," says the old miner, and so they are, outwardly: you cannot spot them on the sidewalks of Centralia (unless they happen to be crippled: empty sleeves and twisted backs are common in the crowd), and you cannot tell their houses from the railroaders'. On pay day you may find the miners in John's saloon near their union hall, cashing their checks and hoisting a few, but on other nights you will not find them gambling or drinking at the wide-open roadhouses, you will find them home in bed. They are not by nature roisterers or drifters; they are substantial men, and most of them around Centralia own their own homes. They rise before dawn and drive to work with friends; they go down in the mine and cut the coal and, after it is blasted, load it; they are highly skilled and sometimes seem not wage workers but men in business for themselves; and at 4:00 P.M. they go home and eat and work around the house till dark, putting up hay or installing a septic tank or rebuilding the chicken coop, then go to bed.

Miners live daily with a hundred dangers; rock can fall on them, coal can fall, a coal car can crush them, a wire can electrocute them. And this breeds in miners a contempt for danger and for men in safer trades. It breeds a deep-rooted fatalism, which their women reflect, and a clannishness. Why do they persist in following so dangerous a calling? Old miners will tell you, hopelessly, "I'd quit tomorrow but I don't know nothing else." Young ones will tell you that no other job they could get pays so well. But others will simply say, "I'm a miner, that's all," and this sums it up: mining is a way of living, as is farming.

The Centralia Mine No. 5 was opened two miles south of Centralia in 1907. Because of its age, its maze of underground workings is extensive, covering perhaps six square miles, but it is regarded as a medium-small mine since it employs but 250 men and produces but 2,000 tons of coal daily. It was owned by the Centralia Coal Company, an appendage of the Bell & Zoller empire, one of the Big Six among Illinois coal operators. In 1947 Herbert E. Bell, the empire's founder, was still chairman of the Bell & Zoller Coal & Mining Company and of the Centralia Company, but he was seventy-eight years old, rich, retired in California. The active, operating vice-president was William P. Young, a slender, tough-minded, graying man who lived in a fashionable suburb of Chicago. The Bell & Zoller home office was in Chicago (most of the big coal operators' home offices are in Chicago or St. Louis); no Bell & Zoller officers or directors lived at Centralia.

There are in coal mines two main explosion hazards—coal dust and gas. Coal dust is unhealthy to breathe and highly explosive. Some of the dust raised by machines in cutting and loading coal stays in suspension in the air. Some subsides to the floor and walls of the tunnels, and a local explosion will kick it back into the air where it will explode and, in turn, throw more dust into the air, which will explode; and as this chain reaction continues the explosion will propagate throughout the mine or until it reaches something that will stop it.

The best method of stopping it, a method in use for some twenty-five years, is rock dusting. Rock dusting is simply applying pulverized stone to the walls and roof of the passageways; when a local explosion occurs it will throw a cloud of rock dust into the air along with the coal dust, and since rock dust is incombustible the explosion will die. Rock dusting will not prevent an explosion but it will localize one. Illinois law requires rock dusting in a dangerously dusty mine. Authorities disagreed as to whether the Centralia mine was gassy but everyone agreed it was exceedingly dry and dusty. The men who worked in it had been complaining about the dust for a long time—one recalls that "the dust was over your shoetops," another that "I used to cough up chunks of coal dust like walnuts after work"—and indeed by 1944, more than two years before the disaster, so widespread had dissatisfaction become that William Rowekamp, as recording secretary of Local Union 52, prepared an official complaint. But even earlier, both state and federal inspectors had recognized the danger.

Let us trace the history of these warnings of disaster to come. For in the end it was this dust which did explode and kill one hundred and eleven men, and seldom has a major catastrophe of any kind been blueprinted so accurately so far in advance.

III

Driscoll O. Scanlan (who led the rescue work after the disaster) went to work in a mine near Centralia when he was 16, studied engineering at night school, and worked 13 years as a mine examiner for a coal company until, in 1941, he was appointed one of 16 Illinois state mine inspectors by Governor Green upon recommendation of the state representative from Scanlan's district. Speaking broadly, the job of a state inspector is to police the mine operators—to see that they comply with the state mining law, including its numerous safety provisions. But an inspector's job is a political patronage job. Coal has always been deeply enmeshed in Illinois politics.

Dwight H. Green, running for Governor the preceding fall, had promised the miners that he would enforce the mining laws "to the letter of the law," and however far below this lofty aim his administration fell (as we shall see), Scanlan apparently took the promise literally. Scanlan is a stubborn, righteous, zealous man of fierce integrity. Other inspectors, arriving to inspect a mine, would go into the office and chat with the company officials. Not Scanlan; he waited outside, and down in the mine he talked with the miners, not the bosses. Other inspectors, emerging, would write their reports in the company office at the company typewriter. Not Scanlan; he wrote on a portable in his car. Widespread rumor had it that some inspectors spent most of their inspection visits drinking amiably with company officials in the hotel in town. Not Scanlan. Other inspectors wrote the briefest reports possible, making few recommendations and enumerating only major violations of the mining law. Scanlan's reports were longer than any others (owing in part to a prolix prose style), he listed every violation however minor, and he made numerous recommendations for improvements even though they were not explicitly required by law.

Scanlan came to consider the Centralia No. 5 mine the worst in his district. In his first report on it he made numerous recommendations, including these: "That haulage roads be cleaned and sprinkled. . . . That tamping of shots with coal dust be discontinued and that clay be used. . . ." Remember those criticisms, for they were made February 7, 1942, more than five years before the mine blew up as a result (at least in part) of those very malpractices.

Every three months throughout 1942, 1943, and 1944 Scanlan inspected the mine and repeated his recommendations, adding new ones: "That the mine be sufficiently rock dusted." And what became of his reports? He mailed them to the Department of Mines and Minerals at Springfield, the agency which supervises coal mines and miners. Springfield is dominated by the Statehouse, an ancient structure of spires and towers and balconies, of colonnades and domes; on its broad front steps Lincoln stands in stone. Inside all is gloom and shabby gilt. The Department of Mines and Minerals occupies three high-ceilinged rooms in a back corner of the second floor. The Director of the Department uses the small, comfortable, innermost office, its windows brushed by the leaves of trees on the Statehouse lawn, and here too the Mining Board meets. In theory, the Mining Board makes policy to implement the mining law, the Director executes its dictates; in practice, the Director possesses considerable discretionary power of his own.

In 1941 Governor Green appointed as Director Robert M. Medill, a genial, paunchy, red-faced man of about sixty-five. Medill had gone to work in a mine at sixteen; he rose rapidly in management. He had a talent for making money and he enjoyed spending it. He entered Republican politics in 1920, served a few years as director of the Department of Mines and Minerals, then returned to business (mostly managing mines); and then, after working for Green's election in 1940, was rewarded once more with the directorship. Green reappointed him in 1944 with, says Medill, the approval of "a multitude of bankers and business men all over the state. And miners. I had the endorsement of all four factions." By this he means the United Mine Workers and its smaller rival, the Progressive Mine Workers, and the two associations of big and little operators; to obtain the endorsement of all four of these jealous, power-seeking groups is no small feat. As Director, Medill received $6,000 a year (since raised to $8,000) plus expenses of $300 or $400 a month. He lived in a sizable country house at Lake Springfield, with spacious grounds and a tree-lined driveway.

To Medill's department, then, came Driscoll Scanlan's inspection reports on Centralia Mine No. 5. Medill, however, did not see the first thirteen reports (1942–44); they were handled as "routine" by Robert Weir, an unimaginative, harassed little man who had come up through the ranks of the miners' union and on recommendation of the union had been appointed Assistant Director of the Department by Green (at $4,000 a year, now $5,200). When the mail brought an inspector's report, it went first to Medill's secretary who shared the office next to Medill's with Weir. She stamped the report in red:

RECEIVED
DEPT. MINES & MINERALS
Springfield, Illinois
Feb 23 1945
AM PM
7 8 9 10 11 12 1 2 3 4 5 6
▲

and put it on Weir's desk. Sometimes, but by no means always, Weir read the report. He gave it to one of a half-dozen girl typists in the large outer office. She edited the inspector's recommendations for errors in grammar and spelling, and incorporated them into a form letter to the owner of the mine, closing:

"The Department endorses the recommendations made by Inspector Scanlan and requests that you comply with same.

"Will you please advise the Department upon the completion of the recommendations set forth above?

"Thanking you . . ."

When the typist placed this letter upon his desk, Weir signed it and it was mailed to the mine operator.

But the Centralia company did not comply with the major recommendations Scanlan made. In fact, it did not even bother to answer Weir's thirteen letters based on Scanlan's reports. And Weir did nothing about this. Once, early in the game, Weir considered the dusty condition of the mine so serious that he requested the company to correct it within ten days; but there is no evidence that the company even replied.

This continued for nearly three years. And during the same period the federal government entered the picture. In 1941 Congress authorized the U.S. Bureau of Mines to make periodic inspections of coal mines. But the federal government had no enforcement power whatever; the inspections served only research. The first federal inspection of Centralia Mine No. 5 was made in September of 1942. In general, the federal recommendations duplicated Scanlan's—rock dusting, improving ventilation, wetting the coal to reduce dust—and the federal inspectors noted that "coal dust . . . at this mine is highly explosive, and would readily propagate an explosion." In all, they made 106 recommendations, including 33 "major" ones (a government official has defined a "major" hazard as one that "could . . . result in a disaster"). Four months passed before a copy of this report filtered through the administrative machinery at Washington and reached the Illinois Department at Springfield, but this mattered little: the Department did nothing anyway. Subsequent federal reports in 1943 and 1944 showed that the "major" recommendations had not been complied with. The federal bureau lacked the power to force compliance; the Illinois Department possessed the power but failed to act.

What of the men working in the mine during these three years? On November 4, 1944, on instructions from Local 52 at Centralia, William Rowekamp, the recording secretary, composed a letter to Medill: "At the present the condition of those roadways are very dirty and dusty . . . they are getting dangerous. . . . But the Coal Co. has ignored [Scanlan's recommendations]. And we beg your prompt action on this matter."

The Department received this letter November 6, and four days later

Weir sent Inspector Scanlan to investigate. Scanlan reported immediately: "The haulage roads in this mine are awful dusty, and much dust is kept in suspension all day. . . . The miners have complained to me . . . and I have wrote it up pretty strong on my inspection reports. . . . But to date they have not done any adequate sprinkling. . . . Today . . . [Superintendent Norman] Prudent said he would fix the water tank and sprinkle the roads within a week, said that he would have had this work done sooner, but that they have 20 to 30 men absent each day." (This last is a claim by the company that its cleanup efforts were handicapped by a wartime manpower shortage. This is controversial. Men of fifty-nine—the average wartime age at the mine—do not feel like spending weekends removing coal dust or rock dusting, a disagreeable task; winter colds caused absenteeism and miners are always laying off anyway. On the other hand, the company was interested in production and profits: as Mine Manager Brown has said, "In the winter you can sell all the coal you can get out. So you want top production, you don't want to stop to rock dust.")

At any rate, Rowekamp's complaint got results. On December 2, 1944, he wrote Scanlan: "Well I am proud to tell you that they have sprinkled the 18th North Entry & 21st So. Entry and the main haulage road. . . . Myself and the Members of Local Union #52 appreciate it very much what you have done for us." It is apparent from this first direct move by Local 52 that Scanlan was working pretty closely with the Local to get something done.

But by the end of that month, December 1944, the mine once more had become so dirty that Scanlan ended his regular inspection report: ". . . if necessary the mine should discontinue hoisting coal for a few days until the [cleanup] work can be done." But all Weir said to the company was the routine "The Department endorses. . . ."

Early in 1945 it appeared that something might be accomplished. Scanlan, emerging from his regular inspection, took the unusual step of telephoning Medill at Springfield. Medill told him to write him a letter so Scanlan did: "The haulage roads in this mine are in a terrible condition.

If a person did not see it he would not believe. . . . Two months ago . . . the local officers [of Local Union 52] told me that . . . if [the mine manager] did not clean the mine up they were going to prefer charges against him before the mining board and have his certificate canceled. I talked them out of it and told them I thought we could get them to clean up the mine. But on this inspection I find that practically nothing has been done. . . . The mine should discontinue hoisting coal . . . until the mine is placed in a safe condition. . . . The coal dust in this mine is highly explosive. . . ."

This stiff letter was duly stamped "Received" at Springfield on February 23, 1945. A few days earlier a bad report had come in from Federal Inspector Perz. And now at last Medill himself entered the picture. What did he do? The Superintendent at Centralia had told Scanlan that, in order to clean up the mine, he would have to stop producing coal, a step he was not empowered to take. So Medill bypassed him, forwarding Scanlan's letter and report to William P. Young, Bell & Zoller's operating vice-president at Chicago: "Dear Bill. . . . Please let me have any comments you wish to make. . . . Very kindest personal regards." From his quiet, well-furnished office near the top of the Bell Building overlooking Michigan Avenue, Young replied immediately to "Dear Bob" [Medill]: "As you know we have been working under a very severe handicap for the past months. The war demand for coal . . . we are short of men. . . . I am hopeful that the urgent demand for coal will ease up in another month so that we may have available both the time and labor to give proper attention to the recommendations of Inspector Scanlan. With kindest personal regards. . . ."

A week later, on March 7, 1945, Medill forwarded copies of this correspondence to Scanlan, adding: "I also talked with Mr. Young on the phone, and I feel quite sure that he is ready and willing. . . . I would suggest that you ask the mine committee [of Local 52] to be patient a little longer, inasmuch as the coal is badly needed at this time."

The miners told Scanlan they'd wait till the first of April but no longer. On March 14 Medill was to attend a safety meeting in Belleville. Scanlan went there to discuss Centralia No. 5 with him. According to

Scanlan, "When I went up to his room he was surrounded with coal operators . . . all having whiskey, drinking, having a good time, and I couldn't talk to him then, and we attended the safety meeting [then] went . . . down to Otis Miller's saloon, and I stayed in the background drinking a few cokes and waited until the crowd thinned out, and went back up to his hotel room with him . . . I told him that the mine was in such condition that if the dust became ignited that it would sweep from one end of the mine to the other and probably kill every man in the mine, and his reply to me was, 'We will just have to take that chance.' " (Medill has denied these words but not the meeting.)

On the first of April the president of Local Union 52 asked Scanlan to attend the Local's meeting on April 4. The miners complained that the company had not cleaned up the mine and, further, that one of the face bosses, or foremen, had fired explosive charges while the entire shift of men was in the mine. There can be little doubt that to fire explosives on-shift in a mine so dusty was to invite trouble—in fact, this turned out to be what later caused the disaster—and now in April 1945 the union filed charges against Mine Manager Brown, asking the State Mining Board to revoke his certificate of competency (this would cost him his job and prevent his getting another in Illinois as a mine manager). Rowekamp wrote up the charges: ". . . And being the Mine is so dry and dusty it could of caused an explosion. . . ."

Weir went to Centralia on April 17, 1945, but only to investigate the charges against Brown, not to inquire into the condition of the mine. He told the miners they should have taken their charges to the state's attorney. Nearly a month passed before, on May 11, Weir wrote a memorandum to the Mining Board saying that the company's superintendent had admitted the shots had been fired on-shift but that this was done "in an emergency" and it wouldn't happen again; and the Board refused to revoke Manager Brown's certificate.

Meanwhile, on April 12 and 13, Scanlan had made his regular inspection and found conditions worse than in February. He told the Superintendent: "Now, Norman, you claim Chicago won't give you the time to shut your mine down and clean it up. Now, I am going to get you some time," and he gave him the choice of shutting the mine down completely or spending three days a week cleaning up. The superintendent, he said, replied that he didn't know, he'd have to "contact Chicago," but Scanlan replied: "I can't possibly wait for you to contact Chicago. It is about time that you fellows who operate the mines get big enough to operate your mines without contacting Chicago." So on Scanlan's recommendation the mine produced coal only four days a week and spent the remaining days cleaning up. For a time Scanlan was well satisfied with the results, but by June 25 he was again reporting excessive dust and Federal Inspector Perz was concurring: "No means are used to allay the dust." Following his October inspection Scanlan once more was moved to write a letter to Medill; but the only result was another routine letter from Weir to the company, unanswered.

Now, one must understand that, to be effective, both rock dusting and cleanup work must be maintained continuously. They were not at Centralia No. 5. By December of 1945 matters again came to a head. Scanlan wrote to Medill, saying that Local 52 wanted a sprinkling system installed to wet the coal, that Mine Manager Brown had said he could not order so "unusual" an expenditure, and that Brown's superior, Superintendent Prudent, "would not talk to me about it, walked away and left me standing." And Local 52 again attempted to take matters into its own hands. At a special meeting on December 12 the membership voted to prefer charges against both Mine Manager Brown and Superintendent Prudent. Rowekamp's official charge, typed on stationery of the Local, was followed next day by a letter, written in longhand on two sheets of dime-store notepaper, and signed by 28 miners (half of them, including Joe Bryant, subsequently killed in the dust explosion). At Springfield this communication too was duly stamped "Received." And another Scanlan report arrived.

Confronted with so many documents, Medill called a meeting of the Mining Board on December 21. Moreover, he called Scanlan to Springfield and told him to go early to the Leland Hotel, the gathering place of Republican politicians, and see Ben H. Schull, a coal operator and one of the operators' two men on the Mining Board. In his hotel room, Schull (according to Scanlan) said he wanted to discuss privately Scanlan's report on Centralia No. 5, tried to persuade him to withdraw his recommendation of a sprinkling system, and, when Scanlan refused, told him "you can come before the board." But when the Mining Board met in Medill's inner office, Scanlan was not called before it though he waited all day, and after the meeting he was told that the Board was appointing a special commission to go to Centralia and investigate.

On this commission were Weir, two state inspectors, and two members of the Mining Board itself, Schull and Murrell Reak. Reak, a miner himself, represented the United Mine Workers of America on the Mining Board. And Weir, too, owed his job to the UMWA but, oddly, he had worked for Bell & Zoller for twenty years before joining the Department, the last three as a boss, so his position was rather ambiguous. In fact, so unanimous were the rulings of the Mining Board that one cannot discern any management-labor cleavage at all but only what would be called in party politics bipartisan deals.

The commission had before it a letter from Superintendent Prudent and Manager Brown setting forth in detail the company's "absentee experience" and concluding with a veiled suggestion that the mine might be forced to close for good (once before, according to an inspector, the same company had abandoned a mine rather than go to the expense entailed in an inspector's safety recommendation). Weir wrote to Prudent, notifying him that the commission would visit Centralia on December 28 to investigate the charges against him and Brown; Medill wrote to the company's vice-president, Young, at Chicago ("You are being notified of this date so that you will have an opportunity to be present or designate some member of your staff to be present"); but Medill only told Rowekamp, "The committee has been appointed and after the investigation you will be advised of their findings and the action of the board"—he did not tell the Local when the commission would visit Centralia nor offer it opportunity to prove its charges.

Rowekamp, a motorman, recalls how he first learned of the special commission's visit. He was working in the mine and "Prudent told me to set out an empty and I did and they rode out." Prudent—remember, the commission was investigating charges against Prudent—led the commission through the mine. Rowekamp says, "They didn't see nothing. They didn't get back in the buggy runs where the dust was the worst; they stayed on the mainline." Even there they rode, they did not walk through the dust. Riding in a mine car, one must keep one's head down. In the washhouse that afternoon the men were angry. They waited a week or two, then wrote to Medill asking what had been done. On January 22, 1946, Medill replied: the Mining Board, adopting the views of the special commission, had found "insufficient evidence" to revoke the certificates of Prudent and Brown.

He did not elaborate. Next day, however, he sent to Scanlan a copy of the commission's report. It listed several important violations of the mining law: inadequate rock dusting, illegal practice in opening rooms, insufficient or improperly placed telephones, more than a hundred men working on a single split, or current, of air. In fact, the commission generally concurred with Scanlan, except that it did not emphasize dust nor recommend a sprinkling system. Thus in effect it overruled Scanlan on his sprinkling recommendation, a point to remember. It did find that the law was being violated yet it refused to revoke the certificates of the Superintendent and the Mine Manager, another point to remember. Weir has explained that the board felt that improvements requiring construction, such as splitting the airstream, would be made and that anyway "conditions there were no different than at most mines in the state." And this is a refrain that the company and the Department repeated in extenuation after the disaster. But actually could anything be more damning? The mine was no worse than most others; the mine blew up; therefore any might blow up!

IV

The miners at Centralia were not satisfied. "It come up at the meeting," Rowekamp recalls. Local 52 met two Wednesday nights a month in its bare upstairs hall. The officers sat at a big heavy table up front; the members faced them, sitting on folding chairs which the Local had bought secondhand from an undertaker. Attendance was heavier now than usual, the men were aroused, some were even telling their wives that the mine was dangerous. They wanted to do something. But what? The state had rebuffed them. Well, why did they not go now to the higher officials of their own union, the UMWA? Why not to John L. Lewis himself?

One of them has said, "You have to go through the real procedure to get to the right man, you got to start at the bottom and start climbing up, you see? If we write to Lewis, he'll refer us right back to Spud White." Spud White is Hugh White, the thick-necked president of the UMWA in Illinois (District 12), appointed by Lewis. Now, Lewis had suspended District 12's right to elect its own officers during the bloody strife of the early 1930s, when the members, disgusted with what they called his "dictator" methods and complaining of secret payrolls, expulsions, missing funds, stolen ballots, and leaders who turned up on operators' payrolls, had rebelled; in the end the Progressive Mine Workers was formed and Lewis retained tight control of the UMWA. A decade later the Illinois officers of UMWA demanded that he restore their self-government, but Lewis managed to replace them with his own men, including Spud White. By 1946 President White, a coal miner from the South, was consulting at high levels with Lewis, he was receiving $10,000 a year plus expenses (which usually equal salary), and he was maintaining a spacious home on a winding lane in the finest residential suburb of Springfield, a white house reached by a circular drive through weeping willows and evergreens.

Evidently the perplexed miners at Centralia already had appealed to District 12 for help, that is to White. Certainly Murrell Reak, the UMWA's man on the Mining Board and a close associate of White's, had asked Weir to furnish him with a copy of the findings of the special commission: "I want them so I may show the district UMWA. So they in turn may write Local Union down there, and show them that their charges are unfounded or rather not of a nature as to warrant the revocation of mine mgr. Certificate. . . ." Jack Ripon, the bulky vice-president of District 12 and White's right-hand man, said recently, "We heard there'd been complaints but we couldn't do a thing about it; it was up to the Mining Department to take care of it."

And yet in the past the UMWA has stepped in when the state failed to act. One unionist has said, "White could have closed that mine in twenty-four hours. All he'd have had to do was call up Medill and tell him he was going to pull every miner in the state if they didn't clean it up. It's the union's basic responsibility—if you don't protect your own wife and daughter, your neighbor down the street's not going to do it."

Perhaps the miners of Local 52 knew they must go it alone. They continued to address their official complaints to the State of Illinois. On February 26 Rowekamp wrote once more to Medill: "Dear Sir: At our regular meeting of local union 52. Motion made and second which carried for rec. secy. write you that the members of local union 52 are dissatisfied with the report of the special investigation commission. . . . " No answer. And so the members of Local 52 instructed Rowekamp to write to higher authority, to their Governor, Dwight H. Green.

V

It took him a long time. Elmer Moss kept asking if he'd finished it and Rowekamp recalls, "I'd tell him, Elmer, I can't do that fast, that's a serious letter, that'll take me a while." He wrote it out first in pencil and showed it to a couple of the boys and they thought it sounded fine. Then, sitting big and awkward at his cluttered little oak desk in the living room of his home outside town, he typed it, slowly and carefully—"Anything important as that I take my time so I don't make mistakes, it looks too sloppified." He used the official stationery of the Local, bearing in one corner the device of the union—crossed shovels and picks—and in the other "Our Motto—Justice for One and All." He impressed upon it the official seal—"I can write a letter on my own hook but I dassen't use the seal without it's official"—and in the washhouse the Local officers signed it. Rowekamp made a special trip to the post office to mail it. It was a two-page letter saying, in part:

Dear Governor Green:

We, the officers of Local Union No. 52, U.M.W. of A., have been instructed by the members . . . to write a letter to you in protest against the negligence and unfair practices of your department of mines and minerals . . . we want you to know that this is not a protest against Mr. Driscoll Scanlan . . . the best inspector that ever came to our mine. . . . But your mining board will not let him enforce the law or take the necessary action to protect our lives and health. This protest is against the men above Mr. Scanlan in your department of mines and minerals. In fact, Governor Green this is a plea to you, to please save our lives, to please make the department of mines and minerals enforce the laws at the No. 5 mine of the Centralia Coal Co. . . . before we have a dust explosion at this mine like just happened in Kentucky and West Virginia. For the last couple of years the policy of the department of mines and minerals toward us has been one of ignoring us. [The letter then recited the story of the useless special commission.] We are writing you, Governor Green, because we believe you want to give the people an honest administration and that you do not know how unfair your mining department is toward the men in this mine. Several years ago after a disaster at Gillespie we seen your pictures in the papers going down in the mine to make a personal investigation of the accident. We are giving you a chance to correct the conditions at this time that may cause a much worse disaster. . . . We will appreciate an early personal reply from you, stating your position in regard to the above and the enforcement of the state mining laws.

The letter closed "Very respectfully yours" and was signed by Jake Schmidt, president; Rowekamp, recording secretary; and Thomas Bush and Elmer Moss, mine committee. Today, of these, only Rowekamp is alive; all the others were killed in the disaster they foretold.

And now let us trace the remarkable course of this letter at Springfield.

It was stamped in red ink "Received March 9, 1946, Governor's Office." In his ornate thick-carpeted offices, Governor Green has three male secretaries (each of whom in turn has a secretary) and it was to one of these, John William Chapman, that the "save our lives" letter, as it came to be called, was routed. Two days later Chapman dictated a memorandum to Medill: ". . . it is my opinion that the Governor may be subjected to very severe criticism in the event that the facts complained of are true and that as a result of this condition some serious accident occurs at the mine. Will you kindly have this complaint carefully investigated so I can call the report of the investigation to the Governor's attention at the same time I show him this letter?" Chapman fastened this small yellow memo to the miners' letter and sent both to Medill. Although Medill's office is only about sixty yards from the Governor's, the message consumed two days in traversing the distance.

The messenger arrived at the Department of Mines and Minerals at 9:00 A.M. on March 13 and handed the "save our lives" letter and Chapman's memorandum to Medill's secretary. She duly stamped both "Received" and handed them to Medill. He and Weir discussed the matter, then Medill sent the original letter back to the Governor's office and dictated his reply to Chapman, blaming the war, recounting the activities of the special commission, saying: "The complaint sounds a good deal worse than it really is. The present condition at the mine is not any different than it has been during the past ten or fifteen years. . . . I would suggest the Governor advise Local Union No. 52, U.M.W. of A., that he is calling the matter to the attention of the State Mining Board with instructions that it be given full and complete consideration at their next meeting."

This apparently satisfied Chapman for, in the Governor's name, he dictated a letter to Rowekamp and Schmidt: "I [i.e., Governor Green] am calling your letter to the attention of the Director of the Department of Mines and Minerals with the request that he see that your complaint is taken up at the next meeting of the State Mining Board. . . ." This was signed with Governor Green's name but it is probable that Green himself never saw the "save our lives" letter until after the disaster more than a year later. Nor is there any evidence that the Mining Board ever considered the letter. In fact, nothing further came of it.

One of the most remarkable aspects of the whole affair was this: An aggrieved party (the miners) accused a second party (Medill's department) of acting wrongfully, and the higher authority to which it addressed its grievance simply, in effect, asked the accused if he were guilty and, when he replied he was not, dropped the matter. A logic, the logic of the administrative mind, attaches to Chapman's sending the complaint to the Department—the administrative mind has a pigeonhole for everything, matters which relate to law go to the Attorney General, matters which relate to mines go to the Department of Mines and Minerals, and that is that—but it is scarcely a useful logic when one of the agencies is itself accused of malfunction. Apparently it did not occur to Chapman to consult Inspector Scanlan or to make any other independent investigation.

And Jack Ripon, Spud White's second-in-command at the District UMWA, said recently, "If I get a letter here I turn it over to the department that's supposed to take care of it, and the same with Governor Green—he got some damn bad publicity he shouldn't have had, he can't know everything that's going on." Ripon's sympathy with Green is understandable—he must have known how Green felt, for he and Spud White received a copy of the same letter. Ripon says, "Oh, we got a copy of it. But it wasn't none of ours, it didn't tell us to do anything. So our hands was tied. What'd we do with it? I think we gave it to Reak." Perhaps Murrell Reak, the UMWA's man on the Mining Board, felt he already had dealt with this matter (it was Reak who, to Scanlan's astonishment, had joined the other members of the special commission in upholding the Superintendent and Mine Manager in their violations of the law and then had been so anxious to help White convince the members of Local 52 "that their charges are unfounded"). At any rate, Reak apparently did not call the Board's attention to the "save our lives" letter, even though it was a local of his own union which felt itself aggrieved. And White took no action either.

As for Medill, on the day he received the letter he called Scanlan to Springfield and, says Scanlan, "severely reprimanded" him. According to Scanlan, Medill "ordered me to cut down the size of my inspection report," because Medill thought that such long reports might alarm the miners, "those damn hunks" who couldn't read English (Medill denied the phrase); but Scanlan took this order to mean that Medill wanted him to "go easy" on the operators—"it is the same thing as ordering you to pass up certain things." And one day during this long controversy, Medill buttonholed Scanlan's political sponsor in a corridor of the Statehouse and said he intended to fire Scanlan; Scanlan's sponsor refused to sanction it and but for this, Scanlan was convinced, he would surely have lost his job.

VI

But now hundreds of miles away larger events were occurring which were to affect the fate of the miners at Centralia. In Washington, D.C., John L. Lewis and the nation's bituminous coal operators failed to reach an agreement and the miners struck, and on May 21, 1946, President Truman ordered the mines seized for government operation. Eight days later Lewis and Julius A. Krug, Secretary of the Interior, signed the famous Krug-Lewis Agreement. Despite strenuous protests by the operators, this agreement included a federal safety code. It was drawn up by the Bureau of Mines (a part of the U.S. Department of the Interior). And now for the first time in history the federal government could exercise police power over coal mine safety.

Thus far the efforts of the miners of Local 52 to thread the administrative maze in their own state had produced nothing but a snowfall of memoranda, reports, letters, and special findings. Let us now observe this new federal machinery in action. We shall learn nothing about how to prevent a disaster but we may learn a good deal about the administrative process.

"Government operation of the mines" meant simply that the operators bossed their own mines for their own profit as usual but the UMWA had a work contract with the government, not the operators. To keep the 2,500 mines running, Secretary Krug created a new agency, the Coal Mines Administration. CMA was staffed with only 245 persons, nearly all naval personnel ignorant of coal mining. Theirs was paper work. For technical advice they relied upon the Bureau of Mines plus a handful of outside experts. More than two months passed before the code was put into effect, on July 29, 1946, and not until November 4 did Federal Inspector Perz reach Centralia to make his first enforceable inspection of Centralia No. 5. Observe, now, the results.

After three days at the mine, Perz went home and wrote out a "preliminary report" on a mimeographed form, listing 13 "major violations" of the safety code. He mailed this to the regional office of the Bureau of Mines at Vincennes, Indiana. There it was corrected for grammar, spelling, etc., and typed; copies then were mailed out to the Superintendent of the mine (to be posted on the bulletin board), the CMA in Washington, the CMA's regional office at Chicago, the District 12 office of the UMWA at Springfield, the UMWA international headquarters at Washington, the Bureau of Mines in Washington, and the Illinois Department at Springfield. While all this was going on, Perz was at home, preparing his final report, a lengthy document listing 57 violations of the safety code, 21 of them major and 36 minor. This handwritten final report likewise went to the Bureau at Vincennes where it was corrected, typed, and forwarded to the Bureau's office in College Park, Maryland. Here the report was "reviewed," then sent to the Director of the Bureau at Washington. He made any changes he deemed necessary, approved it, and ordered it processed. Copies were then distributed to the same seven places that had received the preliminary report, except that the UMWA at Springfield received two copies so that it could forward one to Local 52. (All this was so complicated that the Bureau devised a "flow sheet" to keep track of the report's passage from hand to hand.)

We must not lose sight of the fact that in the end everybody involved was apprised of Perz's findings: that the Centralia Company was violating the safety code and that hazards resulted. The company, the state, and the union had known this all along and done nothing, but what action now did the new enforcing agency take, the CMA?

Naval Captain N. H. Collisson, the Coal Mines Administrator, said that the copy of the inspector's preliminary report was received at his office in Washington "by the head of the Production and Operations Department of my headquarters staff . . . Lieutenant Commander Stull. . . . Lieutenant Commander Stull would review such a report, discuss the matter with the Bureau of Mines as to the importance of the findings, and then . . . await the final report"—unless the preliminary report showed that "imminent danger" existed, in which case he would go immediately to Captain Collisson and, presumably, take "immediate action." And during all this activity in Washington, out in Chicago at the CMA's area office a Captain Yates also "would receive a copy of the report. His duty would be to acquaint himself with the findings there. If there was a red check mark indicating it fell within one of the three categories which I shall discuss later, he would detail a man immediately to the mine. If it indicated imminent danger . . . he would move immediately." The three categories deemed sufficiently important to be marked with "a red check mark" were all major hazards but the one which killed 111 men at Centralia No. 5 was not among them.

These, of course, were only CMA's first moves as it bestirred itself. But to encompass all its procedures is almost beyond the mind of man. Let us skip a few and see what actually resulted. The CMA in Washington received Perz's preliminary report November 14. Eleven days later it wrote to the company ordering it to correct one of the 13 major violations Perz found (why it said nothing about the others is not clear). On November 26 the CMA received Perz's final report and on November 29 it again wrote to the company, ordering it to correct promptly *all* violations and sending copies of the directive to the Bureau of Mines and the UMWA. Almost simultaneously it received from Superintendent Niermann a reply to its first order (Niermann had replaced Prudent, who had left the company's employ): "Dear Sir: In answer to your CMA8-gz of November 25, 1946, work has been started to correct the violation of article 5, section 3c, of the Federal Mine Safety Code, but has been discontinued, due to . . . a strike. . . ." This of course did not answer the CMA's second letter ordering correction of all 57 violations, nor was any answer forthcoming, but not until two months later, on January 29, 1947, did the CMA repeat its order and tell the company to report its progress by February 14.

This brought a reply from the company official who had been designated "operating manager" during the period of government operation, H. F. McDonald. McDonald, whose office was in Chicago, had risen to the presidency of the Centralia Coal Company and of the Bell & Zoller Coal Company through the sales department; after the Centralia disaster he told a reporter, "Hell, I don't know anything about a coal mine." Now he reported to CMA that "a substantial number of reported violations have been corrected and others are receiving our attention and should be corrected as materials and manpower become available." For obvious reasons, CMA considered this reply inadequate and on February 21 told McDonald to supply detailed information. Three days later McDonald replied ("Re file CMA81-swr"): He submitted a detailed report—he got it from Vice-President Young, who got it from the new General Superintendent, Walter J. Johnson—but McDonald told the CMA that this report was a couple of weeks old and he promised to furnish further details as soon as he could get them. The CMA on March 7 acknowledged this promise but before any other correspondence arrived to enrich file CMA81-swr, the mine blew up.

Now, the Krug-Lewis Agreement set up two methods of circumventing this cumbersome administrative machinery. If Inspector Perz had found what the legalese of the Agreement called "imminent danger," he could have ordered the men removed from the mine immediately (this power was weakened since it was also vested in the Coal Mines Administrator, the same division of authority that hobbled the state enforcers). But Perz did not report "imminent danger." And indeed how could he? The same hazardous conditions had obtained for perhaps twenty years and the mine hadn't blown up. The phrase is stultifying.

In addition, the Krug-Lewis Agreement provided for a safety committee of miners, selected by each local union and empowered to inspect the mine, to make safety recommendations to the management, and, again in case of "an immediate danger," to order the men out of the mine (subject to CMA review). But at Centralia No. 5 several months elapsed before Local 52 so much as appointed a safety committee, and even after the disaster the only surviving member of the committee didn't know what his powers were. The UMWA District officers at Springfield had failed to instruct their Locals in the rights which had been won for them. And confusion was compounded because two separate sets of safety rules were in use—the federal and the state—and in some instances one was the more stringent, in other instances, the other.

Meanwhile another faraway event laid another burden upon the men in the mine: John L. Lewis's combat with Secretary Krug. It ended, as everyone knows, in a federal injunction sought at President Truman's order and upheld by the U.S. Supreme Court, which forbade Lewis to order his miners to strike while the government was operating the mines. (Subsequently Lewis and the UMWA were fined heavily.) The members of Local 52 thought, correctly or not, that the injunction deprived them of their last weapon in their fight to get the mine cleaned up—a wildcat strike. A leader of Local 52 has said, "Sure we could've wildcatted it—and we'd have had the Supreme Court and the government and the whole public down on our necks."

The miners tried the state once more: Medill received a letter December 10, 1946, from an individual miner who charged that the company's mine examiner (a safety man) was not doing what the law required. Earlier Medill had ignored Scanlan's complaint about this but now he sent a department investigator, who reported that the charges were true and that Mine Manager Brown knew it, that Superintendent Niermann promised to consult Vice-President Young in Chicago, that other hazards existed, including dust. Weir wrote a routine letter and this time Niermann replied: The examiner would do his job properly. He said nothing about dust. This letter and one other about the same time, plus Young's earlier equivocal response to Medill's direct appeal, are the only company compliance letters on record.

There was yet time for the miners to make one more try. On February 24, 1947, the safety committee, composed of three miners, wrote a short letter to the Chicago area office of the Coal Mines Administration: "The biggest grievance is dust. . . ." It was written in longhand by Paul Compers (or so it is believed: Compers and one of the two other committee members were killed in the disaster a month later) and Compers handed it to Mine Manager Brown on February 27. But Brown did not forward it to the CMA; in fact he did nothing at all about it.

VII

And now almost at the last moment, only six days before the mine blew up, some wholly new facts transpired. Throughout this whole history one thing has seemed inexplicable: the weakness of the pressure put on the company by Medill's Department of Mines and Minerals. On March 19, 1947, the St. Louis *Post-Dispatch* broke a story that seemed to throw some light upon it. An Illinois coal operator had been told by the state inspector who inspected his mine that Medill had instructed him to solicit money for the Republican Chicago mayoralty campaign. And soon more facts became known about this political shakedown.

Governor Dwight H. Green, a handsome, likeable politician, had first made his reputation as the young man who prosecuted Al Capone. By 1940 he looked like the white hope of Illinois Republicans. Campaigning for the governorship, Green promised to rid the state of the Democratic machine ("there will never be a Green machine"). He polled more votes in Illinois than Roosevelt; national Republican leaders began to watch him. Forthwith he set about building one of the most formidable machines in the nation. This task, together with the concomitant plans of Colonel Robert R. McCormick of the Chicago *Tribune* and others to make him President or Vice-President, has kept him occupied ever since. He has governed but little, permitting subordinates to run things. Re-elected in 1944, he reached the peak of his power in 1946 when his machine succeeded in reducing the control of the Democratic machine over Chicago. Jubilant, Governor Green handpicked a ward leader to run for mayor in April of 1947 and backed him hard.

And it was only natural that Green's henchmen helped. Among these was Medill. "Somebody," says Medill, told him he was expected to raise "$15,000 or $20,000." On January 31, 1947, he called all his mine inspectors to the state mine rescue station in Springfield (at state expense), and told them—according to Inspector Scanlan who was present—that the money must be raised among the coal operators "and that he had called up four operators the previous day and two of them had already come through with a thousand dollars . . . and that he was going to contact the major companies, and we was to contact the independent companies and the small companies." Medill's version varied slightly: he said he told the inspectors that, as a Republican, he was interested in defeating the Democrats in Washington and Chicago, that if they found anybody of like mind it would be all right to tell them where to send their money, that all contributions must be voluntary.

After the meeting Scanlan felt like resigning but he thought perhaps Governor Green did not know about the plan and he recalled that once he had received a letter from Green (as did all state employees) asking his aid in giving the people an honest administration: Scanlan had replied to the Governor "that I had always been opposed to corrupt, grafting politicians and that I wasn't going to be one myself; and I received a nice acknowledgment . . . the Governor . . . told me that it was such letters as mine that gave him courage to carry on. . . ." Scanlan solicited no contributions from the coal operators.

But other inspectors did, and so did a party leader in Chicago. So did Medill: he says that his old friend David H. Devonald, operating vice-president of the huge Peabody Coal Company, gave him $1,000 and John E. Jones, a leading safety engineer, contributed $50 (Jones works for another of the Big Six operators and of him more later). No accounting ever has been made of the total collected. The shakedown did not last long. According to Medill, another of Governor Green's "close advisers" told Medill that the coal operators were complaining that he and his inspectors were putting pressure on them for donations and if so he'd better stop it. He did, at another conference of the inspectors on March 7.

Since no Illinois law forbids a company or an individual to contribute secretly to a political campaign we are dealing with a question of political morality, not legality. The Department of Mines and Minerals long has been a political agency. An inspector is a political appointee and during campaigns he is expected to contribute personally, tack up candidates' posters, and haul voters to the polls. Should he refuse, his local political boss would have him fired. (Soliciting money from the coal operators, however, apparently was something new for inspectors.) Today sympathetic Springfield politicians say: "Medill was just doing what every other department was doing and always has done, but he got a tough break." But one must point out that Medill's inspectors were charged with safeguarding lives, a more serious duty than that of most state employees, and that in order to perform this duty they had to police the coal operators, and that it was from these very operators that Medill suggested they might obtain money. A United States Senator who investigated the affair termed it "reprehensible."

What bearing, now, did this have on the Centralia disaster? Nobody, probably, collected from the Centralia Coal Company. But the shakedown is one more proof—stronger than most—that Governor Green's department had reason to stay on friendly terms with the coal operators when, as their policeman, it should have been aloof. As a miner at Centralia said recently: "If a coal company gives you a thousand dollars, they're gonna expect something in return."

Here lies Green's responsibility—not that, through a secretary's fumble, he failed to act on the miners' appeal to "save our lives" but rather that, while the kingmakers were shunting him around the nation making speeches, back home his loyal followers were busier building a rich political machine for him than in administering the state for him. Moreover, enriching the Green machine dovetailed nicely with the personal ambitions of Medill and others, and Green did not restrain them. By getting along with his old friends, the wealthy operators, Medill enhanced his personal standing. Evidence exists that Bell & Zoller had had a hand in getting him appointed Director, and remember, Weir had worked as a Bell & Zoller boss. By nature Medill was no zealous enforcer of laws. As for the inspectors, few of them went out of their way to look for trouble; some inspectors after leaving the Department have obtained good jobs as coal company executives. Anyway, as one inspector has said, "If you tried to ride 'em, they'd laugh at you and say, 'Go ahead, I'll just call up Springfield.' " As one man has said, "It was a cozy combination that worked for everybody's benefit, everybody except the miners." And the miners' man on the Board, Murrell Reak of the UMWA, did not oppose the combination. Nor did Green question it.

As the Chicago campaign ground to a close, down at Centralia on March 18 Federal Inspector Perz was making another routine inspection. General Superintendent Johnson told him the company had ordered pipe for a sprinkler system months earlier but it hadn't arrived, "that there would be a large expenditure involved there . . . they had no definite arrangements just yet . . . but he would take it up with the higher officials of the company" in Chicago. Scanlan and Superintendent Niermann were there too; they stayed in the bare little mine office, with its rickety furniture and torn window shades, till 7:30 that night. No rock dusting had been done for nearly a year but now the company had a carload of rock dust underground and Scanlan got the impression it would be applied over the next weekend. (It wasn't.) Perz, too, thought Johnson "very conscientious . . . very competent." Scanlan typed out his report—he had resorted wearily to listing a few major recommendations and adding that previous recommendations "should be complied with"—and mailed it to Springfield. Perz went home and wrote out his own report, acknowledging that 17 hazards had been corrected but making 52 recommendations most of which he had made in November (the company and the CMA were still corresponding over that November report). Perz finished writing on Saturday morning and mailed the report to the Vincennes office, which presumably began processing it Monday.

The wheels had been turning at Springfield, too, and on Tuesday, March 25, Weir signed a form letter to Brown setting forth Scanlan's latest recommendations: "The Department endorses. . . ." But that day, at 3:26 P.M., before the outgoing-mail box in the Department was emptied, Centralia Mine No. 5 blew up.

VIII

Scanlan was inside a mine at Venedy when his wife called him. He hurried to Centralia and so did others—Perz, Medill, Young, union and company and state and federal officials. They went sleepless day after day, and on the minds of many lay heavily the knowledge of what had gone before. Some of the warnings—Scanlan's and Perz's reports—were still thumbtacked to the bulletin board outside the washhouse.

Tempers grew short. Medill and Scanlan engaged in an unseemly row over rescue operations. Scanlan talked bitterly to newspapermen. Governor Green's office announced he was ill with a cold in Chicago, confined to the Union League Club. A Democratic legislator demanded his impeachment and newspapers attacked him. He went to Centralia. In the hotel there he was confronted by Rowekamp (Rowekamp met him reluctantly, at the behest of Spud White, the UMWA president now suddenly greatly interested in Centralia); neither had much to say, and Rowekamp felt sorry for the Governor, ill with a cold. Green announced he was appointing a committee to investigate, told Medill he must resign, overrode Medill's objections, announced the appointment of Medill's successor, and departed. Green's candidate lost the Chicago mayoralty; most experts said the explosion was simply the *coup de grâce* to his ambitions, and perhaps to Green's. In Washington, Lewis prepared to rumble, and Secretary Krug's aides tried to locate Perz's last report, which was somewhere being processed. Investigations began. Politicians scrambled desperately to deflect blame. The public uproar mounted and mounted.

And around the tipple in the snow stood the silent crowd of friends and relatives, wives and children of the men underground. The women sat in the washhouse beneath their husbands' clothing, waiting. They did not give up hope even when the first sixteen bodies were found and they were told that the rest were trapped much farther back. But most of the miners knew the truth. Nobody was rescued alive after the first day. Those who died of gas were horribly bloated, those whom violence killed were mangled beyond facial identification. All the ambulances in Centralia and nearby towns had arrived, and they stood drawn up in a semicircle before the tipple, their drivers sitting behind the steering wheels, having a smoke and running the engine to keep the heater going; and now and then the bell at the shaft would sound and the cage would come rumbling up and men would carry a stretcher off it, and one of the ambulances would move up fast, stop beside the shaft-head, then whirl away to the Greyhound bus garage, which had been converted into a temporary morgue; and sometimes several bodies would be brought up at one time and the ambulances would move up, stop, and speed away as smartly as though on military maneuvers. As one, a shiny big limousine, departed bearing its dead miner, a friend of his in the crowd said: "I bet it's the only time he ever rode in a Cadillac." Even after the battered bodies began to come to the surface, the wives still hoped. Might their men not be holed up, awaiting rescue?

One of these men was Joe Bryant. His wife was a very large woman of forty-four, with weary features but soft, kind eyes, who had been reared on a farm, a woman who had borne eleven children to Joe Bryant and who was pregnant with the twelfth. They lived in a little four-room house at a dreary gray settlement north of Centralia called Glenridge, a cluster of houses huddled around the shaft of another coal mine, the Glenridge Mine. Joe Bryant had been born near the mine 48 years earlier and at 14 had gone to work in it. At 24 he got married. Later he took other jobs, and he worked five years in the Indiana oil fields. "But the only steady job he could depend on was the mines," his wife says, and so he went back. The pay was better than anywhere else and surely he needed money, for their first child, Harold, had been born a year after their marriage, their second, Melvin, a year later, and after that nine more were born, one every couple of years or so (two died in infancy). "The big family kept us a skimpin' and a goin'," Mrs. Bryant said. Sometimes in the nineteen-thirties Joe Bryant's weekly pay was five dollars. In 1942 they bought a vacant weed-grown lot beside a gravel road and Joe and his oldest sons, Harold and Melvin, built a small house for about $1,000.

Harold Bryant, Joe's oldest boy, got out of the Army on December 5, 1945, and Melvin on the 18th. Their father got them jobs at the mine, where he was now a motorman. During the strike in the spring of 1946—which ended in government seizure—Melvin went to work at the Illinois Central shops, and he stayed there. Harold, however, returned to the mine. One night that January, Harold had met a baby-sitter at some friends' house, a small, sharp girl of fifteen; and in September, Ruth being then sixteen and out of grade school, he married her. They rented rooms at Glenridge not far from the house of his father, Joe Bryant; soon Ruth was pregnant, as was Mrs. Joe Bryant. Harold made about $120 every two weeks. He and Ruth went to movies a good deal; he liked Westerns—"he didn't care much about love movies," his bride recalls. They didn't dance. One or two nights a week they'd walk over to Fritz's Place, a small tavern in Glenridge with a juke box and three slot machines, the walls hung with signs like "Keep Smiling" and "Boisterous and Profane Language Is Objectionable." Nights they stayed home they went to bed at seven. Saturday afternoons they'd drive to Centralia to shop for clothes for the baby that was coming. Saturday nights they'd go over to his parents' home; Sundays they'd go to hers; Monday morning at 5:45 he'd go back to work. One day down in the mine a chunk of rock fell from the roof and hit Harold on the neck but did not hurt him seriously and then a little later he got his foot smashed between the cars underground. It frightened Ruth. "I always was just scared of the mine. I always wanted him to quit. But he said he couldn't find no other job paid as good. And he always said if he was going to die he might as well die in the mine." He was twenty-three.

On the morning of the explosion, Harold drove his V-8 coupé over to his father's house. His foot was still swollen—he hadn't laced his shoe—and his father didn't feel very good either, he'd had all his teeth pulled. Joe's wife asked them why they didn't lay off but Joe said he thought the union was going to pull them out on strike soon and they'd better work while they could. Harold agreed; he and his bride wanted to build a home. So they got into Joe's Model A and drove to the mine.

Like many miners' wives, Mrs. Joe Bryant thought a good deal about death in the mine, not consciously perhaps, but the thought was always there. Joe was a quiet man. "He didn't talk to me much about the mine. I guess he figured I had the children and had problems of my own and he wouldn't bother me with his." Her second son Melvin heard about the explosion soon after he got off work at the Illinois Central shops at 3:30. He picked up his wife at the dress factory and drove out to his mother's house. "He asked me if I heard it yet," Mrs. Bryant recalls, "and I hadn't. I was fixing supper, frying potatoes and sausage." Melvin went over to Harold's house and said, "Ruth, there's been an explosion at the mine." Ruth, who was just seventeen, recalls, "Something told me I wouldn't see him no more." They all went over to Mrs. Joe Bryant's and sat down to wait for news.

They made a houseful. Neighbors dropped in throughout the evening to see if Mrs. Bryant had heard anything and all night long Melvin kept driving Harold's V-8 back and forth to the mine, but there was no news. Next morning at 9:00 A.M. Ruth's sister came to the house. She took Mrs. Bryant's oldest daughter into the kitchen and whispered to her, then *she* took Mrs. Bryant out into the kitchen. Mrs. Bryant recalls, "It was Harold, they'd found him, they'd talked to a man who had seen him. I just said, well, I guess it's true." Nobody knew how to tell Ruth, Harold's bride and widow, so nobody did tell her; if she went into the kitchen the whispering stopped.

That night two "merchant men," business men from Centralia, arrived; they asked for Harold's description, and they were more interested in what his clothes looked like than in what his face looked like. They intended to talk to Harold's mother, but his bride and widow Ruth spoke up. "I thought it was my place to." They went away. "Everybody knew he was gone but me," Ruth recalls. She waited all week. She recalls, "When they brought the last bunch up, I got in the car even if I don't know how to drive and I said I will go myself if somebody don't take me." So they took her to the vast Greyhound bus garage but the man in charge said she was in no condition to go in. Her brother went in and returned a few minutes later with a belt. It was Harold's. "He's got on a red jacket," her brother added, and Ruth said, "It's him, then," and they went back to his mother's house at Glenridge. She never saw his body; he had been working right at the heart of the explosion. "I'm glad he went like he did, not like his father did."

His father, Joe—what of him? They had waited all week, from Tuesday afternoon till past midnight Saturday, and then the business men returned—how had Joe Bryant been dressed? Mrs. Bryant said he had been wearing overalls and a white sweatshirt—she was sure because she had just fixed them for him, and she wept, remembering—and he had been carrying a pocket knife, a white cigarette case, and a whistle with a chain on it. The two business men left, and Mrs. Bryant, knowing now for sure her oldest son was dead, waited the rest of that night to hear whether her husband was dead. At 9:00 A.M. the same business men returned; they had Joe's cigarette case and his whistle.

They brought something else, too, some notes Joe Bryant had written. He had been working with a gang of fourteen men about a half-mile south of the flash point and at the day's end they were sitting in the mine cars, ready to head for the shaft, when the concussion hit them. They dropped their aluminum dinner buckets and scrambled from the cars and into the labyrinth of rooms and corridors. Apparently they were trying to grope their way to another entry. They stopped in a room at the face of the coal, lay down on the fireclay floor where the air would longest support life, and wrote notes on old envelopes and pages torn from the timebook.

A few attempted to describe what was going on—"I am fine at 5:30 P.M. It looks better, getting some air"—but most were worried about what their wives would do—"See about security insurance" and "if I don't make it, sell the house and go live with your folks"—or they were preoccupied with long thoughts—"Please get the baby baptized. . . . Well, I love you all and please take care of them and raise them a good Christian"—and all said this or something like it: "Dear wife: God bless you and your baby." As for Joe Bryant, he must have taken quite a long time to write his notes in the complete darkness; the letters are formed carefully, not scribbled. One of his notes was addressed to some of his children: "Sammie Raymond Be good Boys Jackie [this was his nickname for Harold, his oldest child who was, though Joe Bryant didn't know it, already dead a half-mile away] Melvin Help Mom Please your father Joe Bryant O Lord Help me."

On another page of the timebook he wrote to Mrs. Bryant: "Dear Wife fro Give me Please all love you Be shure and don't sign any Paper see Vick Ostero [a warning against signing away the compensation money which would be due her because of his death, so imminent] My Dear wife good By. Name Baby Joe so you will have a Joe love all dad."

The baby was born three months later, it was a girl but she named it Joedy.

IX

The last of the bodies was recovered at 5:30 A.M. on the fifth day after the explosion. On "Black Monday" the flag on the new city hall flew at half staff and all the businesses in town closed. Already the funerals had begun, 111 of them. John L. Lewis cried that the 111 were "murdered by the criminal negligence" of Secretary Krug and declared a national six-day "mourning period" during this Holy Week, and though some said he was only achieving by subterfuge what the courts had forbidden him—a strike and defiance of Krug—nonetheless he made the point that in the entire nation only two soft coal mines had been complying completely with the safety code; and so Krug closed the mines.

Six separate investigations began, two to determine what had happened and four to find out why. Federal and state experts agreed, in general, that the ignition probably had occurred at the extreme end, or face, of the First West Entry, that it was strictly a coal-dust explosion, that the dust probably was ignited by an explosive charge which had been tamped and fired in a dangerous manner—fired by an open-flame fuse, tamped with coal dust—and that the resulting local explosion was propagated by coal dust throughout four working sections of the mine, subsiding when it reached rock-dusted areas.

The four broader investigations sought to determine who was to blame and how another such disaster might be prevented. But months passed before anything came of them. Let us now see how in the meanwhile the "reconstituted" state Department of Mines and Minerals was functioning.

To replace Medill, Green had appointed not a politician but, temporarily, the head of the Department of Mining and Metallurgical Engineering at the University of Illinois, Harold L. Walker. But Weir, though soon he was indicted, remained as Assistant Director and the inspectors, including those who had collected campaign funds, stayed too.

On July 24, 1947, a gas explosion in another mine—the Old Ben Coal Corporation's No. 8 mine near West Frankfort—killed 27 men. They had been "pulling pillars"—extracting coal previously left to support the roof—near some caved-in abandoned workings. Gas formed in the caved area and no fresh ventilation reached it to dissipate it. It was ignited, perhaps by a miner's smoking (illegal in a gassy mine).

John E. Jones, the widely-known Safety Director of Old Ben (who had given Medill a campaign contribution), said the accident looked like an act of God. Walker said he could find no violation of the state law (except for smoking, and any man whose cigarette caused the explosion was dead). Murrell Reak, the UMWA's man on the Mining Board, said he found no violation of the law at all. So once again the trinity was unanimous. But the department's records show that the mine had been inspected only twice in 1947 before the explosion, not three times as the law requires. Moreover the safety code in the UMWA's contract with the operators was being violated. Yet John L. Lewis, personally visiting the scene of this second disaster in four months, was silent. Why? Well, it is worth noting that Lewis's brother, Howard Lewis, was a superintendent at the mine. By contrast, when a few days later a gas explosion at still another mine killed three men, the UMWA demanded that the night mine manager's certificate of competency be suspended; and although in this latter case 286 of the 300 men who worked for the mine manager signed a petition defending him, this time the Mining Board put through the suspension (though it reinstated him later).

Subsequently, Governor Green replaced Walker with a new permanent director, a management man. And Scanlan has since resigned in disgust.

And what resulted from all the investigations into the Centralia disaster? The Washington County Grand Jury returned no-bills—that is, refused to indict Inspector Scanlan and five company officials ranging upward in authority through Brown, Niermann, Johnson, Young, and McDonald. The Grand Jury did indict the Centralia Coal Company, as a corporation, on two counts of "wilful neglect" to comply with the mining law—failing to rock dust and working more than 100 men on a single split of air—and it also indicted Medill and Weir for "palpable omission of duty." The company pleaded nolo contendere—it did not wish to dispute the charge—and was fined the maximum: $500 on each count, a total of $1,000 (or less than $10 per miner's life lost). The law also provides a jail sentence of up to six months but of course you can't put a corporation in jail.

At this writing the indictments against Medill and Weir are still pending, and amid interesting circumstances. Bail for Medill was provided by Charles E. Jones, John W. Spence, G. C. Curtis, and H. B. Thompson; and all of these men, oddly enough, are connected with the oil and gas division of the Department from which Medill was fired. And one of them is also one of Medill's defense attorneys. But this is not all. Medill and Weir filed a petition for a change of venue, supported by numerous affidavits of Washington County residents that prejudice existed. These affidavits were collected by three inspectors for the oil and gas division. They succeeded in getting the trial transferred to Wayne County, which is dominated by a segment of Governor Green's political organization led locally by one of these men, Spence. Not in recent memory in Illinois has the conviction of a Department head on a similar charge been sustained, and there is little reason to suppose that Medill or Weir will be convicted. Medill performed an act of great political loyalty when he shouldered most of the blame at Centralia, in effect stopping the investigation before it reached others above him, and this may be his reward.

Why did nobody close the Centralia mine before it exploded? A difficult question. Medill's position (and some investigators') was that Inspector

Scanlan could have closed it. And, legally, this is true: The mining law expressly provided that an inspector could close a mine which persisted in violating the law. But inspectors have done so very rarely, only in exceptional circumstances, and almost always in consultation with the Department. Scanlan felt that had he closed the Centralia mine Medill simply would have fired him and appointed a more tractable inspector. Moreover, the power to close was not his exclusively: it also belonged to the Mining Board. (And is not this divided authority one of the chief factors that produced the disaster?) Robert Weir has said, "We honestly didn't think the mine was dangerous enough to close." This seems fantastic, yet one must credit it. For if Scanlan really had thought so, surely he would have closed it, even though a more pliable inspector reopened it. So would the federal authorities, Medill, or the company itself. And surely the miners would not have gone to work in it.

Governor Green's own fact-finding committee laid blame for the disaster upon the Department, Scanlan, and the company. The Democrats in the Illinois joint legislative committee submitted a minority report blaming the company, Medill, Weir, and Green's administration for "the industrial and political crime. . . ."; the Republican majority confessed itself unable to fix blame. After a tremendous pulling and hauling by every special interest, some new state legislation was passed as a result of the accident, but nothing to put teeth into the laws: violations still are misdemeanors (except campaign solicitation by inspectors, a felony); it is scarcely a serious blow to a million-dollar corporation to be fined $1,000. Nor does the law yet charge specific officers of the companies—rather than the abstract corporations—with legal responsibility, so it is still easy for a company official to hide behind a nebulous chain of command reaching up to the stratosphere of corporate finance in Chicago or St. Louis. It is hard to believe that compliance with any law can be enforced unless violators can be jailed.

As for the Congress of the United States, it did next to nothing. The Senate subcommittee recommended that Congress raise safety standards and give the federal government power to enforce that standard—"Immediate and affirmative action is imperative." But Congress only ordered the

Bureau of Mines to report next session on whether mine operators were complying voluntarily with federal inspectors' recommendations.

The subcommittee said the nation has a stake in coal mine safety. We need coal. But young men are not going into the mines, for mining coal is America's most dangerous trade. About 1,887 miners have been killed at work *each year* since 1910. Mechanization has increased the hazards but safety has not advanced. The coal industry is backward, economically sick, chaotic.

One must conclude that coal miners generally are not as safe as the operators could make them, that it would cost money to make them safer, and that it is difficult to expect mine owners to be eager to incur such expenses at the risk of financial failure. But one must conclude also that so long as men go under the earth to get coal they must be safeguarded, and that if costs (or indifference) deter the operators from safeguarding them voluntarily, some other agency must enforce safety. Above all it is clear that, whatever agency may be assigned this task, some one person must be clearly charged with responsibility. When many persons and agencies are involved, as a witness told the Senate subcommittee, "What is everybody's business is nobody's business."

It also seems clear that no board in Springfield or Washington can decide whether a mine is dangerous, and this means that the inspector, whether state or federal, must be given the power to close a mine. But there must be assurance that one fine morning your inspector, needing money to meet a mortgage payment on his home, will not abuse his great power. Two ways to guard against this appear open: To make his decisions reviewable by an absent board (with public hearings mandatory), and to pay the inspectors well, raise high their qualifications, and make their appointments permanent during good behavior and beyond the reach of party politicians.

But all this may fail. Well, then, who benefits by the safety laws? Obviously, the miners. If we cannot expect much of petty politicians with campaigns to run, nor of operators with profits to earn, can we not turn, finally, to the miners themselves? Indeed, here, as almost nowhere else, is an opportunity for a labor union to demonstrate its usefulness. We can "take the Department out of politics," we can jail the operators who violate the law, we can clarify the authority of government bureaus, and still the best safeguard that the miners will have is a powerful, vigilant union sincere in its single-minded desire to protect the lives of its members. But the UMWA has no effective safety program, and it has consistently dodged responsibility. White, asked by the Senate subcommittee for suggestions on legislation, replied, "Well, Senator, I have not given that any study." In Illinois the union bargained away its right to improve the mining law: in 1941 it agreed with the operators that neither would seek to change the law without consent of the other. (Again, one is reminded of the "cozy combination that works to everybody's advantage except the miners'.") John L. Lewis used the Centralia disaster only as a club in his personal feud with Secretary Krug, not as a weapon in the broad battle for mine safety; and White did nothing but echo Lewis. Before the explosion neither had done a thing to help the miners. It was afterward that they were very righteous, and Lewis cried, "There is too much blood on our coal."

After the Centralia disaster each man responsible had his private hell, and to escape it each found his private scapegoat—the wartime manpower shortage, the material shortage, another official, the miners, or, in the most pitiable cases, "human frailty." Surely a strange destiny took Dwight Green from a federal courtroom where, a young crusader, he overthrew Capone to a hotel in Centralia where, fifteen years older, he came face to face with William Rowekamp, who wanted to know why Green had done nothing about the miners' plea to "save our lives." But actually responsibility here transcends individuals. The miners at Centralia, seeking somebody who would heed their conviction that their lives were in danger, found themselves confronted with officialdom, a huge organism scarcely mortal. The State Inspector, the Federal Inspector, the State Board, the Federal CMA, the company officials—all these forever invoked "higher authority," they forever passed from hand to hand a stream of memoranda and letters, decisions and laws and rulings, and they lost their own identities. As one strives to fix responsibility for the disaster, again and again one is confronted, as were the miners, not with any individual but with a host of individuals fused into a vast, unapproachable, insensate organism. Perhaps this immovable juggernaut is the true villain in the piece. Certainly all those in authority were too remote from the persons whose lives they controlled. And this is only to confess once more that in making our society complex we have made it unmanageable.

X

And how is Mrs. Joe Bryant faring, she with seven children at home under eighteen, including Joe Bryant's new daughter, Joedy, the daughter he never saw? "There ain't much to say," she says. "It don't pay to say much. We was pretty lucky—our home ain't fixed up like we'd want it, it ain't much, but we own it." Like other widows with children, Mrs. Bryant received in lump sums $1,000 from the UMWA's new health and welfare fund and nearly as much from other private and union sources. Funeral expenses and bills took most of this. As income, for about the next five years she will receive about $44 a week—$20 Social Security and $24 state industrial compensation. Then the $24 will stop, leaving only $20 Social Security. This too will end when the children become eighteen; after that there will be nothing at all for her until she is sixty-five. "The girls will help me out, I guess," she says. "We been a gettin' by. I ain't very much on spendin' money."

On the walls now hang two new pictures, tinted in color and framed in gilt, one of her son Harold in his corporal's uniform, the other of her husband in his working clothes; to them are affixed little metal plates: "Know Ye These Presents Certify That This is an Heirroom Portrait of Joe Bryant made from a photograph taken in the year 1935 and faithfully portrayed by the artist in a manner and quality befitting a work to be passed on to future generations as a priceless heirloom." Mrs. Bryant says, "A man from Chicago came round selling them." She paid $18 for each frame and $18.75 for Joe's picture; the man from Chicago "threw the boy's picture in." On the wall over the cluttered dresser is a framed Resolution passed by the Legislature: "Whereas, the horror of their sudden death and the shock to parents, wives, and children to whom these men were so devoted, is one of the greatest tragedies ever to have struck the State of Illinois: . . . therefore, be it Resolved . . . that we express our profound grief and sorrow at the deaths of the men who were stricken by this awful disaster . . . that we direct the Secretary of State to prepare copies of this resolution . . . and as a mark of further respect to those whose memory we today honor, that this House do now adjourn." (The legislators also spent $1,000 for an oil painting, "The Coal Miner," as a memorial to the Centralia dead, and a Centralia widow said, "Why didn't they give the money to us?" The legislators voted down several bills appropriating money for the widows.)

Whom does Mrs. Bryant blame for the disaster? "I don't know nothin' about the mine, I wouldn't blame no one, them accidents happen, seems like it just has to be." But her daughter-in-law, Harold's wife, rearing her own baby that her husband never saw, says, "Everybody says it was just one of those things, it was their time to go, but I don't believe it. If that mine'd been safe they'd still be here."

A half mile away, beyond the tipple and the barren gray fields, a locomotive is coming up the grade from Centralia, blowing steam hard, pulling forty-eight cars of coal, cars of the CB&Q, and the Pennsy, the Lehigh Valley and the IC. Just across the highway is the Hillcrest Memorial Cemetery, with so many new graves on the gentle sloping hill, the words in granite: "March 25, 1947. At Rest." And in a saloon in a neighboring town a young miner is having a beer, his hair neatly combed, his sport jacket of latest cut. "I got a wife and one kid. It takes a lot of money to raise kids. Where else could I make thirteen-o-five a day? The railroads pay eight, nine dollars. And that's all there is around here." At a table in a corner a couple of old miners are arguing quietly, and behind the bar the lady bartender is listening sympathetically to a lady customer whose husband is always crabbing about what she cooks. The young miner says, "Sometimes I'd like to leave for good. But where'd I go? I don't know anything else. I don't like mining. It's not really life," and he laughed shortly. "I don't know what in hell you would call it. Well, it is life, in a way too. I just wish my life away, when I go below I just wish it was tomorrow. Wish my life away. And I guess the others are the same way, too."

Marvel Cooke

Well into her nineties, Marvel Cooke (1903–2000) would warmly greet oral historians, students, and journalists who tracked her down on Edgecome Avenue in Harlem, recalling decades at the heart of African-American literary and journalistic life in New York. Richard Wright shared his manuscript for Native Son *over Cooke's kitchen table; she was W. E. B. DuBois's deputy at his journal* The Crisis; *her first great love affair was with NAACP leader Roy Wilkins; Paul Robeson counted her a close personal friend. As a reporter at New York's* Amsterdam News *Cooke organized the first African-American chapter of the Newspaper Guild. When the* New York Compass *hired Cooke in 1950, she became the first black woman to work as a reporter at a white-owned New York daily. A member of the Communist party from her Newspaper Guild days, Cooke remained active in the American-Soviet Friendship Committee.*

In the 1930s, Cooke and the NAACP's Ella Baker first investigated conditions facing domestic workers, focusing on what they called "The Bronx Slave Market"—the street-corner lots where affluent housewives would come to bid for casual labor. At the Compass, *she returned to the Slave Market as an undercover reporter, jobbing herself out for eighty cents an hour. Her stories, combining her first-person experiences with statistical analysis, reveal the special dynamic of black working women's poverty, and the daily humiliation faced by domestic workers.*

THE BRONX SLAVE MARKET
PART I

From the *New York Compass*, 1950

I WAS A PART OF THE BRONX SLAVE MARKET

I was a slave.

I was part of the "paper bag brigade," waiting patiently in front of Woolworth's on 170th St., between Jerome and Walton Aves., for someone to "buy" me for an hour or two, or, if I were lucky, for a day.

That is The Bronx Slave Market, where Negro women wait, in rain or shine, in bitter cold or under broiling sun, to be hired by local housewives looking for bargains in human labor.

It has its counterparts in Brighton Beach, Brownsville and other areas of the city.

Born in the last depression, the Slave Markets are products of poverty and desperation. They grow as employment falls. Today they are growing.

They arose after the 1929 crash when thousands of Negro women, who before then had a "corner" on household jobs because they were discriminated against in other employment, found themselves among the army of the unemployed. Either the employer was forced to do her own household chores or she fired the Negro worker to make way for a white worker who had been let out of less menial employment.

The Negro domestic had no place to turn. She took to the streets in search of employment—and the Slave Markets were born.

Their growth was checked slightly in 1941 when Mayor LaGuardia ordered an investigation of charges that Negro women were being exploited by housewives. He opened free hiring halls in strategic spots in The Bronx and other areas where the Slave Markets had mushroomed.

They were not entirely erased, however, until World War II diverted labor, skilled and unskilled, to the factories.

Today, Slave Markets are starting up again in far-flung sections of the city. As yet, they are pallid replicas of the depression model; but as unemployment increases, as more and more Negro women are thrown out of work and there is less and less money earmarked for full-time household workers, the markets threaten to spread as they did in the middle '30s, when it was estimated there were 20 to 30 in The Bronx alone.

The housewife in search of cheap labor can easily identify the women of the Slave Market. She can identify them by the dejected droop of their shoulders, or by their work-worn hands, or by the look of bitter resentment on their faces, or because they stand quietly leaning against store fronts or lamp posts waiting for anything—or for nothing at all.

These unprotected workers are most easily identified, however, by the paper bag in which they invariably carry their work clothes. It is a sort of badge of their profession. It proclaims their membership in "the paper bag brigade"—these women who can be bought by the hour or by the day at depressed wages.

The way the Slave Market operates is primitive and direct and simple—as simple as selling a pig or a cow or a horse in a public market.

The housewife goes to the spot where she knows women in search of domestic work congregate and looks over the prospects. She almost undresses them with her eyes as she measures their strength, to judge how much work they can stand.

If one of them pleases her, the housewife asks what her price is by the hour. Then she beats that price down as low as the worker will permit. Although the worker usually starts out demanding $6 a day and carfare, or $1 an hour and carfare, the price finally agreed upon is pretty low—lower than the wage demanded by public and private agencies, lower than the wage the women of the Slave Market have agreed upon among themselves.

FEW CHANGES

I know because I moved among these women and made friends with them during the late 1930s. I moved among them again several days ago, some ten years later. And I worked on jobs myself to obtain first-hand information.

There is no basic change in the miserable character of the Slave Market. The change is merely in the rate of pay. Ten years ago, women worked for as little as 25 cents an hour. In 1941, before they left the streets to work in the factories, it was 35 cents. Now it is 75 cents.

This may seem like an improvement. But considering how the prices of milk and bread and meat and coffee have jumped during the past decade, these higher wages mean almost no gain at all.

And all of the other evils are still there.

The women of the "paper bag brigade" still stand around in all sorts of weather in order to get a chance to work. They are still forced to do an unspecified amount of work under unspecified conditions, with no guarantee that, at the end of the day, they will receive even the pittance agreed upon.

They are still humiliated, day after day, by men who frequent the market area and make immoral advances.

Pointing to this shameful fact, civic and social agencies have warned that Slave Market areas could easily degenerate into centers of prostitution.

So they could, were it not for the fact that the women themselves resent and reject these advances. They are looking for an honest day's work to keep body and soul together.

THE BRONX SLAVE MARKET PART II

WHERE MEN PROWL AND WOMEN PREY ON NEEDY JOB-SEEKERS

I was part of the Bronx Slave Market long enough to experience all the viciousness and indignity of a system which forces women to the streets in search of work.

Twice I was hired by the hour at less than the wage asked by the women of the market. Both times I went home mad—mad for all the Negro women down through the ages who have been lashed by the stinging whip of economic oppression.

Once I was approached by a predatory male who made unseemly and unmistakable advances. And I was mad all over again.

My first job netted me absolutely nothing. My employer on this occasion was a slave boss and I quit cold soon after I started.

My second job netted me $3.40 for a full day of the hardest kind of domestic work. My "madam"—that is how the "slaves" describe those who hire them—on this occasion was a gentle Mrs. Simon Legree, who fed me three crackers, a sliver of cream cheese, jelly and a glass of coffee while she ate a savory stew.

The brush with the man was degrading and unspeakable.

These are everyday experiences in the Bronx Slave Market and in the markets elsewhere in the city.

• • •

I took up my stand in front of Woolworth's in the early chill of a December morning. Other women began to gather shortly afterwards. Backs pressed to the store window, paper bags clutched in their hands, they stared bleakly, blankly, into the street. I lost my identity entirely. I was a member of the "paper bag brigade."

Local housewives stalked the line we had unconsciously formed, picked out the most likely "slaves," bargained with them and led them off down the street. Finally I was alone. I was about to give up, when a short, stout, elderly woman approached. She looked me over carefully before asking if I wanted a day's work. I said I did.

"How much you want?"

"A dollar." (I knew that $1 an hour is the rate the Domestic Workers Union, the New York State Employment Service and other bona fide agencies ask for work by the hour.)

"A dollar an hour!" she exclaimed. "That's too much. I pay 70 cents."

The bargaining began. We finally compromised on 80 cents. I wanted the job.

"This way." My "madam" pointed up Townsend Ave. Silently we trudged up the street. My mind was filled with questions, but I kept my mouth shut. At 171st St., she spoke one of my unasked questions:

"You wash windows?"

'NOT DANGEROUS'

I wasn't keen on washing windows. Noting my hesitation, she said: "It isn't dangerous. I live on the ground floor."

I didn't think I'd be likely to die from a fall out a first-floor window, so I continued on with her.

She watched me while I changed into my work clothes in the kitchen of her dark three-room, ground-floor apartment. Then she handed me a pail of water and a bottle of ammonia and ordered me to follow her into the bedroom.

"First you are to wash this window," she ordered.

Each half of the window had six panes. I sat on the window ledge, pulled the top section down to my lap and began washing. The old woman glanced into the room several times during the 20 minutes it took me to finish the job. The window was shining.

I carried my work paraphernalia into the living room, where I was ordered to wash the two windows and the venetian blinds.

As I set about my work again, I saw my employer go into the bedroom. She came back into the living room, picked up a rag and disappeared again. When she returned a few moments later, I pulled up the window and asked if everything was all right.

"You didn't do the corners and you missed two panes." Her tone was accusing.

I intended to be ingratiating because I wanted to finish this job. I started to answer her meekly and offer to go back over the work. I started to explain that the windows were difficult because the corners were caked with paint. I started to tell her I hadn't missed a single pane. Of this I was certain. I had checked them off as I did them, with great precision—one, two, three—.

Then I remembered a discussion I'd heard that very morning among members of the "paper bag brigade." I learned that it is a common device of Slave Market employers to criticize work as a build-up for not paying the worker the full amount of money agreed upon.

"They'll gyp you at every turn if you let 'em," one of the women had said.

"They'll even take 25 cents off your pay for the measly meal they give you. You have to stand up for yourself every inch of the way."

Suddenly I was angry—angry at this slave boss—angry for all workers everywhere who are treated like a commodity. I slipped under the window and faced the old woman. The moment my feet hit the floor and I dropped the rag into the pail of water, I was no longer a slave.

My voice shaking with anger, I exclaimed: "I washed every single pane and you know it."

Her face showed surprise. Such defiance was something new in her experience. Before she could answer, I had left the pail of dirty water on the living room floor, marched into the kitchen and put on my clothes. My ex–slave boss watched me while I dressed.

"I'll pay you for the time you put in," she offered. I had only worked 40 minutes. I could afford to be magnanimous.

"Never mind. Keep it as a Christmas present from me."

With that, I marched out of the house. It was early. With luck, I could pick up another job.

Again I took up my stand in front of Woolworth's.

THE BRONX SLAVE MARKET PART III

'PAPER BAG BRIGADE' LEARNS HOW TO DEAL WITH GYPPING EMPLOYERS

I had quit my first job in revolt and now, at 10:30 A.M., I was back in The Bronx Slave Market, looking for my second job of the day.

As I took my place in front of Woolworth's, on 170th St. near Walton Ave., I found five members of the "paper bag brigade" still waiting around to be "bought" by housewives looking for cheap household labor.

One of the waiting "slaves" glanced at me. I hoped she would be friendly enough to talk.

"Tough out here on the street," I remarked. She nodded.

"I had one job this morning, but I quit," I went on. She seemed interested.

"I washed windows for a lady, but I fired myself when she told me my work was no good."

It was as though she hadn't heard a thing I said. She was looking me over appraisingly.

"I ain't seen you up here before," she said. "You're new, ain't you?"

ON THE OUTSIDE

I was discovering that you just can't turn up cold on the market. The "paper bag brigade" is like a fraternity. You must be tried and found true before you are accepted. Until then, you are on the outside, looking in.

Many of the "new" women are fresh from the South, one worker told me, and they don't know how to bargain.

"They'll work for next to nothing," she said, "and that makes it hard for all of us."

My new friend, probably bored with standing around, decided to forgive my newness and asked about the job I had left. I told her how the fat old lady had accused me of neglecting the window I had so painstakingly washed.

"Oh, that's the way they all act when they don't want to give you your full pay." She brushed off the incident as if it were an everyday occurrence.

"Anyway, you shouldn't-a agreed to work by the hour. That's the best way to get gypped. Some of them only want you for an hour or so to clean the worst dirt out of their houses. Then they tell you you're through. It's too late by that time to get another job."

"What should I have done?"

"Just don't work by the hour," she repeated laconically. "Work by the day. Ask six bucks and carfare for a three-room apartment."

EXPERT ADVICE

My new friend proved helpful. She told me all manner of things for which to be on the alert.

"Don't let them turn the clock back on you," she warned. "That's the easiest way to beat you out of your dough. Don't be afraid to speak up for yourself if they put more work on you than you bargained for."

I asked whether she had tried to get jobs at the New York State Employment Service on Fordham Road. She said she had a "card," but that "there are just no jobs up there. . . . And anyway, I don't want my name on any records."

When I asked what she meant by that, she became silent and turned her attention to another woman standing beside her. I guessed that she was a relief client.

There seemed little likelihood of another job that morning. I decided to call it a day. As I turned to leave, I saw a woman coming down the street with the inevitable bag under her arm. She looked as if she knew her way around.

"Beg your pardon," I said as I came abreast of her. "Are you looking for work, too?"

"What's it to you?" Her voice was brash and her eyes were hard as steel. She obviously knew her way around and how to protect herself. No foolishness about her.

"Nothing," I answered. I felt crushed.

"I'm new up here. Thought you might give me some pointers," I went on.

"I'm sorry, honey," she said. "Don't mind me. I ain't had no work for so long, I just get cross. What you want to know?"

When I told her about my morning's experience, she said that "they (the employers) are all bitches." She said it without emotion. It was spoken as a fact, as if she had remarked, "The sun is shining."

"They all get as much as they can out your hide and try not to pay you if they can get away with it."

She, too, worked by the job—"six bucks and carfare." I asked if she had ever tried the State Employment Service.

"I can't," she answered candidly. "I'm on relief and if the relief folks ever find out I'm working another job, they'll take it off my check. Lord knows, it's little enough now, and it's going to be next to nothing when they start cutting in January."

She went on down the street. I watched her a moment before I turned toward the subway. I was half conscious that I was being followed. At the corner of 170th St. and Walton Ave., I stopped a moment to look at the Christmas finery in Jack Fine's window. A man passed me, walked around the corner a few yards on Walton Ave., retraced his steps and stopped by my side.

I crossed Walton Ave. The man was so close on my heels that when I stopped suddenly on the far corner, he couldn't break his stride. I went back to Jack Fine's corner. When the man passed me again, he made a lewd, suggestive gesture, winked and motioned me to follow him up Walton Ave.

I was sick to my stomach. I had had enough for one day.

Stetson Kennedy

In 1973 a young group of North Carolina journalists needed a name for their new muckraking magazine. They chose Southern Exposure*—a tribute to Stetson Kennedy's fierce and exhaustive investigation of racism, rural economic exploitation, and political corruption in the South published under that title in 1946.*

Kennedy (1916–) grew up the son of a Jacksonville, Florida, furniture merchant and the nephew of a Klansman. Sent by his father to collect layaway payments from hard-pressed black and white families, he began collecting their folk tales and songs instead. Kennedy dropped out of the University of Florida to join the WPA Florida Writers Project, and by the age of twenty-one was in charge of its folklore and oral history departments. As a folklorist he employed Zora Neale Hurston and befriended Woody Guthrie. By the end of World War II, Kennedy turned his research skills to segregation and Southern poverty. Under the alias John Perkins—and with his uncle's name as a calling-card—he joined the Klan, tracking its brutal violence and political connections (all the way up to nationally prominent figures like Georgia's Governor Gene Talmadge) across several states, at great personal risk.

In 1950 Kennedy ran for the U.S. Senate on an independent antisegregationist ticket. During a sojourn in Europe he was championed by Jean-Paul Sartre, then returned to Florida to cover the civil rights movement. Stetson Kennedy still lives and writes in Beluthahachee, Florida. At the age of seventy-nine he published After Appomattox, *an investigative history of how the gains of emancipation were reversed during Reconstruction.*

THE KLAVALIERS RIDE TO A FALL

From *The Klan Unmasked*, 1954

This job for tonight is a cinch," Carter declared. "As y'all know, there's a law against coloured cab-drivers carrying white folks. But near 'bout every week we get reports that the law ain't being enforced. When the law fails, it's time for the Klan to step in . . . "

He paused, and there was a supercharged silence in the den as the Klavaliers waited for their briefing to continue.

"One nigger cab-driver especially, who operates out of the bus station, is in the habit of pickin' up white ladies. Tonight we're going to put a stop to it. I've got it all set up. There's a Klanswoman down at the bus station right now. She's going to get in his cab, throw a gun on him, and hold him for us."

Then he looked directly at me. "Perkins, I'm going to give you your first chance to show us what you're made of. I want you to report to the bus station right away, and relieve Brother Jim Meeks, who's on duty there. Keep an eye on a woman in a canary yellow blouse with a silver spider breast-pin. When she gets in the cab, you come out the side door of the station and give a long, low whistle. Then stand by for the boys to pick you up!"

"Just watch my smoke!" I said, starting for the door. I wanted to get to a phone as fast as I could to put in a riot call for Duke's men.

"Hold on!" Carter shouted. "No need to charge off like a bull moose going to crap! Brother Randal here will drive you over to the station. He's got a fast car, and I want it to be on hand."

Just my luck, I thought, to get sent out on a flog party and not even be able to try to stop it. I resolved to make every effort to put in the call to Duke after I got to the station.

When we got there, Randal put me out, and drove off into the dark side street leading up to the side entrance. I soon spotted Meeks, who threw out his left palm in the Klan's secret sign of recognition.

"Clearwater gave me instructions to relieve you, and to give the signal when our girl friend climbs into the cab," I said to him.

"There she is, right over there—" Meeks indicated with a jerk of his head. I looked, and saw a buxom peroxide blonde of the sort generally found in third-rate bars. She gave me a wink, and I winked back. She's a Klanswoman, all right, I said to myself, and I'll bet she knows how to use the pistol in her purse.

"The nigger's cab is parked in the taxi stand out front right now," Meeks went on. "How long do you reckon it'll be before the rest of the boys get here?"

"Clearwater didn't say—he must've given our girl friend some kind of cue. My orders are to follow her lead."

"O.K.—I think I'll duck out the side door and see if I can spot the boys when they drive up."

This, I thought, would give me a chance to phone Duke! As soon as Meeks disappeared through the side door, I headed for the phone booths. Just before stepping into one, something told me to look back. Meeks was watching me like a hawk through the window! Instead of entering the booth, I cocked one leg against it and pretended to tie my shoelace.

So Clearwater was testing me in more ways than one . . . I wondered if every new recruit into the Klavaliers was given the same treatment, or whether I was under suspicion. Of course, I could claim I was phoning a girl friend—but I would need a far better excuse than that if Duke's men pounced and caught them in the act. For a moment I debated with myself—was this the time for a showdown—or should I hold my fire for some more serious occasion? Remembering what Carter had said about getting along without the bullwhip, I decided that relatively minor "punishment" was to be meted out. I had no way of knowing that the night would end with murder . . .

I straightened up and walked back to the centre of the waiting room. About fifteen minutes went by before the woman in the canary blouse suddenly went into action. I watched as she walked quickly through the front door and climbed into the Negro's cab. Hurrying to the side door, I walked over to the darkness of the side street and whistled. . . .

The Klavaliers must have been waiting with motors running—in a matter of seconds they pulled up beside me in two cars.

"Get in!" I heard Randal bark.

I climbed into the back seat of his car, and we drove around in front of the station. The cab had already disappeared. There must have been a prearranged plan, however, for the woman to direct the cab to a certain spot, for we had scarcely driven a half-mile before we pulled into a deserted street to find the cab parked at the kerb. Cutting our lights, we coasted up behind it, climbed out and walked up to the cab.

The Klanswoman was sitting on the edge of the back seat, pressing a huge pearl-handled Police Special .45 revolver into the back of the driver's neck! Her chubby hands with their long red fingernails held the baby cannon firmly.

"Here's your meat, boys!" she said with a grin.

"Good girl! " Randal said, taking the pistol from her.

"You've done a good night's work—you can run along now, and we'll take care of the rest!"

He opened the front door of the cab, shoved the Negro aside, and climbed in behind the steering wheel.

"Let's get going!" he ordered. We piled into the back seat, and Randal handed Slim the .45. Without being told, Slim stuck the barrel back into the Negro's neck.

"White folks, what y'all want with me?" he said with dignity. "I ain't done nothing to be treated like this. . . . You must be got the wrong man. . . ."

"You're wrong, but we're goin' to set you right!" Slim said, jabbing him savagely with the gun barrel. "Meanwhile, keep your mouth shut or I'll blow your head off!"

We drove off, followed by the other carload of Klavaliers. "Pass the whisky," Slim said. "Nigger-killin' is hard work, and a man needs a little nip now and then. . . . "

The other Klavalier on the back seat fished out a bottle of cheap blended whisky and handed it to Slim. Slim tilted it to his mouth and let it gurgle.

"Don't kill it!" the Klavalier said.

"Hell, ain't I doin' all the work so far?" Slim asked, handing the bottle to Randal. Randal took a short pull, and passed it to us in the back seat again. It was my turn next, and I pretended to drink deeply. The keeper of the bottle drank last.

"Damn' thing's 'most empty!" he complained bitterly. "You'd think Clearwater would come across with a bigger bottle."

"We just crossed the county line," Randal said. "You can put on your robes now."

The man with the bottle had a robe for me. As we got into them, the Negro man watched out of the corner of his eye. But the fear he must have felt upon discovering he was in the hands of the Klan did not show in his face.

We turned off the highway and on to a clay road that threaded off through the pine flatwoods. When we came to a clump of hardwood trees at the head of a branch, Randal stopped the cab. Reaching over and opening the door, he gave the Negro a shove that sent him sprawling face first on to the ground. Almost before I knew what was happening, both carloads of Klavaliers had swarmed around him, and were kicking at his prostrated form amid a torrent of profanity. The Negro groaned and doubled over to protect his groin, but he made no plea for mercy. I felt like vomiting, and was glad my face was masked to hide my disgust. With great effort I kicked in the direction of the Negro, missing deliberately. Randal, meanwhile, was standing on the sidelines, calmly putting on his robe. That done, he stepped up, and the kicking subsided.

"You'd better say your prayers, nigger!" he said. "Your time has come."

"I don't know why y'all are treating me like this," he groaned.

"You know better than to pick up a white woman!" Randal said. "And now you're going to pay the penalty. Are you going to pray or not?"

"I never was no prayin' man . . ." the Negro replied, with more hatred than fear showing in his eyes.

"Let's stop foolin' around and get on with the killin'," Slim said, emptying the whisky bottle and heaving it off into the woods. The bottle struck a tree and broke with a loud smash.

"We got to change this nigger's attitude first," Randal said. "We got to put the fear of the Klan and God both in him! Get up!" He kicked the man fiercely in the ribs.

The Negro groaned and struggled painfully to his feet.

"We're callin' the tune, and you're goin' to dance!" Randal said. "Get goin'!" He took the .45 from Slim's hand and began firing at the Negro's feet, kicking up puffs of red dust. "Come on, boys, help me provide the music!"

All of the Klavaliers pulled pistols from beneath their robes and began firing at his feet. I was glad I was just a novice, and, as far as the Klavaliers knew, unarmed.

"Dance, damn you!" Randal cried in a rage.

Mechanically, but still not showing the fear the Klavaliers longed to see, the man began to jog up and down. Suddenly he stopped.

"If you're aimin' to kill me, you'll just have to kill me," he said.

"I'm givin' you one more chance!" Randal snarled. "Start running down that road—but don't dare leave the road, or your running days will be over!"

Randal climbed back into the cab and motioned for us to get in. The Negro started on a slow, painful lope down the road, and Randal began to follow. Leaning out of the window, he fired at the Negro's heels.

"Step on it!" he yelled, increasing the speed of the car. Slim and the others followed suit, leaning out of the windows, firing and cursing. We kept going faster and faster, and the distance between the cab and the fleeing form grew perilously shorter. The Negro had been running in the centre of the road, between the ruts, when suddenly he started to cross the road and head for the woods. He stumbled in the rut and fell. Randal jammed on the brakes, but there was a sickening thud and the car passed over the Negro's body. I turned away, sick. Without looking, I knew he was dead.

"The black bastard had it comin' to him!" Randal said bitterly. "He wouldn't pay no attention to nothin' we said. We'd better get out of here!"

I looked through the rear window. The other Klavaliers in the car behind us, seeing what had happened, made a wide detour around the body. Together we raced back to Atlanta, and abandoned the cab where we had first commandeered it.

"Disperse, and keep a tight lip!" Randal ordered.

It was after 1 A.M. I hurried to Atlanta's only all-night drug store and put in a call to Duke's home. His wife answered the phone.

"Dan's not here," she said sleepily. "He's down in Macon on business, and won't get back until tomorrow . . . "

"Thanks," was all I could say.

I felt completely frustrated. I had seen a murder committed, and yet there was no one to whom I could turn. There was not even any point in reporting the matter to the F.B.I., which has no jurisdiction over murder. For the first time in my life, I had a real insight into how it must feel to be a Negro in a part of the country where there is no authority to whom one can appeal for justice.

After a restless night reliving the tragedy, I was awakened by the thud of the morning paper being delivered. I brought it in and scanned it hurriedly, Just as I was about to give up, I found what I was looking for. It was a one-inch notice buried on a back page:

> BODY FOUND
>
> The body of a Negro man, with head and chest crushed, apparently the victim of a hit-and-run driver, was found in the early morning hours on Pryor Road by Rockledge County Police. From papers on the man's body he was identified as James Martin, a driver for the Lincoln Cab Company.

So that was how it was being written off! I wondered how many Negroes had died similarly violent deaths in the South, only to have one-inch obituaries bury the atrocities as "accidents." James Martin, I swore to myself, was not going to be buried that way.

Fred J. Cook

In 1930s New Jersey, Fred J. Cook once told an interviewer, "protection could be purchased for everything—including murder." Cook learned that as a shoe-leather crime reporter in his home state. In the 1950s he moved his career across the Hudson to the World-Telegram, *covering the politics behind slum clearance, the mafia, and other quintessential New York stories.*

In the mid-1950s, Carey McWilliams of The Nation *approached Cook and asked him to bring his hard-nosed reporter's instincts to bear on cold war security cases—most notoriously spy charges against former State Department aide Alger Hiss. Cook was one of the few journalists in the paranoid 1950s to systematically examine loyalty scandals. That, in turn, led him to the actions of the F.B.I., and in 1958* The

Nation *devoted a special issue to his comprehensive evaluation of the Bureau's history and record. In this excerpt, Cook goes back to his crime-reporter roots, dismantling J. Edgar Hoover's reputation as a mob-buster.*

Cook has enjoyed a prolific and diverse career as a maverick reporter on subjects ranging from the death penalty to New York political corruption to military contractors. His forty-five books include children's literature as well as journalism and autobiography. Like I. F. Stone, Cook evolved from daily reporter into a careful reader of public documents, and combined his original research with astute synthesis of others' journalism. In 1980, after nearly fifty years in the business, he won a fourth Headline Award from the New York Press Club for a Nation *series on the energy crisis.*

FROM THE BIG ONES GET AWAY

From *The Nation*, 1958

On September 29, 1935, J. Edgar Hoover announced, in the words of the *New York Times*, "a national campaign against racketeers comparable to the successful drive against perpetrators of violent crimes." Hoover had just returned to Washington from a "bird-dog expedition" to New York, where he had spent several days sniffing out possible violations of federal law. The rackets, he estimated, were costing New York businesses alone $50 million annually. A blanket of super-secrecy was being thrown about the new FBI racket drive, the *Times* reported, but agents all over the country were sending information to headquarters. In May, 1936, in the flush of victory after his personal capture of Karpis, Hoover denounced "the link of the so-called underworld to politics," which he said was the real "Public Enemy No. 1." And later in the same month, announcing that only one kidnaper remained at large, he indicated again that the G-men were going to concentrate on the big rackets and racket ties to politics.

On June 11, 1958, Hoover's new chief in the Justice Department, Attorney General Rogers, declared in a speech in Chicago that crime was costing the country $20 billion annually; organized rings, he said (telling the public nothing that hadn't been reported in eight-column headlines for years), were reaping a harvest by maintaining remote control over lucrative rackets. The Department of Justice, however, was going to set matters straight; it had undertaken a long-range campaign aimed at wiping out syndicates and jailing top racketeers.

In the context of these two statements, separated by more than twenty years, it seems fair to ask: What happened in the interim?

The inevitable answer has to be: Not much.

The FBI scored its greatest successes over the stumble-bums of crime—the trigger-happy desperadoes, the vicious kidnapers who were usually lone wolves and often rank amateurs. But with rare exceptions—Al Capone and Lepke Buchalter are two—it did not curb the dark emperors of the underworld. In these years of the FBI's dominance, the Syndicate perfected an organization that gave gangland virtual status as a forty-ninth state. Frank Costello reigned untouched until his nervously twitching fingers were exposed to the gaze of millions by the Kefauver Committee's television cameras. Even after his downfall, the Syndicate continued doing business as usual. It cut itself in on the lush Las Vegas gambling revenues. It went into virtual partnership with Dictator Fulgencio Batista in Cuba. And in November, 1957, it demonstrated the extent and nature of its organization by rallying sixty mobsters to a national crime conclave in a hilltop mansion at Apalachin, N.Y.

The evidence seems indisputable that, whatever happened to the stooges, the real powers of the underworld flew high, wings unclipped by the FBI. This is a picture shockingly different from the publicity-induced image. Didn't Attorney General Cummings proclaim in the thirties that the FBI, with its broadened powers, was going to get the big shots of the underworld? But, as was pointed out at the time, his conception of what constituted a big shot was schoolboyish.

ENTER THE SYNDICATE

The extensive powers bequeathed to the FBI by the first Roosevelt Congress in 1934 were predicated upon the idea, valid enough in itself, that crime was becoming interstate in character; that the automobile and the airplane gave gangsters mobility, enabled them to commit a crime and then hop across state lines to far-distant hideouts. For this reason, the FBI was specifically given jurisdiction in cases in which a person crossed a state line to avoid prosecution or to avoid giving testimony—a sweeping provision that, it would seem, would cover a multitude of cases and would embrace, if the effort were made, most of the major activities of the Syndicate.

But Attorney General Cummings and Hoover himself weren't so much concerned at the time with the secretive and important machinations of the underworld; they were preoccupied with the obvious, the sensational, the spectacular. In speech after speech, Cummings proclaimed the thesis that huge underworld gangs had been built up by bootlegging millions in Prohibition days, which was true; and that these gangs, deprived by repeal of bootlegging as a source of livelihood, were turning to kidnaping—a patently false and ridiculous theory.

As Milton Mayer pointed out in his *Forum* article:

> Kidnaping is largely an amateur sport. Unlike bootlegging, it is desperate and dangerous. It attracts two kinds of men: nuts and the kinds of men person who shoots up banks. It does not attract the kind of man who peddles illicit goods or murders fellow hoodlums for hire under the tolerant eye of both police and public. "Good" criminals, the foundation blocks of the underworld, avoid it because it is a one-shot racket; kidnaping is easier to solve than any other major crime; the life of a "kidnaping gang" has never been shown to be more than one kidnaping.

William Seagle in *Harper's* phrased the same thought this way: "The opinion of at least the New York Police Department is that kidnaping is an amateur crime, and this impression is certainly borne out by most of the front-page stories of kidnapings. . . . It is true that the record of the Division of Investigation of the Department of Justice has been very brilliant in the kidnaping cases in which it has assumed jurisdiction. But it has conveniently forgotten that the record of local police forces has been brilliant too, the Lindbergh case to the contrary notwithstanding."

BUSINESS AS USUAL

Time has proved the validity of these analyses. The famous kidnapers were not the big names of the underworld. Hauptmann was an impoverished carpenter; Angelo John La Marca, recently executed for the kidnap-murder of the Weinberger baby on Long Island, was an impecunious laborer driven to the border of insanity by the crushing pressure of debts. The record of the years makes it obvious that the dreaded powers of gangdom, the men who directed vast enterprises and held life and death in their hands—Lucky Luciano, Vito Genovese, Costello, Joe Adonis, Dandy Phil Kastel, Albert Anastasia, Meyer Lansky—never were so stupid as to mess with a cheap thug's crime like kidnaping. While the FBI was garnering its headlines with its successful pursuit of kidnapers and its gun battles with the Dillingers and the Floyds and the Nelsons, the really big-league operators of the underworld continued to amass their untold millions, their rackets in such lucrative fields as narcotics, the numbers, bookmaking and gambling casinos that rivaled the plush of Monte Carlo—and ran as openly.

Some of these enterprises, of course, were intrastate in nature and so beyond the pale of federal prosecution. But many more were not. Indeed, it would seem that the majority of the Syndicate's maneuvers violated the sanctity of state lines and made it, in one way or another, a sitting-duck for federal police agents really eager to join battle with the masterminds of crime. For example, it is a virtual axiom in law-enforcement circles that the big gang murders of the last twenty years have involved cross-continental planning. If a Bugsy Siegel is to be bumped off in California, a Willie Moretti in New Jersey, an Albert Anastasia in New York City, it is a cinch that the triggerman is not a home-grown product, but an imported expert who runs little danger of recognition. And once the bloody deed is done, the murderer hops car and plane and is speedily away, not across one state line but many. No clearer opportunity could be offered—under the provision of crossing state lines either to escape prosecution or to avoid giving testimony—for the vigorous entry by the FBI into the difficult field of big-time criminal prosecutions, the kind of prosecutions that would really matter. Yet the FBI, which has built up its statistics with the stolen cars recovered in interstate commerce, has seen fit only on extremely rare occasions to inject itself into the hunt for interstate syndicate murderers.

Capone an Exception

One of the notable exceptions was Al Capone. The notorious czar of Chicago gangdom had ruled untouched throughout the Prohibition era, and his mob had chalked up a gory tally of more than 200 murders before the FBI, in 1929, put the first crimp in his career. The immediate reason for intervention was that Capone had failed to answer a subpoena to appear as a witness in Chicago in a Prohibition case. Capone argued, with a doctor's affidavit to support him, that he had been too ill to appear; but the FBI's investigation showed that, at the time he was supposed to have been bedridden, he had been enjoying himself at the races and even taking off by air to the Bahamas. A contempt of court charge was lodged against Capone, the first of numerous legal troubles. He was subsequently arrested for carrying a gun in Pennsylvania, and the sleuths of the Internal Revenue Service ultimately put the seal on his career when they nailed him on an income-tax rap and sent him up for ten years.

Capture by Radio

The other exception to the FBI's generally inconsequential record in the field of big-league crime is Louis (Lepke) Buchalter. Lepke's had been a dread name in the New York underworld for years; he sat in the inner council of Eastern crime; his mob reputedly extorted a million dollars from the bakery industry alone. Yet he had led the charmed life of the untouchable until, in the late 1930s, Dewey began to ride herd on the New York rackets. Dewey wanted Lepke's scalp in the worst way, and the city of New York posted a $25,000 reward for his capture. Even with this indictment Lepke wasn't to be found, and it was obvious to any schoolboy that he was a fugitive beyond the pale of New York's jurisdiction. And so the FBI stepped in. It announced it, too, would pay $25,000 if information leading to Lepke's capture came to it *first;* otherwise, all it would dish out would be its standard $5,000 reward for the apprehension of a top fugitive.

This was the situation when Walter Winchell came to the aid of Hoover. He pleaded on his radio program for Lepke to give himself up. The indications are that Lepke, fearing the feds less than he did Dewey, was only too happy to oblige provided he could make a deal. He contacted Walter Winchell, was assured he wouldn't be double-crossed by being handed over to Dewey if he surrendered, and so on August 24, 1939, at a designated rendezvous, Lepke walked up to Winchell's car, sat down beside the columnist and was driven away to be delivered personally to Hoover.

Federal agents questioned Buchalter for hours and finally held him on a narcotics rap. New York's Mayor Fiorello H. LaGuardia and the local gendarmes were furious because they learned of these interesting developments only by reading their morning newspapers. Dewey, too, was considerably put out because his detectives were firmly barred from the presence of the prisoner. The only way he could get access to Lepke, Dewey was told, was to develop some charge that would take precedence over the federal narcotics case. Ultimately, Dewey did just that. He had Lepke indicted for murder, tried him, convicted him and sent him to the electric chair in Sing Sing.

To generations reared in the comfortable belief that the FBI represents the Nemesis of crookedness in every form, it may seem incredible that the scalps of Al Capone and Lepke Buchalter represent virtually the only exhibits the bureau has to offer in the really top echelon of crime. But so it is. The names of Costello, Adonis, Luciano, Anastasia do not even appear in *The FBI Story.* Yet the national ramifications of the Syndicate would seem to have offered some ideal opportunities for an alert and eager federal law-enforcement agency to lay some major demons by the heels. Take, for example, the history of the interstate New York–New Jersey gangland operation that ran brazenly, openly, in utter contempt of all law during the entire decade of the 1940s.

BRIDGE TO CRIME

The peculiar geography, the colossal wealth and the temporary political climate of New York City were the factors that led the Syndicate to create a bi-state capital of Eastern crime. Dewey and LaGuardia had made Manhattan uncomfortable for the hoods; William O'Dwyer in Brooklyn picked up the Dewey formula of crusading to political success and exposed the macabre, incredible story of Murder Inc., the enforcement arm of gangdom. O'Dwyer's probe stopped at the threshold of the throne room where Albert Anastasia, known throughout the underworld as the Lord High Executioner, ruled the sadistic thugs of Murder Inc. It was a strategic pause that made O'Dwyer no less a local hero and that naturally gratified the only slightly-inconvenienced Anastasia.

The boss of murderers moved his operations just a short hop away, across the George Washington Bridge to northern New Jersey, where, atop the beautiful Palisades, he set up home and shop. Joe Adonis, another major power in the Brooklyn rackets, joined him there, and the activities of this grim pair were supplemented by two ambassadors of crime who already had been tilling the Bergen County pastures—Willie and Solly Moretti, widely and justly famed as smoothies with solid-gold local contacts.

The setup was perfect for the Syndicate. New York throughout the forties was bulging with the financial loot of war profits and post-war boom. The Syndicate could not be expected to let such a fat cow go bleating in pain from not being milked, especially when the solution was so ridiculously easy. A string of gambling casinos was established throughout the Bergen County countryside, a fleet of gleaming Cadillacs with liveried chauffeurs was maintained in New York, and nightly the Cadillac parade crossed the bridge to Jersey, ferrying the well-heeled suckers to the Syndicate's houses of lost chance.

This interstate traffic was not a secret. Mayor LaGuardia, his voice rasping on the radio, proclaimed frequently that the "tinhorns" (what a misnomer!) had been driven "across the bridge to Jersey." Newspapers headlined the fact. On one occasion, during the gasoline-rationing days of World War II, federal agents from the Office of Defense Transportation checked up on the suspicious stream of Jersey-bound Cadillacs and found themselves being led right to the door of a gambling hall. This was a much-publicized discovery, though of course all the gambling paraphernalia had been whisked away by the time the Jersey cops poked dilatory noses into the scene.

BANKING THE HAUL

Nothing happened to interfere with the gangland paradise in New Jersey's Bergen County, fed by literally millions in revenue from the sidewalks of New York. And very probably nothing would have happened to this day, had it not been for the fortuitous combination of two nearly simultaneous probes—one conducted by District Attorney Frank S. Hogan in New York; the other by Senator Estes Kefauver, whose crime committee picked up Hogan's sensational discoveries and catapulted them into the headlines.

Hogan, of course, is strictly a local prosecutor, with no authority at all in New Jersey. But in the summer of 1948 his curiosity was aroused by a Park Avenue charity gambling party that seemed to have professional overtones. He ordered an investigation. And his staff came upon the trail of one of the most fabulous money men in criminal history.

He was a three-chinned check-casher named Max Stark, of Teaneck, New Jersey. The Manhattan charity gambling checks had been deposited with Stark, but they represented little more than nickel-and-dime business, as Hogan's detectives quickly realized when they began to examine Max Stark's bank account. This looked almost like a page torn from the federal ledger. The detectives learned that daily Max Stark would descend upon the Merchants Bank of New York with a sack of crumpled, sweat-stained greenbacks—the haul from the previous night's losing agony in the Syndicate's Jersey halls of chance. It was a poor day when Stark showed up with a mere $30,000 in cash to be sorted and tallied; often, he lugged $90,000 through the bank's doors in a single morning. Handling this tidal wave of currency tied up the operations of the branch bank to which Stark first repaired to such an extent that little other business could be transacted, and arrangements were made with Stark to transfer his business to the main office, where a special teller was assigned to his exclusive use. After all, the Merchants Bank had to be polite to Max Stark, for there were just 20,000 shares of bank stock outstanding—and Stark held 2,000 of them!

Fantastic as this daily cash transaction sounds, it was only half of the Max Stark story. For Hogan's investigators found that Stark's check business rivaled his cash business. In the twenty-five months from July 1, 1946, through July 31, 1948, he had banked $6,810,847 worth of checks. When Hogan's fiscal experts added a conservatively estimated $200,000-a-week flow of cash to Stark's check business, they came up with a minimum figure for the gambling play in New Jersey: $13,500,000 a year. Actually, Hogan believed, the total wagered annually in the Jersey casinos was probably closer to $20 million.

3,000 Telephones

And even this was only part of the story!

In addition to gambling casinos, the Syndicate's master bookmaker, Frank Erickson, established payoff headquarters for the nation in the well-protected Bergen County paradise. To handle the tremendous betting on the horses, Erickson's agents rented the phones of some 3,000 householders in the county. They would call each afternoon, use the phone for a few hours, and depart as quietly and unobtrusively as they came by the time the family was sitting down to the evening meal. For accommodating such gentlemanly businessmen, each householder was paid a weekly phone rental of $50—a seemingly bounteous reward for a courtesy that could hardly be described as entailing even a minor inconvenience.

Board of Directors

It is obvious that the management of such vast enterprises required skillful direction. After all, General Motors does not run without board meetings and staff conferences; neither does crime. Hogan's detectives, by much careful and peripheral sleuthing, ultimately established to their satisfaction that the Syndicate had set up a daily functioning Council of

Five that administered the affairs of crime from a closely-guarded inner sanctum in the now-defunct Duke's Restaurant in Cliffside Park, almost opposite the entrance to the Palisades Amusement Park.

Joe Adonis was chairman of the board, and his fellow councilors were the Moretti brothers, Albert Anastasia and Anthony (Tony Bender) Strollo, a power on the Jersey docks and in New York's Greenwich Village area. When major decisions were to be made, underworld minions would be summoned from New York and New Jersey; they would congregate in the bar and while away the hours while the Council of Five deliberated, decided and ultimately issued its orders. So autocratically did Adonis and his fellow chieftains operate that frequently three times as many hoods would be summoned as were needed—just to make certain that the right men were present to handle any chore that might arise.

This governing nerve center of gangdom was as well known to the underworld as the corridors of City Hall are to the ward heeler. Protected by a security screen worthy of the FBI itself, Duke's became famed as a secure haven to masterminds of crime across the nation. Frequently, when major decisions were to be made, Costello would be chauffeured across the bridge from New York to meet with the Council of Five. Or Abner (Longie) Zwillman, the old bootleg czar, would drive over from Newark. Or Meyer Lansky would fly in by plane from his swank gambling casinos in Hollywood, Florida and Saratoga Springs, New York.

Getting the evidence on such a well-protected capital of the underworld wasn't easy. So solid were the Syndicate's local contacts that Hogan's detectives, trying to watch the homes of some of the gang lords along the Palisades, actually were chased out of town by local police. Treasury agents on similar missions also found that the law wasn't on their side. Watchful local cops spotted them the instant they poked their noses into Bergen County and tailed them until they left the scene. Such handicaps were overcome by Hogan's office in a patient and dogged investigation that lasted for months. Witnesses who had played and lost in the Syndicate's gambling halls were summoned before a grand jury; more than 700 pages of detailed testimony finally were amassed. Even so, with ironclad evidence in his possession, Hogan had only a slim legal entering wedge that, just possibly, might justify criminal action—the charge of conspiracy to commit a crime in another state.

KEFAUVER'S EXPOSÉ

This was the situation when, in 1950, Kefauver focused a spotlight on the ramifications of big-league crime. He picked up and highlighted Hogan's reports on Max Stark's multi-million-dollar check-cashing business. He threatened to bring his investigation to New Jersey. Thus menaced, Jersey cleaned up. Using Hogan's records, it indicted Joe Adonis, Solly Moretti and some of the lesser gambling henchmen. Willie Moretti, incensed at the imprisonment of his brother, threatened to blow the lid off the ties between the mob and politics. He declared that a payoff of $228,000 had gone directly to the State House in Trenton in one period of nineteen months. Not long after he committed this verbal indiscretion—it was on October 4, 1951—Willie Moretti went to a late-morning rendezvous in a public restaurant with some supposed friends; and when the waitress and help weren't looking, one of the "friends" placed the business end of a gun close to Willie's noggin and blasted him into eternity.

Cars with New York license plates were seen driving from the site of the public execution, fairly reliable evidence of the interstate nature of the crime; but from that day to this, no law-enforcement agency on any level has exhibited any great eagerness to track down the slayers of Willie Moretti. The crime remains unsolved—an ending that can be written almost automatically whenever the top powers of gangdom execute one of their own.

TWILIGHT OF THE GODS

The Kefauver exposé raised havoc with the rulers of the Eastern mobs. After Willie Moretti was murdered, his brother Solly died in prison; Joe Adonis came out of jail only to be deported; Costello ran afoul of a contempt rap and then an income-tax evasion charge; Frank Erickson went to the pen; and Albert Anastasia, the dark emperor of death, jailed briefly by the Treasury tax sleuths, gained his freedom only to become, on October 25, 1957, the victim of his own copyright. In the bright light of that fine autumn morning, Anastasia was reclining in a barber's chair in a midtown New York hotel when two fast-stepping gunmen strode in from the lobby. They walked up behind the Lord High Executioner and gave him the works from two fast-talking gats. They then strode out again, discarded their guns, became lost in the subway crowds. The guns, later recovered, were traced back to Illinois, to the suburbs of Chicago where the old Capone mob still rules. The mute evidence of the murder weapons would seem to italicize again the interstate nature of the Syndicate murder, would seem to indicate that the killers, mission completed, had probably hopped the New York state line for the good old purpose of escaping prosecution. Yet the FBI has shown no public disposition to ride to the roundup as it did in the days when it envisioned kidnapers and trigger-happy gunmen as the great menaces to the republic. And Anastasia's murder, like Moretti's, like the legion of murders that preceded them, remains unsolved.

Now no one supposes that the FBI is in complete ignorance of the facts of life in the underworld, of the organization of the Syndicate. Definitely, it knows—and knows in great detail—the names of the underworld barons, their ties, their interests. Some years ago, for example, its dossier on Anthony (Tony Bender) Strollo ran to three fat manuscript tomes, each thicker than *Gone With the Wind.* More recently, in May, 1957, when the underworld made an abortive attempt on Costello's life, one of the compelling reasons for the shooting was that the Syndicate feared the FBI was learning too much. Costello was temporarily out of prison and was much aggrieved because the boys, instead of according to him and his old authority, had virtually read him into limbo as a man too hot to direct the affairs of state. In his cups in one of his favorite East Side hangouts, Costello couldn't refrain from muttering to a very dear friend about the injustice of it all. The element that he hadn't considered, astute as he is, was that his particular friend was also a particular friend of J. Edgar Hoover. The underworld through its own grapevine learned that Uncle Frank was babbling—and bounced a bullet off his skull as a pointed warning to him to shut up. Such incidents show that the FBI is well-informed about the major operations of gangdom. And, equally, they throw into startling relief the FBI's uncharacteristic silence, its apparent failure to turn all its batteries on the real masterminds of organized crime.

APALACHIN CONCLAVE

Probably no incident of recent years has underlined so graphically the FBI's role as a virtual spectator of gangland crime as the Apalachin conclave on November 14, 1957, just three weeks after Anastasia's murder. Obviously, when a power like Anastasia, with the vast interests of an Anastasia, is suddenly erased from the gangland scene, a vacuum is created. Obviously, the Syndicate could not tolerate such a vacuum; obviously it had to straighten out its organization, delineate new territories and new spheres of influence. The result was the convention of sixty top gangland figures.

This by now famous meeting took place in the hilltop mansion of Joseph Barbara, Sr. Any skeptics who doubted the sweep of gangland power and its close-knit organization must have been convinced of the reality of the Syndicate by the impressive evidence furnished by the list of delegates.

Representatives were present from the Eastern Seaboard, from the Midwest, from California, from Cuba, from Puerto Rico. And at least two were recent arrivals from Italy, where they were believed to have had contact with the international narcotics czar, the notorious Lucky Luciano.

The mere fact of Apalachin was enough to trigger investigations that continue today, nearly a year later. And the mere fact has been almost all there was to go on. Almost no evidence was gathered, for the mobsters were startled into premature flight and, ever since, efforts to put them under oath and make them talk have demonstrated merely how firmly they could wrap themselves in the Fifth Amendment. Yet the mere knowledge of Apalachin, the public outcry that it raised, has been important. And even this little we would not have had except for a New York State police trooper, Sergeant Edgar L. Croswell, who became suspicious when he found too many out-of-state Cadillacs parked at motels. Croswell rounded up a force of state troopers, got the help of a couple of Federal Alcohol Tax Division agents, and started setting up a roadblock. It wasn't the best way to find out what the mob was planning, for it flushed the quarry too soon. But it did demonstrate clearly, for all to see, the monstrous fact of the multi-million-dollar controlled conspiracy of the underworld.

In the wake of Apalachin came the usual spate of suggestions about what could be done to curb the mob. The New York *Herald Tribune* felt that the FBI ought to be able to do the job and that the only reason it hadn't was that it lacked men and money. Even the *Herald Tribune* acknowledged, however, that "Congress has never yet refused anything J. Edgar Hoover said he had to have. Let him demand the funds to take on this job. Let Congress provide them, plus stronger laws on national crime." The McClellan Senate Rackets Committee drew the usual clam-up from Apalachin gangsters and listened to a number of police experts expound on possible remedies. The committee itself seemed to lean toward the formation of a permanent federal crime commission to keep track of things, and some of the expert witnesses acknowledged that such a body would be valuable if it just clipped the newspapers and collected racket intelligence so that the FBI, the Secret Service, the Alcohol Tax Division and the Bureau of Narcotics could be informed quickly when gangsters were committing violations in their jurisdictions.

THE SILENT BUGLE

All of these years-late proposals might not have been necessary, it would seem, had the FBI exhibited the same fervor in pursuing the big-shots of gangdom as it did in building up its record against the lower-rank hoodlums in the thirties. After all, the FBI budget today runs to more than $100 million annually, some twelve times what it was just prior to the outbreak of World War II. And, after all, it didn't take Apalachin to demonstrate the reality of what the *Herald Tribune* calls the Invisible Government. The Syndicate had flexed its muscles in public more than ten years ago when it practically annexed Bergen County to the underworld, when brazenly and openly it ran a nightly interstate business for fat-cat gamblers. All of this must have been obvious to an agency so well-informed as the FBI, and as the *Herald Tribune* says, Congress never refused J. Edgar Hoover anything. All that was needed was for the infallible policeman to sound the clear bugle call for the charge. But instead of a call, there was silence.

RALPH NADER

The press usually calls him "consumer advocate"; he named his own organization "Public Citizen." Either way, Ralph Nader (1934–) is today recognized as the preeminent champion of corporate accountability. Less obvious, perhaps, is Nader's significant influence on investigative journalism. Nader's careful trawl through corporate records in Unsafe at Any Speed *became the model for documenting how corporations endanger public interest, and projects run through Public Citizen have nurtured many aspiring reporters' research skills.*

This article, "The Safe Car You Can't Buy," appeared in The Nation *in 1959. It launched Nader—then a recent law school graduate—on his career, leading him to write* Unsafe at Any Speed *and setting in motion latter-day corporate muckraking.*

THE SAFE CAR YOU CAN'T BUY

From *The Nation*, 1959

The Cornell Aeronautical Laboratory has developed an exhibition automobile embodying over sixty new safety concepts which would enable an occupant to withstand a head-on collision at 50 mph with at most only minor scratches. In its design, six basic principles of crash protection were followed:

1. The car body was strengthened to prevent most external blows from distorting it against the passengers.
2. Doors were secured so that crash impacts could not open them, thereby saving passengers from ejection and maintaining the structural strength of the side of the car body.
3. Occupants were secured to prevent them from striking objects inside the car.
4. Interior knobs, projections, sharp edges and hard surfaces have been removed and the ceiling shaped to produce only

glancing blows to the head (the most vulnerable part of the body during a crash).

5. The driver's environment was improved to reduce accident risk by increasing visibility, simplifying controls and instruments, and lowering the carbon monoxide of his breathing atmosphere.
6. For pedestrian safety, dangerous objects like hood ornaments were removed from the exterior.

This experimental car, developed with funds representing only a tiny fraction of the annual advertising budget of, say, Buick, is packed with applications of simple yet effective safety factors. In the wraparound bumper system, for instance, plastic foam material between the front and rear bumpers and the back-up plates absorbs some of the shock energy; the bumpers are smoothly shaped to convert an increased proportion of blows from direct to glancing ones; the side bumpers are firmly attached to the frame, which has been extended and reinforced to provide support. Another feature is the installment of two roll-over bars into the top of the car body as added support.

It is clear that Detroit today is designing automobiles for style, cost, performance and calculated obsolescence, but not—despite the 5,000,000 reported accidents, nearly 40,000 fatalities, 110,000 permanent disabilities and 1,500,000 injuries yearly—for safety.

Almost no feature of the interior design of our current cars provides safeguards against injury in the event of collision. Doors that fly open on impact, inadequately secured seats, the sharp-edged rear-view mirror, pointed knobs on instrument panel and doors, flying glass, the overhead structure—all illustrate the lethal potential of poor design. A sudden deceleration turns a collapsed steering wheel or a sharp-edged dashboard into a bone- and chest-crushing agent. Penetration of the shatterproof windshield can chisel one's head into fractions. A flying seat cushion can cause a fatal injury. The apparently harmless glove-compartment door has been known to unlatch under impact and guillotine a child. Roof-supporting structure has deteriorated to a point where it provides scarcely more protection to the occupants, in common roll-over accidents, than an open convertible. This is especially true of the so-called "hardtops." Nor is the automobile designed as an efficient force moderator. For example, the bumper does not contribute significantly to reduction of the crash deceleration forces that are transmitted to the motorist; its function has been more to reflect style than absorb shock.

These weaknesses of modern automobile construction have been established by the investigation of several groups, including the Automotive Crash Injury Research of the Cornell University Medical College, the Institute of Transportation and Traffic Engineering of the University of California and the Motor Vehicle Research of Lee, New Hampshire. Careful coverage of all available reports do not reveal a single dissent from these findings:

1. There are direct causal relationships between automotive design and the frequency, type and severity of injuries.
2. Studies of body tolerances to abrupt deceleration show that the forces in most accidents now fatal are well within the physiological limits of survival under proper conditions.
3. Engineering improvement in safety design and restraining devices would materially reduce the injury and fatality rate (estimates range from twenty to thirty thousand lives saved annually).
4. Redesign of injury-causing automotive components is well within the capabilities of present engineering technique and would require no radical changes in present styling.
5. Many design improvements have already been developed but are not in production.

The remarkable advances in crash-protection knowledge achieved by these research organizations at a cost of some $6 million stands in marked contrast to the glacier-like movements of car manufacturers, who spend that much to enrich the sound of a door slam. This is not due to any dearth of skill—the industry possesses many able, frustrated safety engineers whose suggestions over the years invariably have taken a back seat to those of the stylist. In 1938, an expert had this to say in *Safety Engineering:*

> The motor industry must face the fact that accidents occur. It is their duty, therefore, to so design the interiors of automobiles that when the passenger is tossed around, he will get an even break and not suffer a preventable injury in accidents that today are taking a heavy toll.

In 1954, nearly 600,000 fatalities later, a U.C.L.A. engineer could conclude that "There has been no significant automotive-engineering contribution to the safety of motorists since about the beginning of World War II. . . ." In its 1955 annual report, the Cornell crash-research group came to a similar conclusion, adding that "the newer model automobiles [1950–54] are increasing the rate of fatalities in injury-producing accidents."

In 1956, Ford introduced the double-grip safety-door latch, the "dished" steering wheel, and instrument panel-padding; the rest of the industry followed with something less than enthusiasm. Even in these changes, style remained the dominant consideration, and their effectiveness is in doubt. Tests have failed to establish, for example, an advantage for the "deep-dish" steering wheel compared with the conventional wheel; the motorist will still collapse the rim to the hub.

This year, these small concessions to safety design have virtually been discontinued. "A square foot of chrome sells ten times more cars than the best safety-door latch," declared one industry representative. Dashboard padding remains one of a few safety accessories available as optional equipment. This is like saying to the consumer: "Here's a hot car. Now, if you wish to be safe in it, you'll have to pay more."

None of this should be construed as placing the increasingly popular mites from abroad in a more favorable light. Most foreign cars offer far less protection to the motorist than domestic ones.

Prevailing analyses of vehicular accidents circulated for popular consumption tend to impede constructive thinking by adherence to some monistic theory of causation. Take one of the more publicized ogres—speed. Cornell's findings, based on data covering 3,203 cars in injury-producing accidents, indicate that 74 per cent of the cars were going at a *traveling* speed under 60 mph and about 88 per cent involved *impact* speeds under 60 mph. The average impact speed on urban roads was 27 mph; on rural roads, 41 mph. Dangerous or fatal injuries observed in accidents when the traveling speed was less than 60 mph are influenced far more by the shape and structure of interior car components with which the body came into contact than by the speed at which the cars were moving. Many fatalities have been recorded which occurred in panic stops or collisions at a speed under 25 mph. Cornell's concluding statement:

> Statistical tests indicated that even if a top speed limit of 60 mph could be uniformly and absolutely maintained, 73 per cent of the dangerous and fatal injuries observed would still be expected to occur . . . the control of speed alone would have only limited effect on the frequency of dangerous and fatal injuries.

In brief, automobiles are so designed as to be dangerous at any speed.

Our preoccupation has been almost entirely with the cause of accidents seen primarily in terms of the driver and not with the instruments that produce the injuries. Erratic driving will always be characteristic, to some degree, of the traffic scene; exhortation and stricter law enforcement have at best a limited effect. Much more significant for saving life is the application of engineering remedies to minimize the lethal effects of human error by designing the automobile so as to afford maximum protection to occupants in the event of a collision. In a word, the job, in part, is to make accidents safe.

The task of publicizing the relation between automotive design and highway casualties is fraught with difficulties. The press, radio and television are not likely to undertake this task in terms of industry responsibility when millions in advertising dollars are being poured into their coffers. Private researchers are reluctant to stray from their scholarly and experimental pursuits, especially when cordial relations with the industry are necessary for the continuation of their projects with the maximum of success. Car manufacturers have thought it best to cooperate with some of these programs and, in one case, when findings became embarrassing, have given financial support. The industry's policy is bearing fruit; most investigators discreetly keep their private disgust with the industry's immobility from seeping into the public limelight. They consider themselves fact-finders and leave the value judgments to others. This adherence to a rigid division of labor provides a convenient rationalization for the widespread amorality among our scholarly elite, who appear insensitive to the increased responsibility as citizens which their superior knowledge should require them to shoulder.

For the past three years, a Special Congressional House Subcommittee on Traffic Safety has been conducting extensive hearings on automobile design. The industry and research organizations have all submitted their testimony and reports. Some revealing facts came out of these hearings, but the press, by and large, has chosen to ignore them. In any case, the subcommittee is proceeding too cautiously for so urgent a matter. It has been too solicitous of recommendations for delay advanced by some academicians who see automotive design from the viewpoint of engineering perfection rather than as a national health emergency requiring immediate, even if not perfect, engineering remedy. Better techniques will be developed, but at least for the present, there will be added protection from remedying known design hazards. This has been the point that many safety engineers and physicians have vainly been urging.

Even if all the facts, laid before the public, did not increase consumer demand for safety design (which is unlikely), the manufacturers should not be relieved of their responsibility. Innumerable precedents show that the consumer must be protected at times from his own indiscretion and vanity. Dangerous drugs cannot be dispensed without a licensed physician's prescription; meat must pass federal inspection before distribution;

railroads and other interstate carriers are required to meet safety standards regarding their equipment.

State motor-vehicle codes set minimum standards for certain vehicular equipment. This legislation has not compelled manufacturers to adopt known safety-design features (with the exception of safety glass), but has merely endorsed previous standards long employed by the car producers. Examples: brake requirements, headlight specifications, horns, mufflers, windshield wipers, rear-view mirrors. Thus the impact of these requirements falls primarily on the operator, who has to keep this equipment functioning. The legislative purpose is directed to accident *prevention* and only peripherally to implementing standards that might *prevent injuries.*

But state laws do not begin to cope with design defects of the postwar car which increase the *risk of collision.* Examples: the terrific visual distortion of the wrap-around windshield; leakage of carbon monoxide; rear-end fishtailing in hard turns; undue brake fade and the decreased braking area of the recent fourteen-inch wheel; the tinted windshield condemned as violative of all basic optical principles to the extent that visual loss at night ranges from 15 per cent to 45 per cent; and the fire hazard of the undercoating and some upholstery.

Motor vehicles have been found to be poorly designed with regard to human capacities and limitations both physical and psychological. For example, there are—especially in truck cabs—unnecessary difficulties in reaching and operating control levers, in reading half-hidden dials and gauges; there are seats that induce poor posture or discomfort, mirrors whose poor placement and size impair vision, visors inadequately shielding eyes from bright light, and uncomfortable temperature, humidity and noise levels. The cumulative effects lead to fatigue, deterioration of driving efficiency and reaction time, and frequently to an accident which cannot be attributed, in the light of such poor design, to the driver.

Recourse to the courts for judgment against a manufacturer by a plaintiff injured by the defective interior design of his car while involved in an accident stands a dim chance of success. While the courts have hung liability on manufacturers for injuries due to defectively designed products, the closest they have come in motor-vehicle cases has been to hold the producer liable for a design defect instrumental in causing the accident, e.g., the braking system. The question of automotive death-traps cannot be dealt with adequately by the limited authority and resources of the judiciary, although a few pertinent decisions would have a salutary effect.

By all relevant criteria, a problem so national in scope and technical in nature can best be handled by the legislative process, on the federal level, with delegation to an appropriate administrative body. It requires uniformity in treatment and central administration, for as an interstate matter, the job cannot be left to the states with their dissimilar laws setting low requirements that are not strictly enforced and that do not strike at the heart of the malady—the blueprint on the Detroit drawing board. The thirty-three-year record of the attempt to introduce state uniformity in establishing the most basic equipment standards for automobiles has been disappointing.

Perhaps the best summation of the whole issue lies in a physician's comment on the car manufacturer's design policy: "Translated into medicine," he writes, "it would be comparable to withholding known methods of life-saving value."

IV.

A FORCE TO BE RECKONED WITH: 1960–1990

FRANK DONNER

"The truth is bad enough," Frank Donner (1911–1993) liked to say: the careful and sardonic watchwords of a writer and attorney immersed for decades in the task of documenting political surveillance and repression by law-enforcement agencies.

Donner began his career as a New Deal lawyer specializing in equal pay for women. By the 1940s he was counsel to the United Electrical Workers Union, and when the UE's leaders were subpoenaed by the House Un-American Activities Committee he emerged as a leading civil-liberties attorney. He defended Communist party members and other individuals charged with sedition under the Smith Act, held in contempt of Congress and otherwise at risk in the paranoid McCarthy era. In 1961 he wrote The Un-Americans, *from which this chapter is taken, documenting the corruption of anti-Communist informants and the ties of HUAC investigators to far-right hate groups. Donner's antiauthoritarian muckraking in* The Un-Americans *presages the growing skepticism of the early 1960s.*

In 1971 Donner established the American Civil Liberties Union Project on Political Surveillance, rummaging newly released FBI files and other records showing the massive, and sometimes violent, extent of government interference in political activism. In The Age of Surveillance *(1980) Donner not only dissected specific abuses by the FBI and CIA but also proposed that pervasive spying on citizens amounts to a secret "mode of governance" used by authorities to maintain social control. His final book,* Protectors of Privilege *(1990) examined civil-liberties abuses by local police departments.*

Though Donner considered himself an attorney first and foremost, his articles and books set the standard—in depth of research, in clarity of thought, and in grace of prose—for journalists covering civil liberties abuses.

FROM ANATOMY OF A HATE GROUP

From *The Un-Americans,* 1962

For the 23 years of its existence HUAC has had close and continuous ties with the hate underworld and the more "respectable" pressure groups which work with it. The Dies Committee's first investigator was

Edward F. Sullivan, a publicity specialist for native Fascist groups and a former professional labor spy. Two years before his appointment he was the principal speaker at an Asheville, North Carolina, convention of native Fascists. (Sullivan's speech was described in the local press as "what Hitler would have said had he been speaking.") He also was a prominent speaker at Nazi Bund and Coughlinite gatherings. Another Committee collaborator was Harry Jung, Chicago propagandist of anti-Semitism. J. B. Matthews, the scholar of the patrioteer hate underworld, and Walter S. Steele, one of its principal spokesmen, were pillars of the Dies Committee.

One of Dies's strongest admirers and collaborators was Joseph P. Kamp, a professional hate merchant who was editor and publisher of a Fascist magazine, *The Awakener.* Kamp's Constitutional Educational League had a working relationship with the Committee. Kamp had access to the Committee's files, in return for which he supplied the Committee with thousands of names. The Educational League gave Dies an "Americanism" award; it was subsequently mentioned in a Federal conspiracy indictment.[1]

Dies enjoyed a similar relationship with Father Charles E. Coughlin, Fascist priest, leader of the Christian Front. Through his radio program and his publication, *Social Justice,* Father Coughlin disseminated quantities of Nazi propaganda. He too provided Dies with lists of names and propaganda material. In 1939 he issued these instructions to his followers:

> In your appreciation of the work accomplished by Dies employ some of your leisure moments to write him a letter of encouragement. In fact, a million letters brought to his desk would be an answer to those who are bent on destroying him and the legislative body he represents.

1 When HUAC's continuance was threatened, Kamp wrote in *The Awakener,* "The League began a nationwide drive on its behalf, secured over 4 million signatures to petitions and deluged Congress with an avalanche of letters from aroused patriots."

Paid Nazi agents were enthusiastic about HUAC and its work. A banquet for Dies was given by Fascist propagandist Merwin K. Hart in December 1939 (Mr. Hart, incidentally, was a contributor to Chairman Walter's most recent congressional campaign. His National Economic Council was charged a few years ago by the Buchanan Committee with "ill-concealed anti-Semitism.") Among those who did honor to Dies were Bundist James Wheeler Hill, and German-American Bund leader, Fritz Kuhn. When asked what he thought of the Committee, Kuhn replied, "I am in favor of it being appointed again and I want them to get more money." Convicted Nazi agent George Sylvester Viereck said, "I have the highest respect for the Committee and sympathize with its program." The Federal Communications Commission reported that "Representative Dies received as many favorable references in Axis propaganda in this country as any other living American public figure." This was during the war.

Dies shared speaking platforms with Fascist James True, inventor of a special blackjack called the "kike-killer," and Reverend Edward Lodge Curran, Father Coughlin's lieutenant. Under Dies, the Committee fed material and articles by its members to Reverend Gerald B. Winrod's *Defender* and Reverend Gerald L. K. Smith's *The Cross and the Flag,* both anti-Semitic hate sheets. Smith and Winrod showered Dies with praise—as did the entire hate underworld.

For example, Wiliam Dudley Pelley, the head of the pro-Nazi Silver Shirts, said, "I formed the Silver Legion in 1933 . . . to propagandize exactly the same principles." The Ku Klux Klan's Imperial Wizard, James Colescott, asserted, "[The Committee's] program so closely parallels the program of the Klan that there's no distinguishable difference between them." In 1942, Imperial Wizard Colescott arranged a private interview with Dies which resulted in his urging Klansmen everywhere "to support the work of the Dies Committee." In the Klan's publication, *The Fiery Cross,* for January 1942, he praised the Committee's "great service to our country."

It is hardly surprising that Representative Samuel Dickstein told the House in 1941: "110 Fascist organizations in the United States have had, and have now, the key to the back door of the Un-American Activities Committee."

Dies was under constant attack by liberal forces for his failure to investigate Fascist organizations. But Dies used his powers to shield these groups and made token investigations only to preserve the appearance of impartiality.[2]

These critics failed to appreciate the underlying realities of the Dies Committee's relationship to the hate underworld. They had become partners in a joint enterprise. The hate groups gave HUAC names, propaganda and political support. HUAC used the power of the government to strike at the hatists' targets. Then this material, fed into the Committee's files and burnished with the prestige of officialdom, was used by the underworld in its press. As David Wesley has summed it up:

> What these long years did, was to create a solid establishment: an acre of files, a thoroughly indoctrinated staff, a firm tradition, a network of contacts and sources of information, a conditioned pattern of behavior, a methodology, all intricately interwoven into the whole fabric of the underworld of the peddlers of hate, with its interlocking directorship and its broad, cross-pollinating system of propaganda organs.

After HUAC was reconstituted in 1945, it continued its collaboration with hate groups. The Committee was dominated by Congressman John

2 In June 1947, HUAC, in response to liberal pressure, set up a subcommittee on Fascism, headed by Representative John McDowell, himself an anti-Semite, of Pennsylvania. The subcommittee was promptly challenged by Representative Sabath to take action by investigating a group of prominent Fascist organizations. The subcommittee met for ten minutes and decided there was nothing to investigate.
Chairman Velde, in 1945, in a move to win support for HUAC, then under the severe criticism for its attack on the clergy, carefully selected for investigation the two smallest hate outfits he could find: The National Renaissance Party and the magazine Common Sense, both of whose supporters could be housed in the same telephone booth. No witnesses were called, but a report was issued.

Rankin[3] of Mississippi, one of the most virulent anti-Semites ever to sit in Congress. Rankin had been honored by the Nazis and did not hesitate to attack Jews and Negroes as inferior peoples whenever he found an opportunity. On November 18, 1943, he announced that I. F. Stone, a Washington liberal journalist who had attacked him for his anti-Semitism, was really named Isidore Feinstein.[4] When a group of women called on him to protest his bill denying the right of franchise to all American soldiers, Mr. Rankin said of these ladies: "If I am any judge, they are Communists, pure and simple, probably more simple than pure. They looked like foreigners to me. I never saw such a wilderness of noses in my life." Speaking on the floor of the House on February 21, 1944, he referred to Walter Winchell as "the communistic little kike."

In the first major debate on the new HUAC in the House, members of Congress complained that HUAC was doing business at the same old stand. Representative Hook of Michigan described the Committee as a "sounding board for the un-American Fascist groups," and he informed the House that "Gerald L. K. Smith [the notorious anti-Semite] is not only the Committee's adviser on un-Americanism, he is also the confidante of the Committee's plans." Representative Savage of Washington complained: "It seems to me all Gerald L. K. Smith has to do is yell 'sic 'em' and the Committee's counsel takes after whatever party Mr. Smith is peeved at." Representative O'Toole of New York said: "The Committee has permitted itself to become a forum for the dissemination of racial and religious theories that are not part of our democracy."

The Wood-Rankin Committee's hate-group connections sparked a number of investigations in the forties. One of the first was the attempt to purge the radio of a group of liberal commentators who were critical of the hate groups. In October 1945 the Committee obtained 78 scripts

3 The nominal Chairman was Representative Edward J. Hart of New Jersey, who resigned in July 1945 and was succeeded by Representative John J. Wood of Georgia.

4 Interestingly enough, Chairman Walter told the House the same thing when Stone criticized the Committee.

of radio commentators. In December the Committee introduced a bill which would "by proper and frequent announcements clearly separate and distinguish programs consisting of news items from those programs based upon, or consisting of, personal opinion or propaganda." On February 2, 1946, Rankin said, "I want to tell you now, some of this stuff that is going over the air should be stopped. Of all the dirt and filth I ever heard, those filthy attacks on me and the Committee on Un-American Activities by Walter Winchell are the worst."

The Committee then turned its investigative talents to proving that the United States is not a democracy—the favorite thesis of the lunatic fringe. Early in 1946 liberal organizations which had concerned themselves with "democracy" were reminded in letters from Committee Counsel Adamson that "this country was not organized as a democracy." Adamson wrote as follows to columnist Drew Pearson: "Several people have called to my attention the closing line of your Sunday night broadcast, 'Make democracy work.' I should like very much to have your definition of the word 'democracy' as you are using it over the radio. If you will be good enough to supply this information, I will give the matter further consideration to determine whether it should be called to the attention of the members of the committee for such action as they deem proper."

The Hollywood probe of 1947 also had strong hatist links. The files on Hollywood had been developed by Fascist publicist Edward F. Sullivan, and the pressure for the investigation had come from an assortment of native Fascists. Gerald L. K. Smith finally turned the trick. In 1948 he wrote in *The Cross and the Flag,* "We do take credit, we Christian Nationalists, for the recent investigation into Hollywood."

In 1949 HUAC made a sally into the field of education. It asked more than 100 schools and colleges to submit textbooks for a check on subversive content. This probe, too, was inspired by a lunatic-fringe outfit, the National Council for American Education, which was run by the notorious anti-Semite Allen A. Zoll. It boasted on its Board of Governors the Coughlinite priest Edward Lodge Curran and a Committee member, Representative (late Senator) Karl Mundt.

With the emergence of McCarthyism, HUAC was no longer limited to old-fashioned hatist and crackpot sects for investigative suggestions and support.[5] Hate became everybody's business. The function of the private organization in HUAC's operation continued to be important. Its principal role was to act as HUAC's agent and collaborator in the hearing held to expose HUAC's targets. The old-line professional hate groups together with patriotic societies, reactionary fraternal orders, individual bigots and patrioteers (the Network),[6] undertook the punishment of HUAC's victims, a perfect outlet for the aggressive action the hate group craves. The primary weapons used against HUAC's victims are denunciation and discharge pressures. The hatist adds to these his own special weapons: the anonymous telephone call, the "crank" letter, boycott, vandalism and physical violence. During the fifties, too, HUAC's dossiers and files—the house that hate groups built—multiplied fantastically. The two-way flow—of names into the Committee and of "official" smears back to their hatist source—became a vast standardized operation.[7] In addition, these files were being stocked with names and propaganda from new sources: the FBI files and ex-Communists. Every hate group was able to become a little do-it-yourself HUAC. These groups, too, emerged as the major consumers and distributors of HUAC propaganda, which they disseminated in millions of copies. It costs them nothing and gives the cachet of official support to their own programs. HUAC, on its part, is a national clearinghouse for the merchandise of hate.

5 The most striking of HUAC's present relationships to the classic hate groups are in the field of religion. These are discussed in a later chapter.

6 Throughout this book I use the term "the Network" as a shorthand description of a large group of organizations and movements which cooperate with HUAC in a variety of ways. HUAC's network covers the ultra-rightist ("the radical right") segments of the political spectrum, the patriotic and nationalist organizations and their "Americanism" commissions, the crackpot hate sects, the irredentist refugee formations, certain religious movements and groupings, and specialized blacklisting services and organizations.

These organizations are HUAC's "public" in the theatrical sense—its wildly approving audience. They are also HUAC's political base and its collaborators in the exposure process.

7 See Chapter 14, "Big Brother Is Watching You."

Rachel Carson

It is difficult to appreciate, from today's vantage point, the radical impact Rachel Carson's Silent Spring *had upon its publication in 1962. Her indictment of chemical companies and government regulators not only warned of the dangers of pollution; Carson challenged scientists to engage in democratic debate over technology, and insisted that the dangers of pesticides required a new definition of humanity as part of a vulnerable ecosystem.*

Yet behind Silent Spring*'s revolutionary conclusions lies meticulous science journalism. Trained as an aquatic biologist, Carson found her first work—like Stetson Kennedy and Frank Donner—in Franklin Roosevelt's New Deal government, in the Department of Commerce's Bureau of Fisheries, later the Fish and Wildlife Service. For extra income she began writing features and essays on marine life, culminating in* The Sea Around Us *(1951), a critical success and best-seller. When she turned her attention to pesticides in the late 1950s, Carson drew on scientific literature and documents collected in a lawsuit against the federal government's insect-eradication program. The chemical industry mounted a $250,000 campaign against* Silent Spring *but were unable to discredit Carson's reporting or conclusions.*

The triumph of Silent Spring *was accompanied by personal tragedy for Carson: afflicted by breast cancer and arthritis, she died eighteen months after the book's publication.*

AND NO BIRDS SING

From *Silent Spring,* 1962

Over increasingly large areas of the United States, spring now comes unheralded by the return of the birds, and the early mornings are strangely silent where once they were filled with the beauty of bird song. This sudden silencing of the song of birds, this obliteration of the color and beauty and interest they lend to our world have come about swiftly, insidiously, and unnoticed by those whose communities are as yet unaffected.

From the town of Hinsdale, Illinois, a housewife wrote in despair to one of the world's leading ornithologists, Robert Cushman Murphy, Curator Emeritus of Birds at the American Museum of Natural History.

> Here in our village the elm trees have been sprayed for several years [she wrote in 1958]. When we moved here six years ago, there was a wealth of bird life; I put up a feeder and had a steady stream of cardinals, chickadees, downies and nuthatches all winter, and the cardinals and chickadees brought their young ones in the summer.
>
> After several years of DDT spray, the town is almost devoid of robins and starlings; chickadees have not been on my shelf for two years, and this year the cardinals are gone too; the nesting population in the neighborhood seems to consist of one dove pair and perhaps one catbird family.
>
> It is hard to explain to the children that the birds have been killed off, when they have learned in school that a Federal law protects the birds from killing or capture. "Will they ever come back?" they ask, and I do not have the answer. The elms are still dying, and so are the birds. *Is* anything being done? *Can* anything be done? Can *I* do anything?

A year after the federal government had launched a massive spraying program against the fire ant, an Alabama woman wrote: "Our place has been a veritable bird sanctuary for over half a century. Last July we all remarked, 'There are more birds than ever.' Then, suddenly, in the second week of August, they all disappeared. I was accustomed to rising early to care for my favorite mare that had a young filly. There was not a sound of the song of a bird. It was eerie, terrifying. What was man doing to our perfect and beautiful world? Finally, five months later a blue jay appeared and a wren."

The autumn months to which she referred brought other somber reports from the deep South, where in Mississippi, Louisiana, and Alabama the *Field Notes* published quarterly by the National Audubon Society and the United States Fish and Wildlife Service noted the striking phenomenon of "blank spots weirdly empty of virtually *all* bird life." The *Field Notes* are a compilation of the reports of seasoned observers who have spent many years afield in their particular areas and have unparalleled knowledge of the normal bird life of the region. One such observer reported that in driving about southern Mississippi that fall she saw "no land birds at all for long distances." Another in Baton Rouge reported that the contents of her feeders had lain untouched "for weeks on end," while fruiting shrubs in her yard, that ordinarily would be stripped clean by that time, still were laden with berries. Still another reported that his picture window, "which often used to frame a scene splashed with the red of 40 or 50 cardinals and crowded with other species, seldom permitted a view of as many as a bird or two at a time." Professor Maurice Brooks of the University of West Virginia, an authority on the birds of the Appalachian region, reported that the West Virginia bird population had undergone "an incredible reduction."

One story might serve as the tragic symbol of the fate of the birds—a fate that has already overtaken some species, and that threatens all. It is the story of the robin, the bird known to everyone. To millions of Americans, the season's first robin means that the grip of winter is broken. Its coming is an event reported in newspapers and told eagerly at the breakfast table. And as the number of migrants grows and the first mists of green appear in the woodlands, thousands of people listen for the first dawn chorus of the robins throbbing in the early morning light. But now all is changed, and not even the return of the birds may be taken for granted.

The survival of the robin, and indeed of many other species as well, seems fatefully linked with the American elm, a tree that is part of the history of thousands of towns from the Atlantic to the Rockies, gracing their streets and their village squares and college campuses with majestic archways of green. Now the elms are stricken with a disease that afflicts them throughout their range, a disease so serious that many experts believe all efforts to save the elms will in the end be futile. It would be tragic to lose the elms, but it would be doubly tragic if, in vain efforts to save them, we plunge vast segments of our bird populations into the night of extinction. Yet this is precisely what is threatened.

The so-called Dutch elm disease entered the United States from Europe about 1930 in elm burl logs imported for the veneer industry. It is a fungus disease; the organism invades the water-conducting vessels of the tree, spreads by spores carried in the flow of sap, and by its poisonous secretions as well as by mechanical clogging causes the branches to wilt and the tree to die. The disease is spread from diseased to healthy trees by elm bark beetles. The galleries which the insects have tunneled out under the bark of dead trees become contaminated with spores of the invading fungus, and the spores adhere to the insect body and are carried wherever the beetle flies. Efforts to control the fungus disease of the elms have been directed largely toward control of the carrier insect. In community after community, especially throughout the strongholds of the American elm, the Midwest and New England, intensive spraying has become a routine procedure.

What this spraying could mean to bird life, and especially to the robin, was first made clear by the work of two ornithologists at Michigan State University, Professor George Wallace and one of his graduate students, John Mehner. When Mr. Mehner began work for the doctorate in 1954, he chose a research project that had to do with robin populations. This was quite by chance, for at that time no one suspected that the robins were in danger. But even as he undertook the work, events occurred that were to change its character and indeed to deprive him of his material.

Spraying for Dutch elm disease began in a small way on the university campus in 1954. The following year the city of East Lansing (where the university is located) joined in, spraying on the campus was expanded, and, with local programs for gypsy moth and mosquito control also under way, the rain of chemicals increased to a downpour.

During 1954, the year of the first light spraying, all seemed well. The following spring the migrating robins began to return to the campus as usual. Like the bluebells in Tomlinson's haunting essay "The Lost Wood," they were "expecting no evil" as they reoccupied their familiar territories. But soon it became evident that something was wrong. Dead and dying robins began to appear on the campus. Few birds were seen in their normal foraging activities or assembling in their usual roosts. Few nests were built; few young appeared. The pattern was repeated with monotonous regularity in succeeding springs. The sprayed area had become a lethal trap in which each wave of migrating robins would be eliminated in about a week. Then new arrivals would come in, only to add to the numbers of doomed birds seen on the campus in the agonized tremors that precede death.

"The campus is serving as a graveyard for most of the robins that attempt to take up residence in the spring," said Dr. Wallace. But why? At first he suspected some disease of the nervous system, but soon it became evident that "in spite of the assurances of the insecticide people that their sprays were 'harmless to birds' the robins were really dying of insecticidal poisoning; they exhibited the well-known symptoms of loss of balance, followed by tremors, convulsions, and death."

Several facts suggested that the robins were being poisoned, not so much by direct contact with the insecticides as indirectly, by eating earthworms. Campus earthworms had been fed inadvertently to crayfish in a research project and all the crayfish had promptly died. A snake kept in a laboratory cage had gone into violent tremors after being fed such worms. And earthworms are the principal food of robins in the spring.

A key piece in the jigsaw puzzle of the doomed robins was soon to be supplied by Dr. Roy Barker of the Illinois Natural History Survey at Urbana. Dr. Barker's work, published in 1958, traced the intricate cycle of events by which the robins' fate is linked to the elm trees by way of the earthworms. The trees are sprayed in the spring (usually at the rate of 2 to 5 pounds of DDT per 50-foot tree, which may be the equivalent of as much as *23 pounds per acre* where elms are numerous) and often again in July, at about half this concentration. Powerful sprayers direct a stream of poison to all parts of the tallest trees, killing directly not only the target organism, the bark beetle, but other insects, including pollinating species and predatory spiders and beetles. The poison forms a tenacious film over the leaves and bark. Rains do not wash it away. In the autumn the leaves fall to the ground, accumulate in sodden layers, and begin the slow process of becoming one with the soil. In this they are aided by the toil of the earthworms, who feed in the leaf litter, for elm leaves are among their favorite foods. In feeding on the leaves the worms also swallow the insecticide, accumulating and concentrating it in their bodies. Dr. Barker found deposits of DDT throughout the digestive tracts of the worms, their blood vessels, nerves, and body wall. Undoubtedly some of the earthworms themselves succumb, but others survive to become "biological magnifiers" of the poison. In the spring the robins return to provide another link in the cycle. As few as 11 large earthworms can transfer a lethal dose of DDT to a robin. And 11 worms form a small part of a day's rations to a bird that eats 10 to 12 earthworms in as many minutes.

Not all robins receive a lethal dose, but another consequence may lead to the extinction of their kind as surely as fatal poisoning. The shadow of sterility lies over all the bird studies and indeed lengthens to include all living things within its potential range. There are now only two or three dozen robins to be found each spring on the entire 185-acre campus of Michigan State University, compared with a conservatively estimated 370 adults in this area before spraying. In 1954 every robin nest under observation by Mehner produced young. Toward the end of June, 1957, when at least 370 young birds (the normal replacement of the adult population) would have been foraging over the campus in the years before spraying began, Mehner could find *only one young robin.* A year later Dr. Wallace was to report: "At no time during the spring or summer [of 1958] did I see a fledgling robin anywhere on the main campus, and so far I have failed to find anyone else who has seen one there."

Part of this failure to produce young is due, of course, to the fact that one or more of a pair of robins dies before the nesting cycle is completed. But Wallace has significant records which point to something more sinister—the actual destruction of the birds' capacity to reproduce. He has, for example, "records of robins and other birds building nests but laying no eggs, and others laying eggs and incubating them but not hatching them. We have one record of a robin that sat on its eggs faithfully for 21 days and they did not hatch. The normal incubation period is 13 days. . . . Our analyses are showing high concentrations of DDT in the testes and ovaries of breeding birds," he told a congressional committee in 1960. "Ten males had amounts ranging from 30 to 109 parts per million in the testes, and two females had 151 and 211 parts per million respectively in the egg follicles in their ovaries."

Soon studies in other areas began to develop findings equally dismal. Professor Joseph Hickey and his students at the University of Wisconsin, after careful comparative studies of sprayed and unsprayed areas, reported the robin mortality to be at least 86 to 88 per cent. The Cranbrook Institute of Science at Bloomfield Hills, Michigan, in an effort to assess the extent of bird loss caused by the spraying of the elms, asked in 1956 that all birds thought to be victims of DDT poisoning be turned in to the institute for examination. The request had a response beyond all expectations. Within a few weeks the deep-freeze facilities of the institute were taxed to capacity, so that other specimens had to be refused. By 1959 a thousand poisoned birds from this single community had been turned in or reported. Although the robin was the chief victim (one woman calling the institute reported 12 robins lying dead on her lawn as she spoke), 63 different species were included among the specimens examined at the institute.

The robins, then, are only one part of the chain of devastation linked to the spraying of the elms, even as the elm program is only one of the multitudinous spray programs that cover our land with poisons. Heavy mortality has occurred among about 90 species of birds, including those most familiar to suburbanites and amateur naturalists. The populations of nesting birds in general have declined as much as 90 per cent in some of the sprayed towns. As we shall see, all the various types of birds are affected—ground feeders, treetop feeders, bark feeders, predators.

It is only reasonable to suppose that all birds and mammals heavily dependent on earthworms or other soil organisms for food are threatened by the robins' fate. Some 45 species of birds include earthworms in their diet. Among them is the woodcock, a species that winters in southern areas recently heavily sprayed with heptachlor. Two significant discoveries have now been made about the woodcock. Production of young birds on the New Brunswick breeding grounds is definitely reduced, and adult birds that have been analyzed contain large residues of DDT and heptachlor.

Already there are disturbing records of heavy mortality among more than 20 other species of ground-feeding birds whose food—worms, ants, grubs, or other soil organisms—has been poisoned. These include three of the thrushes whose songs are among the most exquisite of bird voices, the olive-backed, the wood, and the hermit. And the sparrows that flit through the shrubby understory of the woodlands and forage with rustling sounds amid the fallen leaves—the song sparrow and the white-throat—these, too, have been found among the victims of the elm sprays.

Mammals, also, may easily be involved in the cycle, directly or indirectly. Earthworms are important among the various foods of the raccoon, and are eaten in the spring and fall by opossums. Such subterranean tunnelers as shrews and moles capture them in some numbers, and then perhaps pass on the poison to predators such as screech owls and barn owls. Several dying screech owls were picked up in Wisconsin following heavy rains in spring, perhaps poisoned by feeding on earthworms. Hawks and owls have been found in convulsions—great horned owls, screech owls, red-shouldered hawks, sparrow hawks, marsh hawks. These may be cases of secondary poisoning, caused by eating birds or mice that have accumulated insecticides in their livers or other organs.

Nor is it only the creatures that forage on the ground or those who prey on them that are endangered by the foliar spraying of the elms. All of the treetop feeders, the birds that glean their insect food from the leaves, have disappeared from heavily sprayed areas, among them those woodland sprites the kinglets, both ruby-crowned and golden-crowned, the tiny gnatcatchers, and many of the warblers, whose migrating hordes flow through the trees in spring in a multicolored tide of life. In 1956, a late spring delayed spraying so that it coincided with the arrival of an exceptionally heavy wave of warbler migration. Nearly all species of warblers present in the area were represented in the heavy kill that followed. In Whitefish Bay, Wisconsin, at least a thousand myrtle warblers could be seen in migration during former years; in 1958, after the spraying of the elms, observers could find only two. So, with additions from other communities, the list grows, and the warblers killed by the spray include those that most charm and fascinate all who are aware of them: the black-and-white, the yellow, the magnolia, and the Cape May; the oven-bird, whose call throbs in the Maytime woods; the Blackburnian, whose wings are touched with flame; the chestnut-sided, the Canadian, and the black-throated green. These treetop feeders are affected either directly by eating poisoned insects or indirectly by a shortage of food.

The loss of food has also struck hard at the swallows that cruise the skies, straining out the aerial insects as herring strain the plankton of the sea. A Wisconsin naturalist reported: "Swallows have been hard hit. Everyone complains of how few they have compared to four or five years ago. Our sky overhead was full of them only four years ago. Now we seldom see any. . . . This could be both lack of insects because of spray, or poisoned insects."

Of other birds this same observer wrote: "Another striking loss is the phoebe. Flycatchers are scarce everywhere but the early hardy common phoebe is no more. I've seen one this spring and only one last spring. Other birders in Wisconsin make the same complaint. I have had five or six pair of cardinals in the past, none now. Wrens, robins, catbirds and screech owls have nested each year in our garden. There are none now. Summer mornings are without bird song. Only pest birds, pigeons, starlings and English sparrows remain. It is tragic and I can't bear it."

The dormant sprays applied to the elms in the fall, sending the poison into every little crevice in the bark, are probably responsible for the severe reduction observed in the number of chickadees, nuthatches, titmice, woodpeckers, and brown creepers. During the winter of 1957–58, Dr. Wallace saw no chickadees or nuthatches at his home feeding station for the first time in many years. Three nuthatches he found later provided a sorry little step-by-step lesson in cause and effect: one was feeding on an elm, another was found dying of typical DDT symptoms, the third was dead. The dying nuthatch was later found to have 226 parts per million of DDT in its tissues.

The feeding habits of all these birds not only make them especially vulnerable to insect sprays but also make their loss a deplorable one for economic as well as less tangible reasons. The summer food of the white-breasted nuthatch and the brown creeper, for example, includes the eggs, larvae, and adults of a very large number of insects injurious to trees. About three quarters of the food of the chickadee is animal, including all stages of the life cycle of many insects. The chickadee's method of feeding is described in Bent's monumental *Life Histories* of North American birds: "As the flock moves along each bird examines minutely bark, twigs, and branches, searching for tiny bits of food (spiders' eggs, cocoons, or other dormant insect life)."

Various scientific studies have established the critical role of birds in insect control in various situations. Thus, woodpeckers are the primary control of the Engelmann spruce beetle, reducing its populations from 45 to 98 per cent and are important in the control of the codling moth in apple orchards. Chickadees and other winter-resident birds can protect orchards against the cankerworm.

But what happens in nature is not allowed to happen in the modern, chemical-drenched world, where spraying destroys not only the insects but their principal enemy, the birds. When later there is a resurgence of the insect population, as almost always happens, the birds are not there to keep their numbers in check. As the Curator of Birds at the Milwaukee Public Museum, Owen J. Gromme, wrote to the Milwaukee *Journal*: "The greatest enemy of insect life is other predatory insects, birds, and some small mammals, but DDT kills indiscriminately, including nature's own safeguards or policemen. . . . In the name of progress are we to become victims of our own diabolical means of insect control to provide temporary comfort, only to lose out to destroying insects later on? By what means will we control new pests, which will attack remaining tree species after the elms are gone, when nature's safeguards (the birds) have been wiped out by poison?"

Mr. Gromme reported that calls and letters about dead and dying birds had been increasing steadily during the years since spraying began in Wisconsin. Questioning always revealed that spraying or fogging had been done in the area where the birds were dying.

Mr. Gromme's experience has been shared by ornithologists and conservationists at most of the research centers of the Midwest such as the Cranbrook Institute in Michigan, the Illinois Natural History Survey, and the University of Wisconsin. A glance at the Letters-from-Readers column of newspapers almost anywhere that spraying is being done makes clear the fact that citizens are not only becoming aroused and indignant but that often they show a keener understanding of the dangers and inconsistencies of spraying than do the officials who order it done. "I am dreading the days to come soon now when many beautiful birds will be dying in our back yard," wrote a Milwaukee woman. "This is a pitiful, heartbreaking experience. . . . It is, moreover, frustrating and exasperating, for it evidently does not serve the purpose this slaughter was intended to serve. . . . Taking a long look, can you save trees without also saving birds? Do they not, in the economy of nature, save each other? Isn't it possible to help the balance of nature without destroying it?"

The idea that the elms, majestic shade trees though they are, are not "sacred cows" and do not justify an "open end" campaign of destruction against all other forms of life is expressed in other letters. "I have always loved our elm trees which seemed like trademarks on our landscape," wrote another Wisconsin woman. "But there are many kinds of trees. . . . We must save our birds, too. Can anyone imagine anything so cheerless and dreary as a springtime without a robin's song?"

To the public the choice may easily appear to be one of stark black-or-white simplicity: Shall we have birds or shall we have elms? But it is not as simple as that, and by one of the ironies that abound throughout the field of chemical control we may very well end by having neither if we continue on our present, well-traveled road. Spraying is killing the birds but it is not saving the elms. The illusion that salvation of the elms lies at the end of a spray nozzle is a dangerous will-o'-the-wisp that is leading one community after another into a morass of heavy expenditures, without producing lasting results. Greenwich, Connecticut, sprayed regularly for ten years. Then a drought year brought conditions especially favorable to the beetle and the mortality of elms went up 1,000 per cent. In Urbana, Illinois, where the University of Illinois is located, Dutch elm disease first appeared in 1951. Spraying was undertaken in 1953. By 1959, in spite of six years' spraying, the university campus had lost 86 per cent of its elms, half of them victims of Dutch elm disease.

In Toledo, Ohio, a similar experience caused the Superintendent of Forestry, Joseph A. Sweeney, to take a realistic look at the results of spraying. Spraying was begun there in 1953 and continued through 1959. Meanwhile, however, Mr. Sweeney had noticed that a city-wide infestation of the cottony maple scale was worse after the spraying recommended by "the books and the authorities" than it had been before. He decided to review the results of spraying for Dutch elm disease for himself. His findings shocked him. In the city of Toledo, he found, "the only areas under any control were the areas where we used some promptness in removing the diseased or brood trees. Where we depended on spraying the disease was out of control. In the country where nothing has been done the disease has not spread as fast as it has in the city. This indicates that spraying destroys any natural enemies.

"We are abandoning spraying for the Dutch elm disease. This has brought me into conflict with the people who back any recommendations by the United States Department of Agriculture but I have the facts and will stick with them."

It is difficult to understand why these midwestern towns, to which the elm disease spread only rather recently, have so unquestioningly embarked on ambitious and expensive spraying programs, apparently without waiting to inquire into the experience of other areas that have had longer acquaintance with the problem. New York State, for example, has certainly had the longest history of continuous experience with Dutch elm disease, for it was via the Port of New York that diseased elm wood is thought to have entered the United States about 1930. And New York State today has a most impressive record of containing and suppressing the disease. Yet it has not relied upon spraying. In fact, its agricultural extension service does not recommend spraying as a community method of control.

How, then, has New York achieved its fine record? From the early years of the battle for the elms to the present time, it has relied upon rigorous sanitation, or the prompt removal and destruction of all diseased or infected wood. In the beginning some of the results were disappointing, but this was because it was not at first understood that not only diseased trees but all elm wood in which the beetles might breed must be destroyed. Infected elm wood, after being cut and stored for firewood, will release a crop of fungus-carrying beetles unless burned before spring. It is the adult beetles, emerging from hibernation to feed in late April and May, that transmit Dutch elm disease. New York entomologists have learned by experience what kinds of beetle-breeding material have real importance in the spread of the disease. By concentrating on this dangerous material, it has been possible not only to get good results, but to keep the cost of the sanitation program within reasonable limits. By 1950 the incidence of Dutch elm disease in New York City had been reduced to 2/10 of 1 per cent of the city's 55,000 elms. A sanitation program was launched in Westchester County in 1942. During the next 14 years the average annual loss of elms was only 2/10 of 1 per cent a year. Buffalo, with 185,000 elms, has an excellent record of containing the disease by sanitation, with recent annual losses amounting to only 3/10 of 1 per cent. In other words, at this rate of loss it would take about 300 years to eliminate Buffalo's elms.

What has happened in Syracuse is especially impressive. There no effective program was in operation before 1957. Between 1951 and 1956 Syracuse lost nearly 3,000 elms. Then, under the direction of Howard C. Miller of the New York State University College of Forestry, an intensive drive was made to remove all diseased elm trees and all possible sources of beetle-breeding elm wood. The rate of loss is now well below 1 per cent a year.

The economy of the sanitation method is stressed by New York experts in Dutch elm disease control. "In most cases the actual expense is small compared with the probable saving," says J. G. Matthysse of the New York State College of Agriculture. "If it is a case of a dead or broken limb, the limb would have to be removed eventually, as a precaution against possible property damage or personal injury. If it is a fuel-wood pile, the wood can be used before spring, the bark can be peeled from the wood, or the wood can be stored in a dry place. In the case of dying or dead elm trees, the expense of prompt removal to prevent Dutch elm disease spread is usually no greater than would be necessary later, for most dead trees in urban regions must be removed eventually."

The situation with regard to Dutch elm disease is therefore not entirely hopeless provided informed and intelligent measures are taken. While it cannot be eradicated by any means now known, once it has become established in a community, it can be suppressed and contained within reasonable bounds by sanitation, and without the use of methods that are not only futile but involve tragic destruction of bird life. Other possibilities lie within the field of forest genetics, where experiments offer hope of developing a hybrid elm resistant to Dutch elm disease. The European elm is highly resistant, and many of them have been planted in Washington, D.C. Even during a period when a high percentage of the city's elms were affected, no cases of Dutch elm disease were found among these trees.

Replanting through an immediate tree nursery and forestry program is being urged in communities that are losing large numbers of elms. This is important, and although such programs might well include the resistant European elms, they should aim at a variety of species so that no future epidemic could deprive a community of its trees. The key to a healthy plant or animal community lies in what the British ecologist Charles Elton calls "the conservation of variety." What is happening now is in large part a result of the biological unsophistication of past generations. Even a generation ago no one knew that to fill large areas with a single species of tree was to invite disaster. And so whole towns lined their streets and dotted their parks with elms, and today the elms die and so do the birds.

Like the robin, another American bird seems to be on the verge of extinction. This is the national symbol, the eagle. Its populations have dwindled alarmingly within the past decade. The facts suggest that something is at work in the eagle's environment which has virtually destroyed its ability to reproduce. What this may be is not yet definitely known, but there is some evidence that insecticides are responsible.

The most intensively studied eagles in North America have been those nesting along a stretch of coast from Tampa to Fort Myers on the western coast of Florida. There a retired banker from Winnipeg, Charles Broley, achieved ornithological fame by banding more than 1,000 young bald eagles during the years 1939–49. (Only 166 eagles had been banded in all the earlier history of birdbanding.) Mr. Broley banded eagles as young birds during the winter months before they had left their nests. Later recoveries of banded birds showed that these Florida-born eagles range northward along the coast into Canada as far as Prince Edward Island, although they had previously been considered nonmigratory. In the fall they return to the South, their migration being observed at such famous vantage points as Hawk Mountain in eastern Pennsylvania.

During the early years of his banding, Mr. Broley used to find 125 active nests a year on the stretch of coast he had chosen for his work. The number of young banded each year was about 150. In 1947 the production of young birds began to decline. Some nests contained no eggs; others contained eggs that failed to hatch. Between 1952 and 1957, about 80 per cent of the nests failed to produce young. In the last year of this period only 43 nests were occupied. Seven of them produced young (8 eaglets); 23 contained eggs that failed to hatch; 13 were used merely as feeding stations by adult eagles and contained no eggs. In 1958 Mr. Broley ranged over 100 miles of coast before finding and banding one eaglet. Adult eagles, which had been seen at 43 nests in 1957, were so scarce that he observed them at only 10 nests.

Although Mr. Broley's death in 1959 terminated this valuable series of uninterrupted observations, reports by the Florida Audubon Society, as well as from New Jersey and Pennsylvania, confirm the trend that may well make it necessary for us to find a new national emblem. The reports of Maurice Broun, curator of the Hawk Mountain Sanctuary, are especially significant. Hawk Mountain is a picturesque mountaintop in southeastern Pennsylvania, where the easternmost ridges of the Appalachians form a last barrier to the westerly winds before dropping away toward the coastal plain. Winds striking the mountains are deflected upward so that on many autumn days there is a continuous updraft on which the broad-winged hawks and eagles ride without effort, covering many miles of their southward migration in a day. At Hawk Mountain the ridges converge and so do the aerial highways. The result is that from a widespread territory to the north birds pass through this traffic bottleneck.

In his more than a score of years as custodian of the sanctuary there, Maurice Broun has observed and actually tabulated more hawks and eagles than any other American. The peak of the bald eagle migration comes in late August and early September. These are assumed to be Florida birds, returning to home territory after a summer in the North. (Later in the fall and early winter a few larger eagles drift through. These are thought to belong to a northern race, bound for an unknown wintering ground.) During the first years after the sanctuary was established, from 1935 to 1939, 40 per cent of the eagles observed were yearlings, easily identified by their uniformly dark plumage. But in recent years these immature birds have become a rarity. Between 1955 and 1959, they made up only 20 per cent of the total count, and in one year (1957) there was only one young eagle for every 32 adults.

Observations at Hawk Mountain are in line with findings elsewhere. One such report comes from Elton Fawks, an official of the Natural Resources Council of Illinois. Eagles—probably northern nesters—winter along the Mississippi and Illinois Rivers. In 1958 Mr. Fawks reported that a recent count of 59 eagles had included only one immature bird. Similar indications of the dying out of the race come from the world's only sanctuary for eagles alone, Mount Johnson Island in the Susquehanna River. The island, although only 8 miles above Conowingo Dam and about half a mile out from the Lancaster County shore, retains its primitive wildness. Since 1934 its single eagle nest has been under observation by Professor Herbert H. Beck, an ornithologist of Lancaster and custodian of the sanctuary. Between 1935 and 1947 use of the nest was regular and uniformly successful. Since 1947, although the adults have occupied the nest and there is evidence of egg laying, no young eagles have been produced.

On Mount Johnson Island as well as in Florida, then, the same situation prevails—there is some occupancy of nests by adults, some production of eggs, but few or no young birds. In seeking an explanation, only one appears to fit all the facts. This is that the reproductive capacity of the birds has been so lowered by some environmental agent that there are now almost no annual additions of young to maintain the race.

Exactly this sort of situation has been produced artificially in other birds by various experimenters, notably Dr. James DeWitt of the United States Fish and Wildlife Service. Dr. DeWitt's now classic experiments on the effect of a series of insecticides on quail and pheasants have established the fact that exposure to DDT or related chemicals, even when doing no observable harm to the parent birds, may seriously affect reproduction. The way the effect is exerted may vary, but the end result is always the same. For example, quail into whose diet DDT was introduced throughout the breeding season survived and even produced normal numbers of fertile eggs. But few of the eggs hatched. "Many embryos appeared to develop normally during the early stages of incubation, but died during the hatching period," Dr. DeWitt said. Of those that did hatch, more than half died within 5 days. In other tests in which both pheasants and quail were the subjects, the adults produced no eggs whatever if they had been fed insecticide-contaminated diets throughout the year. And at the University of California, Dr. Robert Rudd and Dr. Richard Genelly reported similar findings. When pheasants received dieldrin in their diets, "egg production was markedly lowered and chick survival was poor." According to these authors, the delayed but lethal effect on the young birds follows from storage of dieldrin in the yolk of the egg, from which it is gradually assimilated during incubation and after hatching.

This suggestion is strongly supported by recent studies by Dr. Wallace and a graduate student, Richard F. Bernard, who found high concentrations of DDT in robins on the Michigan State University campus. They found the poison in all of the testes of male robins examined, in developing egg follicles, in the ovaries of females, in completed but unlaid eggs, in the oviducts, in unhatched eggs from deserted nests, in embryos within the eggs, and in a newly hatched, dead nestling.

These important studies establish the fact that the insecticidal poison affects a generation once removed from initial contact with it. Storage of poison in the egg, in the yolk material that nourishes the developing embryo, is a virtual death warrant and explains why so many of DeWitt's birds died in the egg or a few days after hatching.

Laboratory application of these studies to eagles presents difficulties that are nearly insuperable, but field studies are now under way in Florida, New Jersey, and elsewhere in the hope of acquiring definite evidence as to what has caused the apparent sterility of much of the eagle population. Meanwhile, the available circumstantial evidence points to insecticides. In localities where fish are abundant they make up a large part of the eagle's diet (about 65 per cent in Alaska; about 52 per cent in the Chesapeake Bay area). Almost unquestionably the eagles so long studied by Mr. Broley were predominantly fish eaters. Since 1945 this particular coastal area has been subjected to repeated sprayings with DDT dissolved in fuel oil. The principal target of the aerial spraying was the salt-marsh mosquito, which inhabits the marshes and coastal areas that are typical foraging areas for the eagles. Fishes and crabs were killed in enormous numbers. Laboratory analyses of their tissues revealed high concentrations of DDT—as much as 46 parts per million. Like the grebes of Clear Lake, which accumulated heavy concentrations of insecticide residues from eating the fish of the lake, the eagles have almost certainly been storing up the DDT in the tissues of their bodies. And like the grebes, the pheasants, the quail, and the robins, they are less and less able to produce young and to preserve the continuity of their race.

From all over the world come echoes of the peril that faces birds in our modern world. The reports differ in detail, but always repeat the theme of death to wildlife in the wake of pesticides. Such are the stories of hundreds of small birds and partridges dying in France after vine stumps were treated with an arsenic-containing herbicide, or of partridge shoots in Belgium, once famous for the numbers of their birds, denuded of partridges after the spraying of nearby farmlands.

In England the major problem seems to be a specialized one, linked with the growing practice of treating seed with insecticides before sowing. Seed treatment is not a wholly new thing, but in earlier years the chemicals principally used were fungicides. No effects on birds seem to have been noticed. Then about 1956 there was a change to dual-purpose treatment; in addition to a fungicide, dieldrin, aldrin, or heptachlor was added to combat soil insects. Thereupon the situation changed for the worse.

In the spring of 1960 a deluge of reports of dead birds reached British wildlife authorities, including the British Trust for Ornithology, the Royal Society for the Protection of Birds, and the Game Birds Association. "The place is like a battlefield," a landowner in Norfolk wrote. "My keeper has found innumerable corpses, including masses of small birds—Chaffinches, Green-finches, Linnets, Hedge Sparrows, also House Sparrows . . . the destruction of wild life is quite pitiful." A gamekeeper wrote: "My Partridges have been wiped out with the dressed corn, also some Pheasants and all other birds, hundreds of birds have been killed. . . . As a lifelong gamekeeper it has been a distressing experience for me. It is bad to see pairs of Partridges that have died together."

In a joint report, the British Trust for Ornithology and the Royal Society for the Protection of Birds described some 67 kills of birds—a far from complete listing of the destruction that took place in the spring of 1960. Of these 67, 59 were caused by seed dressings, 8 by toxic sprays.

A new wave of poisoning set in the following year. The death of 600 birds on a single estate in Norfolk was reported to the House of Lords, and 100 pheasants died on a farm in North Essex. It soon became evident that more counties were involved than in 1960 (34 compared with 23). Lincolnshire, heavily agricultural, seemed to have suffered most, with reports of 10,000 birds dead. But destruction involved all of agricultural England, from Angus in the north to Cornwall in the south, from Anglesey in the west to Norfolk in the east.

In the spring of 1961 concern reached such a peak that a special committee of the House of Commons made an investigation of the matter, taking testimony from farmers, landowners, and representatives of the

Ministry of Agriculture and of various governmental and nongovernmental agencies concerned with wildlife.

"Pigeons are suddenly dropping out of the sky dead," said one witness. "You can drive a hundred or two hundred miles outside London and not see a single kestrel," reported another. "There has been no parallel in the present century, or at any time so far as I am aware, [this is] the biggest risk to wildlife and game that ever occurred in the country," officials of the Nature Conservancy testified.

Facilities for chemical analysis of the victims were most inadequate to the task, with only two chemists in the country able to make the tests (one the government chemist, the other in the employ of the Royal Society for the Protection of Birds). Witnesses described huge bonfires on which the bodies of the birds were burned. But efforts were made to have carcasses collected for examination, and of the birds analyzed, all but one contained pesticide residues. The single exception was a snipe, which is not a seed-eating bird.

Along with the birds, foxes also may have been affected, probably indirectly by eating poisoned mice or birds. England, plagued by rabbits, sorely needs the fox as a predator. But between November 1959 and April 1960 at least 1,300 foxes died. Deaths were heaviest in the same counties from which sparrow hawks, kestrels, and other birds of prey virtually disappeared, suggesting that the poison was spreading through the food chain, reaching out from the seed eaters to the furred and feathered carnivores. The actions of the moribund foxes were those of animals poisoned by chlorinated hydrocarbon insecticides. They were seen wandering in circles, dazed and half blind, before dying in convulsions.

The hearings convinced the committee that the threat to wildlife was "most alarming"; it accordingly recommended to the House of Commons that "the Minister of Agriculture and the Secretary of State for Scotland should secure the immediate prohibition for the use as seed dressings of compounds containing dieldrin, aldrin, or heptachlor, or chemicals of comparable toxicity." The committee also recommended more adequate controls to ensure that chemicals were adequately tested under field as well as laboratory conditions before being put on the market. This, it is worth emphasizing, is one of the great blank spots in pesticide research everywhere. Manufacturers' tests on the common laboratory animals—rats, dogs, guinea pigs—include no wild species, no birds as a rule, no fishes, and are conducted under controlled and artificial conditions. Their application to wildlife in the field is anything but precise.

England is by no means alone in its problem of protecting birds from treated seeds. Here in the United States the problem has been most troublesome in the rice-growing areas of California and the South. For a number of years California rice growers have been treating seed with DDT as protection against tadpole shrimp and scavenger beetles which sometimes damage seedling rice. California sportsmen have enjoyed excellent hunting because of the concentrations of waterfowl and pheasants in the rice fields. But for the past decade persistent reports of bird losses, especially among pheasants, ducks, and blackbirds, have come from the rice-growing counties. "Pheasant sickness" became a well-known phenomenon: birds "seek water, become paralyzed, and are found on the ditch banks and rice checks quivering," according to one observer. The "sickness" comes in the spring, at the time the rice fields are seeded. The concentration of DDT used is many times the amount that will kill an adult pheasant.

The passage of a few years and the development of even more poisonous insecticides served to increase the hazard from treated seed. Aldrin, which is 100 times as toxic as DDT to pheasants, is now widely used as a seed coating. In the rice fields of eastern Texas, this practice has seriously reduced the populations of the fulvous tree duck, a tawny-colored, gooselike duck of the Gulf Coast. Indeed, there is some reason to think that the rice growers, having found a way to reduce the populations of blackbirds, are using the insecticide for a dual purpose, with disastrous effects on several bird species of the rice fields.

As the habit of killing grows—the resort to "eradicating" any creature that may annoy or inconvenience us—birds are more and more finding themselves a direct target of poisons rather than an incidental one. There is a growing trend toward aerial applications of such deadly poisons as parathion to "control" concentrations of birds distasteful to farmers. The Fish and Wildlife Service has found it necessary to express serious concern over this trend, pointing out that "parathion treated areas constitute a potential hazard to humans, domestic animals, and wildlife." In southern Indiana, for example, a group of farmers went together in the summer of 1959 to engage a spray plane to treat an area of river bottomland with parathion. The area was a favored roosting site for thousands of blackbirds that were feeding in nearby cornfields. The problem could have been solved easily by a slight change in agricultural practice—a shift to a variety of corn with deep-set ears not accessible to the birds—but the farmers had been persuaded of the merits of killing by poison, and so they sent in the planes on their mission of death.

The results probably gratified the farmers, for the casualty list included some 65,000 red-winged blackbirds and starlings. What other wildlife deaths may have gone unnoticed and unrecorded is not known. Parathion is not a specific for blackbirds: it is a universal killer. But such rabbits or raccoons or opossums as may have roamed those bottomlands and perhaps never visited the farmers' cornfields were doomed by a judge and jury who neither knew of their existence nor cared.

And what of human beings? In California orchards sprayed with this same parathion, workers handling foliage that had been treated *a month* earlier collapsed and went into shock, and escaped death only through skilled medical attention. Does Indiana still raise any boys who roam through woods or fields and might even explore the margins of a river? If so, who guarded the poisoned area to keep out any who might wander in, in misguided search for unspoiled nature? Who kept vigilant watch to tell the innocent stroller that the fields he was about to enter were deadly—all their vegetation coated with a lethal film? Yet at so fearful a risk the farmers, with none to hinder them, waged their needless war on blackbirds.

In each of these situations, one turns away to ponder the question: Who has made the decision that sets in motion these chains of poisonings, this ever-widening wave of death that spreads out, like ripples when a pebble is dropped into a still pond? Who has placed in one pan of the scales the leaves that might have been eaten by the beetles and in the other the pitiful heaps of many-hued feathers, the lifeless remains of the birds that fell before the unselective bludgeon of insecticidal poisons? Who has decided—who has the *right* to decide—for the countless legions of people who were not consulted that the supreme value is a world without insects, even though it be also a sterile world ungraced by the curving wing of a bird in flight? The decision is that of the authoritarian temporarily entrusted with power; he has made it during a moment of inattention by millions to whom beauty and the ordered world of nature still have a meaning that is deep and imperative.

I. F. Stone

"I decided to cut the cloth to fit the market," I. F. Stone (1907–1989) recalled of his decision to start his Weekly. *It was the height of the McCarthy era and Stone, formerly political columnist for the bankrupt liberal* Daily Compass *and Washington editor for the nearly-broke* Nation, *decided to strike out on his own, with a four-page investigative weekly.*

It was partly medical accident that turned Stone from a political columnist into a path-breaking investigative journalist. Growing hard of hearing in the 1950s, he came to rely upon hearing transcripts, government reports, the Congressional Record, and other documentary sources—leading him to conclude that "all the information is available to the public if you know where to look." Stone evolved a distinct method, employed to devastating effect: challenging the official lies of politicians and generals with evidence gleaned by careful scrutiny of the public record. That method made him a legend during the Vietnam War, when he regularly shredded the Pentagon's public assessments. In this 1967 dispatch, he uses documentary sources to undermine official accounts of the Tonkin Gulf incident, which had been seized upon by the Johnson administration to justify a wider war.

ALL WE REALLY KNOW IS THAT WE FIRED THE FIRST SHOTS

From *I. F. Stone's Weekly*, March 4, 1968

A major, if inadvertent, revelation in McNamara's new testimony on the Tonkin Gulf affair has been overlooked. If there was indeed an attack involving two U.S. destroyers on the night of Aug. 4, 1964, we began the attack, we opened fire first. Indeed the only shots we are completely sure of beyond any shadow of doubt even at this late date are those which came from our own vessels. McNamara's new version of the attack contradicts the melodramatic account he gave four years ago, two days after the incident, behind the closed doors of a joint executive session of the Senate's Foreign Relations and Armed Services Committees. It was this graphic, but (as it now appears) untrue version which helped stampede the Senate into voting the Tonkin Gulf resolution.

A Mendacious Melodrama

That earlier testimony was given Aug. 6, 1964. When the transcript of that hearing is now compared with the new one held by the Senate Foreign Relations Committee, one can begin to get some idea of the full dimensions of the mendacity by which the Johnson Administration obtained that resolution which was its blank check for war in Southeast Asia. "The attack," McNamara told the Senate committees four years ago, "occurred at night. It appeared to be a deliberate attack in the nature of an ambush. Torpedoes were launched, automatic weapons fire was directed against the vessels (the Maddox and the Turner Joy). They returned the fire." (Our italics.)

The Secretary put it even more vividly when Senator Lausche asked him, "Do you know how many of the torpedoes were set in motion and what small arms were used?"

Secretary McNamara: It is difficult to estimate. This was a very dark night. The attack was carried out during the night, the hours of darkness. It was a premeditated attack, a pre-planned attack. It was described as an ambush in the reports from the commanders, but because it was night it is very difficult to estimate the total amount of fire.

Senator Lausche: The shots were again initiated by the North Vietnamese?

Secretary McNamara: Yes.

General Wheeler: That is correct.

Thus drawn a picture of "unprovoked aggression." It was magnified and emotionalized by President Johnson, who went on TV after the attack and declared, "This new act of aggression, aimed directly at our own forces, again brings home to all of us in the United States the importance of the struggle for peace and security in Southeast Asia." This was echoed in the same high dramatic vein by Adlai Stevenson at the UN Security Council next day: "Without any shadow of doubt . . . planned deliberate military aggression against vessels lawfully present in international waters" was Stevenson's description.

The rhetoric made it sound like a new Pearl Harbor.

But when McNamara appeared before the Senate Foreign Relations Committee a few days ago on February 20 he knew that the Committee had in its possession documents from Defense Department files which cast doubt on every aspect of that earlier version. He had to tone down his own presentation to fit. So in his prepared statement, as given out to the press that day, he gave a very different picture from that drawn four years ago.

"At about 9:39 P.M.," McNamara now related, "both Maddox and Turner opened fire on the approaching craft *when it was evident from their maneuvers* [our italics—not from any shots but from their maneuvers] that they were pressing in for attack positions. At about this time, the boats were at a range of 6,000 yards from Maddox when the radar tracking indicated *that the contact had turned away and begun to open in range* [our italics]. Torpedo noises were then heard by the Maddox's sonar. A report of the torpedo noise was immediately passed to the Turner Joy by inter-ship radio (and both ships took evasive action to avoid the torpedo. A torpedo wake was then sighted passing abeam Turner Joy from after to forward.

Even this scaled-down version was still a deceptive picture of what actually had transpired. McNamara released his statement during the noon recess of the February 20 hearing, which was held behind closed doors. He thus jumped the gun on the committee by getting his version out first, perhaps hoping that it might be some time before the Committee could publish the full transcript.[1] Fortunately Senator Morse, to whom the country owes so much in this whole affair, courageously defied security regulations and in a Senate speech next day made public much of the intramural Pentagon messages obtained by the Committee. This and the Committee's anger over McNamara's tricky action in releasing his own testimony brought about the swift publication of the whole record, with some security deletions.

TRICKY TEXT AND TRICKY TACTICS

If the transcript of the two hearings and the text of McNamara's prepared statement are now placed side by side, it is quite clear that he and Secretary Rusk and General Wheeler lied—there is no other word for it—to the Senate committees four years ago, and that McNamara is still trying hard to lie about it now. His whole performance is the shameful climax of what many had believed to be an honorable record as Secretary of Defense. He withheld from the committees then—and in his prepared statement tried to withhold from the public now—many crucial facts which cast doubt on the whole story of the Aug. 4 attack. You have to go from his tricky language to the Morse speech and to the hearing transcript to learn that three or four hours after the supposed attack, the task force commander on the Maddox cabled a warning that "freak weather," an "overeager sonarman" and the absence of any "visual sightings" cast doubt on the attack stories and called for "complete evaluation before any further action." No one would know from his accounts then or now that no debris had been found, though we claimed to have sunk two and possibly three enemy vessels, and that we ordered our retaliatory attack without waiting to learn the outcome of a belated order to search for debris.

You have to go back to that master of shyster lawyer language, John Foster Dulles, to match McNamara's performance. If an attack occurred,

1 Pentagon and State managed to tie up the transcript of the August 6, 1964, hearing in so many security snafus that it was not finally released until more than two years later, on November 24, 1966—Thanksgiving Day, when it was calculated to attract as little attention as possible.

how is it that not a single captured North Vietnamese naval man, including one who was very cooperative denied knowledge of any such attack? How is it that Hanoi, which boasted of the August 2 attack, has always denied the August 4 attack? If Hanoi attacked on August 4, in the face of Johnson's warning after August 2, how is it that its entire tiny fleet was caught by surprise in our retaliatory attack the next day? "Why," as North Vietnam asked in its own White Paper which has been kept from the U.S. public, "does this small country with its negligible naval forces embark on a systematic provocation of the U.S. 7th Fleet with its 125 vessels and 650 airplanes?" And then take no precautions against a counter-attack?

Familiar Military Habits

Fake incidents are hardly new in the history of military bureaucracies. The Japanese military staged one near Mukden in 1931 to begin its seizure of Manchuria despite parliamentary disapproval. The Pueblo incident illustrates another notorious military tactic: they play incidents up or down like an organist depending on whether they want to make or avoid war. Faked or exaggerated, the Tonkin incidents were used for a war buildup the White House and Pentagon wanted. The full truth is still hidden and we applaud Senator Gruening's demand that the staff study prepared by the Fulbright Committee be released. We are told that McNamara urged "a decisive commitment" in Vietnam on Johnson a few days after the Kennedy assassination. If the Foreign Relations committee digs further, it will find that both the bombing of the North and the commitment of combat troops to Vietnam were planned at the Pentagon several months before the Tonkin Gulf incidents, that the Tonkin Gulf resolution was prepared beforehand, and that the course pursued beginning in July, 1964, was calculated to create some kind of incident sooner or later, to justify the expansion of the conflict already decided upon. A Rostow Plan No. 6 for "PT-boat raids on North Vietnamese coastal installations and then by strategic bombing raids flown by U.S. pilots under either the U.S. or South Vietnamese flags" was disclosed in *Newsweek* as early as March 9, 1964. The coastal raids began in July

1964, by vessels we supplied the South Vietnamese, with crews we trained, backstopped by intelligence our planes and ships provided. The collection of such information was the business of those "routine patrols" on which we sent our destroyers.

We cannot claim freedom of the seas for such missions. If Russian vessels backstopped Cuban naval attacks on Florida, we would take counteraction even if they stayed outside our 3-mile limit. There are no territorial limits in war, and this would be war. We merely compounded the offense and assured an "incident" by instructing our destroyers to ignore North Vietnam's 12-mile limit. McNamara in his prepared statement fell back on the disingenuous argument that we had no "official documentary" evidence of this 12-mile limit. Even the Geographer's Office at the State Department admitted to us in a telephone inquiry that it had always been assumed that North Vietnam's limit, like China's and North Korea's, was 12 miles. What was McNamara waiting for—an affidavit from Ho Chi Minh? Men who can so twist the truth are a menace to national security. In the pages of this special issue, as gleaned from the Senate hearings, Morse's speech and the North Vietnamese White Paper, one can begin to see what I believe will prove to be one of the great military frauds of world history, the curtain raiser for our disastrous Vietnamese adventure, which may easily and soon turn into a wider and nuclear war. There are no limits to what such leadership may cook up. Khesanh may provide the excuse.

ROBERT SCHEER, WARREN HINCKLE, AND SOL STERN

The 1960s transformed American journalism, and nowhere was that transformation more evident than at San Francisco–based Ramparts *magazine. Founded as a Catholic public affairs quarterly, in 1964 its editorship fell to Warren Hinckle, a newspaper veteran with a restless sense of troublemaking. By the mid-'60s* Ramparts *was virtually a house organ for the New Left and was breaking story after story on subjects the mainstream would not touch: CIA sponsorship of campus organizations; killing of civilians by American troops in Vietnam; Pentagon stockpiles of chemical weapons.*

Ramparts *challenged "establishment" journalism in tone as well as substance. The cool, distant stance of conventional reporting and the stuffy righteousness of the old left both seemed inadequate to the upheavals of the civil rights movement, the sexual revolution, the escalating war. The story that follows, by Hinckle (1938–) and fellow* Ramparts *editor Robert Scheer (1936–), shows the magazine at its best, exposing how covert government activity was implicating a major public university in human-rights abuses in Southeast Asia.*

THE UNIVERSITY ON THE MAKE

From *Ramparts,* April 1966

The Vietnamese soldier in the sentry box stood at attention as the chauffeured limousine bearing license plate No. 1 from the government motor pool roared down the long driveway of the French villa, picked up speed and screeched off along the road towards the palace where the President was waiting breakfast.

The year was 1957, the city was Saigon, and the man who lived in the huge villa with its own sentry box was no Batman of the diplomatic corps. He was only Wesley Fishel of East Lansing, Michigan, assistant professor of political science at Michigan State University.

Peasants who scrambled off the road to make way for the speeding professor might have wondered what was happening, but Fishel's academic compatriots could have no doubt: he was "making it." To make it, in the new world of Big University politics, was no longer as elemental as publishing or perishing. You needed "contact" with the outside world. You had to get a government contract. You had to be an operator. And some people viewed Professor Fishel in South Vietnam in the mid-1950s as the Biggest Operator of them all.

Some professors on the make have had a bigger press, but none deserves notoriety more than Wesley Fishel. Eugene Burdick, for instance, got a lot of publicity out of his quickie novels and underwater beer commercials on television. But no academician has ever achieved Fishel's distinction in getting his school to come through with enough professors, police experts and guns to secure his friend's dictatorship.

That was what Wesley Fishel was about on that humid Saigon morning, burning rubber to visit Ngo Dinh Diem. The presidential palace was known informally and with some degree of jealousy by the United States Mission in Saigon as the "breakfast club," because that was where Diem and Fishel and Wolf Ladejinsky, the agricultural expert left over from the New Deal, ate morning melons several times a week and discussed the state of the nation.

Leland Barrows, the United States Mission chief, was disturbed because he couldn't get to see Diem anywhere near that often. And Fishel was particularly closed-mouthed about his regular morning conferences. Saigon in the early days of the Diem regime was a status-minded city, and Fishel had a bigger villa than Barrows, bigger, even, than the American ambassador's. This residential ranking attests to Fishel's importance as head of the Michigan State University Group in Vietnam, an official university project under contract to Saigon and Washington, with responsibility for the proper functioning of Diem's civil service and his police network, shaping up the 50,000-man "ragamuffin" militia, and supplying guns and ammunition for the city police, the civil guard, the palace police and the dreaded Sûreté—South Vietnam's version of the FBI. No small task for a group of professors, but one which Michigan State took to as if it were fielding another national championship football team.

One less-known and perhaps more unpleasant task of the MSU professors was to provide a front for a unit of the United States Central Intelligence Agency. This is a role that both Professor Fishel and Michigan State University have now chosen to forget. It is described here as a specific, if shocking, documentation of the degree of corruption and abject immorality attending a university which puts its academic respectability on lend-lease to American foreign policy.

JOHN A. HANNAH, THE PRESIDENT AS COACH

The decay of traditional academic principles found in the modern university on the make may well be traced to Harold Stassen and Clark Kerr, but it is best exemplified by President John A. Hannah of Michigan State University. Stassen, in the International Cooperation Administration, was responsible for the concept that American universities should be tapped as "manpower reservoirs" for the extension of Americanism abroad, and Clark Kerr, the embattled Berkeley savant, first came up with the vision of the large university as a "service station" to society. Hannah, an Eisenhower liberal with a penchant for public service, has made these concepts the raison d'être of MSU.

Hannah, in a blustery way, represents the best traditions of the American Success Story. The son of an Iowa chicken farmer, he took a degree in poultry husbandry from Michigan Agricultural College in 1922. Then, like the football hero who works for 30 years in the college bookstore because he can't bear to leave the campus, Hannah stayed on in East Lansing. He taught chicken farming, married the president's daughter, got his first taste of public service during a stint with the Department of Agriculture as an NRA administrator, came back to campus and in 1941 succeeded his father-in-law as president.

MSU, under President Hannah's tutelage, is more service oriented than the average Standard Oil retail outlet. MSU's School of Agriculture aids farmers, its School of Hotel Management turns out educated room clerks, its School of Police Administration graduates cops sophisticated in the social sciences. MSU once offered a Bachelor of Science degree with a major in Mobile Homes under a program financed by the trailer industry.

But it is in the field of international service that Michigan State has really made it. A shiny new building on campus houses MSU's Center for International Programs—an edifice built, incidentally, with funds from the administrative allowance on the seven-year Vietnam contract. The University has over 200 faculty members every year out in the boondocks of the world running "educational projects" in 13 countries including Columbia, Taiwan, Turkey, Brazil and Okinawa. *Time* magazine recently acknowledged the MSU president's extensive influence on the role of American universities overseas by recording Hannah's boast that he can "tap his campus specialists, get an answer to most any question for government or research groups within 30 minutes." Now that is service.

The list of countries MSU is presently "helping" is lopsided with military dictatorships, but it is not President Hannah's style to question the assignment his country gives him. A former assistant secretary of defense under General Motors' Charles Wilson, Hannah sees the military, like football, as an important character-building element in life. His view of the modern university is tied to the liberal concept of America as the defender of the free world. That the university must prepare young citizens to assume this proud task, and to be a leader abroad in areas chosen for it by the government, is Hannah's educational credo.

Despite Hannah's obvious pride in the work his University is doing overseas, he is particularly reticent in discussing its most extensive foreign operation. In a colorful brochure about MSU's international programs, given away free to visitors, there is only one sentence about the Vietnam Project—despite the fact that this was the largest single project ever undertaken by an American university abroad, a project that spent the incredible amount of 25 million in American taxpayers' dollars giving "technical assistance" to the Republic of South Vietnam under Ngo Dinh Diem. This one-sentence treatment of MSU's Vietnam operation is like reducing to a photo caption in the school yearbook the story of the prize-winning basketball team—because the coach was caught taking bribes.

A key to MSU's apparent official desire to forget about the Vietnam experience, dubbed the "Vietnam Adventure" by some professors who worked on the Project, might be found in the unexpressed fear that the details of the University's "cover" for the CIA may become public knowledge. If pressed for an answer, Fishel denies any such role and so does President Hannah. "CIA agents were not knowingly on our staff—if that were true we didn't know about it," Hannah said recently in his office, sitting beneath the portrait that hangs above his desk. But this assertion of innocence is flatly contradicted by the disclosures of other professors who held administrative positions in the Project. Indeed, the weight of evidence is that MSU finally had to ask the CIA unit to go elsewhere because its presence had become such embarrassing general knowledge in Saigon and East Lansing.

Economist Stanley K. Sheinbaum, the campus coordinator of MSU's Vietnam operation for three years, was flabbergasted by Hannah's denial: "If John Hannah can make up something like that, he calls into question his competence as a university president," he said.

WESLEY FISHEL, THE PROFESSOR AS PROCONSUL

One indication of Wesley Fishel's power in Saigon in the heyday of the Diem era was provided by a veteran of that period who recently paid a return visit to Saigon. "I heard people talking about what 'Westy' would think," he said, "and for a minute I thought that Wesley was back."

"Westy," in the Saigon vernacular, is General William Westmoreland, but those in the know used to talk about "Wesley" in the same awe-struck fashion. There is one public reminder of the transfer of power. "Westy" is now running the war out of the same office building, a reconverted apartment house at 137 Pasteur Street, that used to be "Wesley's" headquarters.

Like most fateful alliances, the Diem-Fishel axis had humble beginnings. The pair met in Tokyo in July of 1950 when each was going nowhere in his chosen field. Diem was an exiled Vietnamese politician with a mandarin personality and a strong sense of predestination but few tangible hopes of assuming power in his war-ravaged country. Fishel was just a run-of-the-mill academician, a young political scientist from UCLA who had written a nondescript thesis on Chinese extra-territoriality and was about to accept a position at Michigan State.

Both were ambitious, looking for an angle, and Napoleon-sized. Diem was 5'4" tall; Fishel, a well-built, curly-haired man with the stance of a bantam rooster, appears to be about the same size. The men became friends and a relationship developed by extensive correspondence over the ensuing year. They exchanged favors early. Fishel had his friend appointed consultant to Michigan State's Governmental Research Bureau and helped arrange a long stay in the United States, where Diem picked up substantial backing among prominent Americans from Cardinal Spellman to Senator Mike Mansfield [*Ramparts*, July 1965]. In return, Diem in 1952 asked the French to let Michigan

State furnish technical aid to Vietnam at United States expense, but the French refused.

Fishel, however, had ultimate faith. An East Lansing colleague recalls that one day Fishel cornered him in the faculty lounge and, with the exuberance of one who could no longer restrain himself, whispered excitedly, "My friend Diem is going to be Premier of Vietnam one of these days!" The prediction was taken lightly; Fishel had neither the swagger nor the stripes of a kingmaker.

But when Diem was named Premier in July 1954, one of his first official acts was to request Washington to send Wesley to Saigon to advise him. Fishel arrived within weeks, and just weeks later Diem asked for the second time that MSU set up a technical-assistance program in Vietnam. The request, this time, had smooth sailing.

With Fishel already in Saigon, there was virtually no one on the East Lansing campus with any knowledge about Vietnam when Diem's assistance request was relayed through official Washington channels. President Hannah, not one to let the possibility of a substantial contract go by, tapped four faculty members for an "inspection team" and put them on a plane to Saigon in almost whirlwind fashion.

The four were Arthur Brandstatter, an ex-MSU football hero who now heads the Police Administration School; James Dennison, the University's public relations man; Edward Weidener, then chairman of the Political Science Department; and Economics Department Chairman Charles Killingsworth. None of these men had any experience in academic or technical assistance roles overseas, nor did they have any expertise in Far Eastern affairs, a deficiency they attempted to repair by reading newspaper clippings about Vietnam during the plane ride. The first time they met as a group was when they fastened their seat belts.

Saigon was a city in ferment in September 1954, when MSU's "inspection team" arrived. Diem was nominally in power, but he had no real support except among a small number of middle-class Catholics and Saigon merchants. The French were preparing to pull out, the Saigon police were controlled by the Binh Xuyen pirate sect, the private armies of the religious sects were in substantial control of the Vietnamese lowlands, the Vietnamese Army was in fledgling revolt against Diem, and the civil service machinery was in a state of stagnation.

The professors found their colleague Fishel and General Edward Lansdale of the CIA maneuvering furiously to consolidate Diem's support, an effort that culminated in the endorsement of Diem by the United States Security Council in the spring of 1955. The professors also learned that Diem was suspicious of the members of the United States Mission in Saigon, many of whom, he felt, held pro-French sentiments. The one American Diem really trusted was Wesley Fishel, and this trust was reflected two weeks later when the MSU inspection team returned to East Lansing and recommended a massive technical-assistance contract, unprecedented in the history of university operations overseas. This contract committed Michigan State to do everything for Diem, from training his police to writing his Constitution.

Contract negotiations bogged down over technical matters, but the jam was broken in the early spring of 1955 by a telephone call from Washington to Hannah requesting that the red tape be cut and MSU involve itself in Vietnam—in a hurry. Fishel once indicated in an interview that the request came from former Vice President Nixon, but he now denies this, and so does President Hannah. The phone call, Hannah told the *Detroit News,* came from an authority "even higher than Nixon." This leaves a choice of John Foster Dulles; his brother, CIA chief Allen Dulles; or Eisenhower himself. At any rate, President Hannah did his duty as he saw it. The first MSU professors joined Wesley Fishel in Saigon in late May of 1955.

In 1956 Fishel abandoned his role as "advisor" to Diem, and assumed the title of Chief of Mission of the MSU Group. For the next four years, he was the most important American in Vietnam. "Wesley was the closest thing to a proconsul that Saigon had," said one of the MSU professors. The assistant professor of political science entertained frequently and lavishly in his opulent villa, and if his parties got a little out of hand the Saigon police obliged by cordoning off the street. No professor had ever made it so big; in the academic world, Fishel was sovereign.

But if the proconsul lived well, so did his lieutenants. East Lansing is hardly a midwestern Paris, and for most of the professors the more exotic and free-wheeling life in Saigon was the closest thing to the high life they had known. Academicians and their families, at first a little uncomfortable, assumed the easy ways of the former French colonial masters. They moved into spacious, air-conditioned villas, rent-free, in the old French section of Saigon, bought the better Scotches at the American commissary at $2 a bottle, hired servants at $30 a month, were invited to all the better cocktail parties because they knew "Wesley," went tiger hunting for laughs and, with various "hardship" and "incentive" salary hikes, made close to double their normal salaries. (A professor earning $9,000 for teaching class at East Lansing got $16,500 a year for "advising" in Vietnam—tax free.)

The "Vietnam Adventure" also did wonders for the professors' tenure. Despite the activist nature of their work in Vietnam and the lack of any substantial scholarly research during the Project, two-thirds of the MSU faculty who went to Saigon got promotions either during their tour of duty or within a year of their return. Professor Fishel, in particular, scored points. His published work was virtually nonexistent and he was absent from his classes for years at a time. But in 1957 MSU promoted him to the rank of full professor.

Hear-No-CIA, See-No-CIA

Central Intelligence Agency men were hidden within the ranks of the Michigan State University professors. They were all listed as members of the MSU Project staff and were formally appointed by the University Board of Trustees. Several of the CIA men were given academic rank and were paid by the University Project.

The CIA agents' instructions were to engage in counterespionage and counterintelligence. Their "cover" was within the police administration division of the Michigan State Group. The CIA unit was self-contained and appeared on an official organization chart of the MSU Project as "VBI Internal Security Section." This five-man team was the largest section within the police administration division of the MSU Vietnam operation. The police administration division in turn was by far the largest of the three divisions of MSUG.

"VBI" was Michigan State shorthand for "Vietnamese Bureau of Investigation," the new name the professors had given the old Sûreté, the Vietnamese special police. The head of the "Internal Security Section" of the VBI under the Michigan State operation was Raymond Babineau, who was in Saigon from the outset of the MSU Project. The other men were hired later by the University and listed on its staff chart as "Police Administration Specialists." All four—Douglas Beed, William Jones, Daniel Smith and Arthur Stein—gave their previous employment as either "investigator" or "records specialist" in the Department of the Army.

The CIA contingent, despite the continued denials of Fishel and Hannah, was identified by two former Project officials—Stanley Sheinbaum and Professor Robert Scigliano, an MSU political scientist who was assistant project chief of the MSU Vietnam Group from 1957–1959. It is also confirmed, in writing, by Scigliano and Professor Guy H. Fox, a former MSU Project chief, in a book titled *Technical Assistance in Vietnam: The Michigan State University Experience,* published by Praeger in 1965.

Sheinbaum, as part of his duties as campus coordinator, hired Stein, Smith and Jones. At the time, all he knew about the men was that they came from the "Department of the Army." Sheinbaum recalls that he was proceeding to investigate the backgrounds of the three applicants before accepting them when he was told "that it wouldn't be necessary to check out these guys." The message came from Professor Ralph Smuckler, a former Vietnam Project head.

Sheinbaum said he was on the job for 18 months before he was taken into the administration's confidence and told about the CIA men. "Smuckler pulled me aside one day and told me that I should know that these CIA guys were there, but that we didn't talk about them," he said.

Professor Scigliano's first brush with the CIA came during his first meeting with the police advisory group in Saigon. He said that Babineau, whom he knew from the organizational chart as head of the VBI Internal

Security, was introduced as a CIA man. The other CIA agents were also introduced, and Babineau made a short speech in which he expressed hope that the professors and his people would get along well. Scigliano recalls Babineau saying, "We hope we don't get in your way."

A professor and his wife became friends with one of the CIA men and his wife, and the couples often dined together. "We talked about books and music," he said, but there was an unspoken rule that they would never mention the CIA. The entire unit operated on an identical hear-no-CIA, see-no-CIA basis. They worked out of offices in one corner of the police administration floor of the beige converted apartment building that housed the MSU Project. The CIA men came in early in the morning, stayed for about an hour and then locked their offices and left for the day. They all drove their own cars and their French was the most fluent on the Project.

If the CIA men got nothing else from their fraternization with Michigan State University, they became the first persons in the spy business to gain academic recognition. "Some of the CIA guys attained faculty status at MSU—some as lecturers, some as assistant professors, depending on their salaries. I know, because I remember signing the papers that gave them faculty rank," Sheinbaum said.

The CIA unit operated within its Michigan State "cover" until 1959. Scigliano and Fox state in their book, in what must rank as one of the more terse statements of the decade: "USOM [United States Operations Mission] also absorbed at this time [1959] the CIA unit that had been operating within MSUG [Michigan State University Group]."

In plain language, Michigan State threw the CIA men out. One of the principal factors leading to the MSU decision was that by 1959 just about everybody in the know was cognizant of the CIA operation. This was not only embarrassing to the legitimate professors, but it served to taint the reputation of the limited amount of solid academic work that was done during the Project. For instance, an anthropologist working far out in the Vietnamese flatlands was flabbergasted to find a local police chief interrupt his work on the grounds that he was digging up bones on behalf of the United States Central Intelligence Agency. The decision to terminate the CIA unit was brought to Professor Scigliano by Smuckler. Babineau was not in Saigon at the time, so Professor Scigliano gave Jones the bad news. He recalls that Jones was "quite upset," as was the United States Mission which wanted the CIA unit to stay right where it was—sheltered by the groves of academe.

Within weeks, the entire "VBI Internal Security Section" had moved over to the offices of the United States Mission to operate, presumably, more in the open. By 1959, the United States was making little pretense of following the Geneva Accords anyway.

ACADEMICS IN ARMORED CARS

In the spring of 1955, Diem gained control of the Army. The United States, which was (and still is) providing the entire South Vietnam Army payroll, said it wouldn't give out any more checks unless the Army played ball with our boy. Diem then used the Army to crush the sect that had controlled the Saigon police and elements of the far-flung Sûreté. The gargantuan task of rebuilding the entire Vietnam police apparatus, from traffic cop to "interrogation expert," as a loyal agency of the Diem government then fell to Michigan State University.

Diem, lacking popular support, could only retain power through an effective police and security network. The American Embassy urgently signaled the MSU contingent to concentrate on this problem, and, like good team players from a school with a proud football tradition, the professors went along.

The professors not only trained Diem's security forces but, in the early years of the Project, actually supplied them with guns and ammunition. In doing so, the East Lansing contingent helped to secure Diem's dictatorship and to provide the base and the arms for the "secret police" which were to make Madame Nhu and her brother infamous.

If not academic, the professors were at least professional. Many supplies—revolvers, riot guns, ammunition, tear gas, jeeps, handcuffs, radios—were requisitioned by the East Lansing School of Police Administration from stocks left over from America's aid to the French

Expeditionary Corps. These supplies were then turned over to the Vietnamese who would strive to achieve Diem's own form of "consensus" government—a consensus gained largely by hauling the dissenters off to jail. Despite the largess left by the French, the professors found it necessary to order some $15 million in additional "equipment" from the United States Mission.

Listen to some of the official progress reports sent home to East Lansing by the professors:

> November 8, 1955: "During the month of October we received notice of Washington's approval of the recommended expanded police program. . . . Conferences were held at USOM on October 10 and the Embassy on October 23 and 24, trying to coordinate Internal Security Operations in Vietnam in which our government has an interest."
>
> April 17, 1956: "The training of the commando squads of Saigon-Cholon police in riot control formations has continued during the month. . . . A report on riots and unlawful assembly is nearing completion."
>
> June 5, 1957: "Training of the Presidential Security Guard in revolver shooting began during the month. Thirty-four VBI agents completed the revolver course."
>
> September 11, 1957: "Eight hundred pairs of Peerless handcuffs arrived in Saigon, but distribution is being delayed pending arrival of 400 additional cuffs."
>
> February 17, 1958: "The training of 125 military and Civil Guard fingerprint technicians at the VBI proceeds satisfactorily. The Palace Guard is being put through another class in revolver training, with 58 men receiving instruction. Forty members of the VBI completed firearm training."

As befits a university project, many of the professors indulged in their academic specialties. Ralph Turner, a professor of police administration, feels that one of the Project's most singular achievements was the program whereby every Vietnamese citizen would be given an identification card—with a special American touch. The cards were laminated so the poor, plasticless Viet Cong would have difficulty forging them.

Dean Brandstatter did not move lock, stock and pistol to Saigon, but he managed frequent "inspection trips"—as did some 11 of the University officials, including President Hannah, all of course at government expense. Brandstatter, a former military policeman, utilized his expertise to immediate effect during one of his first trips. Rumors of a coup against Diem were escalating, and the East Lansing official personally inspected the Palace Guard to see that they had enough guns to meet the threat.

Brandstatter, a large, jovial man in his early fifties, and a devoted follower of MSU's football fortunes, played talent scout for the police operation. The services that the MSU team was called upon to perform for Diem's security apparatus were so esoteric that even its heralded School of Police Administration wasn't up to the job. Brandstatter had to recruit specially trained cops from all over the country. Fingerprint experts, small-arms experts and intelligence experts came from the Detroit police force, the New York police force, the FBI and even the Department of Defense. Other professors, doing civil service work, felt a little left out and labeled the onslaught of police experts "mercenaries." This might seem a little unkind, but the term seems somewhat applicable since, at one point in the Project, only four of the 33 police advisors had roots at the Michigan campus; the others were nomads. The Project, of course, still bore the name—or the "cover"—of the MSUG, since these "mercenaries" were all put on the MSU payroll and provided with faculty status. In the action-filled world of the service station university, not only do the professors become activists, but the cops aspire to professorships.

DECLINE AND FALL

Ngo Dinh Diem was a nice man to buy guns for, but in other areas of human endeavor, the professors discovered that he could be a tough man to do business with. Even Wolf Ladejinsky, who broke bread regularly with Diem, was subject to occasional indignities. When an issue of the *New Republic* appeared in Saigon containing an article mildly critical of the Diem regime, the President sent Ladejinsky packing off from the palace to buy up all the copies from the dozen English-language kiosks in Saigon.

The game in Saigon was to cater to Diem's pettiness and paranoia, and for the most part the men from Michigan State played it. There appeared to be a conscious effort within the Project administration to prepare reports pleasing, or at least palatable, to the President. Milton Taylor, an MSU economics professor who went to Vietnam as a tax advisor, said that his reports were often rewritten by the Project head. When he questioned this practice he was told that there were "higher considerations" at stake; other universities were in hot pursuit of the juicy Vietnam contract.

It became necessary to forsake principles for the good of the Project. At times, in the Saigon of the late 1950s, that must have been difficult. Professor Adrian Jaffe of the MSU English Department, one of the most persistent critics of his University's "Vietnam Adventure," recalls some vivid street scenes. Each morning, men, and more often than not women and children, were hauled out of the jail directly across from his office at the Faculty of Letters of the University of Saigon, handcuffed, thrown into a van, and driven away to an island concentration camp known as a sort of Devil's Island à la Diem. Professors in the Project, because of their intimacy with the Vietnamese security apparatus, knew this was happening, Jaffe said, but his colleagues said and did nothing.

The moral question raised by Jaffe is dismissed by many veterans of the Project as "unprofessional." Perhaps more professional was the work of Wesley Fishel, who, as late as the fall of November 1959, wrote an article in the *New Leader* with the obfuscating title, "Vietnam's One-Man Democratic Rule." The text requires no recounting, except to observe that Fishel uses adjectives for Diem that only Jack Valenti might dare use for Johnson.

The failure of the MSU professors to bear witness against what are now known to be Diem's outrageous violations of civil liberties raises serious questions about them as men. But their failure as professionals to exercise the traditional role of the independent scholar as critic accounted in large part for the general ignorance of the United States public about the true nature of Diem's regime. Professors, presumed to be men of principle, were on the scene in Vietnam and had to be accepted as the best unprejudiced source of information. David Halberstam, after all, simply could have been mad at Madame Nhu.

The same disastrous vacuum of information occurred in this country only a decade before when the China experts, almost to a man, were purged as Reds and comsymps, and yahoos were all the public had left to hear.

In Vietnam, at least, there was a Buddhist monk with the fortitude to burn himself—and the public suddenly wondered how what they had been reading about Diem for six years could have been so wrong. But the professors, by this time, were long back in East Lansing. The MSU Vietnam Project ended rather abruptly in 1962. The University claims that it terminated the arrangement in the name of academic freedom—but the truth is, unfortunately, more complex.

Diem, painfully aware of the slightest criticism, was infuriated by the modicum of critical material published in the United States in the early '60s by veterans of the MSU "experience." Professor Jaffe and economist Milton Taylor wrote an essay for the *New Republic* in 1961 that set Diem's paranoia percolating. The author dared to suggest that the President rid himself of the Nhus. The contract between Diem and Michigan State stipulated that members of the Project could not use materials gathered on the job "against the security or the interests of Vietnam." In other words, they were to keep quiet. Taylor recalls that many of his colleagues in Vietnam felt he was being "disloyal" in publicly criticizing Diem.

The President was also miffed that in 1959 MSU had drastically curtailed its police work after being urged by both Diem and the United States Mission to plunge more deeply into paramilitary work than it already had. MSU's reluctance was understandable, since a greater degree of involvement would just about require its professors to shoot off howitzers and drill troops in the jungle.

Nevertheless, the University genuinely believed that its contract would be renewed in 1962. President Hannah even sent a special envoy, Alfred Seelye, dean of the Business College, to Saigon to smooth things out by telling Diem that the University was prepared to weed out any future troublemakers in the Project by selecting personnel more likely to "write scholarly scientific studies and not sensational journalistic articles." Diem, however, surprised everybody. He was adamant: no more MSU.

With no deal in sight, the business dean proceeded to make a strong declaration in defense of the academic freedom of MSU professors and beat Diem in announcing that the contract would not be renewed.

The Ruins

Like a factory that has contracted for a job and then completed it, there is little evidence on the MSU campus that it was ever involved in Vietnam. Thousands of pages of mimeographed reports and documents sent from Saigon have been piled haphazardly in out-of-the-way files in the University library, uncatalogued and unused. MSU has not a single course, not even a study program, to show for its six years in Vietnam.

Professor Wesley Fishel still flies in and out of East Lansing, but now he goes to Washington and advises the administration on Vietnam, a role which allows him to visit Saigon occasionally—where he has the look of a man who would like another try. But there is nothing for him to do. Fishel has been careful to exclude the infamous *New Leader* article from the otherwise thorough 64-page bibliography on Vietnam and Southeast Asia which he distributes to his students.

MSU is still big on police. There are, literally, policemen all over the campus, almost beyond the wildest expansion of the human retina. There are the campus police—a complement of roughly 35 men in blue uniforms. Then there are the professors and visiting firemen at the School of Police Administration. Finally, it is hard to find a parking spot on campus since so many police cars are occupying the stalls; state police headquarters adjoins MSU.

With all this protection, the University officials should feel safe. But they do not. President Hannah has lately been publicly worried about the possibilities of what he terms a "Berkeley-style" revolt. The vice-president of student affairs bluntly stated that MSU had been "selected" as the "next Berkeley." Hannah, fearful of "outside agitators," has suggested that there is an "apparatus" at work on campus that is a "tool for international communism." The University police have a special detail charged with keeping tabs on student political activities, especially anything "radical." Several years ago a member of this "Red squad" endeared himself to the student daily newspaper by trapping homosexuals in a state-built bathroom.

These conditions would be sufficient enough for the light-hearted to suggest that MSU is a Lilliputian police state, but that is silly. Professor Alfred Meyer of the Political Science Department, during his course on the Soviet political system, always gets a good laugh by telling the students to take a good look around campus if they want to know what the Soviet system is like.

Hannah's concern over Berkeley is more than apocryphal. If the Berkeley experience meant any one thing, it meant that the University wasn't doing its job. It had lost its sense of purpose; it no longer had meaning to the students. In that sense East Lansing is, assuredly, another Berkeley. The university on the make has little time for nonconforming students and rarely enough for conforming students. Its service function is the first priority. The students are, in Clark Kerr's idiom, only the "raw material" that has to be processed. That was the cause of the Berkeley revolt, and the ingredients are available in excess portions at Michigan State.

Acting dean of international programs, Ralph T. Smuckler, is perhaps the one person at MSU who got something lasting out of the "Vietnam Adventure." He derived an ideology, and it is an ideology that goes Clark Kerr one better. Smuckler sees the future of the social sciences in the world-wide scope of the "action" projects he is now directing—in Formosa as he did in Vietnam. "Classroom teaching is a tame business," said Smuckler, "and anybody who doesn't see how his discipline fits into the overseas operations of the University is already obsolete."

To question the assumption that the academician of tomorrow must be an operator is to ask but part of the essential question about MSU's "Vietnam Adventure." And to ask whether the University officials are liars, or whether the MSU Project broke the spirit of the Geneva Accords, is also neglecting the primary question.

The essential query, which must be asked before the discussion of Michigan State's behavior can be put into any rational perspective, is this: what the hell is a university doing buying guns, anyway?

Seymour Hersh

It is notable that the single most influential investigative report on U.S. conduct in the course of the war in Southeast Asia was broken not by the legions of correspondents "in country" but by a freelance Washington journalist, former AP Pentagon reporter Seymour Hersh. Hersh was a protégé of I. F. Stone, from whom he learned, he has said, that "you can't write without reading."

Hersh's shattering exposé of Charlie Company's 1968 massacre of 567 villagers in a hamlet called My Lai 4 began with a tip from a public-interest lawyer, who had heard rumors of an officer court-martialed for the killing of seventy-five civilians. A Washington foundation, the Fund for Investigative Journalism, provided Hersh with a small grant to cover his travel. In Claremont College, California, he located Ron Ridenhour, a recently returned Vietnam veteran who had spoken with participants in the massacre and had tried without success to interest Congress and the Pentagon in the case. (Ridenhour went on to his own distinguished career in journalism.) In Fort Benning he interviewed Lieutenant William Calley, who implicated superior officers; he obtained more details from other members of Charlie Company and even from the military judge overseeing Calley's court-martial. Life *and* Look *both turned down the story—their editors refused to believe it could be true—so Hersh turned to a twenty-three-year-old neighbor who ran a tiny alternative syndicate,* Dispatch News Service. *His story gained momentum two days after its initial publication, when a* Cleveland Plain Dealer *reporter named Joe Eszterhas—today a celebrated screenwriter—obtained and published grisly photos of the massacre from an Army photographer who had been on the scene. On November 21, one of the members of Charlie Company who had been interviewed by Hersh confirmed his story to Walter Cronkite on the CBS evening news.*

The story of the My Lai massacre won Hersh a Pulitzer Prize for international reporting. Lieutenant Calley was sentenced to life in prison, but served less than four years. Other officers escaped prosecution in what Hersh, in one of four books he wrote on the incident, termed a Pentagon cover-up.

Hersh remains at this writing the country's foremost investigative journalist on national-security affairs. As a reporter for the New York Times *in the 1970s he exposed domestic spying by the CIA, and in the years since he has written books on subjects ranging from Kissinger's role in the illegal bombing of Cambodia to Israeli nuclear weapons. Since the Al-Qaeda attacks of September 11, 2001, Hersh has written for the* New Yorker *on U.S. military and intelligence operations.*

THE MY LAI MASSACRE

Three articles from the *St. Louis Post-Dispatch*, 1969

LIEUTENANT ACCUSED OF MURDERING 109 CIVILIANS

FORT BENNING, GA., Nov. 13—Lt. William L. Calley Jr., 26 years old, is a mild-mannered, boyish-looking Vietnam combat veteran with the nickname "Rusty." The Army is completing an investigation of charges that he deliberately murdered at least 109 Vietnamese civilians in a search-and-destroy mission in March 1968 in a Viet Cong stronghold known as "Pinkville."

Calley has formally been charged with six specifications of mass murder. Each specification cites a number of dead, adding up to the 109 total, and charges that Calley did "with premeditation murder . . . Oriental human beings, whose names and sex are unknown, by shooting them with a rifle."

The Army calls it murder; Calley, his counsel and others associated with the incident describe it as a case of carrying out orders.

"Pinkville" has become a widely known code word among the military in a case that many officers and some Congressmen believe will become far more controversial than the recent murder charges against eight Green Berets.

Army investigation teams spent nearly one year studying the incident before filing charges against Calley, a platoon leader of the Eleventh Brigade of the Americal Division at the time of the killings.

Calley was formally charged on or about Sept. 6, 1969, in the multiple deaths, just a few days before he was due to be released from active service.

Calley has since hired a prominent civilian attorney, former Judge George W. Latimer of the U.S. Court of Military Appeals, and is now awaiting a military determination of whether the evidence justifies a general court-martial. Pentagon officials describe the present stage of the case as the equivalent of a civilian grand jury proceeding.

Calley, meanwhile, is being detained at Fort Benning, where his movements are sharply restricted. Even his exact location on the base is a secret; neither the provost marshal, nor the Army's Criminal Investigation Division knows where he is being held.

The Army has refused to comment on the case, "in order not to prejudice the continuing investigation and rights of the accused." Similarly, Calley—although agreeing to an interview—refused to discuss in detail what happened on March 16, 1968.

However, many other officers and civilian officials, some angered by Calley's action and others angry that charges of murder were filed in the case, talked freely in interviews at Fort Benning and Washington.

These factors are not in dispute:

The Pinkville area, about six miles northeast of Quang Ngai, had been a Viet Cong fortress since the Vietnam war began. In early February 1968, a company of the Eleventh Brigade, as part of Task Force Barker, pushed through the area and was severely shot up.

Calley's platoon suffered casualties. After the Communist Tet offensive in February 1968, a larger assault was mounted, again with high casualties and little success. A third attack was quickly mounted and it was successful.

The Army claimed 128 Viet Cong were killed. Many civilians also were killed in the operation. The area was a free fire zone from which all non–Viet Cong residents had been urged, by leaflet, to flee. Such zones are common throughout Vietnam

One man who took part in the mission with Calley said that in the earlier two attacks "we were really shot up."

"Every time we got hit it was from the rear," he said. "So the third time in there the order came down to go in and make sure no one was behind.

"We were told to just clear the area. It was a typical combat assault formation. We came in hot, with a cover of artillery in front of us, came down the line and destroyed the village.

"There are always some civilian casualties in a combat operation. He isn't guilty of murder."

The order to clear the area was relayed from the battalion commander to the company commander to Calley, the source said.

Calley's attorney said in an interview: "This is one case that should never have been brought. Whatever killing there was was in a firefight in connection with the operation."

"You can't afford to guess whether a civilian is a Viet Cong or not. Either they shoot you or you shoot them.

"This case is going to be important—to what standard do you hold a combat officer in carrying out a mission?

"There are two instances where murder is acceptable to anybody: where it is excusable and where it is justified. If Calley did shoot anybody because of the tactical situation or while in a firefight, it was either excusable or justifiable."

Adding to the complexity of the case is the fact that investigators from the Army inspector general's office, which conducted the bulk of the investigation, considered filing charges against at least six other men involved in the action March 16.

A Fort Benning infantry officer has found that the facts of the case justify Calley's trial by general court-martial on charges of premeditated murder.

Pentagon officials said that the next steps are for the case go to Calley's brigade commander and finally to the Fort Benning post commander for findings on whether there should be a court-martial. If they so hold, final charges and specifications will be drawn up and made public at that time, the officials said.

Calley's friends in the officer corps at Fort Benning, many of them West Point graduates, are indignant. However, knowing the high stakes of the case, they express their outrage in private.

"They're using this as a Goddamned example," one officer complained. "He's a good soldier. He followed orders.

"There weren't any friendlies in the village. The orders were to shoot anything that moved."

Another officer said, "It could happen to any of us. He has killed and has seen a lot of killing. . . . Killing becomes nothing in Vietnam. He knew that there were civilians there, but he also knew that there were VC among them."

A third officer, also familiar with the case, said: "There's this question—I think anyone who goes to (Viet) Nam asks it. What's a civilian? Someone who works for us at day and puts on Viet Cong pajamas at night?"

There is another side of the Calley case—one that the Army cannot yet disclose. Interviews have brought out the fact that the investigation into the Pinkville affair was initiated six months after the incident, only after some of the men who served under Calley complained.

The Army has photographs purported to be of the incident, although these have not been introduced as evidence in the case, and may not be.

"They simply shot up this village and (Calley) was the leader of it," said one Washington source. "When one guy refused to do it, Calley took the rifle away and did the shooting himself."

Asked about this, Calley refused to comment.

One Pentagon officer discussing the case tapped his knee with his hand and remarked, "Some of those kids he shot were this high. I don't think they were Viet Cong. Do you?"

None of the men interviewed about the incident denied that women and children were shot.

A source of amazement among all those interviewed was that the story had yet to reach the press.

"Pinkville has been a word among GIs for a year," one official said. "I'll never cease to be amazed that it hasn't been written about before."

A high-ranking officer commented that he first heard talk of the Pinkville incident soon after it happened; the officer was on duty in Saigon at the time.

Why did the Army choose to prosecute this case? On what is it basing the charge that Calley acted with premeditation before killing? The court-martial should supply the answers to these questions, but some of the men already have their opinions.

"The Army knew it was going to get clobbered on this at some point," one military source commented. "If they don't prosecute somebody, if this stuff comes out without the Army taking some action, it could be even worse."

Another view that many held was that the top level of the military was concerned about possible war crime tribunals after the Vietnam war.

As for Calley—he is smoking four packs of cigarettes daily and getting out of shape. He is 5-foot-3, slender, with expressionless gray eyes and thinning brown hair. He seems slightly bewildered and hurt by the charges against him. He says he wants nothing more than to be cleared and return to the Army.

"I know this sounds funny," he said in an interview, "but I like the Army . . . and I don't want to do anything to hurt it."

Friends described Calley as a "gung-ho Army man . . . Army all the way." Ironically, even his staunchest supporters admit, his enthusiasm may be somewhat to blame.

"Maybe he did take some order to clear out the village a little bit too literally," one friend said, "but he's a fine boy."

Calley had been shipped home early from Vietnam, after the Army refused his request to extend his tour of duty. Until the incident at Pinkville, he had received nothing but high ratings from his superior officers. He was scheduled to be awarded the Bronze and Silver Stars for his combat efforts, he said. He has heard nothing about the medals since arriving at Fort Benning.

Calley was born in Miami, Fla., and flunked out of the Palm Beach Junior College before enlisting in the Army. He became a second lieutenant in September 1967, shortly after going to Vietnam. The Army lists his home of record as Waynesville, N.C.

An information sheet put out by the public affairs officer of the Americal Division the day after the March 16 engagement contained this terse mention of the incident: "The swiftness with which the units moved into the area surprised the enemy. After the battle the Eleventh Brigade moved into the village searching each hut and tunnel."

HAMLET ATTACK CALLED "POINT-BLANK MURDER"

WASHINGTON, Nov. 20—Three American soldiers who participated in the March 1968 attack on a Vietnam village called Pinkville said in interviews made public today that their Army combat unit perpetrated, in the words of one, "point-blank murder" on the residents.

"The whole thing was so deliberate. It was point-blank murder and I was standing there watching it," said Sgt. Michael Bernhardt, Franklin Square, N.Y., now completing his Army tour at Fort Dix, N.J.

Bernhardt was a member of one of three platoons of an Eleventh Infantry Brigade company under the command of Capt. Ernest Medina. The company entered the Viet Con–dominated area on March 16, 1968, when on a search-and-destroy mission. Pinkville, known to Vietnamese as Song My village, is about six miles northeast of Quang Ngai.

The Army has charged Lt. William L. Calley Jr., Miami, one of Medina's platoon leaders, with the murder of 109 South Vietnamese civilians in the attack. A squad leader in Calley's platoon, Sgt. David Mitchell, St. Francisville, La., is under investigation for assault with intent to murder.

At least four other men, including Medina, are under investigation in connection with the incident. Calley and his attorney, George W.

Latimer, Salt Lake City, have said that the unit was under orders to clear the area.

Bernhardt, interviewed at Fort Dix, said he had been delayed on the operation and fell slightly behind the company, then led by Calley's platoon, as it entered the village. This is his version of what took place:

"They (Calley's men) were doing a whole lot of shooting up there, but none of it was incoming—I'd been around enough to tell that. I figured they were advancing on the village with fire power.

"I walked up and saw these guys doing strange things. They were doing it three ways. One: They were setting fire to the hootches and huts and waiting for people to come out and then shooting them up. Two: They were going into the hootches and shooting them up. Three: They were gathering people in groups and shooting them.

"As I walked in, you could see piles of people all through the village . . . all over. They were gathered up into large groups.

"I saw them shoot an M-79 (grenade launcher) into a group of people who were still alive. But it (the shooting) was mostly done with a machine gun. They were shooting women and children just like anybody else.

"We met no resistance and I only saw three captured weapons. We had no casualties. It was just like any other Vietnamese village—old Papa-san, women and kids. As a matter of fact, I don't remember seeing one military-age male in the entire place, dead or alive. The only prisoner I saw was about 50."

An Army communiqué reporting on the operation said that Medina's company recovered two M-1 rifles, a carbine, a short-wave radio and enemy documents in the assault. The Viet Cong body count was listed as 128 and there was no mention of civilian casualties.

Bernhardt, short and intense, told his story in staccato fashion, with an obvious sense of relief at finally talking about it. At one point he said to his interviewer: "You're surprised? I wouldn't be surprised at anything these dudes (the men who did the shooting) did."

Bernhardt said he had no idea precisely how many villagers were shot. He said that he had heard death counts ranging from 170 to more than 700.

Bernhardt also said he had no idea whether Calley personally shot 109 civilians, as the Army has charged. However, he said, "I know myself that he killed a whole lot of people."

Residents of the Pinkville areas have told newspapermen that 567 villagers were killed in the operation.

Why did the men run amuck?

"It's my belief," the sergeant said, "that the company was conditioned to do this. The treatment was lousy. . . . We were always out in the bushes. I think they were expecting us to run into resistance at Pinkville and also expecting them (the Viet Cong) to use the people as hostages."

A few days before the mission, he said, the men's general contempt for Vietnamese civilians intensified when some GIs walked into a landmine, injuring nearly 20 and killing at least one member of the company.

Why didn't he report the incident at the time?

"After it was all over, some colonel came down to the firebase where we were stationed and asked about it, but we heard no further. Later they (Medina and some other officers) called me over to the command post and asked me not to write my Congressman."

(The Army subsequently substantiated Bernhardt's accusation. In a private letter dated Aug. 6, 1969, Col. John G. Hill Jr., a deputy for staff action control in the office of Army Chief of Staff William C. Westmoreland, wrote that Medina acknowledged that he had requested Bernhardt to wait until a brigade investigation of the incident was completed. Nothing came of the investigation.)

Bernhardt said that about 90 per cent of the 60 to 70 men in the short-handed company were involved in the shootings. He took no part, he said. "I only shoot at people who shoot at me," was his explanation.

"The Army ordered me not to talk," Bernhardt told the interviewer. "But there are some orders that I have to personally decide whether to obey; I have my own conscience to consider.

"The whole thing has kind of made me wonder if I could trust people any more."

His opinion, he said, is that a higher ranking officer must have ordered the destruction of Pinkville. "Calley's just a small fry," he said.

Bernhardt said the Army must have known at high levels just what did happen at Pinkville.

"They've got pictures. Some dude went along on the mission and shot pictures," he said.

Bernhardt said the photographs were shown to him in the Article 32 proceeding, which concluded that the charges against Calley were justified.

"They showed a mass of people . . . this pile-up of people. I don't see how anybody could say it was artillery or crossfire that killed those people," he said.

(The *Cleveland Plain Dealer* printed today photographs showing South Vietnamese civilians allegedly killed in the incident. It said the photographs came from a former Army combat photographer, Ronald L. Haeberle, Cleveland.

(Haeberle said in a copyright story that he joined the company just before it entered the village and heard from the men the villagers were suspected of being Viet Cong sympathizers. He said he saw men, women and children killed.)

Another witness to the shootings was Michael Terry, Orem, Utah, then a member of the C Platoon of Medina's company and now a sophomore at nearby Brigham Young University. Interviewed at his home, Terry said he, too, came on the scene moments after the killings began.

"They just marched through shooting everybody," he said. "Seems like no one said anything. . . . They just started pulling people out and shooting them."

At one point, he said, more than 20 villagers were lined up in front of a ditch and shot.

"They had them in a group standing over ditch—just like a Nazi-type thing. . . . One officer ordered a kid to machine-gun everybody down, but the kid just couldn't do it. He threw the machine gun down and the officer picked it up . . ." Terry said.

"I don't remember seeing any men in the ditch. Mostly women and kids."

Later, he and the platoon team he headed were taking a lunch break near the ditch when, Terry said, he noticed "some of them were still breathing. . . . They were pretty badly shot up. They weren't going to get any medical help, and so we shot them. Shot maybe five of them . . ."

Why did it happen?

"I think that probably the officers didn't really know if they were ordered to kill the villagers or not. . . . A lot of guys feel that they (the South Vietnamese civilians) aren't human beings, we just treated them like animals."

Apparently one officer, who was not from Medina's company, attempted to halt the shootings. Terry and Bernhardt both reported that a helicopter pilot from an aviation support unit landed in the midst of the incident and attempted to quell it.

The officer warned that he would report the shootings. On the next day, the pilot was killed in action and the subsequent investigation started by officials of the Eleventh Brigade was dropped after one and a half days because of insufficient evidence.

Terry said he first learned of the present investigation when he was interviewed last spring by a colonel from the Army Inspector General's office. Bernhardt was not questioned until a team from the Army's Criminal Investigation Division visited him two months ago.

The third witness to the Pinkville shootings cannot be identified. He is still on active duty with the Army on the West Coast. But he corroborated in detail the Bernhardt and Terry descriptions of that day in March 1968.

"I was shooting pigs and a chicken while the others were shooting people," he said. "It isn't just a nightmare; I'm completely aware of how real this was.

"It's something I don't think a person would understand—the reality of it just didn't hit me until recently, when I read about it again in the newspapers."

All three GIs were read key excerpts from a three-page letter sent in March by a former GI, Ronald Ridenhour, to the Army and 30 other officials, including some Senators. The letter outlined the Pinkville incident as he understood it. It was Ridenhour's persistence that prompted the Army to begin its high-level investigation in April.

Ridenhour, now a student at Claremont (Calif.) Men's College, was not in Medina's company and did not participate in the shootings. He relied on information from Terry and Bernhardt, among many others, to draft his letter.

Calley's attorney refused to comment on the new charges brought out in the interviews. But another source, discussing Calley's position, said, "Nobody's put the finger yet on the man who started it."

The source said also that he understood that Calley and other officers in the company initially resisted the orders but eventually did their job. Calley's platoon led the attack on the village, with the other units forming a horseshoe-shaped cordon around the area, to prevent enemy troops from fleeing.

"I don't care whether Calley used the best judgment or not—he was faced with a tough decision," the source said.

EX-GI TELLS OF KILLING CIVILIANS AT PINKVILLE

TERRE HAUTE, IND., Nov. 25—A former GI told in interviews yesterday how he executed, under orders, dozens of South Vietnamese civilians during the United States Army attack of the village of Song My in March 1968. He estimated that he and his fellow soldiers shot 370 villagers during the operation in what has become known as Pinkville.

Paul Meadlo, 22 years old, West Terre Haute, Ind., a farm community near the Illinois border, gave an eyewitness account—the first made available thus far—of what happened when a platoon led by Lt. William L. Calley Jr. entered Pinkville on a search-and-destroy mission. The Army has acknowledged that at least 100 civilians were killed by the men; Vietnamese survivors had told reporters that the death total was 567.

Meadlo, who was wounded in a mine accident the day after Pinkville, disclosed that the company captain, Ernest Medina, was in the area at the time of the shootings and made no attempt to stop them.

Calley, 26, Waynesville, N.C., has been accused of the premeditated murder of 109 civilians in the incident. Medina, as commander of the Eleventh Infantry Brigade unit, is under investigation for his role in the shootings. Last week the Army said that at least 24 other men were under investigation, including Calley's chief noncommissioned officer, Sgt. David Mitchell, 29, St. Francisville, La., who is being investigated for assault with intent to commit murder. Calley was ordered yesterday to stand general court-martial.

Here is Meadlo's story as given in interviews at his mother's home near Terre Haute:

"There was supposed to have been some Viet Cong in Pinkville and we began to make a sweep through it. Once we got there we began gathering up the people . . . started putting them in big mobs. There must have been about 40 or 45 civilians standing in one big circle in the middle of the village . . . Calley told me and a couple of other guys to watch them.

'You know what I want you to do with them,' he said," Meadlo related. He and the others continued to guard the group. "About 10 minutes later Calley came back. 'Get with it,' he said. 'I want them dead.'

"So we stood about 10 or 15 feet away from them, then he (Calley) started shooting them. Then he told me to start shooting them. . . . I started to shoot them, but the other guys (who had been assigned to guard the civilians) wouldn't do it.

"So we (Meadlo and Calley) went ahead and killed them. I used more than a whole clip—actually I used four or five clips," Meadlo said. (There are 17 M-16 shells in a clip.) He estimated that he killed at least 15 civilians—or nearly half of those in the circle.

Asked what he thought at the time, Meadlo said, "I just thought we were supposed to do it." Later, he said that the shooting "did take a load off my conscience for the buddies we'd lost. It was just revenge, that's all it was."

The company had been in the field for 40 days without relief before the Pinkville incident on March 16, and had lost a number of men in mine accidents. Hostility to the Vietnamese was high in the company, Meadlo said.

The killings continued.

"We had about seven or eight civilians gathered in a hootch, and I was going to throw a hand grenade in. But someone told us to take them to the ditch (a drainage ditch in the village into which many civilians were herded—and shot).

"Calley was there and said to me, 'Meadlo, we've got another job to do.' So we pushed our seven to eight people in with the big bunch of them. And so I began shooting them all. So did Mitchell, Calley . . . (at this point Meadlo could not remember any more men involved). I guess I shot maybe 25 or 20 people in the ditch."

His role in the killings had not yet ended.

"After the ditch, there were just some people in hootches. I knew there were some people down in one hootch, maybe two or three, so I just threw a hand grenade in."

Meadlo is a tall, clean-cut son of an Indiana coal mine worker. He married his high-school sweetheart in suburban Terre Haute, began rearing a family (he has two children) and was drafted. He had been in Vietnam four months at the time of Pinkville. On the next day, March 17, his foot was blown off, when, while following Calley on an operation, a land mine was set off.

As Meadlo was waiting to be evacuated, other men in the company had reported that he told Calley that "this was his (Meadlo's) punishment for what he had done the day before. He warned, according to onlookers, that Calley would have his day of judgment too. Asked about this, Meadlo said he could not remember.

Meadlo is back at a factory job now in Terre Haute, fighting to keep a full disability payment from the Veterans' Administration. The loss of his right foot seems to bother him less than the loss of his self-respect.

Like other members of his company, be had been called just days before the interview by an officer at Fort Benning, Ga., where Calley is being held, and advised that he should not discuss the case with reporters. But, like other members of his company, he seemed eager to talk.

"This has made him awful nervous," explained his mother, Mrs. Myrtle Meadlo, 57, New Goshen, Ind. "He seems like he just can't get over it.

"I sent them a good boy and they made him a murderer."

Why did he do it?

"We all were under orders," Meadlo said. "We all thought we were doing the right thing. . . . At the time it didn't bother me."

He began having serious doubts that night about what he had done at Pinkville. He says he still has them.

"The kids and the women—they didn't have any right to die.

"In the beginning," Meadlo said, "I just thought we were going to be murdering the Viet Cong." He, like other members of his company, had attended a squad meeting the night before, at which time Company Commander Medina promised the boys a good firefight.

Calley and his platoon were assigned the key role of entering the Pinkville area first.

"When we came in we thought we were getting fired on," Meadlo said, although the company suffered no casualties, apparently because the Viet Cong had fled from the area during the night.

"We came in from this open field, and somebody spotted this one gook out there. He was down in a shelter, scared and huddling. . . . Someone said, 'There's a gook over here,' and asked what to do with him. Mitchell said, 'Shoot him,' and he did. The gook was standing up and shaking and waving his arms when he got it.

"Then we came onto this hootch, and one door was hard to open."

Meadlo said he crashed through the door and "found an old man in there shaking.

"I told them, 'I got one,' and it was Mitchell who told me to shoot him. That was the first man I shot. He was hiding in a dugout, shaking his head and waving his arms, trying to tell me not to shoot him."

After the carnage, Meadlo said, "I heard that all we were supposed to do was kill the VC. Mitchell said we were just supposed to shoot the men."

Women and children also were shot. Meadlo estimated that at least 310 persons were shot to death by the Americans that day.

"I know it was far more than 100 as the U.S. Army now says. I'm absolutely sure of that. There were bodies all around."

He has some haunting memories, he says. "They didn't put up a fight or anything. The women huddled against their children and took it. They brought their kids real close to their stomachs and hugged them, and put their bodies over them trying to save them. It didn't do much good," Meadlo said.

Two things puzzled him. He vigorously disputes the repeated reports of an artillery barrage before the village was approached.

"There wasn't any artillery barrage whatsoever in the village. Only some gunships firing from above," he said.

The South Vietnamese government said Saturday that 20 civilians were killed in the Pinkville attack, most of them victims of tactical air strikes or an artillery barrage laid down before the U.S. troops moved in. The government denied reports of a massacre.

Meadlo is curious also about the role of Capt. Medina in the incident.

"I don't know if the C.O. (Company Commander) gave the order to kill or not, but he was right there when it happened. Why didn't he stop it? He and Calley passed each other quite a few times that morning, but didn't say anything. Medina just kept marching around. He could've put a stop to it anytime he wanted."

The whole operation took about 30 minutes, Meadlo said.

As for Calley, Meadlo told of an incident a few weeks before Pinkville.

"We saw this woman walking across this rice paddy and Calley said, 'Shoot her,' so we did. When we got there the girl was alive, had this hole in her side. Calley tried to get someone to shoot her again; I don't know if he did."

In addition, Calley and Medina had told the men before Pinkville, Meadlo said, "that if we ever shoot any civilians, we should go ahead and plant a hand grenade on them."

Meadlo is not sure, but he thinks the feel of death came quickly to the company once it got to Vietnam.

"We were cautious at first, but as soon as the first man was killed, a new feeling came through the company . . . almost as if we all knew there was going to be a lot more killing."

NEIL SHEEHAN AND HEDRICK SMITH

On June 13, 1971, recently inaugurated President Richard Nixon awoke in a cheerful mood: he had celebrated his daughter's marriage the evening before. The day soured when he received a call from his national security advisor, Henry Kissinger, about a massive story in that morning's New York Times*: revelation of a secret Pentagon study on the roots of the Vietnam conflict. The study had been leaked to the* Times*'s Neil Sheehan by Daniel Ellsberg, a former Pentagon advisor who had grown disillusioned by the war. At Kissinger's urging, the Nixon administration went to Federal Judge Murray Gurfein, arguing that further publication of excerpts from the study would inflict "grave and irreparable harm to the nation's security." Judge Gurfein issued the first restraining order against a news story in American history. The* Washington Post *began publication from its own copy of the Pentagon Papers, and Judge Gurfein extended his injunction. It would be nearly three weeks before a six-justice majority of the Supreme Court threw out the injunction, saying that the Nixon administration had not met the "heavy burden" the Constitution requires for prior censorship of the news.*

As assembled by Sheehan (1936–), Hedrick Smith (1933–) and other Times *reporters, the Pentagon Papers story counts as the single most consequential "leak" on record. Fury at the disclosures led Nixon and Kissinger to establish a secret White House team—the Plumbers—to control future leaks and to find damaging information on Ellsberg. Thus one investigative scoop, the Pentagon Papers, set in motion the pattern of secret White House operations that would be revealed two years later in the* Washington Post*'s Watergate coverage.*

VAST REVIEW OF WAR TOOK A YEAR

From the *New York Times*, 1971

In June, 1967, at a time of great personal disenchantment with the Indochina war and rising frustration among his colleagues at the Pentagon, Secretary of Defense Robert S. McNamara commissioned a major study of how and why the United States had become so deeply involved in Vietnam.

The project took a year to complete and yielded a vast and highly unusual report of Government self-analysis. It was compiled by a team of 30 to 40 Government officials, civilian and military, many of whom had helped to develop or carry out the policies that they were asked to evaluate and some of whom were simultaneously active in the debates that changed the course of those policies.

While Mr. McNamara turned over his job to Clark M. Clifford, while the war reached a military peak in the 1968 Lunar New Year offensive, while President Johnson cut back the bombing of North Vietnam and announced his plan to retire, and while the peace talks began in Paris, the study group burrowed through Government files.

The members sought to probe American policy toward Southeast Asia from the World War II pronouncements of President Franklin D. Roosevelt into the start of Vietnam peace talks in the summer of 1968. They wrote nearly 40 book-length volumes backed up by annexes of cablegrams, memorandums, draft proposals, dissents and other documents.

MANY INCONSISTENCIES

Their report runs to more than 7,000 pages—1.5 million words of historical narratives plus a million words of documents—enough to fill a small crate.

Even so, it is not a complete or polished history. It displays many inconsistencies and lacks a single all-embracing summary. It is an extended internal critique based on the documentary record, which the researchers did not supplement with personal interviews, partly because they were pressed for time.

The study emerged as a middle-echelon and official view of the war, incorporating material from the top-level files of the Defense Department into which flow papers from the White House, the State Department, the Central Intelligence Agency and the Joint Chiefs of Staff.

Some important gaps appear in the study. The researchers did not have access to the complete files of Presidents or to all the memorandums of their conversations and decisions.

Moreover, there is another important gap in the copy of the Pentagon study obtained by the *New York Times*: It lacks the section on the secret diplomacy of the Johnson period.

But whatever its limitations, the Pentagon's study discloses a vast amount of new information about the unfolding American commitment to South Vietnam and the way in which the United States engaged itself in that conflict. It is also rich in insights into the workings of government and the reasoning of the men who ran it.

Throughout the narrative, there is ample evidence of vigorous, even acrimonious, debate within the Government—far more than Congress, the press and the public were permitted to discover from official pronouncements.

But the Pentagon account and its accompanying documents also reveal that once the basic objective of policy was set, the internal debate on Vietnam from 1950 until mid-1967 dealt almost entirely with how to reach those objectives rather than with the basic direction of policy.

The study related that American governments from the Truman Administration onward felt it necessary to take action to prevent Communist control of South Vietnam. As a rationale for policy, the domino theory—that if South Vietnam fell, other countries would inevitably follow—was repeated in endless variations for nearly two decades.

CONFIDENCE AND APPREHENSIONS

Especially during the nineteen-sixties, the Pentagon study discloses, the Government was confident that American power—or even the threat of its use—would bring the war under control.

But the study reveals that high officials in the Johnson Administration were troubled by the potential dangers of Chinese Communist intervention and felt the need for self-restraint to avoid provoking Peking, or the Soviet Union, into combat involvement.

As some top policy makers came to question the effectiveness of the American effort in mid-1967, the report shows, their policy papers began not only to seek to limit the military strategies on the ground and in the air but also to worry about the impact of the war on American society.

"A feeling is widely and strongly held that 'the Establishment' is out of its mind," wrote John T. McNaughton, Assistant Secretary of Defense, in a note to Secretary McNamara in early May, 1967. Mr. McNaughton, who three years earlier had been one of the principal planners of the air war against North Vietnam, went on to say:

"The feeling is that we are trying to impose some U.S. image on distant peoples we cannot understand (any more than we can the younger generation here at home) and that we are carrying the thing to absurd lengths. Related to this feeling is the increased polarization that is taking place in the United States with seeds of the worst split in our people in more than a century."

At the end of June, 1967, Mr. McNamara—deeply disillusioned with the war—decided to commission the Pentagon study of Vietnam policy that Mr. McNaughton and other high officials had encouraged him to undertake.

Mr. McNamara's instructions, conveyed orally and evidently in writing as well, were for the researchers to pull together the Pentagon's documentary record and, according to one well-placed former official, to produce an "objective and encyclopedic" study of the American involvement.

Broadest Possible Interpretation

The Pentagon researchers aimed at the broadest possible interpretation of events. They examined not only the policies and motive of American administrations, but also the effectiveness of intelligence, the mechanics and consequences of bureaucratic compromises, the difficulties of imposing American tactics on the South Vietnamese, the governmental uses of the American press, and many other tributaries of their main story.

The authors reveal, for example, that the American intelligence community repeatedly provided the policy makers with what proved to be accurate warnings that desired goals were either unattainable or likely to provoke costly reactions from the enemy. They cite some lapses in the accuracy of reporting and intelligence, but give a generally favorable assessment of the C.I.A. and other intelligence units.

The Pentagon researchers relate many examples of bureaucratic compromise forged by Presidents from the conflicting proposals of their advisers.

In the mid-fifties, they found, the Joint Chiefs of Staff were a restraining force, warning that successful defense of South Vietnam could not be guaranteed under the limits imposed by the 1954 Geneva accords and agreeing to send in American military advisers only on the insistence of Secretary of State John Foster Dulles.

In the nineteen-sixties, the report found, both Presidents Kennedy and Johnson chose partial measures, overriding advice that some military proposals were valid only as packages and could not be adopted piecemeal.

In examining Washington's constant difficulties with the governments in Saigon, the study found the United States so heavily committed to the regime of the moment and so fearful of instability that it was unable to persuade the South Vietnamese to make the political and economic reforms that Americans deemed necessary to win the allegiance of the people.

Though it ranges widely to explain events, the Pentagon report makes no summary effort to put the blame for the war on any single administration or to find fault with individual officials.

The writers appear to have stood at the political and bureaucratic center of the period, directing their criticisms toward both left and right.

In one section, Senator Eugene J. McCarthy, the antiwar candidate for the 1968 Democratic Presidential nomination, is characterized as "impudent and dovish," and as an "upstart challenger." At another point in the same section the demands of Adm. U.S. Grant Sharp, commander of Pacific forces, for all-out bombing of North Vietnam, are characterized as "fulminations."

For the most part, the writers assumed a calm and unemotional tone, dissecting their materials in a detached and academic manner. They ventured to answer key questions only when the evidence was at hand. They found no conclusive answers to some of the most widely asked questions about the war, including these:

- Precisely how was Ngo Dinh Diem returned to South Vietnam in 1954 from exile and helped to power?

- Who took the lead in preventing the 1956 Vietnam elections required under the Geneva accords of 1954—Mr. Diem or the Americans?

- If President Kennedy had lived, would he have led the United States into a full-scale ground war in South Vietnam and an air war against North Vietnam as President Johnson did?

- Was Secretary of Defense McNamara dismissed for opposing the Johnson strategy in mid-1967, or did he ask to be relieved because of disenchantment with Administration policy?

- Did President Johnson's cutback of the bombing to the 20th Parallel in 1968 signal a lowering of American objectives for the war or was it merely an effort to buy more time and patience from a war-weary American public?

The research project was organized in the Pentagon's office of International Security Affairs—I.S.A., as it is known to Government insiders—the politico-military affairs branch, whose head is the third-ranking official in the Defense Department. This was Assistant Secretary McNaughton when the study was commissioned and Assistant Secretary Paul C. Warnke when the study was completed.

'It Remained McNamara's Study'

In the fall of 1968, it was transmitted to Mr. Warnke, who reportedly "signed off" on it. Former officials say this meant that he acknowledged completion of the work without endorsing its contents and forwarded it to Mr. Clifford.

Although it had been completed during Mr. Clifford's tenure, "in everyone's mind it always remained Mr. McNamara's study," one official said.

Because of its extreme sensitivity, very few copies were reproduced—from 6 to 15, by various accounts. One copy was delivered by hand to

Mr. McNamara, then president of the World Bank. His reaction is not known, but at least one other former policy maker was reportedly displeased by the study's candor.

Other copies were said to have been provided to President Johnson, the State Department and President Nixon's staff, as well as to have been kept for Pentagon files.

The authors, mostly working part-time over several months, were middle-level officials drawn from I.S.A., Systems Analysis, and the military staffs in the Pentagon, or lent by the State Department or White House staff. Probably two-thirds of the group had worked on Vietnam for the Government at one time or another.

Both the writing and editing were described as group efforts, though individuals with academic qualifications as historians, political scientists and the like were in charge of various sections.

For their research, the Pentagon depended primarily on the files of Secretary McNamara and Mr. McNaughton. William P. Bundy, former Assistant Secretary of State for Far Eastern Affairs, provided some of his files.

For extended periods, probably the most serious limitation of the Pentagon study is the lack of access to White House archives. The researchers did possess the Presidential decision papers that normally circulated to high Pentagon officials, plus White House messages to commanders or ambassadors in Saigon. These provide insight into Presidential moods and motives, but only intermittently.

An equally important handicap is that the Pentagon researchers generally lacked records of the oral discussions of the National Security Council or the most intimate gatherings of Presidents with their closest advisers, where decisions were often reached.

As the authors themselves remark, it is common practice for the final recommendations drafted before a key Presidential decision to be written to the President's spoken specifications on the basis of his reactions to earlier proposals. The missing link is often the meeting of the Administration's inner circle.

Also, because the Pentagon study draws almost entirely on internal

Government papers, and primarily papers that circulated through the Defense Department, the picture of so important a figure as Secretary of State Dean Rusk remains shadowy. Mr. Rusk was known as a man who rarely committed himself to paper and who, especially during the Johnson Administration, saved his most sensitive advice for solitary talks with the President.

In the late months of the Johnson Administration, the lack of records of such meetings is a considerable weakness because, as the survey comments, Mr. Johnson operated a split-level Government. Only his most intimate advisers were aware of the policy moves he was contemplating, and some of the most important officials at the second level of government—Assistant Secretaries of State and Defense—were late to learn the drift of the President's thinking.

The Pentagon account notes that at times the highest Administration officials not only kept information about their real intentions from the press and Congress, but also kept secret from the Government bureaucracy the real motives for their written recommendations or actions.

"The lesson in this," one Pentagon analyst observes, "is that the rationales given in such pieces of paper (intended for fairly wide circulation among the bureaucracy, as opposed to tightly held memoranda limited to those closest to the decision maker), do not reliably indicate why recommendations were made the way they were." The words in parentheses are the analyst's.

Another omission is the absence of any extended discussion of military or political responsibility for such matters as civilian casualties or the restraints imposed by the rules of land warfare.

NECESSARILY FRAGMENTED ACCOUNT

The approach of the writers varies markedly from section to section. Some of the writers are analytical and incisive. Others offer narrative compendiums of the most important available documents for their periods, with little comment or interpretation.

As a bureaucratic history, this account is necessarily fragmented. The writers either lacked time or did not choose to provide a coherent, integrated summary analysis for each of the four administrations that became involved in Vietnam from 1950 to 1968.

The Pentagon account divides the Kennedy period, for example, into five sections—dealing with the key decisions of 1961, the strategic-hamlet programs, the buildup of the American advisory mission in Vietnam, the development of plans for phased American withdrawal, and the coup d'etat that ousted President Diem.

In the Johnson era, four simultaneous stories are told in separate sections—the land war in South Vietnam, the air war against the North, political relations with successive South Vietnamese governments and the secret diplomatic search for negotiations. There is some overlapping, but no single section tries to summarize or draw together the various strands.

The overall effect of the study, nonetheless, is to provide a vast storehouse of new information—the most complete and informative central archive available thus far on the Vietnam era.

JACK ANDERSON

As a young reporter Jack Anderson (1922–) was hired to assist Drew Pearson on his syndicated Washington Post *column "Washington Merry-Go-Round," soon becoming Pearson's partner and co-author. Anderson took over "Washington Merry-Go-Round" upon Pearson's death in 1969, becoming one of Washington's most-feared conduits for disclosures of official misconduct in a column distributed to some four hundred newspapers. Though Anderson's reporting ranges widely—his subjects vary from foreign policy to the NRA—his most notable contributions came during the Nixon presidency. In the following series of 1972 columns, Anderson reveals how the administration colluded with the International Telephone and Telegraph company, settling a lawsuit in return for $400,000 in campaign contributions. Anderson's ITT columns earned him a place on Nixon's "enemies list," and in retrospect are the first harbingers of the pervasive financial scandals that drove Nixon from office.*

Anderson was never an analyst of issues or institutions; instead, he is in the tradition of reporters focusing on individual acts of corruption in politics. The ITT columns (with much of the reporting actually done by Anderson's legman Brit Hume, today a Fox News anchor) are notable not only for their specific charges but because they show how Anderson strategically built one scoop upon another—first an initial revelation of wrongdoing, then uncovering lies in the official response.

SECRET MEMO BARES MITCHELL-ITT MOVE

From the *Washington Post, February 29,* 1972

We now have evidence that the settlement of the Nixon administration's biggest anti-trust case was privately arranged between Attorney General John Mitchell and the top lobbyist for the company involved.

We have this on the word of the lobbyist herself, crusty, capable Dita Beard of the International Telephone and Telegraph Co. She acknowledged the secret deal after we obtained a highly incriminating memo, written by her, from ITT's files.

The memo, which was intended to be destroyed after it was read, not only indicates that the anti-trust case had been fixed but that the fix was a payoff for ITT's pledge of up to $400,000 for the upcoming Republican convention in San Diego.

Confronted with the memo, Mrs. Beard acknowledged its authenticity. The next night, badly shaken and acting against the wishes of ITT officials who wanted her to leave town, she met with my associate Brit Hume at her home to try to explain the document.

By this time, she said, ITT security officers from company headquarters in New York had put most of her office files through a document shredder to prevent their being subpoenaed after disclosure of the memo.

She said she met with Mitchell at the Governor's mansion in Kentucky during a dinner reception given by Republican Gov. Louie Nunn last May after the Kentucky Derby.

At the governor's reception, she said, Mitchell took her and Nunn aside and to her astonishment and shock, launched into an hour-long diatribe against her. He criticized her for putting pressure through Congress and the on the Justice Department White House on the anti-trust cases [*sic*].

She said Mitchell confided to her he was sympathetic to ITT but had been prevented until then from helping the company because of the zeal of the Justice Department's anti-trust chief, Richard McLaren.

After his harangue, Mrs. Beard said, Mitchell agreed to discuss the anti-trust matters and asked bluntly, "What do you want?" meaning what companies did ITT most want to keep if the anti-trust cases were settled.

"We have to have Hartford Fire because of the economy," Mrs. Beard recalled saying.

She said she also told Mitchell ITT wanted to keep "part of the Grinnell Corporation," a manufacturing concern. She said Mitchell at first replied, "You can't have part of Grinnell," but he subsequently relented.

And, she said, when the Justice Department announced its settlement with ITT on July 31, more than two months later, it conformed to the agreement she had made with Mitchell.

Mrs. Beard insisted the subject of the GOP convention never came up with Mitchell and was never a factor in the anti-trust matter. But this clearly contradicts her memorandum, which was written six weeks after the Kentucky Derby dinner.

It is addressed to W. R. (Bill) Merriam, head of ITT's Washington office. It is marked "Personal and Confidential," and its last line asks, "Please destroy this, huh?"

The memo warns Merriam to keep quiet about the ITT cash pledge for the Republican convention. "John Mitchell has certainly kept it on the higher level only," the memo says, "we should be able to do the same . . . "

"I am convinced, because of several conversations with Louie (Gov. Nunn) re Mitchell that our noble commitment has gone a long way toward our negotiations on the mergers coming out as Hal (ITT President Harold Geneen) wants them.

"Certainly the President has told Mitchell to see that things are worked out fairly. It is still only McLaren's mickey-mouse we are suffering . . .

"If (the convention commitment) gets too much publicity, you can believe our negotiations with Justice will wind up shot down. Mitchell is definitely helping us, but cannot let it be known."

KLEINDIENST ACCUSED IN ITT CASE

From the *Washington Post,* March 1, 1972

We have now established that Attorney General-designate Richard Kleindienst told an outright lie about the Justice Department's sudden out-of-court settlement of the Nixon Administration's biggest anti-trust case.

The case involved the International Telephone and Telegraph conglomerate, which appeared on the way to Supreme Court showdown with the Justice Department over ITT's takeover of the huge Hartford Fire Insurance Co.

Last July, however, the case was abruptly settled. The terms, considered highly favorable to ITT, were announced at the same time ITT secretly pledged up to $400,000 to support the Republican convention in San Diego this year. A check for $100,000 has already been written.

Denying any connection between the convention cash and the anti-trust settlement, Kleindienst insisted that the Justice Department's anti-trust staff had been free from any political pressure from above.

"The settlement between the Department of Justice and ITT was handled and negotiated exclusively by Assistant Attorney General Richard W. McLaren (then head of the anti-trust division)," Kleindienst said in a letter to Democratic Nation Chairman Larry O'Brien.

However, we have now learned that Kleindienst himself held roughly a half-dozen secret meetings on the ITT case with a director of the company before the settlement was reached.

The director, Wall Street financier Felix Rohatyn, conceded to us that he met in private with Kleindienst, who was then Deputy Attorney General, at the same time McLaren was negotiating with ITT's lawyers.

"I was supposed to make the case on the economic side of it," Rohatyn told my associate Brit Hume. He said he particularly stressed to Kleindienst ITT's arguments for keeping Hartford Fire.

Kleindienst Duplicity

Kleindienst's duplicity is further evidence that the administration has much to hide in the ITT affair, which looks more suspicious the more we investigate it.

Not only Kleindienst, but his boss, outgoing Attorney General John Mitchell, has now been linked to the settlement. Mitchell had officially disqualified himself from the case because of an old relationship with ITT. Yet Dita Beard, the company's top lobbyist, has know acknowledged that she arranged the settlement with Mitchell in a private conversation at the governor's mansion in Kentucky after last year's Kentucky Derby.

Her admission came after we obtained an extraordinary confidential memo, written by her, from ITT's files. The memo suggested strongly that the settlement was made in exchange for ITT's pledge of cash support for the Republican convention.

Mrs. Beard also told us that the day after we confronted her with the memo, ITT security men from New York shredded many of her office files because they feared the papers might be subpoenaed when the memo became public.

Mitchell would not discuss the matter with us. Josh Hushen, a Justice Department spokesman, told us there was "no truth" to Mrs. Beard's story. He acknowledged, however, that Mitchell had spoken to Mrs. Beard at the governor's mansion.

We gave Hushen specific questions to ask the Attorney General. But four hours later, after conferring with Mitchell, he called us back without the answers.

Instead, he urged that we withhold our story on Mrs. Beard's version of events until, as Hushen put it, "we get all our ducks in a row." He said

Mitchell would "prove" the falsehood of Mrs. Beard's incriminating memo, but three days later, no proof had appeared.

REPUBLICAN NAMES

The June 25, 1971 memo is studded with such big Republican names as President Nixon, Mitchell, California Lt. Gov. Ed Reinecke, San Diego Congressman Bob Wilson, White House aide Bob Haldemen and H. S. (Hal) Geneen, ITT's president.

It is addressed to W. R. (Bill) Merriam, manager of ITT's Washington office. "I thought you and I had agreed very thoroughly that under no circumstances would anyone in this office discuss with anyone our participation in the Convention, including me," Mrs. Beard wrote.

"Other than permitting John Mitchell, Ed Reinecke, Bob Haldeman and Nixon (besides Wilson, of course) no one has known from whom that 400 thousand commitment had come . . . John Mitchell has kept it on the higher level only, we should be able to do the same . . .

"I am convinced, because of several conversations with Louie (Nunn) re Mitchell that our noble commitment has gone a long way toward our negotiations on the mergers eventually coming out as Hal (Geneen) wants them. Certainly the President has told Mitchell to see that things are worked out fairly. It is still only McLaren's mickey-mouse we are suffering . . .

"If (the convention cash) gets too much publicity you can believe our negotiations with Justice will wind up shot down. Mitchell is definitely helping us, but cannot let it be known. Please destroy this, huh?"

CONTRADICTIONS CITED IN ITT CASE

From the *Washington Post,* March 3, 1972

The Justice Department and International Telephone and Telegraph are now trying to lie their way out of a scandal over the suspicious, sudden settlement of a landmark anti-trust suit against ITT.

In earlier columns, we disclosed a remarkable ITT memo indicating the Justice Department granted the favorable settlement in exchange for cash support of the upcoming Republican convention in San Diego.

The author of the memo, ITT lobbyist Dita Beard, told us she arranged the settlement herself in a private conversation with Attorney General John Mitchell at a Kentucky dinner party.

Mitchell refused to talk to us. A spokesman, John Hushen, urged us to withhold our information until he could "get our ducks in a row." He then waited three days before calling us back with a terse statement from Mitchell.

The statement says the Attorney General "was not involved in any way with the Republican National Committee convention negotiations and had no knowledge of anyone from the committee or elsewhere dealing with International Telephone and Telegraph."

This is false. In mid-May last year, California Lt. Gov. Ed Reinecke and an aide, Edgar Gillenwaters, met with Mitchell in his Washington office to discuss efforts to hold the convention in San Diego.

Mitchell Misleads

We could not reach Reinecke, but Gillenwaters told us he and Reinecke personally informed Mitchell that ITT had offered to put up as much as $400,000 to support a GOP convention in San Diego.

"He liked the idea of (having the convention in) San Diego," Gillenwaters said of Mitchell. "He didn't need any persuading. He said, 'If you can do it, more power to you.'"

ITT also issued a statement on the matter which insisted that only its lawyers were authorized to deal with the Justice Department on the antitrust cases. "Neither Mrs. Beard nor anyone else except legal counsel was authorized to carry on such negotiations," the statement said.

This is also false. Felix Rohatyn, an investment banker and director of ITT, told us he held a series of about a half dozen secret meetings during the merger negotiations with Deputy Attorney General Richard Kleindienst. Rohatyn said he was specifically authorized to "make the case on the economic side" by ITT President Harold S. Geneen.

Rohatyn's acknowledgement also puts the lie to an earlier statement by Kleindienst, who has been named to replace Mitchell as Attorney General. On December 13, Kleindienst wrote to Democratic National Chairman Larry O'Brien to deny that high-level political pressure had been exerted on the Justice Department's anti-trust staff in the ITT case.

"The settlement between the Department of Justice and ITT was handled and negotiated exclusively by Assistant Attorney General Richard W. McLaren (then head of the anti-trust division)," the Kleindienst letter said.

Obviously, if Kleindienst were holding secret talks with Rohatyn on the case, it could not have been "handled" and negotiated "exclusively" by McLaren and ITT's lawyers.

ROBERT WOODWARD AND CARL BERNSTEIN

The Watergate reporting of Carl Bernstein (1944–) and Bob Woodward (1943–) long ago passed into Hollywood legend. Rereading their original Washington Post *stories, what is perhaps most striking is their sheer shoe-leather tenacity. Like Seymour Hersh's exposé of the My Lai massacre, the Watergate scandal eluded far more experienced reporters on the national-affairs beat. Woodward and Bernstein triumphed because they treated the Watergate break-in like a crime story rather than a political story, pursuing Nixon aides with the same tactics and tone a reporter would use investigating a building inspector on the take.*

Woodward and Bernstein's Watergate coverage was a watershed in daily-newspaper investigative journalism. Their success inspired a new generation of reporters who shared their skepticism toward received authority. the Post*'s success ratcheted up the competitive energies of the* New York Times, *which hired Hersh. It also convinced local and regional newspaper editors to make new commitments to investigative reporting, leading to a renaissance in local public-interest reporting later in the decade.*

SPY FUNDS LINKED TO GOP AIDES

From the *Washington Post*, September 17, 1972

Funds for the Watergate espionage operation were controlled by several principal assistants of John N. Mitchell, the former manager of President Nixon's campaign, and were kept in a special account at the Committee for the Re-election of the President, the *Washington Post* has learned.

The Mitchell assistants, all of whom still hold policy-making positions on a high level in President Nixon's re-election campaign, were among 15 persons who had access to the secret fund of more than $300,000 earmarked for sensitive political projects.

Included in those projects was the espionage campaign against the Democrats, for which seven persons—including two former White House aides—were indicted Friday by a federal grand jury.

It could not be learned whether the Mitchell aides, who include persons who once worked at the White House, knew that funds would specifically be expended for the purpose of illegal electronic surveillance. However, associates told the *Post* that the aides were aware that the money would be spent generally on gathering information about the Democrats.

Some of the Mitchell aides are among the persons named by a self-described participant in the Watergate operation as recipients of confidential memos based on the tapped telephone conversations of Democratic Party officials.

A spokesman for President Nixon's re-election committee, informed of the *Post*'s story, said late yesterday afternoon that "there have been and are cash funds in this committee used for various legitimate purposes such as reimbursement for expenditures for advances on travel. However, no one employed by this committee at this time has used any funds (for purposes) that were illegal or improper."

The *Post*'s information about the funds and their relationship to the Watergate case was obtained from a variety of sources, including investigators, other federal sources and officials and employees of the Committee for the Re-election of the President.

The $300,000 fund also was used for travel and entertainment that campaign officials did not want known outside the campaign organization. One source said the money was in part used for routine and legal intelligence gathering about Democrats.

The fund was kept in the safe of former Secretary of Commerce Maurice H. Stans, finance chairman of the President's campaign. It is presumably the same money that the General Accounting Office cited in an Aug. 26 report as a violation of the new campaign disclosure law, because it had not been properly accounted for. The GAO, the investigative arm of Congress, said the fund contained $350,000.

Sources said that Stans had no previous knowledge of the Watergate bugging—a position he has taken in public on numerous occasions, though he has not answered reporters' questions directly.

Stans, according to the sources, was aware of the existence of the secret fund and knew that large amounts of money had been withdrawn in the names of Mitchell aides.

Only one accounting of the special fund—a single piece of lined ledger paper listing the names of 15 persons with access to the money and the amount each received—was maintained. It was purposely destroyed shortly before April 7, the date that the new campaign finance law requiring detailed accounting of election funds took effect, the sources told the *Post.*

A spokesman for the Nixon re-election committee denied late yesterday that such a list ever existed.

On the day it was destroyed, the list showed that the largest individual sums of money were distributed to a handful of campaign aides closest to Mitchell, then still the President's campaign manager.

It was from those withdrawals that Nixon committee money was used for the espionage campaign against the Democrats, according to sources.

Mitchell, formerly Attorney General, resigned as the President's campaign manager on July 1, saying it was because his wife, Martha, insisted he leave politics.

She said at the time that "I love my husband very much, but I'm not going to stand for all those dirty things that go on." The former Attorney General has repeatedly denied any knowledge of the Watergate bugging.

The Mitchell aides who received money from the secret account include individuals who reportedly were sent confidential memos containing information obtained from a tapped telephone at Democratic headquarters.

The names of those Mitchell aides also appear in an account of the espionage operation told by Alfred Baldwin, a self-described participant in the Watergate affair who has been interviewed by both the FBI and lawyers for the Democratic Party.

Baldwin reportedly was granted immunity from prosecution in the Watergate case, in exchange for telling the federal grand jury his version of the espionage conspiracy. He has described himself as a former FBI agent who was hired as a security guard for Martha Mitchell and subsequently was assigned to monitor phone conversations intercepted from the telephone of a Democratic official with offices in the Watergate.

Yesterday the FBI said the only agent who ever worked for the Bureau with the same name is Alfred C. Baldwin III, age 37, who was an agent from 1963 to 1965. Meanwhile, a spokesman for the Nixon re-election committee confirmed that an Alfred Baldwin "worked briefly" as a security guard for Mrs. Mitchell, though his name does not appear on the committee's payroll.

In his account to the Democrats, Baldwin said that one of the men indicted Friday in the Watergate case—James W. McCord Jr., the former security coordinator of the Nixon re-election committee—sent memos and transcript of the bugged conversations to a White House aide and several high officials in the Nixon campaign—including the Mitchell aides.

According to Baldwin's account, McCord brought him into the espionage operation as a wiretap monitor on May 10 or 11 and told him that he would be assigned the same task in Miami during the Democratic National Convention. Baldwin also said he was assigned by McCord to infiltrate Vietnam Veterans Against the War for the purpose of "embarrassing the Democrats" if the veterans demonstrated at the Republican convention.

The secret fund that supplied the money for Baldwin's Watergate activities and other aspects of the intelligence-gathering campaign was managed by the "political side" of the Nixon re-election committee—that part directly under Mitchell's control—but physically kept on the financial side, headed by former Commerce Secretary Stans.

In some cases, individual aides to Mitchell received nearly $50,000 from the secret account. Except for ex–White House aide G. Gordon Liddy, the former finance counsel of the Nixon campaign who was indicted in the Watergate Friday, no other officials of the finance operation are known to have obtained money from the account.

The actual distribution of money from the fund to the intelligence operation was described to the *Washington Post* as being an "extremely complex transaction." It was designed to eliminate the possibility of tracing any of the funds to their original source—thought to be campaign contributions—or to reveal the point of distribution in the Finance Committee for the Re-election of the President.

In the interest of secrecy only one person was assigned to maintain the single-sheet list of transactions. Usually, the money was distributed by Liddy, the sources said.

Besides the Mitchell aides, "very few people" knew that the funds were used for intelligence-gathering and political espionage, according to one source. However others at the Nixon committee knew of the existence of a secret fund earmarked for sensitive political projects.

On June 18, "when we read about the Watergate break-in in the papers," said another source, "we put two and two together."

MITCHELL CONTROLLED SECRET GOP FUND

The *Washington Post,* September 29, 1972

John N. Mitchell, while serving as U.S. Attorney General, personally controlled a secret Republican fund that was used to gather information about the Democrats, according to sources involved in the Watergate investigation.

Beginning in the spring of 1971, almost a year before he left the Justice Department to become President Nixon's campaign manager on March 1, Mitchell personally approved withdrawals from the fund, several reliable sources have told the *Washington Post.*

Those sources have provided almost identical, detailed accounts of Mitchell's role as comptroller of the secret intelligence fund and its fluctuating $350,000–$700,000 balance.

Four persons other than Mitchell were later authorized to approve payments from the secret fund, the sources said.

Two of them were identified as former Secretary of Commerce Maurice H. Stans, now finance chairman of the President's campaign, and Jeb Stuart Magruder, manager of the Nixon campaign before Mitchell took over and now a deputy director of the campaign. The other two, according to the sources, are a high White House official now involved in the campaign and a campaign aide outside of Washington.

The sources of the *Post*'s information on the secret fund and its relationship to Mitchell and other campaign officials include law enforcement officers and persons on the staff of the Committee for the Re-election of the President.

Last night, Mitchell was reached by telephone in New York and read the beginning of the *Post*'s story. He said: "All that crap, you're putting it in the paper? It's all been denied. Jesus. Katie Graham (Katharine Graham, publisher of the *Washington Post*) is gonna get caught in a big fat wringer if that's published. Good Christ. That's the most sickening thing I've ever heard."

Told that the Committee for the Re-election of the President had issued a statement about the story, Mitchell interjected: "Did the committee tell you to go ahead and publish that story? You fellows got a great ball game going. As soon as you're through paying Williams (Edward Bennett Williams, whose law firm represents the Democratic Party, as well as the *Washington Post*), we're going to do a story on all of you." Mitchell then hung up the phone.

Asked to comment on the *Post* report, a spokesman for President Nixon's re-election committee, Powell Moore, said, "I think your sources are bad; they're providing misinformation. We're not going to comment beyond that."

Asked if the committee was therefore denying the contents of the story, Moore responded: "We're just not going to comment."

Later, Moore issued a formal statement that read: "There is absolutely no truth to the charges in the *Post* story. Neither Mr. Mitchell nor Mr. Stans has any knowledge of any disbursement from an alleged fund as described by the *Post* and neither of them controlled any committee expenditures while serving as government officials."

Asked to discuss specific allegations in the story, Moore declined, saying: "The statement speaks for itself."

According to the *Post's* sources, the federal grand jury that investigated the alleged bugging of the Democrats' Watergate headquarters did not establish that the intelligence-gathering fund directly financed the illegal eavesdropping.

Investigators have been told that the only record of the secret fund—a single sheet of lined ledger paper, listing the names of about 15 persons who received payments and how much each received—was destroyed by Nixon campaign officials after the June 17 break-in at the Watergate.

It has been established, however, that G. Gordon Liddy, the former Nixon finance committee counsel who was one of the seven men indicted in the Watergate case, withdrew well in excess of $50,000 in cash from the fund, the sources said.

Some of the still-unrevealed intelligence activities for which the secret fund was used were described by one federal source as potentially "very embarrassing" to the Nixon campaign if publicly disclosed. Other sources said they expect these activities to be revealed during the trial of the seven men indicted in the Watergate case.

Mitchell served as the President's campaign manager for three months and resigned on July 1, citing an ultimatum from his wife that he leave politics.

The former attorney general has repeatedly denied that his resignation was related in any way to the Watergate bugging or that he had any knowledge of it.

When asked whether it would be illegal for an incumbent attorney general to control disbursements from a political campaign fund, one federal attorney involved in the Watergate case said yesterday: "I don't know. There's a question."

A spokesman for the Justice Department said there is no law prohibiting the political activity of a member of the President's cabinet.

Last month, the existence of the secret fund was cited as a "possible and apparent" violation of a new, stricter campaign finance disclosure law in a report by the General Accounting Office, the investigative arm of Congress.

The GAO said the fund contained $350,000 as of May 25 and was possibly illegal, because receipts and expenditures were not publicly reported for a six-week period after the new disclosure law took effect on April 7.

The fund, which was kept in a safe in Stans's office, primarily consisted of cash contributions made to the Nixon campaign over an 18-month period, according to sources.

Although the only record of the fund was destroyed, it is known that investigators were able to reconstruct at least a partial list of recipients.

In addition to Liddy, those who received payments included Magruder, who withdrew about $25,000 from the fund; Herbert L. Porter, scheduling director of the Nixon committee, who received at least $50,000; several White House officials and thus-far unidentified persons who were not on the regular Nixon campaign or White House payroll.

Magruder has denied he received any money from the fund, and Porter has not commented.

At its inception, the secret intelligence fund was wholly controlled by Mitchell, the sources said, with the other four officials gaining authority to approve disbursements later on.

According to the *Post*'s sources, the primary purpose of the secret fund was to finance widespread intelligence-gathering operations against the Democrats. It could not be determined yesterday exactly what individual projects were funded by the secret account.

JESSICA MITFORD

"You may not be able to change the world, but at least you can embarrass the guilty," Jessica Mitford (1917–1996) told an interviewer. No one ever embarrassed the guilty with Mitford's lethal combination of factual precision and mordant wit, which Mitford turned to subjects ranging from the funeral industry to high-end restaurant meals.

Mitford was well into her forties—and already a larger-than-life character—before finding her calling as a muckraker. Born into British aristocracy and a famously idiosyncratic family, Mitford moved with her first husband to the United States in 1939. Her way stations to journalism included the Spanish civil war, the Communist party, the New Deal's Office of Price Administration, the J. Walter Thompson advertising agency, and the Attorney General's list of subversives. She turned to magazine writing in the late 1950s, she said later, because it was the only job that required no credential. In 1963 Simon and Schuster published Miford's exposé of the mortuary business, The American Way of Death, *a runaway best-seller. She followed that up with reporting on prisons (excerpted below), on the prosecution of antiwar protestors, and on obstetrics.*

Like I. F. Stone, Mitford made no claim to confidential sources. Instead she displayed an uncanny knack for interviewing that threw corporate shills off their pitch. (She prepared for interviews, Mitford wrote, by dividing prospective subjects into "friendly witnesses" and "unfriendly witnesses," sardonically borrowing the jargon of congressional witch-hunters in the 1950s.) She carefully mined trade-association journals, in-house educational materials, and other corporate publications, and haunted trade conventions, gleaning not only facts but language revealing her subjects' underlying attitudes and intentions.

Time *magazine called Jessica Mitford "the queen of the muckrakers."* Time *meant it derisively. To Mitford it was a badge of honor.*

THE PRISON BUSINESS

From *Kind and Usual Punishment,* 1973

Riots, work stoppages, hunger strikes in prisons across the nation have opened the eyes of even the most myopic to the shocking and degrading physical conditions to which prisoners are subjected. From Attica we learned that men work for twelve hours a day in temperatures of often more than a hundred degrees, are permitted but one shower a week, one roll of toilet paper every five weeks. We heard the prisoners' vivid descriptions of rotting food, roach-infested cells, gross medical neglect—all ruefully acknowledged by the prison administration and confirmed by subsequent official investigations.

The reflex reaction of the conventional reformer to such revelations is to demand ever bigger appropriations for Corrections, and in this he is heartily seconded by prison officialdom. Facts are marshaled about how much we spend on dispatching astronauts to the moon while men and women prisoners in this, the richest nation in the world, are forced by tightwad legislatures to suffer incredible privations. Ramsey Clark chides us for spending less than $2 billion a year on all Corrections—federal, state, and local—while we squander $9 billion on tobacco and $12.5 billion on liquor. Thus the message from the Corrections men and their reformer-allies to the growing numbers of people who are appalled by the barbarism of prison conditions: in the name of common decency give us a larger slice of the public monies that we may more adequately supply the needs of those in our charge. How best to orchestrate the money pitch, enlisting reformers for the purpose, was explained to a group of us by a public relations man for the American Correctional Association at the 1971 Congress. Discussing the problem of do-gooders who want to go poking about in the prisons, he said: "We shouldn't be afraid of them. We should let them in the prisons, because they can become our best lobbyists for funds. Although they may still go on squawking about all the things they don't like, they are invaluable in getting appropriations out of the legislature."

Instead of climbing on this bandwagon it might be well to take account of the present realities of prison expenditure. At the time of the Attica uprising, Russell G. Oswald, New York commissioner of Corrections, predictably blamed much of the trouble on what he termed "fiscal starvation." The deputy corrections commissioner, Wim van Eekeren, gloomily told the *New York Times* that the department had been "trying to shift to a more nutritional diet, but the effort was slowed by a tight budget."

Yet in 1971 the New York State prison budget was $71.6 million, up from $62.4 million in 1966; in the same period, the convict population dropped from 16,400 to 13,000. Divide $71.6 million by 13,000 and you get a bountiful $5,500 per year per convict. Why then are they denied the most rudimentary necessities of life?

Of the $9.2 million total increase over the five-year period, more than $8 million was accounted for by "salary adjustments." By 1971, staff in the New York prisons numbered 6,306, making the prisoner/employee ratio just over 2 to 1, exclusive of central administration. About 70 percent of this work force was in custody, another 10 percent in maintenance, 7 percent each in clerical and counseling/education, 1 percent professional medical personnel. Commenting on additional funds appropriated in 1971 for New York prisons before Attica erupted, the *New York Times* notes that "much of this year's increase—about $5 million—has gone into administration overhead, including the creation of a number of new top-level and middle-management jobs, and the $200,000 cost of new offices." This, at a time when the food budget was frozen at 72¢ per prisoner per day because of the alleged "fiscal starvation."

So prison money, far from benefiting those at the bottom, floats or is propelled up to the top, there to be converted into jobs for organization men and the latest in office equipment rather than into decent food or sufficient toilet paper for the prisoners. When the inevitable crisis erupts, a cry goes up for additional millions to restore order via more concrete, more hardware, more guards.

Immediately after the Attica uprising, Governor Rockefeller opened up the state coffers and ordered an emergency allocation of $4 million, $3 million of that "to initiate restoration of essential functions for safe and secure operations of the State Correctional Facility at Attica," the balance for investigating committees and purchase of security equipment including, according to the *New York Times,* "the latest things for mob control."

Six months later, Commissioner Oswald reported that a total of 339 new guards had been hired, thousands of gas masks purchased, bidding would shortly begin for "new, diversified metal detectors," sites were being sought for a maxi-maxi security prison (required, he said, "because of the militant tendencies of some inmates")—and under the heading of Inmate Improvements, "an increase in the number of showers permitted, an expanded clothing issue, a better provision of toilet paper." Checking with New York authorities several months later, I learned the prisoners now get *two* showers a week and "toilet paper as requested." For this, 43 men died?

No doubt like schools, old-age homes, mental hospitals, and other closed institutions that house the powerless, prisons afford a very special opportunity to employees at all levels for various kinds of graft and thievery. Convicts will tell you about profitable deals made with local merchants for supplies in which the warden pockets a handsome rakeoff, unexplained shortages in the canteens, the disappearance of large quantities of food from the kitchens. Occasionally scandals break into the press: a prison administrator caught with his hand in the till, the deepfreeze, or the toolbox, pilfering money, meat, or equipment intended for his charges. Yet even these excesses pale beside the legitimate, legislatively sanctioned dissipation of the vast sums appropriated for the prison establishment.

Budgets for tax-supported institutions are tricky territory, whether they be for schools, welfare departments, the Pentagon, your local library, or prisons. Woe to the innocent taxpayer who tries to discover where his money goes; he will find himself in a quagmire of incomprehensible terms and figures. Aware of these perils—and of the danger of generalization—I have endeavored to take a close look at one prison budget, that of California, largest in the nation, in an attempt to get some notion of how prison money circulates and for whose benefit.

Unlike the New York prison administration, the California Department of Corrections does not plead poverty. Mr. L. M. Stutsman, deputy director, told me: "The Department of Corrections has a relationship with the Administration that no other department has. We've got all we asked for, since Reagan took office."

In the nine fiscal years 1964–65 to 1972–73, California's prison budget soared from $61.5 million to a proposed $96.5 million. During this period the prison population dropped from 26,600 to an estimated 20,500; thus the per capita costs more than doubled, from $2,313 to $4,702 per year per inmate.[1] As Table I shows, there has been considerable fluctuation in the prison population, which reached the all-time high of 28,500 in 1968–69 and thereafter fell precipitously to an estimated 20,500 for 1972–73. Not so the budget, which continued in its inexorable rise.

Robin Lamson, chief researcher for the California State Assembly Office of Research, says that today it costs as much to keep a man in San Quentin as it would to send him to Harvard (which suggests the interesting possibility of exchange scholarships between these two institutions). Where does all the money go? In recent years the California budget has become even more difficult to interpret owing to a

1 These estimates consider only General Fund expenditures and do not include other sources of revenue such as California Correctional Industries and Inmate Welfare Fund. Taken together, the total institution costs for 1972–73 are estimated by the Department of Corrections' Management Services Division at $110.5 million, or $5,239 per capita. Because figures including the Industries and the Inmate Welfare Fund are unavailable for some of the years under consideration, Table I on page 394 is based on budgets exclusive of those categories.

changeover in the accounting procedure from "line item" to "program budgeting," a change ordered by Governor Reagan. (This is the same planned program budgeting with which McNamara was going to trim the fat in the Defense Department and obtain "more bang for the buck" in Vietnam.) Costs were formerly expressed in terms of location, by institution, but are now grouped under "program" or "activity" headings: "security," "housekeeping-maintenance," and the like. The new technique, which puts a dollar value on each "program," is supposed to simplify the legislator's task in arriving at intelligent decisions about allocation of funds.

However, a CPA in the state auditor's office told me that while the figure for the year's total expenditures is accurate, the breakdowns by "program" are meaningless because the department does not have an accounting system equipped to handle the new method. "For proper accountability you must have a consistent and rational accounting method of gathering cost information, and that does not exist," he said. "Although they say they do 'program budgeting,' they do not have a program cost-accounting system. They're terribly far off. If you ask how they do it, they can't answer. The figures are a sheer fabrication. That's called fraud where I come from." So the prison administration, adept at obfuscation in all its dealings, has now discovered how to apply this skill where it will yield substantial cash rewards in the dollar-and-cents columns of its annual explanation to the legislature of estimated budgetary needs.

How the conscientious statistician sets about program budgeting in the area of life and death is disclosed in a departmental memorandum from Vida Ryan, senior statistician, to the California director of Corrections, written shortly before the Supreme Court abolished the death penalty. Discussing the budgetary consequences of pending legislation, she writes: "In the computation of costs of 1972 legislative bills involving death penalty, some assumptions must be made or thought be given to the possibility of certain events occurring." Should the legislature replace the death penalty for first degree murder with a life sentence without possibility of parole, the department must, she points out, expect to find a difference in program costs: "Persons received with a death penalty will spend approximately *three* years in prison before execution. If commuted to life without possibility of parole, the additional cost is based upon a period of seventeen years." Computing the programmed cost of life versus death in prison, Ms. Ryan reports that: "In accordance with basic costs, Mr. Ritter estimated (telephone conversation of 1-18-72) that the additional direct costs are: $4,000 annual cost per man, $750 cost per execution." She adds this postscript: "Bills increasing or adding the death sentence for such selected offenses as robbery, burglary, sex, and destruction of property might result in savings for the Department of Corrections, as the length of time in prison would be less."

Despite the obstacles erected by program budgeting, it is possible, by questioning the men in Sacramento who run the prisons, extrapolating from old "line item" budgets, and enlisting the help of researchers privy to the ways of prison budgets, to penetrate some of the mysteries.

The broad categories are fairly predictable. In the 1972–73 proposed budget far and away the largest chunk of money, $42 million or 38 percent, pays for "Security: effective control of the inmates, prevention of riots, escapes, arson, assault, introduction of contraband, and other incidents," as the department describes it. Nearly all of the Security budget (formerly designated Custody) goes for guards' wages: officers, sergeants, lieutenants, and captains who together comprise well over half of all personnel in the prisons. The remaining expenditure for Security buys weapons, ammunition, tear gas, restraint equipment, chains, handcuffs, flashlights, etc. It develops that the crueler the conditions of custody the more expensive it gets: the department estimates the cost of keeping a man caged in "Adjustment Center" solitary confinement for 23 ½ to 24 hours a day at $7,000 a year, compared with $1,970 per prisoner in the minimum security conservation camps.

The next largest budget entry is "Inmate Support," 26 percent of the prison dollar, a catch-all category that includes food, clothing, medical-dental services, housekeeping and maintenance. The latter, and largest, item is budgeted for a surprising $10 million, more than is spent for food—especially surprising when, as the department states, "maintenance of the institutions' physical plants is accomplished by inmate workers," supervised by free personnel. (Indeed, the grounds outside San Quentin and Soledad as seen by the visitor are quite lovely—brilliant expanses of flowers and shrubbery bathed in California sunshine. These, of course, are seldom seen by most prisoners, who must make do with the concrete-enclosed bare blacktop of the prison yard.)

Treatment accounts for $14.5 million, or 13 percent. It comprises academic education, counseling and psychiatry, vocational training, religion, recreation. Of these, academic education and vocational training are allotted $2,600,000 apiece, or $10 per month per inmate; however, only one fourth of the population is actually enrolled in academic education and one seventh in vocational training. Psychiatric and counseling services seem, on the face of it, to have been accorded rather a large share: together they draw down $8.25 million. There are in fact 32 full-time psychiatrists and 24 psychologists in the California prison system, the largest group of these in the California Medical Facility at Vacaville. We have already seen something of the modus operandi of the prison psychiatrist. As for the "counseling services," these consist for the most part of writing reports and are in many cases performed by guards whose jobs have been upgraded to "correctional counselor." The remainder of the treatment budget goes for "Leisure-Time Activities," $415,000 or $1.67 per month per inmate, and Religion, $544,000.

Everything seems to come higher in prisondom. Thus in the 1969 budget "movement processing," meaning busing prisoners from one prison to another, was budgeted at just under $1 million. (This category has disappeared from subsequent budgets, which categories have a habit of doing lately, thus further complicating the task of the would-be budget-fathomer.) Over 30,000 such trips were taken by inmates during the fiscal year, which would bring the average ticket cost to $29. Continental Trailways told me I could get from San Francisco to Salem, Oregon—about 500 miles—for $27.50 (which would leave me $1.50 for a cocktail). This is for their deluxe service and includes hostess, air conditioning, music, magazines, pillows, food and beverage service.

A convict accused of participating in the Folsom work strike describes what it is like to be "movement-processed" as a troublemaker: "First the cold; lying bound, handcuffed, on the ribbed floor of the van, how it bit into the bones! The turning and twisting of half-nude bodies looking for a soft spot on the metal floor. How do four men feel lying trapped and chained in their own sputum, kidneys breaking, backbone trembling?" And he adds: "If you get the chance, find out why the Department of Corrections has such a surplus of men that they can use four of them for a two-day trip with four prisoners. I mean, this would be interesting in light of the department always wanting a budget increase. It cost the taxpayers $400 to transfer four chained men from Folsom to San Luis Obispo. . . ."

What of "Administration"? The budget recognizes about 550 positions under this heading, 200 in Sacramento and 350 in the thirteen prisons. The 550 figure, however, represents only the surface if one is interested in how many bodies warm those chairs from the director and his aides—researchers, business managers, clerks, receptionists, etc.—to people who are doing essentially administrative work under other headings like "Treatment," "Inmate Employment," "Housekeeping."

For example, the California Conservation Camp at Susanville has a total staff of 378, with 28 of those positions logged under "Administration." In the remaining program categories, one locates another 38 assorted clerks, typists, administrators, chiefs, and "III"s (a civil service designation of high rank). That brings the total to 66, and a number more lurk behind ambiguous titles of supervisor or manager—persons who may or may not have much direct contact with inmates. Depending, of course, on how one counts, a reasonable approximation for desk jobs at an institution is 25 percent of all positions.

It is, however, to the more obscure corners of the budget rather than to the broad categories that one must look to discover what happens to the convict trapped at the bottom of this pile of money.

Item: From the $28 million dollar "Inmate Support" budget, $9.5 million is allocated for what the department inelegantly calls "Feeding," of which 20 percent is for staff wages, leaving $7,340,000 for food. So the $96 million budget allows 30¢ per meal for each of 21,000 prisoners.

Item: When a man arrives in prison he is issued clothing worth slightly less than $50, which includes jacket, jeans, shirts, shorts, socks, T-shirts, belt, shoes, and bandanas. The overall clothing budget, including initial issue, is $6 per month per person—on paper. However, since the clothing is all made by prisoners in prison industries and bought back by the department, this arbitrarily set figure is, according to a source in the state audit department, "unrealistic and extremely high."

Item: Out of "Inmate Support" the $7,000-a-year man in solitary confinement gets two helpings per day of "Special Isolation Diet." The recipe for this concoction, which smells and tastes like inferior dog food, was purposely devised, says the department in its official regulation on the subject, to be "monotonous and lacking in taste." Cost per serving? The department declined to divulge this information. Judging from the recipe, 5¢ to 10¢ would be about right.

Item: From the same $28 million "Inmate Support" the indigent prisoner is allowed one stamped envelope a week and one sheet of writing paper for his total correspondence with the outside world.[2] The indigent's envelopes are colored yellow so all may know his special status.

Item: Another category that has disappeared from the current program budget is "Release Program," last heard of in 1969, when it cost $6 million. This is a multifaceted operation consisting of preparation by counselors of elaborate "Inmate Program Reports" for parole board review, lectures to prisoners by parole officers and other law enforcement men, transfer of records from prison to parole agency.

To the cost of all this paper-shuffling must be added the budget of the Adult Authority—close to $1 million a year. (The San Francisco *Examiner* estimates the cost of each few minutes' interview granted to prisoners by the Adult Authority at $34 and suggests that in view of the way the Adult Authority goes about its work it would be far cheaper and just as effective to hire a man with a dice box to decide who gets paroled.) The goal of the Release Program, says the department, is to assure "a successful but conditional release to the community . . . with reasonable expectations of successful parole." Is it? The department is

2 Mr. Philip Guthrie of the California Department of Corrections tells me the allowance was recently increased to five envelopes; prisoners say this news has not yet filtered down into the institutions.

supposed to allow for $68 "gate money" when a man is released. With deductions from those who have money in their Inmate Trust Account, actual gate money doled out in 1971 to the 9,768 prisoners released that year was $563,005.20, or an average of $57.65 per person. From this sum was deducted $8.01 for what the department calls "appropriate apparel," leaving $49.64 in cash, from which the prisoner had to pay the cost of transportation from the prison to his home, and survive as best he might.

Prison administrators all over, one gathers, order their budgetary priorities in much the same fashion. Some information about how the federal prison system spends its money was furnished by George Pickett, superintendent of Marion maximum-security federal prison, testifying before the House of Representatives Select Committee on Crime in December 1971. Describing Marion as a "model institution," built in 1963 at a cost of over $10 million to hold some 500 "adult male felons who are difficult to manage and control," with an average sentence of thirty-four years, he said the cost per prisoner is $7,600 a year, or more than $20 a day. Pressed by the committee's chief counsel to explain how this money is allocated and how much is spent for food, Mr. Pickett answered that the daily cost of food per prisoner is "roughly 77¢. Total cost per man per day is $1.36. But then everything included, salaries and what-have-you, it comes to approximately $20." After thirty-four years, then, the "salaries and what-have-you" generated by a single prisoner would amount to $241,536, during which time $16,864 would have been allocated for his food and upkeep. As Benjamin Franklin might have said, had he known of this, "One man's time is another man's money."

At the same hearing, Mr. Pickett's boss, Norman A. Carlson, director of the U.S. Bureau of Prisons, offered a ready explanation for any shortcomings in his operation: "As is true in most prison systems in the United States, the federal system has been handicapped by antiquated facilities, insufficient staffs, and limited resources with which to provide adequate programs for offenders," he said. Which moved a subsequent witness, Dr. James A. Bax, commissioner of the Community Services Administration of HEW, to make some salty comments about the boundless rapacity of the prison men. Prisons, he said, "are often incestuous bureaucracies existing unto themselves. Their budgets are stoked by legislators, not on the basis of the numbers of citizens they rehabilitate, but on the numbers of prisoners they keep quietly tucked away out of circulation. . . . Institutions are amoral. They are socially irresponsible. They are inherently power-hungry. As every legislator knows, they are always hungry for more public money. In short, institutions are lawless—they themselves must be constantly controlled and rehabilitated. The prison system is no exception. . . ."

Central to the strategies of prison administrations in the era of convict rebellion is construction of new prisons, about which we shall doubtless be hearing a good deal in the coming years. At a 1971 conference on criminal justice sponsored by the Center for Democratic Studies, James V. Bennett said he estimates that, nationwide, Corrections needs a minimum of $18 billion for new buildings alone. These old bastilles should be replaced, say the prison men; some of them are more than a hundred years old, they are too big, unwieldy, unsanitary, overcrowded. The humanitarian reformer will agree, for he has seen the evidence on his television screen and in magazine picture spreads: the tiny, dark cells, rusty iron bars, overflowing toilets, dank concrete, over all an aura of decay. Incomparably worse than any zoo, he will declare! No wonder riots and disturbances are endemic in these places. As long as we must have prisons, let them at least be decent and fit for human habitation.

Significantly, the occupants of these disgraceful dungeons have in no instance joined the chorus of demands for newer and better-built prisons. Search the manifestoes of convict leaders from the Tombs to San Quentin and you will find no such proposal. On the contrary, prisoner and ex-convict groups throughout the country are urging opposition to new prison building, which they see as leading to a vast expansion of the existing prison empire. The economics are simple: x-million dollars are spent for a new jail. It must be kept reasonably full because if the population goes down jailers are thrown out of jobs—or the per capita cost of operating the jail gets so out of hand that taxpayers may begin to take note. As the authors of *Struggle for Justice* say, "When pressures for reform lead to demands to relieve 'overcrowding' by adding new cell or bed space, the result is inevitable: the coercive net of the justice system will be spread over a larger number of people, entrapping them for longer periods of time."

For example, the anouncement in 1971 by the California Department of Corrections that San Quentin was to be "phased out" was applauded by liberal reformers and editorial writers throughout the state. Soon thereafter the department sought, and obtained, a legislative appropriation of $150,000 for capital outlay to produce plans for a new institution. Those liberal assemblymen who supported the appropriation told me they did so because, having visited the rotting cages of San Quentin, they felt no human beings should be lodged therein and that new, sanitary buildings were an absolute necessity.

The prison administration was remarkably closemouthed about the precise nature of the new facilities and produced no written statement of what was intended, although early in 1972 Raymond Procunier, director of Corrections, told a Senate committee, "The prison to replace San Quentin will be a lot tougher, a lot more stringent." Eventually I was informed by the Legislative Analyst's Office that there are to be two 400-man maximum-security prisons for "problem inmates," small "prisons within prisons." They would be "more secure than Soledad" with double instead of single fencing, and would cost approximately $12 million apiece. Thus the budget request for preliminary planning was the first step toward a more repressive long-term, maximum-security lock-up and segregation for prisoners upon whom the department has bestowed the label "problem inmates."

Lucasville Penitentiary in southern Ohio is worth a detour, as the *Guide Michelin* would say, for anybody who might be curious about the costs, design, and purposes of new prison building. I visited Lucasville, then under construction, in August 1971. From back issues of Ohio newspapers I learned that the new prison was planned following a series of riots in the Ohio Penitentiary and subsequent disclosure of deplorable conditions there; the groundbreaking ceremony, presided over by Governor James A. Rhodes, had taken place in 1968, at which time cost was estimated at $15 million, to be raised through a taxpayers' bond issue. By the time of my visit, construction costs of the "Southern

Ohio Correctional Facility" (the designation conferred on the new prison by Governor John J. Gilligan, Governor Rhodes's successor) had risen to $42 million, and according to the superintendent in charge were expected to reach $60 million.

One's first impression of Lucasville is that of a huge, surrealistic barracks rising out of a desolate countryside. It is 90 miles south of Columbus, the nearest town; there is no public transportation available. The superintendent who showed me around enthusiastically plied me with facts and figures: the 80-acre area is surrounded by 2 ½ miles of two double-wire, 16-foot-high security fences topped with seven strands of barbed wire. Twenty feet inside this fence is a concrete wall topped with 14 strands of barbed wire. The 1 ½-mile perimeter is guarded by eight gun towers. The prison proper consists of 22 acres of building under one roof, to accommodate 1,620 convicts in single cells measuring 6 feet 6 inches by 10 feet 6 inches.

We walked through seeming miles of vast, gleaming ceramic-tiled corridors to the cell blocks. There workmen were installing fantastic Rube Goldberg electronic equipment in each cell door, controlled by a central panel of buttons and levers that looked something like an airplane dashboard. Television monitors in three main control rooms allow guards to watch the prisoners' every move. The cells, with their bars and catwalks, were indistinguishable from others I had seen—with one exception: they were variously painted in shades of powder blue, baby pink, canary yellow.

Of the 1,620 cells, 240 were being especially equipped to confine the anticipated quota of troublemakers, with unbreakable stainless steel toilets which, said the superintendent, cost $600 apiece; 550 employees would be recruited from the surrounding Appalachian foothills at a starting wage for guards of $2.77 an hour . . . the very poor, guarding the even poorer.

The eerie sense of observing misery under construction deepened as we approached the 20-cell Death Row, adjacent to which was the execution chamber, complete except for the electric chair which had not yet been delivered. (In 1972, after the Supreme Court ruling against the death penalty, the electric chair was countermanded and Lucasville Superintendent W. J. Whealon told the press, "We'll use the room for special treatment facilities for ungovernable disciplinary problems.")

My subsequent efforts to learn something of the background of Lucasville—who stood to gain and how from this vast enterprise—were unsuccessful; my letters to former Governor Rhodes, former Commissioner of Corrections Maury Koblentz and former Assistant Commissioner Beryl Sacks went unanswered. Apparently members of the Ohio Governor's Task force on Corrections fared no better. One of these, Dr. Harry Allen of Ohio State University, wrote in answer to my inquiry: "I asked a staff assistant to examine the decision-making process by which Lucasville was created and to investigate the implementation procedure, including land purchase, history, and problems of Lucasville. . . . In our final report, the task force concluded that the decision-making process could not be reconstructed at this time. In fact, the Lucasville institution is remarkable, in light of our inability to find any documentation in this area."

Two years after my visit, Ysabel Rennie, another member of the task force, told me of some of the uses to which Lucasville, now open for business, is being put. Following a sitdown strike at the London, Ohio, prison over demands for a democratic election of the inmate council, 91 inmates were "busted," she said. The newly elected council was disbanded by the authorities and its chairman was eventually shipped off to Lucasville, "along with every Black Muslim at London." Shortly before Christmas of 1972, the entire population of Chillecothe minimum-security prison conducted a work strike in which the main issues were unfair parole board practices and failure of the authorities to implement the work-furlough law. "They loaded 52 of the strikers into buses and took them off to Lucasville," said Mrs. Rennie.

In their campaign to halt new prison construction, the prisoners may find some unexpected allies. William Nagel, director of the influential American Foundation Institute of Corrections (a privately funded group that is frequently called on by government agencies to furnish research assistance), describes himself as "a prison man at the very core, with a background of eleven years as a disciplinarian, assistant to the superintendent, and deputy in a major institution." At the request of the Law Enforcement Assistance Administration he visited more than 100 new penal institutions in 26 states. He learned that budgets for prison construction, nationwide, in 1973 amount to over $6 billion and are expected to reach twice that amount. He says the prison building boom has become "a huge bonanza for architects, contractors, hardware companies who are cashing in on building all these better mousetraps with the latest in electronic gadgetry."

Mr. Nagel's efforts to discover what the federal Bureau of Prisons is planning in the way of new facilities were at first frustrated, he told me, as the bureau refused to answer any of his inquiries about details and costs of proposed construction. "Finally, I found somebody in the bureau who was willing to talk. I felt a little like Daniel Ellsberg, getting these super-secret plans! My informant says the bureau's budget for new buildings is already over $600 million. He showed me the architectural designs for Butner—Butner frightens me. There are no rooms or cells in the drawings, they are all labeled 'Behavior Modification Units.' "

Once an enthusiast for more cell space to relieve the desperate overcrowding in most jails and prisons, Mr. Nagel says he underwent an "agonizing reappraisal" during his two-year odyssey of new penal institutions, and has concluded that "prisons don't work, period."

He found demands for new prison building coming from every quarter: "The hard-liners are demanding more, not less cell space. The wardens and sheriffs insist their prisons are inadequate and must be replaced. The idealists, sickened by the inhuman conditions in so many of our jails and prisons, are lobbying for bright new replacements for those intolerable places. Civil libertarians argue that since our jails do not provide the basic protections and rights guaranteed by the Constitution, they should be replaced by new jails which do. Architects and contractors are quick to oblige." He advocates a moratorium on all prison building: "The prison is obsolete, cannot be reformed, should not be perpetuated through the false hope of forced treatment, and should be repudiated and abandoned."

In my view, such a moratorium should be a principal demand of all who are concerned with prisoner welfare. For the new prisons, whether the proposed "maxi-maxi" type that New York authorities are planning in response to Attica, the "tougher, more stringent" prisons for "problem inmates" in California, or the Behavior Modification Center in Butner, North Carolina, for "aggressive" federal prisoners, add up to one proposition: the establishment of a form of legal concentration camp to isolate and contain the rebellious and the political militant.

TABLE I

California Prisons Population and Cost Growth 1959–73

Fiscal year	*Average Institution Population*[1]	*General Fund Expenditure (P&CSD excluded)*[2]	*Per Capita*[3]
1959–60	19,500	$33,164,000	$1701
60–61	21,800	38,551,000	1772
61–62	23,700	43,736,000	1846
62–63	24,200	50,381,000	2085
63–64	26,200	56,887,000	2173
64–65	26,600	61,585,000	2313
65–66	26,300	66,907,000	2539
66–67	27,300	71,674,000	2628
67–68	27,600	73,877,000	2680
68–69[4]	28,500	80,059,000	2811
69–70[4]	27,700	87,359,000	3155
70–71[4]	25,100	90,687,000	3619
71–72[4]	21,400	93,958,000	4384
72–73[4]	20,500	96,364,000	4702

Source of table: *Analysis of the Budget Bill,* 1968–69, with 1972–73 additions; Office of the Legislative Analyst, Sacramento, California.

[1] Includes women and Civil Addicts.

[2] Parole and Community Services Division.

[3] Per capita estimates derived.

[4] Population estimates from 1972–73 *Program Budget.*

Mark Dowie, Barbara Ehrenreich, and Stephen Minkin

By the mid-1970s, American journalism had gone through a period of radical ferment. Feminism, environmentalism, and gay liberation had changed the language and agenda of American politics. Investigative reporting had toppled a president. In cities around the country, alternative weekly newspapers proved that in an era of pop culture it was possible to pursue in-depth, sometimes highly personal reporting on controversial subjects and still turn a profit.

In 1976, amid this heady atmosphere, a group of San Francisco journalists started publishing Mother Jones *magazine, named for a famed union organizer and self-described "hell-raiser."* Mother Jones*—with lively graphic design and a pop sensibility—was aimed at a mass audience, trying to pick up where* Ramparts *(which closed in 1975) had left off. And it was a magazine with an agenda: "We thought the country was ready for a magazine of investigative reporting that would focus on the great unelected power wielders of our time—multinational corporations," cofounder Adam Hochschild recalled on the magazine's twenty-fifth anniversary.*

One of the magazine's first triumphs was Mark Dowie's meticulous and chilling 1977 inquiry into preventable deaths involving the Ford Pinto, revealing how executives sacrificed the lives of car owners to cost-benefit analysis. Dowie, Mother Jones's *business manager, looked and dressed like an executive, securing the confidence of sources for Ford's in-house memos. In 1979 Dowie, biologist-turned-essayist Barbara Ehrenreich, and medical writer Stephen Minkin laid out the lines of accountibility for an even more sweeping corporate crime: the "dumping" of medical products, pesticides, and other goods banned in the United States on Third World countries.*

CORPORATE CRIME OF THE CENTURY

From *Mother Jones,* 1979

THE CHARGE: GYNOCIDE
THE ACCUSED: THE U.S. GOVERNMENT

When Maria Aguirrez woke up on the morning of June 5, 1977, she was, at first, too drenched with sweat to feel the blood. They had warned her at the clinic that there might be some bleeding, but this was more than a period. Her skirt, the worn sheet, the mat, were soaked through—more than after her oldest daughter's birth, when the midwife had, at one point, simply prayed. Dimly, Maria must have realized that the baby was already awake and fussing. He was still fussing an hour later when Maria's sister, summoned by the older children, came running in. Maria was no longer sweating.

The death of Maria Aguirrez (not her real name) does not even figure as a statistic in our story. It was recorded as the result of a fever. That the fever and the bleeding were the result of an intrauterine device (IUD) known to be unsafe was not recorded. Nor would the information have made any difference to the government and corporate officials behind the distribution of the device; they were already well aware of the history of medical problems associated with it.

The U.S. government and U.S. drug companies maintain a systematic and intentional double standard for the sale of contraceptives. Unsafe IUDs, dangerous high-estrogen birth control pills and, most recently, Depo-Provera—an injectable contraceptive not approved for American use—are bought up wholesale by the U.S. government for mass consumption in the Third World. This is the story of how and where and why these contraceptive dumps take place, of the corporations that profit from them and of the government official, Dr. R. T. Ravenholt, who headed the Office of Population of the U.S. Agency for International Development and engineered the dumps.

The contraceptive double standard surfaced as a public issue only in the summer of 1978, when a congressional committee held hearings on the Depo-Provera problem: Should the U.S. government subsidize the export to Third World nations of a contraceptive drug that had been ruled unsafe for American women? Pharmaceutical company spokespeople, officials of the U.S. Agency for International Development (AID) and representatives of private population control agencies stood up one after another to advance the "humanitarian" defense of the double standard. Because the risks of dying in childbirth are so much greater in the Third World than in the United States, they asserted the use of almost *any* contraceptive is justified. Scientists from selected Third World governments, many of them U.S.-sponsored dictatorships like Chile and Thailand, seconded the argument, adding that their "national sovereignty" would be violated if they were denied access to the contraceptive of their choice. Consumer representatives countered that there is no excuse for sending our *least* safe contraceptive abroad and questioned the accountability of the "sovereign" governments, which, it is now known, have received millions of dollars in bribes from U.S. drug companies like Upjohn Co. (maker of Depo-Provera) and G. D. Searle Co. (a manufacturer of birth control pills).

At the bottom the contraceptive issue is no different than the case of Tris-treated pajamas, carcinogenic pesticides or lethal antibiotics: products that had been found unsafe for domestic use are still being sold overseas. There is, however, a crucial difference in the case of contraceptives: dumping them is not only a common business practice; it is part of U.S. foreign policy.

DISCOUNT DALKONS

The dangers of the Dalkon Shield IUD were well known before the dump began in 1972. Only a few months after the Dalkon Shield went on the market in 1971, reports of adverse reactions began pouring into the headquarters of the manufacturer, A. H. Robins Co. (See "A Case of Corporate Malpractice," by Mark Dowie and Tracy Johnston, *MJ,* Nov. '76.) There were cases of pelvic inflammatory disease (an infection of the uterus that can require weeks of bed rest and antibiotic treatment), septicemia (blood poisoning), pregnancies resulting in spontaneous abortions, ectopic (tubal) pregnancies and perforations of the uterus. In a number of cases, the damage was so severe as to require a hysterectomy. There were even medical reports of Dalkon Shields ripping their way through the walls of the uterus and being found floating free in the abdominal cavity far from the uterus. According to a recent and probably conservative U.S. medical estimate, the Dalkon Shield caused over 200,000 cases of serious uterine infections in this country alone. For every million dollars in profit the manufacturer has made on the Shield, U.S. women—those who could afford medical care at all—spent an estimated $20 million for medical care on problems arising from its use. By 1974, there were reports of deaths clearly attributable to the Dalkon Shield—not one or two, but 17.

The Dalkon Shield was turning out to be far more dangerous than any other IUD already on the market. Later research in Canada and Germany showed that microscopic defects helped account for the Shield's ability to slice into the uterine wall. Worse still, the "wicking effect" of its string caused it to conduct bacteria up from the vagina, through the tiny cervical opening and into the uterus. Physicians found insertion was difficult; patients found it almost unbearable. As early as February 1971, a physician wrote to A. H. Robins in reference to the insertion of the Dalkon Shield: "I have found the procedure to be the most traumatic manipulation ever perpetrated on womanhood, and I have inserted thousands of other varieties."

Sometime in 1972, with angry correspondence pouring in and the prospects for increasing U.S. sales looking bleak, A. H. Robins decided to expand its exports. With any other kind of hazardous product, the manufacturer might, at this point, have had to search out some sleazy broker to arrange a secret dump. Not so with a contraceptive device. The Office of Population within AID had a budget of $125 million to spend on the purchase and overseas distribution of contraceptives. Director R. T. Ravenholt was known to be a population control enthusiast who would ask few questions about a good deal on Dalkon Shields. It was only natural for Robins to turn to the government.

Robert W. Nickless, Robins' director of international marketing, wrote to the population office of AID to interest them in placing "this fine product" with population control programs and family planning clinics throughout the Third World. Nickless sweetened the deal with a special discount, which dramatically illustrates the double standard drug companies apply to Third World consumers: the company offered AID the Shield in bulk packages, *unsterilized,* at 48 percent off.

Robins made this offer knowing that the sale of nonsterile IUDs was highly irregular in the United States. One of the greatest hazards associated with the use of any IUD is the possibility of introducing bacteria into the uterus, which is particularly poorly equipped to fight infection. In the United States, IUDs are sold to doctors in individual, sterilized packages, with a sterile, disposable inserter for each device.

Careful to preserve Robins' image, Nickless emphasized that AID could not distribute the nonsterile Dalkon Shields in the U.S. The nonsterile form, he wrote in a January 1973 memo to AID, "is for the purpose of reducing price, and thereby attaining wider use [and] is intended for restricted sale to family planning/support organizations who will limit their distribution to those countries commonly referred to as 'less developed.'" Practitioners in such countries were expected by Robins to sterilize the Shields by the old-fashioned method of soaking them in a disinfectant solution.

In the United States, according to private gynecologists we interviewed, the insertion of an IUD that had merely been soaked in a disinfectant before use would possibly be grounds for a malpractice suit. Robins insists that the "sterilization" procedure it recommended was effective, but it is highly likely that few people ever read the instructions. The company attached only one set of instructions for each pack of 1,000 Shields, and those were printed in only three languages—English, French and Spanish—although the devices were destined for 42 countries from Ethiopia to Malaysia. Worse still—only ten inserters were provided per 100 Shields, adding immeasurably to the possibility of infection.

To their credit, officials within AID did express concern with at least one of the more reckless features of Robins' discount Dalkon dump. They questioned whether the Shields could be reliably inserted by the staffs of remote family planning clinics, who would not have had the benefit of an American medical education.

It should have been an embarrassing question for Robins. In the U.S., the company had repeatedly countered reports of adverse reactions by arguing that the person who had inserted the device, such as an occasional general practitioner, had been unqualified to do so. But Robins was undaunted and nimbly produced a new study which proved beyond a shadow of a doubt that any paramedic could learn to insert a Dalkon Shield in half an hour.

Reassured by this logic, AID approved the deal. Hundreds of shoebox-sized cartons, each filled with 1,000 unsterilized Dalkon Shields paid for by the U.S. Treasury, left the shores of America for clinics in Paraguay, Israel, Tunisia and 39 other countries. The dump was on.

Within months, the agencies that distributed Dalkon Shields for AID, such as the International Planned Parenthood Federation, had discovered more bad news about the device. Company sales monographs and ads in medical journals had boasted of a pregnancy rate with the Shield of no more than 1.1 percent. But the reports coming in from the field told another story: pregnancy rates of 4.5 percent in Israel, 3.8 percent in the United Kingdom, 6.7 percent in Costa Rica and 6.5 percent in Yugoslavia. One clinic in Latin America reported a pregnancy rate of 14.8 percent. From a population controller's point of view, a contraceptive may, if expedient, be unsafe; but it should not, under any circumstances, be ineffective.

Disturbed by the negative reports, A. H. Robins sent Robert Nickless on a whistle-stop tour of Asia in March 1973 to counter the increasing volume of criticism and drum up new business. With him, Robins sent along an "independent expert"—Dr. John Lesinski, a colleague at Johns Hopkins University of the Shield's inventor, Dr. Hugh Davis, and an early Dalkon Shield booster. At a typical stop, the local AID population control officer would assemble a group of physicians, and Lesinski, lending an aura of professional responsibility, would lecture, show slides, and occasionally perform demonstration insertions on a few local women.

While Nickless was peddling the Shield from Pakistan to Hong Kong, time was running out for it in the United States. In August of 1974, the FDA opened hearings on the Dalkon Shield. At that time, the FDA had little jurisdiction over medical devices like IUDs: they could investigate their safety, but they could not ban them from the market. Despite the FDA's lack of authority, the hearings were held simply because, by 1974, the carnage had become too gruesome to ignore. One critical study after another told of women who had suffered infections, septic abortions or emergency hysterectomies.

A. H. Robins had been hardened by years of fighting regulatory agencies, however, and the company went down fighting. "Throughout the entire proceedings," according to Dr. Richard Dickey, a member of the FDA's Ob/Gyn committee, "the halls of the FDA were crawling with Robins men. It was disgusting." Finally evidence was presented at the hearings that could have undercut Robins' defenses in future product liability suits, potentially costing millions of dollars. Only then did the company give up. Robins made no attempt to resume its domestic sales, suspended at the FDA's urging.

When Robins gave in, AID was left holding the bag, or, rather, the bulk pack. International complaints about the effectiveness of the device had been bad enough. With the Shield now considered too dangerous for domestic use, AID had little choice but to issue an international recall. It was an embarrassing moment for the agency, but hardly a major setback. Even without Dalkon Shields, there would be plenty of "discount" contraceptives to dump in the Third World.

THE MAN BEHIND THE DUMPS

That corporations dump to make a profit is no surprise. In the case of contraceptive dumping through the foreign aid program, though, there are other motives as well. What kind of person knowingly stamped the seal of American "goodwill" on this corporate jackpot? To find out, in July 1979, we interviewed Dr. R. T. (Ray) Ravenholt, the head of AID's Office of Population from 1966 to mid-1979 and the man who most represents the government role in contraceptive dumping.

In person, he is a tall, affable Midwesterner with an engaging smile and a marked inability to sit still once he warms up to the subject at hand. No sooner had we gotten through the introductions than he bounded off to one corner of his spacious office and returned with his latest contraceptive enthusiasm: a plastic "gun-styled" laparoscopic device, which, when aimed through the vagina, shoots little plastic bands around the fallopian tubes, resulting in permanent sterilization. He demonstrated by placing one foot up on his chair and shooting bands at his shoelace. Only after he completed the simulated sterilization of his left foot were we able to bring the subject around to the Dalkon Shield.

"Robins didn't know there was any problem with it in 1972," he insisted. When we countered that A. H. Robins had been deluged with reports of adverse reactions by that time, Ravenholt smiled patiently and explained: "You don't really know anything until you have a very, very large number of people who have used it. You might have one kind of impression from 10,000 people, another from 100,000. You might need a million—10 million—before you really know."

You might, in other words, need a few medium-size nations to experiment on.

Ravenholt did concede that AID "had been hearing about infections" associated with the Dalkon Shield prior to Robins' withdrawal of the device. Then, leaning forward with enthusiasm, he confided his own theory about IUD-induced pelvic infections: "Women who frequently change sexual partners have these intercurrent low-grade infections," he told us. "The IUD can't cause an infection. The body tolerates anything that's sterile." Taken aback, we asked whether Dalkon Shield–related infections in the Third World might not have been caused by nonsterile devices, rather than by female promiscuity. "Well," he said, in a classic non sequitur, "it wasn't just the Dalkon Shield that was supplied that way. The Lippes Loop [another variety of IUD] was supplied in a nonsterile form at first too."

Ravenholt has one very good reason to continue to defend the Dalkon Shield: it is still in use throughout the Third World. When the recall order was issued in 1975, AID could hope to recover stocks of unused devices from the warehouses and storage rooms of major international agencies, like the International Planned Parenthood Federation. But it could not, despite any number of memos, recall the AID-supplied Shields from the approximately 440,000 women already using the device. Nor could it hope to recover the thousands of Shields lying in the drawers of countless private practitioners and tiny rural family planning clinics.

Almost five years after the manufacturer's suspension of sales and AID's recall, Dalkon Shields are still being inserted. Dr. A. Goldsmith, a researcher for the AID-funded International Fertility Research Program and a man who could hardly be accused of harboring a consumerist bias, told us in June 1979, "I know they are still inserting the device" in Pakistan, India and possibly in South Africa.

It is impossible to know how frequently this is still taking place, but our own sources have told us of at least two cases. In Nairobi, Kenya, on the wall of the Family Planning Association clinic, there is a poster advertising the Dalkon Shield. In early May 1979, a young woman patient at this clinic was offered, among other birth control options, a Dalkon Shield. In Ottawa, Canada, Pierre Blais, senior consultant to the Bureau of Medical Devices told us, the Shield was being inserted as late as 1977—two years after it had been withdrawn from the U.S. market.

Finally, neither AID nor even the FDA would have any way of stopping A. H. Robins from privately dumping its own unsold stock of Dalkon Shields, if the company was of a mind to do so—and it was. In a recent interview, Robins attorney Franklin Tatum admitted to us that his client was still selling the devices through the first quarter of 1975—even as they were being recalled through AID and allegedly destroyed.

THE INUNDATION APPROACH

Ray Ravenholt winces slightly when he is asked about his critics, who are as numerous and diverse as any salaried civil servant could hope to acquire. "Right to lifers" head his list, along with "Catholics, Communists. . . ." He could have added consumerists, like Ralph Nader's Health Research

Group, and feminists, like the National Women's Health Network and the Feminist Women's Health Centers.

To be fair though, he is a man with a cause, and that cause is ultimately no different from the one that motivates every other hard-working professional in the State Department. "Population explosions, unless stopped, would lead to revolutions," he told the *St. Louis Post-Dispatch* in an April 1977 interview. Population control is required to maintain "the normal operation of U.S. commercial interests around the world. . . . Without our trying to help these countries with their economic and social development, the world would rebel against the strong U.S. commercial presence. The self-interest thing is the compelling element."

More liberal population controllers argue that economic development, health services and an expanded role for women are needed to motivate people to reduce family size, but Ravenholt's approach is single-mindedly contraceptive-oriented. To him, the point is to "get the contraceptives out there."

In the early 1970s Ravenholt pioneered a whole new approach to "getting them out there"—the "inundation approach," which was to provide, among other things, a convenient dump for the Palo Alto, California–based Syntex Corporation. Contraceptive inundation means disseminating contraceptives through any outlets, to any and all takers. Trained personnel can be bypassed; educational programs can be dispensed with. Oral contraceptives were especially well-suited to the inundation approach.

No woman can insert her own IUD, but—the theory was—if you can chew gum, you can swallow a pill. In Bangladesh, site of an intensive AID inundation program, pills are sold, usually at nominal prices and without any semblance of medical supervision, through local shops, alongside cigarettes, bananas and betel nuts.

From the beginning, AID's inundation program in Bangladesh had the markings of a biological disaster. The average Bangladeshi woman weighs 92 pounds and suffers from chronic malnutrition. Even in a 135-pound American woman, the pill is known to deplete the body's supply of vitamins A, B-6, D and folic acid (hence the special vitamins sold in the U.S. as supplements to the pill). Furthermore, no less than 90 percent of the

Bangladeshi women who accepted the pill were breastfeeding. According to a study by the International Planned Parenthood Federation, babies nursed by pill-users grew at an average rate that was only two-thirds that of babies nursed by non-pill-users. Ending world hunger is the most common rationalization for the top-down approach to population control, but in Bangladesh, AID was creating its own kind of chemically induced famine.

All this preceded anything that could, strictly speaking, be called a dump. AID was, after all, distributing a pill that had been judged safe for American women. Not all birth control pills are the same, however, and in 1970 the FDA had advised physicians to prescribe only those with the lowest possible estrogen dose—at that time, 50 micrograms. Sales of high-estrogen pills began to sag. AID had at first been following the FDA's advice, buying 50-microgram pills from G. D. Searle, Wyeth and Parke, Davis. Then, in 1973, AID took its business to the Syntex Corporation and started buying up high-dose, 80-microgram pills. AID explained the switch as a response to "market conditions." Simply put, the high-dose pills were cheaper. According to sources at the George Washington University Medical Center (which was under contract to AID to publish the bulletin *Population Reports*), Syntex offered AID a better deal—a discount on the domestically discredited, high-estrogen pills. Ravenholt bought up millions of dollars' worth of Syntex's stock of 80-microgram pills—for overseas use only, of course.

The dangers of estrogen overdosing don't dismay AID's inundation strategists. Dr. Malcolm Potts, director of the International Fertility Research Program and a key inundation planner, even sees a bright side to one pill side effect—swollen breasts. In a paper presented at the 1977 Tokyo International Symposium on Population, Potts and two colleagues suggested as a catchy slogan for rural pill promotion: "It makes your breasts more beautiful and is good for everyone—including the tailors who have to make bigger brassieres."

AND NOW: DEPO-PROVERA

Depo-Provera, a drug unfamiliar to most Americans, because it is not available here, may determine the future of contraceptive dumping.

Right now, AID is prohibited from shipping it across U.S. borders. But debates that will begin within the next few months will reopen the issue. If this dump is approved by Congress or the FDA, the informal contraceptive double standard will become official U.S. policy.

But AID is not just passively waiting for the go-ahead. Depo's manufacturer (the Upjohn Company) and AID are, even now, getting around the law and dumping the drug through both overt and covert programs. According to Upjohn, five million women in 70 countries have used Depo-Provera for contraception.

There are reasons why AID is so anxious to increase the distribution of Depo-Provera. Most birth control methods, because they depend on consumer cooperation, are considered unreliable by population controllers. Pills, condoms or diaphragms can all be forgotten or rejected. Sterilization would be ideal, but is politically risky. Depo-Provera brings new hope to planners looking for the final solution to fertility, for several reasons.

First, it is long-lasting: one injection prevents conception for three to six months. Second, it requires no effort on the part of the patient. Finally, by being injectable, it is believed to have a special appeal in the Third World, where, according to the AID-funded journal *Population Reports,* "injections are associated with safe, effective, modern medicine."

To the Third World consumer, a new product from the U.S. may seem to represent the latest in scientific research. But the overseas consumer of Depo doesn't know that the "latest research" is what prevented the contraceptive from being approved for use in the United States, and that is why it is being dumped.

The list of known side effects, complications and potentially lethal hazards could fill several magazine-size pages with small print. Depo-Provera causes nodules in the breasts and cancer in the reproductive organs of test animals. It causes "irregular bleeding disturbances," which have been described in one medical journal as "menstrual chaos." It reduces the body's resistance to infection. In some women it causes weight gain, headaches and dizziness. Its effects are not readily reversible: use may be followed by long-term or even permanent sterility. If injected into a pregnant woman (and almost every field study has reported the accidental injection of pregnant women), it can cause birth defects, especially congenital heart defects, and, in the case of female fetuses, masculinization and enlargement of the clitoris. Dr. J. Joseph Speidel, a colleague of Ray Ravenholt's at AID, did concede that excess bleeding induced by Depo "will be a problem where sanitary napkins are in short supply."

For 11 years, starting in 1967, Upjohn battled to get FDA approval for Depo-Provera. But in 1971, after studies done on beagle dogs showed that Depo was carcinogenic in high doses, the FDA was alarmed enough to call a halt to all clinical tests of the drug. On March 7, 1978, the FDA sent Upjohn a letter notifying the company of its final decision: Depo-Provera was "not approvable" for use in the U.S.

The population control community was outraged by the FDA's decision. AID's Ray Ravenholt called it "the tyranny of the beagle dog."

Domestic criticism of Depo-Provera has not prevented a plentiful supply from reaching the Third World. The FDA's refusal to approve Depo only meant that Upjohn could not ship the drug from its U.S. plants. It could, however, ship the drug from its Belgian subsidiary to whatever foreign commercial outlets it could find.

It has found plenty. In Belize, Central America, Depo is freely available at drugstores, despite what our correspondent reports as "many instances of amenorrhea [lack of menstrual periods] or profuse bleeding." A letter from Guatemala City to the Washington-based National Women's Health Network, related that in Honduras, El Salvador, Costa Rica, Nicaragua, Panama and the Dominican Republic "it is completely possible to buy it over the counter with no prescription."

This, apparently, is not enough for some parties. AID would like to be able to buy up huge batches of Depo at bulk rates, and Upjohn would like nothing better. Both testified to that effect to the U.S. Congress. An AID-subsidized dump could mean a four-fold increase in Upjohn's Depo sales.

There are several ways this could happen. First, AID could simply buy Depo from Upjohn's Belgian subsidiary and ship from there, as it has threatened to do. Another possibility is that Congress could pass a new drug reform act allowing for the export of nonapproved drugs. (A bill that may liberalize drug exports has recently been approved by the Senate Health Committee.) Or, the FDA could reverse its position on Depo-Provera and approve it for use in the United States, though perhaps only for special subgroups (the mentally retarded and drug addicts have been proposed). This, believe it or not, is a real possibility.

But with all eyes on Congress and the FDA, the real action is going on under the table. Increased pressure from feminist groups and mounting suspicion in some Third World countries are forcing AID, like the CIA, to carry on its more "sensitive" activities through a thick padding of front groups.

In September 1978, an elite group called the Population Roundtable met at Planned Parenthood World Population Headquarters in New York. Present were representatives of the Population Council, the International Planned Parenthood Federation, the UN Fund for Population Activities and—unbeknownst to the invited participants—two feminist health activists. The principal speaker was AID's Ravenholt, and, according to the two feminists present, "He stated that AID's most sensitive actions frequently cannot be spoken of publicly. He proudly reported that $12 million was secretly funneled to Mexico through Family Planning International Assistance, part of the Planned Parenthood Federation of America, and other organizations . . . that are AID-tainted conduits. He described this as a 'remarkable creative action.'"

AID's willingness to apply similar creativity to the Depo problem was expressed publicly in the May 1978 congressional hearings on population and development. Representative James Scheuer asked Dr. J. Joseph Speidel, then deputy director of AID's Office of Population: "If a health minister or chief of state of a foreign country requested our AID officials to provide Depo-Provera, would there be sufficient protection for our AID organization to make Depo-Provera available?"

Speidel responded: "I think our first action would be to attempt to get the appropriate supplies to them through some other routing. For example, the U.N. Fund for Population Activities might be willing to provide the needed drugs."

The U.N. Fund for Population Activities (UNFPA) has received $204 million, or 35 percent of its income, from AID since the fund's inception in 1969. In its first year of operation, a full 85 percent of UNFPA's money came from AID. Other agencies that might be happy to provide "routing" for covert AID actions include:

- IPPF (International Planned Parenthood Federation): AID has provided 40 percent of its budget since its inception in 1969, or a total of $126 million.
- FPIA (Family Planning International Assistance): AID provides 95 percent of its budget and takes credit for the development of FPIA.
- IFRP (International Fertility Research Program): According to its director, IFRP is "funded by the U.S. AID," so far to the tune of $18 million.
- International Project for the Association for Voluntary Sterilization: $29 million from AID.
- Pathfinder Fund: $50 million from AID.

All of these agencies have the advantage of being officially "private" or "international" despite their heavy dependence on U.S. public funds. Both IPPF and UNFPA are distributing Depo-Provera.

AID itself, we have discovered, continues to supply Depo under the guise of research. According to an AID internal document dated April 1979, three "Operations Research Projects" developed, designed and financed by AID are now supplying Depo-Provera. One, in San Pablo Autopan, Mexico, involves a population of 8,000; the second, in Sri Lanka, involves 120,000 people; and the last, in Matlab Thana, Bangladesh, involves 250,000 people.

AID's resort to undercover stratagems, frustrating as it may be to reformers, is a measure of the agency's increasing public vulnerability. The Dalkon Shield dump in 1972–75 went by almost unnoticed; Depo-Provera in 1979 is the target of international activists. Newspapers throughout the Third World have carried exposés about U.S. drug companies and AID's contraceptive double standard, although the U.S. press has virtually ignored the issue. Representatives of the "independent" population control agencies privately admit that their ties to AID have become an international embarrassment.

Under pressure, even AID has begun to change its tune. No one talks about contraceptive inundation anymore. Ray Ravenholt has been demoted to a still-powerful but ambiguous position as head of population training. And while AID is as committed as ever to the Depo dump, its public statements now link population control to "health and nutrition . . . and the role of the community, including that of women."

DAMNING THE DUMPS

Most of the growing resistance to contraceptive dumping is coming, in fact, from women—both the targets of the dumps and the American women at the more privileged end of the double standard. For thousands of American feminist health activists, Depo-Provera, sterilization abuse, and AID's entire population control program have become immediate issues. Carol Downer, a director of the Los Angeles Feminist Women's Health Center says, "We can fight against some problem here, only to see it exported to women overseas. But we're not going to sit by while a victory at home turns into a tragedy abroad. Feminists here have a responsibility to women all over the world."

Third World women activists agree. At a 1978 conference on Women and Multinational Corporations held in Des Moines, Iowa, a young Filipino woman urged the American women present to "find out everything you can" about American corporations and their products and spread the word. "Living in a dictatorship, we are very limited in our access to information," she said. "You are not."

It's just this kind of process—what Belita Cowan of the Washington Women's Health Network calls "grass-roots-level information sharing"—that will, sooner or later, make contraceptive dumping impossible: a nurse in Guatemala writes to the Boston Women's Health Collective and gets back a packet of information on Depo-Provera; a student from South Korea attends a feminist conference in the U.S. and takes back a stack of literature on U.S. drug companies' overseas operations; a health worker in Honduras discovers Dalkon Shields in a clinic supply room and alerts the local women.

So far, it can't compare with the international network AID runs or the "information sharing" a drug company's public relations department can arrange. But the word is getting out.

JONATHAN KWITNY

Few contemporary investigative reporters have matched the range of Jonathan Kwitny, who died of cancer in 1998 at the age of fifty-seven. In Wall Street Journal *reports, in seven books, and in television documentaries, his subjects ranged from murder investigation to AIDS research; with equal passion, he chronicled corporate scandals, CIA complicity in drug-running, President George H.W. Bush's involvement in savings-and-loan scandals, and (admiringly) the life of Pope John Paul II. Kwitny unraveled complex conspiracies with gumshoe tenacity and transparent storytelling.*

In his book Vicious Circles: The Mafia and the Marketplace, *Kwitny documents emerging partnerships between organized crime and corporate boardrooms. As this excerpt shows, Kwitny eschewed the clichés of mob reporting in favor of meticulous mapping of financial and legal trails and precise character studies.*

STEINMAN

From *Vicious Circles: The Mafia and the Marketplace,* 1979

On April 25, 1970, a scruffy, half-literate little manipulator named Moe Steinman shuffled into a suite at the elegant Stanhope Hotel overlooking Central Park in Manhattan, pulled the blinds, and within a few hours assumed a stature that even the most celebrated racketeers in history hadn't dreamed of.

Other mobsters had gone only partway. Gurrah Shapiro had controlled the garment center, and Joe Bonanno the Brooklyn dairy products district. Steinman had also gone partway—he had dominated the Fourteenth Street meat market. Some racketeers before Steinman had persuaded the heads of rival Mafia families to unite behind a single organized shakedown system. Thus had Steinman united racketeers from three powerful Mafia families, Genovese, Gambino, and Lucchese, and become the meat industry front for all of them. Other racketeers, before Steinman, had achieved nationwide control over certain specialty products, like mozzarella cheese, or over an atomized industry, like trucking.

But on this day, Moe Steinman, as a front for the Mafia, would achieve what no one else had achieved, even in the days of Al Capone or Lucky Luciano. Moe Steinman, who had risen from the gutter only by his lack of scruples, would tighten his fist around one of the biggest corporations in the country, a corporation that dominated a major national industry. It was an industry that almost every American depended on almost every day. It was an industry—unlike trucking—that was clothed with all the garments of Wall Street respectability.

Into this darkened room at the Stanhope Hotel, Moe Steinman would summon Currier J. Holman, founder and head of Iowa Beef Processors Inc., by far the largest meat company in the world. Then, as now, Iowa Beef's name was listed in the upper levels of the Fortune 500 ranking of largest corporations. Its shares were traded on the New York Stock Exchange. Its financing was handled by a syndicate of the biggest banks in the country. Then, as now, its sales were in the billions of dollars, and its food was on the tables of millions of Americans from Bangor to San Diego.

And Currier J. Holman, the tall, graying Notre Dame alumnus and widely-recognized business genius who organized and ran this mammoth operation, was to come crawling all the way from the Great Plains, bringing with him his co-chairman, his executive vice-president, and his general counsel, all at the beck of a foul-mouthed alcoholic hoodlum.

Iowa Beef, though founded only in 1961, already in 1970 dominated the meat industry the way few other industries are dominated by anyone. Since then, in partnership with Steinman and his family and friends, Iowa Beef has grown more dominant still. It was as if the Mafia had moved into the automobile industry by summoning the executive committee of General Motors, or the computer industry by summoning the heads of IBM, or the oil industry by bringing Exxon to its knees. Moe Steinman and the band of murderers and thugs he represented had effectively kidnapped a giant business. Its leaders were coming to pay him the ransom, a ransom that turned out to be both enormous and enduring.

As a result of the meeting in the darkened suite at the Stanhope that day in 1970, Iowa Beef would send millions of dollars to Steinman and his family under an arrangement that continued at least until 1978. After the meeting, millions more would go to a lifelong pal of Steinman and his Mafia friends, a man who had gone to prison for using slimy, diseased meat in filling millions of dollars in orders (he bribed the meat inspectors) and who wound up on Iowa Beef's board of directors. Consequent to the meeting in the Stanhope Hotel, Iowa Beef would reorganize its entire marketing apparatus to allow Steinman's organization complete control over the company's largest market, and influence over its operations coast to coast. In 1975, Iowa Beef would bring Moe Steinman's son-in-law and protégé to its headquarters near Sioux City to run the company's largest division and throw his voice into vital corporate decisions. But, most important, a mood would be struck in the Stanhope that day—a mood of callous disregard for decency and the law. Iowa Beef would proceed to sell its butcher employees out to the Teamsters union, to turn its trucking operations over to Mafia-connected manipulators, and to play fast and loose with anti-trust laws.

Because of their hold on Iowa Beef, the racketeers' control of other segments of the meat industry would expand and harden. And as a result of all this, the price of meat for the American consumer—the very thing Currier Holman had done so much to reduce—would rise. Meyer Lansky once said that the Syndicate was bigger than U.S. Steel. When Iowa Beef Processors caved in on that April day in 1970, the Syndicate, as far as the meat industry was concerned, *became* U.S. Steel.

Moe Steinman is not impressive to look at. He is of average height, but seems shorter. He isn't fat, but there's something overweight about him. He has a sad, doberman-like face, that is pockmarked and ruddy like a drunk's. Steinman is often drunk. His clothes are sometimes flashy, but seldom tasteful. He is appallingly inarticulate when he talks. But everybody knows what he means.

Detective Bob Nicholson once stood near the bar of the Black Angus restaurant and saw a slightly tipsy Moe Steinman point his stubby finger at John "Johnny Dio" Dioguardi, the foremost active labor racketeer in the Lucchese Mafia family. "You listen here, Johnny," Steinman said. "You don't tell me how to run my business. I tell you." The boast rocked

Nicholson (and Dio may not have cared for it, either). Ultimately, the Mafia retained its power, through its violent system of justice. But the fact that Steinman was allowed to get away with such bragadoccio—and he did it repeatedly—showed just how indispensable he had become to the Mafia's designs on controlling the marketplace. There is a story in the industry that once in the late 1960s Steinman brazenly cheated Peter Castellana, a relative and high aide of boss Carlo Gambino. Steinman is said to have shortchanged Castellana on the sale of a load of hijacked turkeys. And nobody raised a finger.

Industry sources also talk about a speech Steinman gave in 1970 at a retirement party for a Grand Union supermarket executive. The party, naturally enough, was at the Black Angus, which was owned by a retired executive from the rival Bohack chain, who had acquired it from the family of the retired head of the butchers' union. While the departing Grand Union official was guest of honor at the party, the center of attention was Johnny Dio, who also was about to depart, in his case for prison, where he was being sent as a result of illegal deals in the kosher meat industry. Steinman, it's said, stood up before the assembled guests, openly recalled how close he was to Dio, and assured everyone that he personally would "take care of the business" while Dio was away.

Only once, in the mid-1960s, is Steinman said to have suffered Mob disfavor. There are reliable reports that he was beaten up once in a supermarket warehouse, and hospitalized. Nobody who is willing to talk seems to know for sure what the beating was about.

Bob Nicholson had been impressed the first time he heard Steinman's name, back in 1964 in the Merkel horsemeat scandal. When Merkel's boss, Nat Lokietz, wanted a connection in government so he could bribe his way out of trouble, he had called Moe Steinman. Steinman didn't arrange the bribe meeting—Tino De Angelis did—because Steinman was out of town. But after the bribery attempt backfired, Lokietz went to Steinman again in a last-ditch effort to keep Merkel afloat. In the spring of 1965, Steinman had met with Lokietz at the Long Island home of a Big Apple supermarket meat buyer, who acted as intermediary. The buyer was in Steinman's pocket; he would later plead guilty to evading income taxes on payoffs he took from Steinman. Through subsequent conversations that were wiretapped, police learned that Lokietz had asked Steinman to get the Mafia to rescue Merkel. Some money, some political clout, and Lokietz could be back on his feet again. Steinman huddled with Dio over the idea one night at the Red Coach Inn in Westchester County, but with the horsemeat scandal all over the papers and Dio involved in some promising new rackets, they decided to let Merkel go on down the drain.

As a result of these meetings, however, Steinman was called in for questioning before the Merkel grand jury. Nicholson was sent to serve the subpoena, and thus got to meet the racketeer for the first time. Immediately Nicholson saw the arrogant conniver that was Steinman, a man who thought he could wheel and deal his way out of anything.

Nicholson found Steinman at the Luxor Baths, the famous old establishment on West Forty-sixth Street where the wealthiest of New York's European immigrant community used to go. There they relived the old-country male ritual of a steam bath, a massage, and a nap. Numerous business and entertainment celebrities had visited the Luxor over the decades. But by the late 1950s, the clientele had cheapened a bit and mobsters were more in evidence. The bathhouse was a frequent hangout for the likes of Johnny Dio, Anthony "Tony Bender" Strollo, and Lorenzo "Chappy the Dude" Brescia. Wiretaps would later reveal that the Luxor served as a convenient location for underworld plotting and the passing of payoffs. It was at the Luxor that Steinman often took care of supermarket executives and butchers' union officials. In 1975, the Luxor Baths closed, and reopened as a house of prostitution.

Nicholson remembers going into the lobby of the Luxor with his subpoena in 1965, and paging Steinman. The stocky (but not fat) racketeer came down in his bathrobe and turned on his crude charm.

"Can you tell me what this is about?" he asked Nicholson.

"Sorry," he was told. "I can't discuss it."

"Why don't we sit down to talk?"

Nicholson looked around at the well-appointed lobby, and then at Steinman in his bathrobe.

"Come on into the steam room. We'll have a nice bath," Steinman said.

Nicholson turned him down, but kept him talking. Maybe there would be an open offer of a bribe.

"After we have a bath," Steinman said, "we can talk. We'll have a few drinks, maybe we can go out to dinner."

Nicholson kept him talking.

"Are you married?" Steinman went on.

Nicholson said he wasn't.

"Do you have a girlfriend? Maybe I could get you a girlfriend. I'm a nice guy. You'll like me."

"I had to say, 'No, thanks,' " Nicholson recalls now. "Anything further would have been a compromise. But that's the way Moe Steinman operates. He never gets caught."

Others have noticed the same phenomenon. Says a partner in a large and long-established New York meat supply company, "Steinman bribes people in the bank not to sign him in or out when he goes to his safety deposit boxes. He has boxes all over the city. Once I was with him on a trip overseas and he bribed the guy at the airline counter $20 to avoid a $50 overweight charge. He didn't need the money. It's just a game with him."

Steinman was wrong when he thought he could bribe Bob Nicholson. But there were ways over Nicholson and around Nicholson. Even when the law had Steinman absolutely dead to rights in 1975, he was able to manipulate his way out of trouble. Bob Nicholson was right about one thing: "He never gets caught."

Moe Steinman has declined numerous requests for an interview. His communications to the author have consisted mostly of grunted greetings and monosyllabic comments in the hallways of various courthouses. There was also a very pregnant stare one day in a visitors' room at the federal Metropolitan Correctional Center in Manhattan when Steinman showed up at what I had been told would be a secret meeting between me and a cellmate of his.

Much of Steinman's story, however, can be told from the public record. He has testified several times about his background (while his veracity has not been constant, certain facts can be verified). And many persons in the meat industry, including his son-in-law Walter Bodenstein, have contributed information to the following sketch.

Steinman was born in Poland around 1918. He came to the United States with his parents at age eight. His father, a butcher, settled in Brooklyn. He quit school after eighth grade and ran off to be a porter or carny worker at the Chicago World's Fair in 1933. He returned to Brooklyn, where a young greengrocer named Ira Waldbaum had decided to lease out sections of his stores to meat dealers. This was, of course, long before Waldbaum's became the major regional supermarket chain it is today.

A dealer who had leased the meat departments in two Waldbaum's stores hired young Moe Steinman to run them, and the budding hoodlum was on his way. Steinman bought his first meat from Sam Goldberger, who would later go to prison for selling adulterated meat and bribing federal food inspectors. And Steinman made connections with two other Polish-Jewish immigrants, Max and Louis Block, who had just left their own Brooklyn butcher business to organize the Amalgamated Meat Cutters' union under rights obtained through mobsters Little Augie Pisano and George Scalise. Pisano and Scalise were of an older generation, but there was a younger, more contemporary Mafia figure whom the Blocks and Steinman and Goldberger began to meet—Johnny Dio.

Soon Steinman was expanding his meat counter operations to the Bronx and Westchester County. When the war came in 1941, Steinman quickly got classified 4-F. He has testified that he doesn't remember why he flunked his physical, though others have observed that if he didn't find a way to put the fix in on the Selective Service System, it would have been uncharacteristic. At any rate, Steinman's 4-F status allowed him to achieve fame and fortune while still in his twenties.

From 1942 to 1945, Steinman was known among meat dealers throughout the five boroughs as "Black Market Moe," the man who never asked for ration coupons and who always had meat to deliver. As Walter Bodenstein, his son-in-law and protégé, put it, "My dad during the black market was in the bakery business. He told me as a boy he had been offered large sums of money for sugar and stuff like that. And he would throw the people out. I guess Moe didn't throw people out."

"If you had meat during the war, there was no problem making money," recalls one prominent wholesaler. He and others in the industry say Steinman was almost certainly a millionaire by the time peace finally forced him to look for other rackets.

The racket he found was one he stayed with a long time. Essentially, it was a disguised way of taking kickbacks from supermarket chains for insuring "labor peace." This he could guarantee through his connections with the labor unions and the Mafia. The disguise required two hats.

First, he would hire himself out as a supermarket executive who could handle "labor problems." Because all the chains were supposed to be competing with each other, for the benefit of the consumer, he could be a payrolled executive for only one of them (it was Shopwell Inc.'s Daitch-Shopwell chain). But in industry-wide bargaining, he would act as lead negotiator for the group of them. One chain alone, however, could not supply Steinman with all the money he would need for the required under-the-table payments to union leaders and Mafiosi, as well as for his own not particularly modest style of living. So it came to pass that the chains all bought substantial quantities of meat from a particular wholesale brokerage firm, and that the firm was controlled by Steinman. The firm would overcharge for its meat, and the overcharge would create enough money to provide for all the people who had to be paid off. This payoff list soon grew to include executives at the various supermarket chains and their relatives, because if the executives were going to participate in graft it seemed unfair for them not to be able to take some of it for themselves.

Steinman's wholesale meat firm would overcharge equally to all the supermarket chains, so that none of them would get a competitive advantage—even the chain for which Steinman was a salaried executive. The customer would pay through the nose for everybody's high living, but that was all right. If any upstart supermarket manager tried to offer the customer a better deal, he would feel the pain of the organization's cleaver in his back. Either the Block brothers' butchers or Johnny Dio's truckers would start making trouble. There could be excessive grievances, or slow-downs, or, if necessary, even a strike.

And this is the way the supermarket system in the New York-New Jersey-Connecticut area works. It is the racket that Moe Steinman began running shortly after the war, when he opened his Mo-Jo meat wholesale business, and simultaneously went to work for the Shopwell supermarket chain (now Daitch-Shopwell). It is the same racket that Steinman was running, with different corporate styles, when Bob Nicholson began chasing him in 1971. And as this is written, there are still trappings of the same deals involving some of the same people and the same corporations that were doing business earlier, and the same Moe Steinman. But in the absence of wiretaps and court subpoenaes, it is impossible to say exactly who is paying how much to whom and for what.

Steinman has always needed a partner to mind his meat operations while he was out engaged in the real business of making payoffs and manipulating the cost of food. In the original Mo-Jo wholesale meat concern, Steinman's partner was Joseph Weinberg. Court testimony later showed Weinberg's own connection to members of the Gambino and Genovese Mafia families, and perhaps it was Steinman who introduced them.

Paul "Constantine" Castellano was the brother-in-law of boss of bosses Carlo Gambino, and succeeded Gambino as head of the Mafia family when Gambino died in 1976. Like Steinman, Castellano was involved in wholesale and retail meat firms in Brooklyn in the 1930s. Others of his blood family entered the industry, and the Castellanos now own many stores and distributorships in Brooklyn and Manhattan. They have a long record of welching on debts; of suffering suspicious hijackings, which can lead to insurance claims; of selling goods that were later found to have been stolen off docks or trucks, and of cheating other firms by receiving the assets of companies about to go into bankruptcy proceedings.

One typical bankruptcy fraud revolved around Steinman's partner Weinberg. A veteran meat dealer, Weinberg was able to open Murray Packing Company in 1959 with a good credit rating. A few months later

Joseph Pagano, a young Genovese henchman and convicted narcotics trafficker became an executive at Murray Packing. (Joseph Valachi testified that Pagano and his brother murdered mobster Eugenio Giannini in New York on September 20, 1952.) Meanwhile, Gondolfo Sciandra, a Gambino soldier and relative by marriage, opened another new meat concern and it began buying supplies from the Weinberg-Pagano company. So did the Castellanos' own company, Pride Wholesale Meat and Poultry Corp. But these favored customers always paid less than Weinberg and Pagano were charged by their own suppliers. For example, Weinberg's Murray Packing would buy hams for fifty cents a pound and sell them to Pride for forty-five cents a pound. Naturally, no business is designed to continue losing money this way.

Murray Packing quickly stepped up its rate of buying meat, but fell further and further behind in paying its bills. Soon the "float" of unpaid-for meat had reached $1.3 million. At that point, in 1961, the creditors sued. Murray Packing was declared bankrupt and there were no assets around to pay the bills, because the Gambino-Castellano firms had received the meat. (The basic concept behind all this is the same one that other Gambino operatives applied to the cheese business in Vermont and elsewhere.)

The exceptional part of the Murray Packing case is that it was prosecuted (because the new U.S. Attorney in Manhattan, Robert Morgenthau, had an unusual interest in crimes of high finance). Joseph Pagano, the young Mafia subordinate, tried to take the entire rap himself by telling a federal court that he had withdrawn some $800,000 from Murray Packing illegally, and had lost it all gambling. The jury dismissed this story. Peter Castellana, scion of the Castellano family,[1] drew five years in prison; it was the only time in at least four similar bankruptcy cases that Castellana was brought to justice at all. Sciandra got eighteen months, and Weinberg, who contended he was just an innnocent dupe, got one year. They were released after serving much less.

Pagano, however, was stunned by civil bankruptcy judge Sidney S.

1 Slight variations of name spelling are common among Mafia kin.

Sugarman, who also refused to believe the gambling story and ordered Pagano to jail for contempt of court until the $800,000 was repaid to Murray Packing's suppliers. Finally, in 1970, after almost six years, the court accepted the Mob's offer of a deal. A lawyer appeared with $75,000—one can only imagine where it came from—and Pagano was released and forgiven the rest of his debt. Over the years, the court had collected just $8,244.30 from the others who helped steal $1.3 million. According to law enforcement reports, Pagano immediately was given command of a big Mafia move into the now illegal business of factoring Medicaid claims; members of Steinman's family also were heavily into the business at that time, as will be described later.

Pride Wholesale Meat & Poultry Corp., the Castellano firm, had to go out of business as a legal entity in order to avoid civil claims in the Murray Packing bankruptcy. But Pride continues to be a trade name of the Castellanos, who are still major distributors of specialty meats and chickens, and occasional creditors in bankruptcy court. Among other things, Peter Castellana runs Ranbar Packing Corp., the region's largest distributor of Paramount chickens (the ones touted on television by Pearl Bailey). Ranbar alone reports annual sales of $30 million.

Moe Steinman's supermarket chains were at the heart of another Gambino family rip-off in the meat industry in the late 1950s. Paul Gambino (Carlo's brother) and Frank Ferro (who later became part of the Gambino cheese operation) briefly took over the business of sharpening knives for retail meat sellers. Their operation, though, amounted to little more than a shakedown of the knife grinders who had previously handled the work. After a brief time in business, the racketeers offered to quit if the knife grinders' organization would pay them $300,000. The organization paid, and the chain stores sent their knives back to the original grinders. (Questioned about this before the New York State Commission of Investigation, Gambino and Ferro invoked the Fifth Amendment right against self-incrimination.)

The Gambino family's long-established ties with Moe Steinman and his partners probably have been useful to other members of the family. For many years, Paul Castellano, Jr., and Joseph Castellano have operated P & H Rendering Company in Brooklyn. P & H buys fat and other meat byproducts from supermarket chains and meat wholesalers, then reprocesses these wastes into cooking lard, or soap, or perhaps an ingredient for pet food. Paul, Jr., and Joseph are first cousins of Peter Castellana, and sons of Paul, Sr., known as "Constantine." All were thus related to boss of bosses Carlo Gambino.

The biggest Castellano racket, by knowledgeable accounts, continues to be loansharking. This high-interest emergency money lending isn't limited to the meat industry, but the Castellanos have used it there to increase the family clout. They are believed to control a large percentage of the independent meat companies in the Fourteenth Street market because of the debts owed to them.

From right after World War II and through the 1950s, while Joseph Weinberg was taking orders for Steinman's Mo-Jo meat firm, Moe Steinman was pursuing a rather unusual career as a supermarket executive. Exactly how his deal worked probably can't be learned at this late date, but clearly he was burning his candle at both ends.

At a court hearing once, he gave the following suspicious version of the story: After the war, he owned and operated eighteen independent meat outlets in Westchester County. In 1949, the owner of the Shopwell supermarket chain asked him to take over the chain's independently-owned meat concession by buying out the existing concession-holder. This Steinman did, for $65,000. Then (Steinman testified), in 1953, Shopwell decided to take over ownership of its own meat departments and bought Steinman out for Shopwell stock. The deal involved no cash, and so presumably left the thirty-five-year-old Steinman a major holder in the Shopwell corporation. He also became a salaried executive at about forty-five thousand postwar dollars a year. Steinman wasn't asked, and didn't choose to tell, what relationship if any his Mo-Jo meat firm had with Shopwell after he became a salaried executive.

The principal owner and manager of the Shopwell chain back then was Lou Taxin, who has long since retired. In an interview for this book, Taxin said he simply did not remember when or how Steinman became associated with Shopwell. He said he also didn't remember whether Steinman, while employed as a salaried meat buyer for the chain, was buying meats from his own wholesale firm. Old-time meat wholesalers say that's exactly what Steinman was doing, and that his unusual status was widely understood throughout the industry as a cover-up for graft. They also say the arrangement dated back to shortly after the war. When Steinman's name came up in criminal charges in 1973, Shopwell was quoted in the press as saying he had been with the company since at least 1947, not 1949 or 1953.

At any rate, the record is clear that by no later than 1953, Steinman had become Shopwell's director of meat operations. He also became its very first "director of labor relations." Everyone noticed that Steinman spent a lot of time with the heads of the butchers' union and the racketeers who controlled various unions. When Moe Steinman was involved in the contract talks, labor problems disappeared. The supermarket chains he protected sometimes went more than a year without paying pension fund contributions for their employees, as the contract required, and the unions didn't object.

In 1956, Shopwell merged with Daitch Crystal Dairies to form the Daitch-Shopwell chain that is a leader in the eastern market today. Daitch's stock shares were traded on the public market, so shares of the merged corporation, which was known as Shopwell Inc., were also publicly tradable. For many years they have been listed on the American Stock Exchange. In recent years, even before Steinman's 1975 "retirement," Shopwell's disclosure statements filed with the S.E.C. contained no reference to Steinman as a top officer or major shareholder. What has happened to the major block of stock he apparently once held in Shopwell can only be wondered at. Despite more than a dozen attempts to interview them on this point for this book, Shopwell's senior officers—Herbert Daitch, Martin Rosengarten and Seymour Simpson—refused to come to the phone or respond to messages.

Whether Steinman helped engineer the Daitch-Shopwell merger wasn't learned either, but the merger was certainly fortuitous for him. Since 1956, the company has been headed by Herbert Daitch, who has been a staunch defender of Steinman throughout various troubles with the law. Daitch could hardly have been a more gracious employer. There certainly wasn't any clock-punching required. Steinman has testified that "I was in for six hours, I was in for an hour, I didn't come in at all sometimes." The detectives who followed him around, or tried to, in the early 1970s, say the six-hour days were rare if they ever even existed.

He slept late. Afternoons he spent with a girlfriend in a hotel, or in an apartment he kept in Queens. For his longtime girlfriend, Steinman picked the wife of an old friend. It was the subject of wide speculation in the industry whether the old friend knew about this liaison—especially after the old friend's name popped up on Steinman's illegal payoff list when it was made public as part of an indictment in 1973. Apparently the old friend was getting $250-a-week "salary" from a Steinman brokerage firm while doing no work for the firm and while his wife, a busty, good-looking brunette, was sleeping around town with Steinman.

What business Steinman did, he did at bars—most frequently the Black Angus, where his hosts were the Block brothers. Though revelations at the McClellan hearings had forced them to resign after twenty-five years' running the butchers' union, they were succeeded in office by men of their choosing, and continued to exercise authority from behind the bar of their restaurant.

Steinman also frequented other bars, notably the Bull & Bear at the Waldorf-Astoria Hotel. It particularly infuriated Bob Nicholson later to see the way Steinman cowed the staff at the prestigious Bull & Bear, where some of the most reputable businessmen in town gather for lunch or a six o'clock scotch. "They bowed down to him," Nicholson recalls with disgust. "The Maitre D' protected him at a table in the corner where he used to sit and talk with union people. Nobody could sit at a table next to him. We (the detectives assigned to follow him) couldn't get near him. He was a big tipper. That was his philosophy. You could get anything you want if you paid for it. He was crude. He had no manners. But when he wanted something"—Nicholson shakes his head—"then he was the charming Moe Steinman."

One law officer puts it this way: "All he [Steinman] ever did was drink, and eat, and fuck."

Well, not all. Steinman negotiated labor contracts with as many as eighteen different locals. Most of the terms were set over the telephone or across a bar table. Formal "negotiations" were staged later in hotel suites, but they hardly appear to have been conducted at arms' length. Steinman became lead negotiator in many labor dealings for a large group of supermarket chains, supposedly competitors, based in or near New York. The owners and executives of these chains were by and large of similar background. They were friendly with each other outside of business. They hung out at the same country club (of course they may have had to do that—the club was owned by the head of the butchers' union).

The membership in this clique of supermarkets was not fixed. Some chains showed more independence than others. But by and large they bought their meats, at least certain cuts, from whatever company Moe Steinman told them to buy from. And the extra money they paid for the meat kept labor problems away, and fattened their own incomes through kickbacks. The chains that supposedly competed with Shopwell, but which were later found to have executives on Steinman's payoff list, included Big Apple, Bohack, Food City, Sloan's, First National Stores (Finast), Foodarama, King Kullen, Shop-Rite (a cooperative whose current central management has refused to deal with Steinman, though many of its stores are run by his cronies), and, of course, Waldbaum's, Steinman's first employer. Food Fair, Grand Union, Great Eastern, Hills, and Key Food were other chains cited in court evidence as being under Steinman's influence, although none of their executives were ever convicted.

The executives who *were* convicted were almost all from the vice-president level. Where were the chief executives all this time? Where were the principal owners of the supermarket chains? None were ever accused in court of getting money from Moe Steinman, or of conspiring to bribe union leaders by overpaying for meat. But human nature has led many people in the industry to assume that at least some of the bosses got their money indirectly. The middle management officials who were convicted had received such enormous payoffs—sometimes more than $100,000 a year each—that it is easy to speculate that they were spreading this money around the office.

People in the industry frequently remark that the president of such-and-such a chain "had to know . . . had to be getting part of it." It hasn't been proven.

One of Moe Steinman's illegal payoff lists was later found to contain the names of close relatives of Herbert Daitch and Martin Rosengarten, the chairman and president of Daitch-Shopwell. (Because the relatives evidently paid taxes on the money they received, they weren't charged with any crime.) Steinman's business protégé and son-in-law, Walter Bodenstein, has stated that the basic decision to buy certain Steinman-promoted products was made directly by the chief executives, even at the largest chains.

But nobody cared—as long as the money was coming from the people who shopped in the supermarkets, and as long as there was no effective competition. (A & P was never part of the clique, but its executives were caught up in similar scandals operating independently.) Because the heads of the supermarkets were not involved directly, they could continue to run their supermarkets, even after Steinman was caught up in a scandal. As of 1977, at least, they were continuing to buy meat from Steinman family brokerages.

While Steinman was at the Black Angus, or the Bull & Bear, or the Luxor Baths, passing out envelopes, his brother Sol handled meat buying for Shopwell. Moe's "boss," Herbert Daitch, evidently was content to settle for a pinch hitter if his last name was Steinman. Then, around 1961, while Moe's wholesaling partner Joe Weinberg was deep in the Murray Packing Company scandal, Sol left Daitch-Shopwell to take over another meat wholesaling operation, Trans-World Fabricators, Inc. More properly, Trans-World was a brokerage. From its office in the Fourteenth Street meat district, Trans-World took telephone meat orders from supermarkets (and other retailers) and made telephone purchases from meat processors to fill the orders. For the most part, there were no warehouses, where product was moved in and out. The firm just took "commissions" on what the supermarkets bought. And if the commissions weren't paid to Trans-World, often the meat couldn't be sold.

Trans-World had been started a couple of years earlier by Herbert Newman, a longtime side-kick of shady characters in the meat industry. He had been partners with Sol Steinman in another meat company in the early 1950s, and also at one point had been involved with Charles Anselmo, the bookie, loanshark, and chief supplier in the Merkel horsemeat scandal. Sources in the industry say that Newman (who died of cancer in 1974) went to jail in the 1940s as a result of meat dealings, though no record of that could be found.

A couple of years after Newman started Trans-World, it was foundering. Newman, a heavy gambler and all-round big spender, effectively gave the company over to the Steinman brothers. He testified once that he needed the Steinmans' help in order to sell meat to supermarkets. Moe, on the other hand, testified that Newman needed better credit, and the people just naturally trusted the Steinmans. At any rate, after Weinberg was gone the Steinmans needed a new commission firm and in Trans-World they got one, without investing so much as a dime. According to Newman's testimony later, the Steinmans simply "declared" that they were partners, and nobody was about to argue with them. For a while, Trans-World shared an address at 408 West Fourteenth Street with Anselmo, who was, at that time, busy trucking diseased meat into New York for Merkel sausages. Anselmo still operates from there; Trans-World eventually found another office around the corner on Gansevoort Street.

True to expectations, the Steinman family brought Trans-World a quick upturn in business. Large orders were placed with Trans-World by Waldbaum's, Hills, King Kullen, Bohack, Grand Union, First National (Finast), Sloan's, Foodorama (which became a large part of the Shop-Rite chain) and, of course, Daitch-Shopwell, where the Steinmans, as official meat buyers, were all too happy to feather the nest of their own meat supply firm with money that belonged to Shopwell's public shareholders. These were the names that came out in testimony as Trans-World customers; undoubtedly there were others. Prices, as always, were puffed up to create a huge kitty for pay-offs to all concerned, including various Mafiosi. The shoppers paid for that. Soon, other commission companies were established under the same ownership, assertedly for tax reasons.

Back in the early 1960s even Moe Steinman probably didn't dream he could grab a commission on *all* the fresh meat that came into chain stores in a three- or four-state area. To accumulate money to handle his payoffs, he claimed the right to commissions on certain easily identified specialty meat items. These included mostly the parts of the cow known in the trade as "offal" (pronounced "awful"); livers, oxtail, tripe, and flank, or "skirt" steak. All of this is meat that does not come from the four standard fresh-meat cuts—the chuck, the ribs, the round, and the loin. But the biggest specialty item by far for Steinman was the brisket, which comes from the belly of the cow, and which most frequently winds up on American dining tables as corned beef.

At first, Steinman simply required that independent corned beef makers buy their briskets from him as part of his control of the offal market. Since corned beef requires processing, which is usually done locally, it was an easy item to control. If the processors didn't buy their briskets from Steinman, the supermarkets wouldn't buy the processed corned beef from *them.* This produced an easy $1 a hundredweight (or $1 commission for every one hundred pounds of corned beef sold). But when Steinman saw how easy it was to control the corned beef market, he decided to nail the manufacturers both coming and going. "You don't sell to the supermarket anymore, you sell to me," he told them.

One New Jersey corned beef maker later told police he had been selling under an exclusive contract to a particular supermarket chain. Then one day Steinman arrived and said, "You can't sell this account any more."

"What do you mean?" demanded the stunned manufacturer.

"Look," Steinman instructed him. "From now on you deliver your corned beef to Trans-World. *I'll* deliver it to the supermarket."

Steinman eventually testified, with his figures scrutinized by federal prosecutors, that he pumped from eight to ten cents a pound into the price of every corned beef sold in a supermarket anywhere near New York. But even that wasn't enough. Steinman also saw that something unusual happens to the corned beef market during the second week in March: every Irish bar and restaurant in town has to have corned beef for St. Patrick's Day, and in New York around St. Patrick's Day every successful bar and restaurant at least pretends to be Irish. So Steinman began holding back corned beef from the market and storing it in coolers well ahead of time. Then, come the second week in March, there was almost no limit to what he could charge for it. To put it simply, by the late 1960s Moe Steinman had put a corner on the corned beef market for much of the northeastern United States. He so restructured the market in New York that Lorenzo "Chappy the Dude" Brescia, Moe's Mafia friend, sent his son into the business, manufacturing corned beefs and selling them through Moe.

It wasn't hard to figure out where Steinman's hold on the supermarkets came from. He controlled the unions. In the words of one meat dealer who started to lose his market until he joined the system, "The union personnel, the foremen, they made certain that nothing but Steinman meat was acceptable. I could sell Bohack meat at fifty cents a pound and it would be rejected. They had to pay Steinman fifty-five cents a pound."

Usually the pressures were subtle, but when disagreements arose, Steinman could interject a heavy hand. Hills, for example, was one chain that apparently tried to buck the system on occasion. Once in 1968 Steinman decided that Hills hadn't been coughing up enough commission money. So, just before Thanksgiving, the unions threw up a picket line around a Hills warehouse full of turkeys. According to Robert Goldman, a lawyer for Hills' meat buyers, Steinman "demanded that Hills purchase seven hundred barrels of corned beef a month and thirty thousand pounds of flank steak." That or no turkeys on Thanksgiving. Hills chose to sell the turkeys, and by the end of the year had become Trans-World's largest customer.

One Fourteenth Street wholesaler recalls a time when a customer of his with several stores was trying to resist unionization. The butchers' union had been defeated in an employee election supervised by the National Labor Relations Board. So the union asked wholesalers to refuse to sell meat to the small chain until it consented to organization. When the wholesaler in question continued to provide supplies, he began getting calls from his major supermarket chain customers: if he didn't stop selling to the boycotted chain, the major chains would stop buying from him. The buyers apologized for this threat, but said the union had given them no choice. "We got people working in our stores using a band saw that aren't supposed to," the big chains said. "We got weighers putting meat in the case. If we run into problems we'd have to put in three or four people per store, and we can't afford it." So the wholesaler fell in line.

In 1967, a big money-making opportunity arose for Steinman. It bore a prophetic similarity to the Iowa Beef Processors shakedown that began three years later. Holly Farms Inc. of Wilkesboro, North Carolina, hadn't been able to break into the New York market even though it was the nation's largest chicken producer. Holly Farms packaged its chickens by a new cryovac process that eliminated the need for re-packaging in the stores. This meant less work for butchers, so the butchers' union barred Holly Farms' product.

Steinman saw an opening. He arranged for Daitch-Shopwell to try the Holly Farms chickens for a few weeks. The union apparently "understood" and didn't complain. Daitch-Shopwell's president, Martin Rosengarten, was delighted, according to Steinman's testimony later: "He called me in and he told me, 'Here is a package that's great. It's beautiful. You can throw it in the case when it comes in. The only problem is, I don't know if the unions will allow it.' " He should have had more confidence.

Steinman immediately went to Al DeProspoe, the man Frank Kissel had selected to run Local 174 when Kissel went off to jail. They made a deal. As described later, the union would let in cryovac chickens if the supermarkets promised not to fire any butchers because of it.[2] By the time Steinman broke the good news to Holly Farms, however, there was more to it. In his own words, "Now I turn around, which my president [Rosengarten] knew about it, and I said to my president that I want to ask them [Holly Farms] for the brokerage for the New York territory. He said, 'If you can get it, go ahead.' I didn't hide anything." Nor did Rosengarten seem to object to Steinman's design to sell the new product to all the chains in town, even though this would cost Shopwell—

2 I tried repeatedly to reach DeProspoe for comment, but he failed to return messages left with the union and with his daughter.

Steinman's employer—its competitive advantage. Steinman's commissions came first.

Holly Farms, of course, was delighted at what Steinman had pulled off, and was easily persuaded to let him have an exclusive brokerage contract—so much for every pound of Holly Farms chicken sold in or near New York. Details of the deal have never been made public. Rather than cut Newman in on the profits, Moe sidestepped Trans-World and set up a separate brokerage firm, Cedar Rapids Fabricators Inc., to receive the commissions from Holly Farms. Then, in his word, he "gave" Cedar Rapids to his son-in-law, Walter Bodenstein, to operate. Holly Farms also was somehow persuaded to hire Bodenstein, a lawyer, as its New York legal counsel, on substantial retainer. A similar practice would be followed three years later with Iowa Beef.

Bodenstein had married Steinman's youngest daughter, Cookie, six years earlier. He had gone on to Brooklyn Law School and had spent the previous several years moving from one small law firm to another, and spending some time in between practicing out of his home. Evidently Steinman decided his daughter's husband needed steadier work. Putting commissions on chickens wasn't the end of it, either. More deals were set up by which Bodenstein could profit from the supermarket chain connection. J. B. Brokerage was established to sell them sawdust powder to clean floors. Linden Overseas Ltd. was established to sell dishes imported from Japan as a sideline. Onto the payroll of these ventures went about two dozen relatives and friends of Steinman and his supermarket employers.

The deal with Holly Farms apparently continues to this day, though the amount of money it involves has been reduced, through no fault of the Steinman family. In the mid-1970s, Frank Perdue's catchy advertisements created a name brand competition that cost Holly Farms its market leadership. Holly Farms' chickens don't carry a brand name in the supermarket case. Perdue's chief brand name competition came from Paramount Chickens, the brand preferred by Pearl Bailey and Carlo Gambino, whose Mafia family distributes them.

In all likelihood, the Holly Farms deal was worth millions over the course of the decade. The sawdust powder and dish deals, however, apparently were too trivial and petered out, especially after Nicholson and his men started looking over everybody's shoulders. By then, though, Bodenstein had found his way into other shady deals, some of them involving Johnny Dio, who had an office at the same Park Avenue address where Bodenstein operated his law practice and chicken brokerage.

In 1968, Frank Kissel was packing his bags for jail, which left a vacuum of bribery in the wholesale meat industry. After more than a dozen meat wholesalers had testified against Kissel and his union colleagues in 1967, union officials were getting edgy about taking money directly from the employers. So Steinman, who already had a lock on the retail (supermarket) end of the corruption, volunteered to fill the vacuum by becoming a middle man in the wholesale industry. "I'll deal with the companies, and you deal with me," he told the union officials.

The threat Steinman used over the wholesalers was not primarily labor trouble, but supermarket trouble. Sure, he controlled the unions, but he also controlled the buyers. Recalled one wholesaler later, "I was already in the chains. Suddenly Moe comes around to me and tells me I have to pay one thousand to this guy, fifteen hundred to that guy, five hundred to that guy. . . ." The wholesalers didn't know with certainty where the money was going. But a huge pool of cash was being accumulated, and problems were being taken care of.

The arrangement depended on phony sales to wholesalers by Steinman's Trans-World brokerage firm. "Moe would bill me for merchandise I didn't get," one wholesaler explained. "I'd pay with a check. . . . I got 10 percent of the cash and Moe would distribute the rest in bribes." (The 10 percent may have been an added inducement to cooperate, or it may have been a way of making sure the wholesaler was taking money illegally and thus wouldn't talk.)

Other wholesalers have explained the same pattern; wiretaps placed later by Nicholson's men confirm it. Of course, Moe kept a goodly share of the bribe money for himself and his Mafia friends. With the help of

Steinman's supermarket network, the Mafia moved into waste hauling, soap distribution and even, of all things, the mass-produced bagel industry. First on the scene, as always, was Johnny Dio.

John Dioguardi was born in New York City on April 28, 1914. He grew up on Forsyth Street in Manhattan's Little Italy. His father, Dominick, owned a bicycle shop. But young John apparently became closer to his uncle and neighbor on Forsyth Street, James "Jimmy Doyle" Plumeri, a prize fighter, racketeer and Mafia member. By the time Dioguardi graduated grade school in 1929, he had learned to terrorize pushcart owners by dumping their wares until they paid him.

In 1930, he got a lesson in justice. One Giovanni Dioguardi, thirty-five, presumably a relative, who lived a few doors down on Forsyth Street, was shot six times and killed on a street in Coney Island. He and the man police arrested for shooting him had recently been acquitted of murdering a widow to steal her jewelry. Now, police said, they were feuding over how to divide up the jewelry. It had been Giovanni Dioguardi's second murder acquittal. The only punishment he ever received was from his fellow criminals.

After a year and a half at Stuyvesant High School, Johnny Dio got work in the garment center through his uncle, Plumeri, assisting the vast shakedown racket headed by Lepke Buchalter and Gurrah Shapiro. Dio and Plumeri ran a trucking association, and garment manufacturers were well advised to hire only truckers who paid dues to it.

In 1932, Plumeri and another mobster were wounded in a shoot-out, which brought a police investigation of the association. Dio and Plumeri were indicted for coercion, but were acquitted. The next year they were indicted again, for extortion, and again were acquitted. The state was having trouble getting victims to talk. Finally, in 1937, Dioguardi got a three-to-five-year stretch at Sing-Sing after being convicted with Plumeri and several other mobsters of extortion and atrocious assault.

Evidence was that they had been getting $500 from every truckman in the garment district, plus a tariff on every suit and coat made in New York. From the *New York Daily Mirror*: "At the trial, frightened witnesses testified how recalcitrant employers and employees were beaten when they refused to pay. . . . One man said he was confined to bed for two weeks after an assault. Another said the hoodlums had threatened to cut off his ears." Midway through the trial, Dio and Plumeri stopped the flow of revelations by pleading guilty.

In 1944, Dio was indicted for operating an illegal still, but the charge was dismissed.

In 1954 he was indicted and convicted for failure to pay state income tax in connection with his continued shakedown receipts in the garment center. The judge gave him sixty days.

It was about at this time that Dio became close to Jimmy Hoffa, as Hoffa sought New York support for his takeover of the Teamsters. Newspaper columnist Victor Riesel began writing about their activities, until, on April 5, 1956, he was permanently blinded in an acid attack outside Lindy's restaurant. Dio was accused of ordering the blinding, but was never convicted of it, although of the five men who took part in the attack, four were convicted and the fifth was murdered by his accomplices a few weeks after the attack. Those convicted served long prison terms, including years of additional time for refusing to testify against Dio (except for one man who did testify as to all he knew).[3]

In November, 1957, Dio went on trial with some Teamster officials for shaking down the owners of various stationery stores. The store owners had been picketed and told that if they wanted to break the

3 The Riesel attack was one of only two carried out over the years against newsmen, the other being the 1976 murder of Don Bolles, a reporter for the *Arizona Republic* in Phoenix. In both cases the attacks backfired badly. Stiff justice was meted out not only to the actual attackers, but to persons at least as high as the middle level of the conspiracies. Perhaps more telling, though, the attacks brought a swift and heavy increase in the very scrutiny and publicity they were designed to squelch, and resulted in far more damage to the Syndicate's activities than Riesel or Bolles could possibly have caused had the attacks not occurred. Despite all the other crimes he's been convicted of, Dio is still best known as "the man who blinded Victor Riesel," and that reputation more than anything else assured that the police, the FBI, and the press would never leave his heels, and that he would spend most of the rest of his prime years in prison for other crimes.

picket they would have to sign their employees up with Teamster Local 295, and hire John Dioguardi's "labor consulting" firm, Equitable Research Associates, for a $3,500 retainer and $200 a month. After a four-week trial, Dio was convicted and sentenced to two years in jail.

In 1958, while in prison for the stationery store shakedown, he went on trial again on similar charges involving shakedowns of the owners of electroplating shops. This time Dio was sentenced to fifteen to thirty years. But one year later, an appeals court overturned the first conviction, and, implicitly, the second, on the ground that Dioguardi never personally issued any threats. In a decision that seemed to legitimate the whole purpose of the Mafia, a divided court ruled that "Extortion cannot be committed by one who does not himself induce fear . . . but who . . . receives money for [the] purpose of removing or allaying . . . pre-existing fear instilled by others." Johnny Dio walked out of jail a free man on June 24, 1959.

In less than a year, the federal government yanked him back to court on charges that he failed to report taxable income from three dress manufacturing companies (all of them non-union) and two labor union locals. By the end of 1960 he was in the slammer again, this time the federal penitentiary in Atlanta, supposedly for four years. But two years later, in March, 1963, he was free again on parole, and in October of the same year he was discharged completely.

That was bad news for kosher meat lovers. Dio's parole had been granted on the contention that he had a good job in legitimate industry—as a salesman for Consumers Kosher Provision Company in Brooklyn. Of course, no industry remains legitimate for very long with people like Johnny Dio involved in it. What had happened was that Dio and several fellow mobsters had managed to convince two rival kosher meat manufacturers that each needed its own group of mobsters to compete effectively with the other's group of mobsters. It was a trick that had worked decades earlier in the garment district. On Fourteenth Street, which supplies kosher meat coast to coast, it worked so well that the *Daily News* took to calling Dio and his colleagues the "Kosher Nostra." They are among the biggest kosher meat suppliers in the country to this day.

Herman Rose, the owner of Consumers Kosher Provision, had let someone in the Dio organization know that he was desperate over the inroads recently made by his chief competitor, American Kosher Provisions Inc. Consumers had been losing many orders to American, which had clearly become lead brand in the supermarkets. It wasn't hard to figure out why. The year before, American had signed up two free-agent sluggers of real all-star class for its sales force: Max Block, who had just been forced to resign as head of the butchers' union but who still exercised effective control over it, and Lorenzo "Chappy" Brescia, the Genovese family Mafioso who had long been close to the union. Who would say "no" to them?

Block received $50,000 a year and a substantial chunk of American Kosher stock. Brescia got $25,000 a year. A good indication of their influence is the fact that their supposed "boss," the sales manager, was getting only $15,000 a year, and later testified that he never saw Block or Brescia except once when the president of the company introduced him to them at a dinner table at the Black Angus.

Dio's son, Dominick Dioguardi, then about twenty-one, and James Plumeri's son Thomas, thirty-two, convinced Herman Rose that in order to compete against the likes of Block and Brescia, Consumers would have to hire Johnny Dio himself—which Rose agreed to do in 1963 for $250 a week. This served, first, to get Dio his parole (the honest job) and, second, to give the Mafia power over not one but two kosher meat companies. As usually happens in such cases, Consumers only fell deeper into debt as the mobsters tried to milk it in every way they could.

It's unlikely the mobsters ever contemplated the kind of competition Rose thought he was buying. Block, Brescia, Dio, and Moe Steinman—whose hands were directly on the strings of the supermarket buyers—had all been buddies for many years and continued to be buddies.

Herman Rose died in July, 1964. The Kleinberg family, which owned American Kosher Provisions, had already been shoved aside. In August, 1964, Dio announced that Consumers and American were going to merge. This allowed for a transfer of assets—namely meat—back and forth. Pretty soon, other firms were created or taken over—First National

Kosher Provisions, Mizrach Kosher Provisions, Tel Aviv Kosher Provisions, Finest Provisions Company. Meat again was transferred back and forth. Supermarket chains went from one to the next as lead supplier. In instance after instance, a kosher firm's debts for meat purchased would climb, and then the income of the debtor company would be cut off by a switch in supermarket loyalties before bills could be paid. The suppliers—western cattle firms and unlucky local wholesalers—took a bath.

In January, 1965, Consumers' suppliers threw the company into involuntary bankruptcy proceedings. The very next month, Consumers was declared formally bankrupt, with tremendous losses. Within a year, American was in bankruptcy proceedings. A few months later, First National's remaining assets were sold at auction to satisfy judgments.

Mizrach became the lead Dio brand. Its trade name was taken from a company that had been producing kosher salami, frankfurters, and baloney for forty years. When the original Mizrach went into reorganization under the bankruptcy law, it became an easy target for a Dio takeover. Milton Sahn, an attorney representing Mizrach's creditors, quickly accepted an offer from Dio whereby young Plumeri would sign on customers for Mizrach in exchange for 5 percent of the gross. Plumeri brought in more than $50,000 a week in new orders. One creditor, at a meeting in March, 1966, objected, "Why do we have to deal with Dio?" According to *New York Post* reporter Marvin Smilon, someone answered him, "Shut up and sit down. You ask too many questions." (Sahn, the attorney who effectively approved Dio's takeover of Mizrach, now represents the wholesale meat industry trade association in New York, and repeatedly put obstacles in the way of this author's efforts to get information from meat dealers. Sahn's co-counsel for the Mizrach creditors, Fred I. Zabriskie, later represented the Castellanos' meat interests.)

While the lawyers marched in and out of bankruptcy court, Dio, with the help of his man Steinman, maintained control of the industry. They had a solid one-two punch, the unions and the supermarkets. Dio took time to develop a close personal relationship with Chaim Horowitz, generally known as Chaim Yiddle (pronounced "Yoodle"). Horowitz was the longtime head of the Kasruth Supervisors Union, an affiliate of the

Amalgamated Meat Cutters, until his death in 1976. The say-so of the rabbis in Horowitz's union is what transforms meat into kosher meat. Though they never found evidence that Horowitz or his men actually took money from Dio, the detectives saw the mobster and the rabbi together often.

Meanwhile, the supermarket chains switched suppliers in perfect step to Dio's needs. An official of American Kosher Provisions later testified that one day, buyers from "many" supermarket chains simply declared that American Kosher was out. American Kosher's managers "were never told who was to replace them or anything of that nature," the official said.

As in other cases, the Hills chain tried briefly to buck the trend. Hills had switched from American to Mizrach with the others. But in 1966, after American had gone through bankruptcy proceedings, the Kleinberg family (its owners) tried to resurrect the company independent of the Mob. They persuaded Hills to switch its business back to American. Moe Steinman immediately announced to George Gamaldi, Hills' meat buyer, that Gamaldi had made a big mistake. Gamaldi found out just how big the mistake was when the butchers' union struck his supermarket chain. Herbie Newman, Steinman's brokerage partner, quickly called Gamaldi and announced that Moe could help straighten out the labor situation. Gamaldi apparently got the message.

Aaron Freedman of Waldbaum's testified that he had switched to Mizrach because of complaints from shoppers about American Kosher's products; he also testified that he had no idea his friend Johnny Dio was behind the Mizrach and Tel Aviv brands he switched to.

Complaints from shoppers may well have occurred. When a Dio brand was getting ready to go off the shelf, its final orders were filled with the cheapest product around—usually spoiled meat. The supermarkets had to sell the product, because Dio's companies expressly forbade returns. One route salesman for Consumers and later American testified that he suddenly started getting merchandise that was "light in color, sometimes green and at all times sweaty." He added that it was "so patently inferior to anything we have had that this is an atrocity to perpetuate on our customers. There is no question in my mind that this is the worst merchandise I have ever seen."

Penny Lernoux

When Penny Lernoux (1940–1989) moved to Bogotá as a wire-service reporter in 1962, most of Latin America was barely on the radar of U.S. media: only the occasional coup, or the stoning of Vice President Nixon's Caracas motorcade, made it to American front pages. Over the next twenty-five years, Lernoux—writing for the National Catholic Reporter *and* The Nation, *among other magazines—took as her beat the undocumented suffering of the region's poor, and how that poverty was perpetuated by oligarchies and corporations in league with religious leadership. "It was not a voice North Americans were accustomed to hearing," wrote British journalist Peter Hebbelthwaite in her obituary. "She wrote from the shantytowns, not air-conditioned hotel rooms."*

Beginning in 1968, Lernoux reported on the emergence of Liberation Theology—a new Latin American Catholicism that attempted to reverse the church's historic alliance with the region's rulers, which Lernoux correctly identified as "the most significant political development in the region in recent decades." Her book Cry of the People *(1980), from which this excerpt is taken, combines evocative reportage with detailed investigation of the church hierarchy's collaboration with dictators, paramilitary terror squads, and the CIA, and remains the greatest piece of English-language journalism on Latin American politics of that era. In her second book,* In Banks We Trust, *Lernoux exposed links between U.S. banks, the Mafia, and the CIA. She died of cancer at a Maryknoll retreat house in New York at age forty-nine.*

VILLAINS AFOOT

From *Cry of the People,* 1980

The CIA goes to church but not to pray.

Popular saying

Adolfo Centeno Alancastro was suitably sympathetic. It really was a shame, he told the Uruguayan Jesuit, how brutish Uruguayan police agents were, but what could you do with people who thought that

Medellín[1] was the name of a person and confused pictures of Christ with Che Guevara.

The police had just ransacked the priest's house in Montevideo, carrying off his entire library to burn, including a rare collection of theological treatises, and here was their boss commiserating with him over the loss of his life's work! According to Centeno, such incidents would never happen if Church officials would only cooperate with educated policemen like himself.

Whatever his claims, Centeno had bona fide credentials, for like his counterparts in Brazil and Chile he could demonstrate an intimate knowledge of theology and Church politics, as well as an expertise in intelligence and "dirty tricks," courtesy of the CIA. After years of using and abusing local and foreign groups in Latin America, the CIA now appears to be seeking a lower profile in this area, partly because of the ruckus caused by indignant Catholic and Protestant organizations in the United States following revelations in 1975 of CIA penetration of missionary groups. More to the point, the Latin-American security agencies can now do the job themselves. Centeno, for example, was trained in the Panama Canal Zone; his boss at the Uruguayan Interior Ministry, Luis Vargas Garmendia, worked with former CIA agent Philip Agee in the 1960s. The pair spent time making life difficult for diplomats from the socialist countries accredited to Uruguay back in the days when Uruguay was still a democracy. Vargas Garmendia was generally thought to have planned the murder of two former Uruguayan senators in Buenos Aires in 1976. He was later made secretary to President Aparicio Méndez, front man for Uruguay's repressive military regime.

Because of his background in Church affairs, acquired during a stint in Central America, Centeno was chosen to monitor and persecute Uruguay's critical Catholic Church. Also useful were his credentials as a militant in Catholic Action, a laymen's movement that was influential in

1 The historic conference of Latin-American bishops held in the Colombian City of Medellín in 1968 that set the hemisphere's Church on a new course for social justice.

Latin America during the 1960s. Centeno professed not to understand why Uruguayan priests were "strangely" reluctant to answer questions, whereas his experience with Catholics in Central America had been "just the opposite." But in view of the regime's arrest and/or expulsion of fifteen religious between 1972 and 1976, the closure of five Church publications, and a smear campaign against Montevideo's Archbishop Carlos Parteli, labeled a communist because he defended human rights, such reticence was well founded. Though an "educated" policeman, Centeno specialized in the "black propaganda" half-truths or outright lies practiced by the CIA in its work with Church groups in Ecuador, Brazil, and Chile during the sixties and early seventies. When such important Montevideo bookstores as Ramos y Mosca refused to stock *The Church of Silence,* a slanderous attack on Chile's bishops by a right-wing Catholic group known as Tradition, Family, and Property (TFP), Centeno threatened the owners. The Uruguayan branch of TFP later came out with its version of the Chilean smear in a dreary tract titled *Leftism in the Church: Communist Fellow Travelers in the Long Adventure of Failures and Changes,* a 384-page denunciation of Uruguay's clergy for "completely abandoning their duty and aiding the enemy of religion and country." (The enemy included such strange bedfellows as the U.S. Democratic Party and the Soviet Union.) Heavily advertised in the government press, *Leftism in the Church* was eulogized as "among the best-selling books in Montevideo," another undocumented exaggeration, according to the bookstore owners.

Men like Centeno owe their skills in part to AID's police training programs, but they also adhere to a long tradition of Church spying that dates to the CIA's forerunner, the Office of Strategic Services (OSS), formed during World War II. Later, during the cold war, U.S. missionaries routinely collaborated with the CIA and, on their return to the United States, visited the State Department to be debriefed. In those days there was nothing conspiratorial about this relationship, nor any suggestion of moral conflict: most missionaries shared the concerns of their government, particularly about the spread of communism. A number of Foreign Service personnel came from missionary backgrounds, and it was not uncommon for missionaries to take sides in military/ideological confrontations, the classic example being John Birch. A Baptist missionary who worked with the OSS in World War II and was later killed by a Chinese communist while leading a patrol of Chinese nationalists, Birch was canonized by Robert Welch and the radical Right as the "first martyr" of the cold war.

Because of their personal relationships with the people they serve and the status of their profession, the forty-five thousand U.S. Catholic and Protestant missionaries stationed abroad were and are an obvious source of intelligence, in some areas perhaps the only source. This was particularly true in Latin America, where twelve thousand U.S. missionaries work and where most of the cases of CIA collaboration have been documented. During the 1960s when the Alliance for Progress was in vogue, nobody questioned this relationship, since Church groups and the U.S. Government were agreed on the twin priorities of economic development and anti-communism. "Part of the problem stems from the fact that the great Latin crusade by the churches in the 1950s and 1960s merged, at times almost totally, with the thrust of the Alliance for Progress and its Truman-Eisenhower predecessors," said Thomas Quigley, assistant director of the Division for Latin America of the U.S. Catholic Conference. "The stated goals were to promote development and contain communism, and few then realized the ambiguities contained in that statement. Only later was it learned that development, as practiced, benefited the rich at the expense of the poor, and that containment of communism was often simplistically equated with protecting an unjust and un-Christian status quo. Now we see those aspects. But at that time, the average missionary—perhaps especially the socially progressive ones—sensed a greater affinity with certain people from the local United States embassy or consulate than with fellow missionaries from another country or even congregation. The prime targets for CIA contact were precisely such pragmatic liberals sent in large numbers during the period to Latin America from the United States churches—the 'concerned' missionaries from the mainline Protestant Churches and from Catholic societies like Maryknoll and the Jesuits."

Typical of this sort of collaboration was the Protestant missionary in Bolivia who regularly met with a CIA agent to pass on "all sorts of information about unions and farmers' cooperatives" according to a highly placed minister in the same denomination. "Now," said the minister, "if a missionary had a similar connection, I would call him in and fire him." U.S. missionaries today wonder how they could have been so easily deceived. Looking back, one priest who had worked in Bolivia at the time when United States Special Forces were combing the jungles for Che Guevara and his guerrillas, explained: "The maneuver was to butter one up as to one's knowledge of the terrain and the people, a kind of anthropological recognition of one's merits as a person who knew the area. At that time, most missionaries were very naive and it usually worked. I don't know what good I was but I talked a lot over beers, feeling flattered by the attention. Later I realized who my drinking companions were."

Darryl Hunt, a Maryknoll missionary who headed the Lima-based *Latinamerica Press* news service covering hemispheric Church affairs, recalled that CIA visits to Maryknoll headquarters in New York were routine up to a decade ago, when the order's superiors were alerted to the agency's intentions. "They tried to get information from the missionaries in the field by developing friendships with them and appearing to ask disinterested questions without identifying themselves as CIA," he added. "U.S. Embassy officials in Lima asked me questions about progressive priests' movements in Peru that later seemed highly suspect."

Jim O'Brien, a former priest who worked in Guatemala in the late 1960s, described how CIA agent Sean Holly used his background as a Maryknoll seminarian to develop contacts with U.S. missionaries Officially listed as the labor attaché, Holly was later kidnapped by a Guatemalan guerrilla group and freed in exchange for four political prisoners held by the Guatemalan Government. Holly's job, said O'Brien, was to keep tabs on U.S. missionaries, particularly Maryknoll priests and nuns.

According to John D. Marks, a former State Department intelligence analyst and co-author of the controversial *The CIA and the Cult of Intelligence,* 30 to 40 percent of the churchmen he interviewed, during an investigation of the subject, knew of a CIA–Church connection. Marks also reported a retired CIA agent as stating: "Hell, I'd use anybody if it was to the furtherance of an objective. I've used Buddhist monks, Catholic priests, and even a Catholic bishop."

It is precisely this amoral—some would say immoral—attitude that altered the thinking of many missionaries: that and political conditions in the countries where they worked. In the days before Vietnam and Watergate, few missionaries questioned U.S. support of right-wing dictatorships because those governments claimed to be anti-communist. But as the United States expanded its role as world policeman, its police methods becoming ever more dubious, the missionary was forced to face the conflict posed by his dual role as American citizen and bearer of Christ's universal Good News. Indigenous Christians were suffering imprisonment, torture, and death, as well as hunger and social discrimination, at the hands of repressive governments; and yet these governments were receiving U.S. economic and military aid, and in some instances had been brought to power by the United States. For the missionaries working and living with these people, this was not a remote issue of foreign relations but a question of neighbors and friends. As one Protestant writer put it, "Most missionaries loved the countries and the people where they worked far too much to knowingly damage them." Thus, when these missionaries realized that they had been used as tools by their own government to harm the interests of the people they had thought to serve, they were shocked and angry. The crux of the matter was the blatant violation of freedom of worship, one of the fundamental guarantees in the United States Constitution, by an agency funded by American taxpayers, and all on behalf of right-wing political interests. According to U.S. Senate investigations, the CIA attempted to play God in Latin America, deciding who should be President, who should be eliminated, how the people should live, and whom they should have as allies and enemies. Foreign missionaries and local religious groups were among the many means used to achieve these ends, but because of what they believed and taught, their manipulation must be viewed as an act of calculated cynicism.

CIA Director William Colby's assertion that CIA use of clergy and churches was "no reflection upon their integrity or mission" was absurd: there is conclusive proof that the CIA used religious groups in Latin

America for its own secret ends. At the same time it contributed to the persecution and division of Latin America's Catholic Church by supporting right-wing Catholic groups and financed and trained police agencies responsible for the imprisonment, torture, and murder of priests, nuns, and bishops, some of them U.S. citizens. That is why missionary groups in the United States have changed from complacent collaborators to harsh critics of the CIA—they have seen the results of the agency's intervention with their own eyes.

ALLAN NAIRN

In 1995, Allan Nairn talked with students at Yale University about the craft of human-rights reporting under dangerous conditions—how to find a stash for your notes, how to talk coolly with perpetrators of atrocity, how to combine on-the-scene reports with precise documentation from government sources.

While still an undergraduate at Princeton in the late 1970s, Nairn (1958–) went to work for Ralph Nader's Public Citizen, researching the Educational Testing Service. In the early 1980s he found himself reporting as a freelancer in Guatemala during a period of widespread political assassination by government-backed paramilitaries. There he learned an important early lesson, which has shaped his career: that a U.S. passport allowed him to name names and tell stories that would cost the lives of local journalists. In Guatemala, El Salvador, and Haiti he documented the chain of accountibility for massacres by U.S.-backed militias. An ability to make sources out of perpetrators as well as victims is one of the hallmarks of Nairn's reporting; he has won the confidence of CIA "assets" in Haiti and written chilling profiles of torturers in Central America.

In 1991, Nairn and radio journalist Amy Goodman smuggled themselves into East Timor, then under brutal Indonesian military occupation, and witnessed a massacre of protestors in Dili by Indonesian troops. Nairn devoted much of the late 1990s to chronicling East Timor's battle for independence and documenting successive U.S. administrations' efforts to prop up Indonesia's rule, returning secretly in 1999 despite being on an Indonesian blacklist.

Nairn is one of a generation of young U.S. journalists whose formative experiences came in Latin America in the 1970s and 1980s, who turned investigative reporting to establishing chains of responsibility for atrocities by regimes created or propped up by the United States during the cold war. To those Yale students, Nairn insisted that his insistent focus on human rights is just a normal impulse of solidarity too often suppressed. "If someone were attacking your mother, you would defend her. If someone is being tortured, you defend them. It comes from the same place."

BEHIND THE DEATH SQUADS

From *The Progressive*, May, 1984

Early in the 1960s, during the Kennedy Administration, agents of the U.S. Government in El Salvador set up two official security organizations that killed thousands of peasants and suspected leftists over the next fifteen years. These organizations, guided by American operatives, developed into the paramilitary apparatus that came to be known as the Salvadoran Death Squads.

Today, even as the Reagan Administration publicly condemns the Death Squads, the CIA—in violation of U.S. law—continues to provide training, support, and intelligence to security forces directly involved in Death Squad activity.

Interviews with dozens of current and former Salvadoran officers, civilians, and official American sources disclose a pattern of sustained U.S. participation in building and managing the Salvadoran security apparatus that relies on Death Squad assassinations as its principal means of enforcement.

Evidence of U.S. involvement covers a broad spectrum of activity. Over the past twenty years, officials of the State Department, the Central Intelligence Agency, and the U.S. armed forces have:

- conceived and organized ORDEN, the rural paramilitary and intelligence network described by Amnesty International as a movement designed "to use clandestine terror against government opponents." Out of ORDEN grew the notorious *Mano Blanco,* the White Hand, which a former U.S. ambassador to El Salvador, Raul H. Castro, has called "nothing less than the birth of the Death Squads";

- conceived and organized ANSESAL, the elite presidential intelligence service that gathered files on Salvadoran dissidents and, in the words of one U.S. official, relied on Death Squads as "the operative arm of intelligence gathering";
- enlisted General Jose Alberto "Chele" Medrano, the founder of ORDEN and ANSESAL, as a CIA agent;
- trained leaders of ORDEN in surveillance techniques and use of automatic weapons, and carried some of these leaders on the CIA payroll;
- provided American technical and intelligence advisors who often worked directly with ANSESAL at its headquarters in the *Casa Presidencial*;
- supplied ANSESAL, the security forces, and the general staff with electronic, photographic, and personal surveillance of individuals who were later assassinated by Death Squads. According to Colonel Nicolas Carranza, director of the Salvadoran Treasury Police, such intelligence sharing by U.S. agencies continues to this day;
- kept key security officials—including Carranza, Medrano, and others—on the CIA payroll. Though the evidence is less conclusive about Major Roberto D'Aubuisson, presidential candidate of the right-wing ARENA party, some of his close associates describe him as a former recipient of CIA funding;
- furnished intelligence files that D'Aubuisson used for a series of 1980 television broadcasts in which he denounced dozens of academics, trade unionists, peasant leaders, Christian Democrats, and members of the clergy as communists or guerrilla collaborators. Many of the individuals D'Aubuisson named in his television speeches were subsequently assassinated. The broadcasts

launched D'Aubuisson's political career and marked the emergence of the paramilitary front which later became ARENA;

- instructed Salvadoran intelligence operatives in the use of investigative techniques, combat weapons, explosives, and interrogation methods that included, according to a former Treasury Police agent, "instruction in methods of physical and psychological torture,"
- and, in the last decade, violated the Foreign Assistance Act of 1974, which prohibits spending U.S. funds "to provide training or advice or provide any financial support for police, prisons, or other law enforcement forces for any foreign government or any program of internal intelligence or surveillance on behalf of any foreign government."

Up to the early 1960s, El Salvador's security forces had been little more than loosely coordinated barracks units in the service of local landowners and political *caudillos.* "They had very, very limited political orientation, if any," says Robert Eugene Whedbee, who served as CIA station chief in El Salvador from 1962 to 1964. That began to change with the Kennedy Administration's Alliance for Progress, founded on the assumption that national security systems working side by side with capitalist development would preempt communist revolution in Latin America.

In El Salvador, the U.S. State Department, the CIA, the Green Berets, and the Agency for International Development (AID) all participated in the effort to suppress dissent.

The United States was "developing within the civil security forces . . . an investigative capability for detecting criminal and/or subversive individuals and organizations and neutralizing their activities," wrote Byron Eagle, director of the AID Public Safety Program, in a 1967 memo to his staff. "This requires a carefully integrated effort between the investigative element and the regular police, paramilitary or military force, operating separately or in conjunction with each other." Engle, himself a former CIA official, referred to thirty-three countries, including El Salvador, in which the Public Safety Program was operating.

The landmark event in the formation of the national security apparatus in El Salvador and the rest of Central America was the Declaration of San Jose, issued on March 19, 1963, at the conclusion of a meeting of six Central American presidents. "Communism is the chief obstacle to economic development in the Central American region," proclaimed President Kennedy, who had chaired the meeting.

The Declaration of San Jose triggered a series of follow-up meetings among Central American ministers of the interior, who held jurisdiction over police and internal security. These meetings—organized and run by the U.S. State Department with assistance from the CIA, AID, the Customs Bureau, the Immigration Service, and the Justice Department—"were designed to develop ways of dealing with subversion," recalls William Bowdler, who represented the State Department at the sessions.

For El Salvador, Washington assigned a central role to General Medrano, then a senior officer of the National Guard and the army general staff.

Medrano is something of a legend in Salvadoran politics. Rank-and-file National Guardsmen still revere him as a fearsome *jefe* and the hero of the 1969 war with Honduras. To his supporters, he is "the founder of Salvadoran nationalism." But to Christian Democrat Jose Napoleon Duarte, Medrano is something else— "the father of the Death Squads, the chief assassin of them all."

Medrano, now retired, prides himself on moving about El Salvador unaccompanied by bodyguards. He drives through the countryside armed only with a .45-caliber pistol and a glove compartment stocked with hand grenades. In a recent series of interviews spanning some twelve hours, he spoke freely about the origins and growth of the security system.

"ORDEN and ANSESAL—the Salvadoran National Security Agency—grew out of the State Department, the CIA, and the Green Berets during the time of Kennedy," Medrano told me. "We created these specialized agencies to fight the plans and actions of international communism."

The meetings of the interior ministers resulted in the formation of ANSESAL and parallel domestic security agencies in Guatemala, Nicaragua, Panama, Honduras, and Costa Rica. These forces "would meet every three months under the supervision of the State Department and exchange information and methods of operation," says Medrano. "They had direct radio teletypes from office to office."

According to a U.S. adviser who helped install the teletype system, known as the Central American Communications Network, it was part of a broader plan "to reorganize the intelligence effort and get Central Americans to work together against subversion. At the meetings, you'd say to them, 'Well, if I had this sort of equipment, I'd do this and this,'—sort of ease them along."

The State Department and AID's Public Safety office in El Salvador had administrative responsibility for establishing the ANSESAL network, Medrano says, but the substantive day-to-day intelligence work was coordinated by the CIA: "The CIA was already participating in connections with us. The CIA would work with us and give us reports."

"Medrano was the CIA's boy," says one current State Department official. Indeed, Medrano himself says he was on the CIA payroll, a fact confirmed by ORDEN colleagues. "He came to my house regularly. He was a close friend," recalls Raul Castro, U.S. ambassador to El Salvador from 1964 to 1968. "And he was a good friend of the United States."

Medrano flew frequently to Washington for consultations at CIA headquarters. In July 1968, he received a silver Presidential medal from Lyndon Johnson "in recognition of exceptionally meritorious service." Medrano refuses to discuss the particular service he performed, though he recalls Johnson's words as the President presented him with the medal: "'I know all about you, Medrano. You're doing good work. I know your pedigree'—like I was a bull!"

The U.S. Government also sent Medrano on a three-month tour of Vietnam, where he traveled with Army units, the Green Berets, and CIA operatives. As he recalls it, Medrano "studied every aspect of warfare from primitive jungle fighting to psychological civic action to strategic bombing."

Medrano gave Washington ample return on its investment. In El Salvador, he organized an intricate, many-tiered intelligence and paramilitary network that extended from the remotest mountain hamlets to the presidential palace. The rural component of this network was ORDEN (Spanish for "Order"), a group founded, in Medrano's words, to "indoctrinate the peasants regarding the advantages of the democratic system and the disadvantages of the communist system."

Green Beret Colonel Arthur Simons was instrumental in the development of ORDEN, says Medrano. In 1963, Simons, then commander of the 8th Special Forces Group in Panama, dispatched a team of counterinsurgency trainers to El Salvador. (According to his service record, Simons had recently completed a stint as commander of the White Star Mobile Training Team, a Green Beret unit that had been sent to Laos to work with indigenous troops. Previously, he had served as chief of staff at the Army Special Warfare Center in Fort Bragg, North Carolina, which was originally called the Psychological Warfare Canter and was later renamed the John F. Kennedy Center for Military Assistance.)

"Colonel Simons sent me ten men to begin training us," recalls Medrano. After "talking among ourselves and with Simons, the idea occurred to us to catechize the people. We talked about how we had to indoctrinate the people, because he who has the population wins the war.

"The army can easily annihilate guerrillas in the urban zone," says Medrano, "but peasants are tough. They are good in the mountains. They can walk at night, see in the dark, see among the trees. We couldn't let them be deceived by the guerrillas."

Medrano says the Green Berets helped him plan the structure and ideology of ORDEN, and then stayed on to train a team of Salvadoran soldiers—among them Colonel Carranza, who now heads the Treasury Police, and Colonel Domingo Monterrosa, currently chief of the Third Brigade and El Salvador's star combat commander. The soldiers went to the countryside to instruct civilian ORDEN leaders, who in turn established the organization's local chapters. At its peak, ORDEN membership reached an estimated 100,000. "It was almost like a religion," Medrano recalls.

ORDEN had the dual mission of teaching anticommunism and gathering information on individuals deemed suspicious. "You discover the communist by the way he talks," says Medrano. "Generally, he speaks against Yankee imperialism, he speaks against the oligarchy, he speaks against military men. We can spot them easily." Once identified, they would be reported to ORDEN's central office, where a staff of eighty would record the information and relay it to ANSESAL. There, "we would study it and pass it on to the president, who would take appropriate actions," says Medrano.

"In this revolutionary war, the enemy comes from our people," Medrano says. "They don't have the rights of Geneva. They are traitors to the country. What can the troops do? When they find them, they kill them."

Sometimes the killings were carried out by ORDEN itself, other times by the army, the National Guard, or the *Mano Blanco* Death Squad. Former Ambassador Castro says *Mano Blanco* "was an offshoot of ORDEN, and the same people in ORDEN were to some extent the same people in the *Mano Blanco.* Even today, some of the same people are in the Death Squads. That was the origin."

According to U.S. and Salvadoran officials, the close relationship between the security forces and the U.S. Government was sustained over the next twenty years.

Edgar Artiga, a civilian leader of ORDEN, says he and eighty other ORDEN officials participated in the two-month CIA course in 1969. The course, held at the headquarters of the Salvadoran National Guard, was taught jointly by General Medrano and three CIA instructors from the U.S. embassy, who brought along movies about life in the Soviet Union. The curriculum, says Artiga, included "anticommunism, democracy, detection and identification, and self-defense." Trainees were instructed in the use of 9-millimeter revolvers and such weapons as the M-16 rifle, which was not yet generally available. All the students were paid daily in cash, according to Artiga. A number of Artiga's classmates continued on CIA payroll after the course was completed, he says.

Training was also conducted in the United States. Among those who received such schooling was Carlos Sosa Santos, the leading explosives expert for the Salvadoran armed forces, who was instructed by the AID Public Safety Program. Sosa has trained dozens of army and security force members in "techniques for secretly placing bombs in houses, cars, and individuals' personal belongings," according to a National Police intelligence officer who studied under Sosa.

The U.S. contribution extends far beyond training. American intelligence services have actually furnished the names, photographs, and whereabouts of suspected dissidents, say Salvadoran security officials.

This March, during a tour of the political intelligence archives of the National Police Center for Analysis and Investigations, I spoke with Captain Rafael Lopez Davila, who displayed files on leftist political leaders. The dossiers included entries reporting on their travels to foreign cities, specifying what flights they took, whom they visited, and where they stayed. The CIA provided such information, Lopez says.

According to General Medrano, the CIA regularly kept ANSESAL posted on the activities of Salvadorans working or studying abroad. In important cases, the CIA supplied photographs and tapes of conversations.

A Salvadoran who served as an aide to a senior intelligence official in the 1970s says he was shown CIA photographic and electronic surveillance reports on many dissidents. "With this information, we knew exactly what we were doing, who was who," he says, adding that many of the subjects were later assassinated by Death Squads.

A former staff member of the *Casa Presidencial* reports that an American CIA officer told him the CIA and the Salvadoran security forces kept Rutilio Grande, a prominent Jesuit priest, under surveillance before his March 1977 assassination. The CIA agent claimed to have seen the dossier on Father Grande, which reportedly included photos and accounts of his visits to other Central American countries as well as his activities in his home parish of Aguilares. A former Treasury Police officer who goes by the name of Rene Hurtado says he was told by ANSESAL members that their agency was responsible for killing Grande.

When a reformist junta briefly came to power in El Salvador in 1979, it abolished ORDEN and ANSESAL and condemned the organizations for committing human rights abuses. Since then, the Salvadoran military have continued to maintain and expand their surveillance and record-keeping activities. And as in the 1960s and 1970s, when the U.S. agents and technicians invented and oiled the intelligence machine, U.S. personnel remain at the center of the system.

According to a Salvadoran colonel involved in the process, the United States routinely receives copies of all major political surveillance reports compiled by Salvadoran security officers. In turn, U.S. officials provide the security forces with information. Colonel Carranza confirmed this relationship.

"The Americans would directly receive all the information on a case even before we had developed the activity, before we had decided how we would terminate a case," Carranza says, referring to the procedure in effect before 1983. "Now we give everything—in relation to captures that the Treasury Police have made—to the general staff and *they* give it to the embassy."

U.S. intelligence officials "have collaborated with us in a certain technical manner, providing us with advice," says Carranza. "They receive information from everywhere in the world, and they have sophisticated equipment that enables them to have better information or at least confirm the information we have. It's very helpful." Carranza says he processes the information with "a small computer, and we also work with the general staff's computer for developing a workable inventory and index."

Colonel Adolfo Blandon, the armed forces chief of staff, says "six or seven" U.S. military advisers—several of them specialists in intelligence and psychological warfare—are currently working with the general staff.

The National Guard now concentrates on monitoring "unions and strikes and the penetration of the education system, where they are brainwashing our students," says Colonel Aristedes Napoleon Montes, director of the National Guard. Reynaldo Lopez Nuilla, director of the National Police, says he has an intelligence staff of 200, including a thirty-man "operations group." He, too, cites unions as an area of concentration, but also mentions the Salvadoran Human Rights Commission (the nongovernmental one, that is; the government maintains its own "human rights commission," of which Lopez Nuilla is a member). And the Catholic organization, Socorro Juridico (legal assistance), "we know to be organized precisely by the guerillas," says Lopez Nuilla. "It's evident in the things they say."

In the National Police political intelligence archive, originally organized by U.S. AID Public Safety advisers, Captain Rafael Lopez Davila, the investigations chief, showed me a special section on unions and their members. The three-story filing room also contained a "library of subversive literature," which, along with Karl Marx's *Das Kapital* and Lenin's collected works, held the publications of UCS, El Salvador's Catholic University.

According to the Salvadoran armed forces *Guide to Normal Operative Procedures,* a confidential policy manual, each army and security force outpost is required to maintain a "Special Archive of S-2 Intelligence." The file covers "the disposition of the subversive delinquents (their location . . . styles of action and mobilization)," lists "militants and sympathizers," and carries a miscellaneous "register of personalities of the enemy."

Names enter the archive through surveillance reports from officers and informants or through reports from troops who have detained an individual for questioning. To qualify for a place in the files, an individual may commit such diverse offenses as "carrying or moving subversive propaganda of whatever type . . . insulting authority . . . carrying notebooks, papers, or symbols related to subversive organizations, [or] traveling in cars destined for points of concentration of the subversive delinquents—unauthorized demonstrations and rallies, etc., especially if the attitude is suspicious."

Surveillance reports compiled by local intelligence units are retained for their own files while a copy is forwarded to the central archives of the service involved. Individual subjects are interrogated, says Colonel Montes, first at the local post and then, if the case warrants it, at the intelligence section of the security force. "All of this information is then turned over to the general staff, with whom we retain a very close coordination," Montes says.

This intelligence system serves as the nerve center of Death Squad operations. "We worked with written orders," recalls one former National Guardsman, a fifteen-year veteran who says he went on Death Squad missions while stationed in the province of La Libertad. "We got names and addresses and were told to pick them up, get information, and kill them later." In important cases, he adds, special troops or security force agents would come from San Salvador with the lists.

"Every garrison of any size had Death Squads. It's that simple," says a U.S. official in San Salvador who studied the Death Squads last year. "All this comes out of a military intelligence function."

When the Reagan Administration launched a publicity campaign against the Death Squads last December, it pointed a finger at individual officers, leaking their names to the press and demanding their removal. Three of those officers were the directors of the intelligence departments of the Treasury Police, the National Guard, and the National Police.

Asked why the Administration chose to blame those specific individuals while leaving the institutions untouched, the U.S. official in San Salvador responded: "Things generated in Washington create certain necessities that don't necessarily reflect the true problems here, but are done for political purposes up there, and this is a good example." The official, heavily involved in the publicity campaign, considered it a success.

"These men were done an injustice," says Colonel Blandon, the chief of staff. "We kept asking the embassy for proof against them but they never gave it. The Americans sacrificed them to avoid their own problems."

The use of the term "Death Squad" has, in some respects, fostered a profound misunderstanding of El Salvador's official terror apparatus.

It conjures up images of discrete bands of gangsters randomly cruising the countryside in search of opportunities to kill. In fact, the term more meaningfully applies to a system that can dispatch a soldier at any time to kill a selected victim.

Another misunderstanding about the Death Squads arises from the fact that they came to public notice in the United States in connection with the spectacular emergence of Roberto D'Aubuisson as a powerful political figure. U.S. officials who want to shield the Salvadoran government from culpability in the Death Squads, as well as some liberals who want to undermine D'Aubuisson's electoral prospects, have promoted the mistaken notion that the Death Squad phenomenon—this sprawling institution with a twenty-year history and tens of thousands of victims—is the political instrument of one diabolical man.

In March, Roberto Eulalio Santivanez, a former colonel who had been paid $50,000 by critics of U.S. policy in El Salvador, began circulating to the mass media a detailed account of Death Squad operations. Speaking as an unnamed source from "the highest level of the security police," Santivanez told the *New York Times* that D'Aubuisson was "the man who organized and continues to direct the death squads."

Santivanez charged that former Defense Minister General Jose Guillermo Garcia and Colonel Carranza, director of the Treasury Police, helped organize and operate D'Aubuisson's Death Squad network. In a *CBS News* interview with Walter Cronkite, Santivanez said Carranza had been on the CIA payroll. The *New York Times* confirmed the CIA connection, citing U.S. intelligence sources. They reported that Carranza had received $90,000 per year for the past five or six years. (Two colleagues of Carranza had said he was a CIA agent weeks before Santivanez did.)

According to Santivanez's version as reported in the *Times,* the Death Squads did not exist before D'Aubuisson rose to prominence in the wake of the 1979 reformist coup. Because of a commitment to protect Santivanez's anonymity, the story identified him as a source with "personal knowledge of these crimes because his government post had put him in direct contact with top military leaders." In fact, Santivanez was the director of ANSESAL and D'Aubuisson's immediate superior from 1977 to 1979, a period of mounting government repression that culminated in the fall of the Carlos Humberto Romero government and the abolition of ANSESAL for its role in the Death Squad killings.

Santivanez was "Romero's black man," says the U.S. embassy official who studied the Death Squads. "He kept the files and took care of people when there was dirty work to be done. His hands are as bloody as anybody's." The official nonetheless confirms that Santivanez's account of involvement in the Death Squads by Carranza and the high command was "substantially correct," though he says it exaggerated D'Aubuisson's personal role.

The story of the relationship between the U.S. Government and the D'Aubuisson branch of the contemporary Death Squads is complex, paradoxical, and far from complete.

D'Aubuisson, a Medrano protégé whom the General remembers as "a fine officer who was loved by the people," made his mark in the ORDEN-ANSESAL network, organizing ORDEN chapters as a National Guard officer and rising to second in command of ANSESAL under Santivanez.

"Roberto was an officer of ANSESAL, which is affiliated with the CIA," says Major Oscar Serrato, one of a small group of Salvadorans who began secretly collaborating with D'Aubuisson soon after the reformist junta came to power in October 1979. Two years later, Serrato helped found ARENA, the rightist political party D'Aubuisson heads. "He worked with the CIA for years, and that's how he was able to learn all the machinations, the people, national as well as international, that were working to establish the communist scheme."

Two of D'Aubuisson's former associates from the National Guard and ANSESAL claim he received U.S. Government money, one saying it came from the CIA, the other from either the CIA or the Defense Intelligence Agency. State Department officials in El Salvador during the 1970s say that although D'Aubuisson had a "disturbingly close relationship" with one U.S. military attaché (who could not be reached for comment), they did not know whether he had received payments.

When D'Aubuisson officially left the army after the 1979 coup, he launched his political movement with a series of television speeches. He assailed the junta for abolishing ORDEN—"born in the bosom of the armed forces," D'Aubuisson declared. "ORDEN has ceased to function with that name," he said, "but its principles live and are newly serving the fatherland with the *Frente Democratica Nacionalista* [Democratic Nationalist Front, D'Aubuisson's new political organization]."

D'Aubuisson openly defended the security forces for their role in the spate of disappearances and assassinations in late 1979 and early 1980. "In no moment should you feel culpable for fighting these terrorists," he said. "If our commanders have captured people like this, they are committing no fault." And he quoted from Napoleon: "Nothing done to defend your country is against the law."

Having established the principle, D'Aubuisson got down to specifics, marshaling charts, photos, videotapes, and computer graphics for an intricately detailed, name-by-name, face-by-face tirade against "El Salvador's terrorist conspiracy."

D'Aubuisson denounced union leaders, priests, academics, peasant organizers, students, professionals, government officials, and Christian Democrats. Among those he named was Archbishop Oscar Romero, whom he told, "You still have time to change your ways." He also attacked Mario Zamora, a leading Christian Democrat and member of the government, who—like others identified in the broadcasts—was assassinated in a matter of weeks.

"Unfortunately, when we mentioned a person, *poom,* they'd shoot them," says Alberto Bondanza, a D'Aubuisson intimate and one of the founders of ARENA. "Then they started linking us with the Death Squads. If by chance the army arrived and happened to shoot one of these people in a battle, then everybody threw the blame on us."

"D'Aubuisson was pointing out the communists so the troops could kill them," Medrano says. "He had good information. He was speaking the truth."

"He had everything—photos and complete personal histories—direct from ANSESAL files," says Major Serrato, who participated in the planning meetings out of which the broadcasts grew. He said D'Aubuisson made copies of the ANSESAL material shortly before the agency was dissolved and its archives transferred to the general staff. "The proofs he presented were concrete and irrefutable: photos and documents that were prepared by the CIA, documents from the archives of the CIA. All of the material was passed back and forth constantly."

D'Aubuisson maintained CIA contacts in 1980 and 1981, according to Jimmy Nixon, an American citizen and ARENA activist who ferried visitors and private messages to D'Aubuisson while he was staying in Guatemala during that period. Nixon says he is uncertain of the current relationship.

Another American closely associated with D'Aubuisson, Billy Murphy, complains of the treatment ARENA received at the hands of the U.S. embassy under the Carter Administration and its last ambassador, Robert White. "Those sons of bitches were doing everything they could against us," he says.

But Murphy adds that ARENA enjoyed amiable relations with one political officer at the embassy who "would always let us know in advance what was going to happen in the junta." He and other D'Aubuisson aides met regularly with "good friends" from the U.S. Military Group and the embassy's military attaché, he says. "You had a wonderful man here" in the Military Group, says Murphy. "He did his best, but he couldn't do anything."

Clandestine U.S. ties with the Salvadoran security apparatus remain firm, and appear to have been strengthened in the 1980s. National Guardsman Luis Alonso Bonilla claims that U.S. military and civilian personnel helped train members of the security forces as bodyguards in 1980. Bonilla, who says he took a similar course in 1975, says it included instruction in combat and ambush techniques. A National Police detective and member of the elite explosives unit established by AID's Public Safety Program says four of his associates visited the United States for an explosives course in November 1983.

"I've been visited by some members of the embassy with whom I've always maintained good relations," Carranza told me last September, "and I have the promise that they are going to help us train our personnel." He said he also needed investigation and interrogation equipment, and was unruffled by the fact that U.S. law prohibits such aid.

"Yes," he remarked, "but by means of other ways, by let's say friendship with some members of the American embassy, I think I can get not only equipment but training." He said he would obtain them through "outside channels," adding, "I don't know whether it would be wise to put this out for the knowledge of the American people."

Once the Treasury Police received the lie detection, fingerprinting, and ballistic equipment he requested, "we would have a better way of doing an investigation than putting pressure on the victim," Carranza said. "Now when you have a prisoner, you have to put pressure on him, questioning him again and again, day and night."

This March, Francis Stanley Martinez, a corporal in the National Police intelligence department, said he and nine colleagues in the security forces—three from the Treasury Police, three from the National Guard, and three from the National Police—were about to depart for an in-depth CIA training course in the United States. He subsequently said the departure date had been postponed until sometime in April. The course would cover investigation, surveillance, weapons, and interrogation, Martinez said.

"You have to know all aspects to work in intelligence here," he said. "It's very different from the United States. Here, intelligence is hard to get, and the delinquent is very different. Here, the first thing you have to do is grab them by the neck."

In the 1960s, when the United States was building a Salvadoran security system based on surveillance and assassination, the enterprise enjoyed unified support within the U.S. Government. With State Department officials and CIA operatives presiding, General Medrano and his counterparts from Anastasio Somoza's Nicaragua and Peralta Azurdia's Guatemala would gather around a table and give speeches about "who the communists were," as Medrano puts it, "what they were up to, and what we should do about them."

Over time, changing political conditions opened something of a rift between the State Department professionals and their Pentagon and CIA colleagues. During the Carter Administration, their disagreements were often clear and pronounced. Under Reagan, the State Department has been brought back into line. Public and Congressional pressures, however, have compelled the Administration to voice public criticism of the Death Squads even as it secretly funnels aid and intelligence to the military and security forces that run them.

U.S. complicity in the dark and brutal work of El Salvador's Death Squads is not an aberration. Rather, it represents a basic, bipartisan, institutional commitment on the part of six American Administrations—a commitment to guard the Salvadoran regime against the prospect that its people might organize in ways unfriendly to that regime or to the United States.

V.

THEMES FOR A NEW CENTURY: 1990–2000

Roy Gutman

"Too many journalists get distracted covering the war," Roy Gutman has said. "Modern conflict is not between armies anymore. It's militaries against civilians."

The collapse of Yugoslavia and the civil war that broke out in 1991 attracted an entourage of international journalists. But while most reporters covered the business of combat—the fall of Vukovar, the siege of Sarajevo—Roy Gutman of Newsday *was among a handful of reporters trying to tell a different story: the systematic ethnic cleansing, largely by Bosnian Serbs, that became the hallmark of the Balkan conflict. Immersing himself in interviews more akin to oral history than conventional reporting, he documented mass deportations of Bosnian Muslims and the pervasive practice of rape by Serb militias. Later, Gutman organized the Crimes of War Project to educate journalists about internationally recognized norms of combat.*

Gutman's work documenting the war crimes of the Balkans embodies the new human-rights investigative journalism that emerged from Latin America in the 1980s. Exposing mass catastrophe requires a new toolbox: witnesses and survivors are deeply traumatized, official corroboration is often nonexistent, and even the usual forms of journalistic narrative can seem unequal to the task. Reporters like Gutman have learned the new psychological vocabulary of traumatic stress; immersed themselves in international law; adopted new, less confrontational interviewing techniques; and found new ways of incorporating eyewitness voices in to their stories.

DEATH CAMP HORRORS

From *Newsday*, 1993

Omarska, Bosnia-Herzegovina, October 18, 1992

The vast mining complex here, with its open pits and ore processing system, looks like anything but a concentration camp. The nondescript buildings in their barren frontier landscape have been cleaned up, and there is no trace of the blood reputedly spilled here. But during the last month dozens of eyewitnesses have provided compelling new evidence of murder and torture on a wide scale at this complex, where the Serbs who conquered Bosnia brought several thousand Muslims and Croats to die.

According to former detainees, the killing went on almost everywhere: Inside the huge hangarlike building that houses earth-moving equipment, armed guards ordered excruciating tortures at gunpoint, sometimes forcing one prisoner to castrate another. The tarmac outside was an open-air prison where 500 to 1,000 men had to lie on their bellies from dawn to dusk. Thousands more packed the offices, workshops and storage rooms in the hangar and a glass-and-brick administration building. All were on starvation diets.

The two most-feared locations were small outbuildings some distance from the main facilities: the "Red House," from which no prisoner returned alive, and the "White House," which contained a torture chamber where guards beat prisoners for days until they succumbed.

Unlike Nazi concentration camps, Omarska kept no real records, making it extremely difficult to determine exactly how many died. Guards often chose victims at whim and had to ask other detainees to identify the corpses. "They never knew how many people were killed from one shift to the next," observed a 22-year-old Omarska survivor who asked that his name not be used.

Newsday first reported mass murders at Omarska and other camps on August 2. Five days later, as television pictures of emaciated prisoners were aired worldwide, Serb authorities closed the camp and dispersed the prisoners. But not until hundreds of survivors reached the West in the last few weeks, aided by the International Red Cross, was it possible to draw up a detailed account.

A month-long *Newsday* investigation, which included extensive interviews with officials who said they were responsible for Omarska and with dozens of former detainees in Croatia, Britain and Bosnia itself, produced these main conclusions:

- Eyewitness accounts of detainees indicate that well over 1,000 people were killed at Omarska, and thousands more probably would have died of beatings, executions, disease or starvation had the camp not been closed.
- A large number of detainees, possibly as many as 1,000, seem to have disappeared without a trace when the camp was closed.

- All but a few detainees were civilians, mostly draft-age Muslim or Croat men, but there were many men under 18 or over 60, and a small number of women.

Newsday's estimate of the death toll of more than 1,000 is based on eyewitness accounts of daily killings by three former detainees who spoke in separate interviews. It does not reflect other, possibly duplicative, first-person reports of mass executions or disappearances; if it did, the toll could easily be twice as high.

Three Bosnian journalists who were detained at Omarska and are now being held in another camp arrived among themselves at an estimated death toll of 1,200 or more. And International Red Cross officials said at least 2,000 people who went to Omarska are unaccounted for.

Nine hundred miles from here, outside London, Edin Elkaz lies awake nights, his head filled with the screams of the men being tortured in the room next door at the White House. During one month at the camp, the 21-year-old said, he witnessed some of the killings next door and the removal of bodies the next day; the guards slaughtered five to 10 men a night, up to 30 on some nights. The guards sang as they beat the Muslim and Croat prisoners to death, sometimes nationalist songs about "Greater Serbia," other times religious melodies from the Serb Orthodox liturgy, he said. E.L., a 26-year-old Muslim, spent two months here and said he helped load between five and 10 corpses daily from the White House into a small yellow pickup truck that removed them to an unknown grave. Like many of those interviewed, he asked that his full name not be used.

And N.J., a 23-year-old Muslim, said he kept a count each night for the final 20 nights of the inmates marched to the Red House. Some days there were as few as 17 or as many as 42. None ever returned.

Interviews with these three detainees, who are among 68 taken to Britain to recover from beatings and shootings, and from several hundred who recently arrived in Karlovac, western Croatia, provide chilling amplification of the original reports of atrocities at the camps in Bosnia.

Reacting to the early accounts, Lawrence Eagleburger, now the acting U.S. secretary of state, said on August 18 that the administration had found no evidence of systematic killing, only of unpleasant conditions. But after conducting its own interviews recently with about 40 former detainees in Karlovac for submission to a special United Nations war crimes panel, the United States Embassy in Zagreb has concluded there were massive atrocities at Omarska and other camps and in the surrounding towns, said an embassy official.

"The Nazis had nothing on these guys. I've seen reports of individual acts of barbarity of a kind that hasn't come up in State Department cable traffic in 20 years," said another top official at the U.S. embassy, who spoke on condition of anonymity.

But even the United States Embassy interviewers have been unable to determine the number of people held at Omarska, the number killed or the number missing.

Extensive *Newsday* interviews with prisoners indicate that at least 2,500 to 3,000 detainees were held in Omarska at any one point. International Red Cross officials have a working estimate that up to 5,000 prisoners were taken to Omarska and that well over 2,000 are accounted for.

Despite the imprecision of the statistics, the story of Omarska and other concentration camps in Bosnia constitutes one of the most savage chapters of modern European history. Serbs from nearby Prijedor set up camps at Omarska and Kereterm, a disused tile factory, on May 25, not quite a month after they seized power by force in the town of 30,000. Officials from Prijedor were eager to present their version of events but acknowledged under questioning by *Newsday* that it was only the official account. "You have your facts. We have our facts. You have a complete right to choose between the two versions," police chief Simo Drljaca said in an interview last month.

Almost nothing in the official version stands up to scrutiny.

During a tour of the administration building at the camp, Zeljko Mejahic, the former commander of the guards, took a visitor to a basement room packed with rows of bunk beds. There were never more than 270 prisoners at Omarska at any one time, Mejahic said, "and this is where they all slept."

But the detainees said they had slept on the ground, on floors or crouching jammed into closets—anywhere but in beds. The beds were brought a few days after the media drew attention to Omarska, according to a foreign humanitarian-aid expert. The authorities raided military barracks for the bunks and the hotels of Banja Luka for the bedding, he said. Only when the bunks were in place were the International Red Cross and reporters allowed to visit.

Milan Kovacevic, the city manager in Prijedor, said Omarska was an investigative facility, set up "to see who did what during the war, to find the guilty ones and to establish the innocent so that they didn't bear the consequences." He said the camp was closed when the investigation was completed.

Drljaca, a little-known law graduate who became police chief when the Serb minority took power, said 3,334 people were arrested on suspicion of resisting or plotting against the new Serb authorities and were taken to Omarska. Drljaca insisted that no one had been killed at Omarska and that only two prisoners died between May 25 and mid-August, both of "natural causes." Another 49 "disappeared," including the former lord mayor of Prijedor, Mohamed Cehajic, and were presumed dead, Drljaca said.

In the official version, detainees were interrogated for four days and shipped out. Drljaca said 800 detainees who were alleged to have "organized the whole thing," among them rich Muslims who financed the Muslim SDA political party, were taken to Manjaca, which was operated by the Bosnian Serb army as a prisoner-of-war camp, to await criminal trial. Taken with them were 600 people who reputedly commanded units of the Muslim and Croat resistance. The remaining 1,900 were found innocent and taken immediately to Trnopolje, which officials said was a transit camp, Drljaca said.

But not one of more than three dozen Omarska survivors whom U.S. embassy officials interviewed at Karlovac said he had been questioned before being taken to Omarska. Only a few of several dozen interviewed by *Newsday* had been interrogated, and they said they were beaten before and during questioning. Most had been held more than two months.

Moreover, nearly every Omarska prisoner sent to Manjaca was a civilian, and only a handful had borne arms against the Serbs—nowhere near the 600 figure given by Drljaca, humanitarian aid sources say.

Drljaca's assertion that prisoners were removed to Manjaca after being interrogated was contradicted by Bozidor Popovic, the commander at Manjaca, who said in an interview last month that 25 busloads of prisoners had arrived in early August.

Slobodan Balaban, an ethnic Serb who was technical director of the mining complex, said Serbs were motivated to operate the camps by revenge for the perceived suffering of Serbs in other conflicts. "The main factor that influenced our conduct has been the treatment of our people who were taken to Croatian camps," he said.

While official accounts are riddled with contradictions, reports by survivors of Omarska of severe deprivation, brutal tortures and routinized slaughter are consistent and corroborative, as well as mind-numbing. According to the reports, some of which follow, savagery enveloped the prisoners from their arrival.

Redzep Tahirovic, 52, said he was brought to Omarska with hundreds of others on May 26 after Serbs destroyed and "cleansed" the nearby Muslim town of Kozarac. In a sworn statement given to the Bosnian State Commission on War Crimes, he said guards called out a dozen people a day for five days and decapitated them with chain saws near one of the main pits. He said Omarska prisoners were forced to witness the massacre as well as the subsequent execution of 20 non-Serb policemen from Prijedor.

D.K., a 25-year-old ethnic Albanian now recovering outside London, had the luck to be shot by accident on arriving at Omarska on May 30. "I was there only 20 minutes," he said. He had been among 15 men standing near the camp entrance who were fired at by a trigger-happy guard. D.K. lifted his pajamas to show seven bullet wounds on his stomach, legs and arm. Three detainees died in the shooting, but D.K. was taken to a hospital in Banja Luka where he was in a coma for 15 days. When he came to, he said, nurses, Serb patients and even Serb children visitors came and beat him. "I had gotten 12 pints of blood, and they beat me because I had Serb blood," he said.

Edin Elkaz was also lucky to be shot by accident on arrival May 30 and taken to a hospital in Prijedor, for it reduced his exposure to the violence in the camp. Elkaz had been a Bosnian soldier, one of the few Omarska prisoners who had actually fought the Serbs. Stuffed with 130 others into a one-car garage, Elkaz was standing near the door when guards seized a friend of his and executed him outside at close range.

The bullet penetrated the door, entered the stomach of Elkaz's brother and finally came to rest in Elkaz's leg. In the hospital for six weeks with his leg suspended from a bar, Elkaz never recovered because Serb ill-wishers came by and poked the wound with a stick, repeatedly reinfecting it.

"I had a very good [Serb] neighbor who came by one day and said hello. I came to regret it," Elkaz said, smiling at the irony. "He brought 15 people to beat me up over six weeks."

Once back in Omarska, he was taken with several other Bosnian soldiers to a room in the "White House." He could see the beatings through a glass door. The guards used wooden clubs and iron bars and usually concentrated on the head, the genitals, the spine and the kidneys. Sometimes they smashed prisoners' heads against radiators. "You'd see pieces of flesh or brain there the next day," Elkaz recalled.

But the worst torture was to stand a prisoner against the wall and beat him with a cable. "I think they killed at least 50 men with that cable," Elkaz said.

Each morning, he said, detainees laid out the corpses on the tarmac in front of the White House. Others then loaded them into the small yellow truck that had just been used to deliver food to the camp kitchen. A four-man burial detail would accompany the truck, but only one would return alive.

No prisoner is known to have survived the "Red House," and only a few even witnessed detainees being taken each night to the outbuilding, well away from the main buildings. From mid-July until Omarska was closed, starting at 8 each night, guards collected men from different locations in the camp and took them to a holding area at the White House, according to the former detainee, N.J. Guards asked them for names and family details, then marched them away individually. At about 4 A.M. prisoners would hear a truck drive up to the Red House, apparently to collect the corpses.

Although guards often combed the many rooms where prisoners were kept and called out names from lists, many of those killed or beaten were selected at random. "The guards would come in at 3 A.M. and take five people out, telling us they were going to be exchanged. Where they took them, God only knows," said M.M., a 28-year-old plumber held with more than 500 men for more than two months in a room adjacent to the giant hangar. "Next morning we would see the dead bodies. I am sure that 50 percent of those who disappeared would be killed."

Often the guards did not know whom they had beaten to death. Elkaz recalled that "sometimes they would call them by name. But sometimes they would ask me afterward, 'Do you know who this is?' " He said he identified many friends who had been beaten to death.

The violence worsened in time as the guards "had already taken everything of value," said a man who called himself by the pseudonym Mrki, aged 40, interviewed at Karlovac. Mrki was taken to the White House because he was standing in a prominent location when a guard came into the room looking for scapegoats. Over two nights, he was beaten unconscious at the White House, both by guards and by villagers invited in for recreational beating. "When I awoke in the morning, there was blood all over the place," he recalled.

There were ways to avoid beatings, detainees said. Rule one was never to look a guard in the eye. Rule two was that if called to an interrogation, to confuse the guards by saying you had just come from one. Prisoners sometimes smeared themselves with blood from a newly beaten detainee "so that we would be spared as much as possible in the next round," Kamber Midho, 31, said in a sworn statement to the Bosnian government. At least one prisoner was burned alive at Omarska.

The burning occurred in late July as detainees lined up for lunch, according to Nedjad Hadzic, 23, an eyewitness now in Karlovac. The man was emerging from an interrogation, and a guard ordered him to run, as if in preparation to shoot him. "You are cowards. You know nothing but cruelty," the man taunted the guard.

When the guards were shoving him on the tarmac, he grabbed a gun from one of them but then gave it up. "They shoved him toward the White House, poured gasoline over him and set him alight," Hadzic said.

And Osman Hamuric, who is now recovering outside London, told *Newsday* he had twice witnessed forced cannibalism at Kereterm camp. On one occasion, he said, guards cut off a prisoner's ear and forced another man to eat it. The second time, a guard cut a piece of flesh off a wounded prisoner and told him to eat it. He refused. "Why not? It's cooked," Hamuric quoted the guard as saying. Hamuric could not say whether the man ate his own flesh. "All I know is that they took him away, and we never saw him again."

Yet nothing was more traumatic for the men than the castrations. United States Embassy officials found a witness to an incident in which a man had his testicles tied with wire to the back of a motorcycle, which took off at high speed. He died of massive blood loss.

Hadzic described a castration in an interview with *Newsday.* The incident began when a guard with a grudge to settle called out Emir Karabasic, a Muslim policeman, from the room in which Hadzic was sleeping and ordered him to strip naked in the hangar in front of parked dump trucks. "Do you remember the time you beat me up in the cafe?" the guard asked. As Hadzic watched from the next room, a second Serb policeman found another Muslim, against whose father he had a grudge, and ordered him to lower his face into a channel cut in the concrete floor and drink old motor oil, then to bite off Karabasic's testicles. "The shrieks were unbearable. Then there was silence," said Hadzic.

Three other men who had been removed from Hadzic's room at the same time and witnessed the castration were then killed by the guards with metal rods, Hadzic said. The man who carried out the castration returned to the room, his face blackened, and could not speak for 24 hours.

Experiences like these have left deep psychic scars on the survivors, among them a Roman Catholic priest from near Prijedor who described his suffering to parishioners in Zagreb. The priest, who spoke briefly with *Newsday* but insisted he not be identified, told them he had been beaten until he vomited blood. Once he said he had been caught trying to give a detainee the last rites, and he swallowed the piece of bread he had consecrated rather than let the guards seize it.

From dawn to dusk he lay out on the tarmac with hundreds of other men. For 32 days, the priest said, he did not have a bowel movement because he had not eaten any food. "It was so terrible that, God forgive me for saying so, we were grateful when someone died. We could take their clothing and place it under us," an attendee at his speech quoted him as saying. The ordeal caused damage to the priest's heart and kidneys, and he is now recovering in Croatia.

During their first five days in Omarska, prisoners were generally given no food, witnesses said. After that time they were taken in groups of 30 to the cafeteria for the sole meal of the day, which consisted of a slice of bread and a bowl of thin soup. After two or three minutes, during which it was possible to wolf down a few spoonfuls of the gruel, it was back to the tarmac.

The beatings that accompanied trips to the toilet were so severe that former detainees said they preferred to defecate in their boots or in the rooms in which they had to sleep. Dysentery was rampant, and conditions were so unclean that some prisoners counted 10 types of lice or vermin on their bodies. "We had lice on our eyelids. They'd fall out of our beards," said Hadzic. Detainees said they bathed only twice all summer. The guards ordered prisoners to disrobe in groups of 50 and then aimed fire hoses at their genitals. "It was pure sadism. They'd laugh if we fell over," Hadzic said.

When Omarska was closed down, camp doctors at Manjaca estimated that of the prisoners transferred there, at least one in 10 had contracted dysentery from bad food or unsanitary conditions, all of whom would have succumbed without immediate treatment. Others suffered from untreated and festering wounds from their beatings.

Many others were close to collapse. "I don't believe I would have lasted another 10 days," said Kemal Husic, 19. "I was reaching a state where I couldn't stand. I had to have two people help me to get to the cafeteria."

Hadzic concurred. "There was so much hunger and dysentery that the whole camp couldn't have lasted another 20 days," he said.

Many detainees never made it to safety and seem to have disappeared "in transit" to or from Omarska. These included two busloads of men who disappeared from Omarska at the end of July. Another 120, according to witnesses, were to be taken from the Kereterm camp to Omarska on August 5 but never turned up. About 11 men who were transferred to Manjaca did not arrive. Guards slit the throats of two and killed another nine, prisoners said.

The Manjaca commander, Bozidor Popovic, disclaimed any knowledge of that alleged atrocity. "I am not interested in what happened outside the gates. My responsibility is only for what happens under my control."

But the biggest mystery is what happened to the people transferred from Omarska at the time of its closing. Prisoners said they reckoned a population of 2,500 to 3,000 at Omarska, basing their estimates on such things as counts of the lunches served on a particular day. Of the prisoners there at the end, 1,374 were transferred to Manjaca, according to the International Red Cross. About 700 others went to Trnopolje, according to prisoners later taken from there to Karlovac. That leaves between 500 and 1,000 missing. Moreover, of the number transferred to Trnopolje in early August, only about 200 made it to Karlovac. Some had been on a convoy into central Bosnia in which more than 250 men were slaughtered by local police.

Were other Omarska prisoners killed in other ways? Were they dispersed to other camps? No one has an answer, not even Thierry Germond, the chief European delegate for the International Red Cross, which has tried to win freedom for all the civilian and military detainees in the war. All Germond could say was, "We understand your concern, and I share it."

Kenneth Armstrong and Steve Mills

In 1998, Illinois death-row inmate Anthony Porter, with an I.Q. of fifty-one, was two days away from execution for a double murder sixteen years earlier. A federal judge ordered a stay to consider whether Porter's mental retardation should have barred him from execution. In the time bought by the stay, Northwestern University journalism professor David Protess assigned his students to investigate Porter's case. The student reporters learned that the only witness against Porter had been threatened by police; they located the actual killer and secured his confession on videotape.

Porter's case—Illinois's tenth exoneration of a death-row inmate—shocked the state. The Chicago Tribune *assigned veteran investigative reporters Steve Mills and Kenneth Armstrong to examine every death-row conviction since Illinois reinstated the death penalty in 1977. Combining sophisticated computer analysis with exhaustive interviews and careful review of court records, they painted a picture of a system so broken that in January 2000 Governor George Ryan, a Republican and former death-penalty supporter, imposed a moratorium on executions. In January 2003, as his final act of office, Governor Ryan commuted to a maximum of life in prison the sentences of all 157 death-row inmates in Illinois.*

The Chicago Tribune *series showed how readily available tools of computer data-analysis have given reporters new techniques for exposing systematic abuses, made all the more effective by compelling case-by-case storytelling. The kind of computer analysis that made the* Tribune*'s series possible was pioneered in the 1970s by the reporters Don Bartlett and James Steele, then of the* Philadelphia Inquirer, *and with the PC revolution has added depth to many newsrooms' investigations. Indeed, computer-assisted reporting challenges the idea of simple "gotcha" journalism by enabling reporters to expose abuses that are hidden only by their sheer pervasiveness. The death-penalty failures Mills and Armstrong exposed in Illinois also suggest that the U.S. criminal-justice system—which experienced massive growth in the 1990s—is likely to become an ever more central subject for investigative reporters.*

DEATH ROW JUSTICE DERAILED

From the *Chicago Tribune,* November 14, 1999

Capital punishment in Illinois is a system so riddled with faulty evidence, unscrupulous trial tactics and legal incompetence that justice has been forsaken, a *Tribune* investigation has found.

With their lives on the line, many defendants have been represented by the legal profession's worst, not its best.

They have been given the ultimate punishment based on evidence that too often is inconclusive, and sometimes nearly nonexistent.

They have seen their fates decided not by juries that reflect the community as a whole but by juries that include not a single member of their racial minority.

They have been condemned to die in trials so rife with error that nearly half of the state's death-penalty cases have been reversed on appeal.

Illinois has claimed the dubious distinction of having exonerated as many Death Row inmates as it has executed. But many of the circumstances that sent 12 innocent men to Death Row have been documented by the *Tribune* in numerous other capital cases.

In the first comprehensive examination of all 285 death-penalty cases since capital punishment was restored in Illinois 22 years ago, the *Tribune* has identified numerous fault lines running through the criminal justice system, subverting the notion that when the stakes are the highest, trials should be fail-safe.

The findings reveal a system so plagued by unprofessionalism, imprecision and bias that they have rendered the state's ultimate form of punishment its least credible.

The *Tribune* investigation, which included an exhaustive analysis of appellate opinions and briefs, trial transcripts and lawyer disciplinary records, as well as scores of interviews with witnesses, attorneys and defendants, has found that:

- At least 33 times, a defendant sentenced to die was represented at trial by an attorney who has been disbarred or suspended—sanctions reserved for conduct so incompetent, unethical or even criminal the lawyer's license is taken away.

In Kane County, an attorney was suspended for incompetence and dishonesty. Ten days after getting his law license back in 1997, he was appointed by the county's chief judge to defend a man's life.

- In at least 46 cases where a defendant was sentenced to die, the prosecution's evidence included a jailhouse informant—a form of evidence so historically unreliable that some states have begun warning jurors to treat it with special skepticism.

  In one Cook County case, the word of a convicted con man, called a "pathological liar" by federal authorities, put a man on Death Row. In exchange for a sharply reduced sentence, the con artist testified that while in jail together the defendant confessed to him, even though a tape recording of their conversation contains no confession.
- In at least 20 cases where a defendant was sentenced to die, the prosecution's case included a crime lab employee's visual comparison of hairs—a type of forensic evidence that dates to the 19th century and has proved so notoriously unreliable that its use is now restricted or even barred in some jurisdictions outside Illinois.
- At least 35 times, a defendant sent to Death Row was black and the jury that determined guilt or sentence all white—a racial composition that prosecutors consider such an advantage that they have removed as many as 20 African-Americans from a single trial's jury pool to achieve it. The U.S. Constitution forbids racial discrimination during jury selection, but courts have enforced that prohibition haltingly.
- Forty percent of Illinois' death-penalty cases are characterized by at least one of the above elements. Sometimes, all of the elements appear in a single case. Dennis Williams, who is black, was sentenced to die by an all-white Cook County jury; prosecuted with evidence that included a jailhouse informant and

> hair comparison; and defended, none too well, by an attorney who was later disbarred.
>
> Williams and three other men—referred to as the Ford Heights Four—were wrongly convicted of the 1978 murders of a south suburban couple. Williams served 18 years, almost all on Death Row, before he was cleared by DNA evidence in 1996. He then filed a lawsuit accusing sheriff's officers of framing him.

"The feeling is emotionally choking," Williams said of being sentenced to die for a crime he did not commit. "It's inhuman. It's something that shouldn't be imaginable. Here are people who are supposed to uphold the law who are breaking it."

Illinois houses its condemned inmates at the Menard and Pontiac correctional centers and at the new prison in Downstate Tamms. They spend 23 hours a day in cells so narrow they can touch opposite walls at the same time.

To be sure, many of Illinois' Death Row inmates are guilty of horrendous crimes. But while lawfully condemning the guilty, the state's system of capital punishment has proved so vulnerable to mistakes that it threatens to execute the innocent as well.

The problems afflicting death-penalty trials in Illinois have generated great concern, even among some supporters of capital punishment, and have prompted the Illinois Supreme Court and the state's legislature to examine possible reforms.

While it is impossible to calculate the exact financial costs imposed by the system's flaws, without question they are staggering. Taxpayers have not only had to finance multimillion-dollar settlements to wrongly convicted Death Row inmates—Williams alone received nearly $13 million from Cook County—but also have had to pay for new trials, sentencing hearings and appeals in more than 100 cases where a condemned inmate's original trial was undermined by some fundamental error.

Illinois Supreme Court Justice Moses Harrison II wrote last year in one Death Row inmate's appeal that he will no longer vote to uphold the death penalty, saying "so many mistakes" have been made in Illinois.

"The system is not working," Harrison wrote. "Innocent people are being sentenced to death. If these men dodged the executioner, it was only because of luck and the dedication of the attorneys, reporters, family members and volunteers who labored to win their release. They survived despite the criminal justice system, not because of it. . . . One must wonder how many others have not been so fortunate."

FLAWED TRIAL, FLAWED EVIDENCE

The case of Madison Hobley exemplifies how a man can be condemned to die in a flawed trial with questionable evidence of guilt.

In the predawn hours of Jan. 6, 1987, an arsonist's fire burned through a three-story apartment building on Chicago's South Side, forcing people to jump from windows and throw children to waiting arms below. Seven people died, including Hobley's wife and baby boy.

The crime was a so-called heater case, one that newspapers and television stations prominently recounted.

Police arrested the 26-year-old Hobley within 24 hours. Three years later, a Cook County jury convicted Hobley and sentenced him to death.

Prosecutors claimed Hobley was having an affair and set the fire to kill his family. Hobley admits the affair. He denies setting the fire.

His appeal alleges that prosecutors suppressed a report saying Hobley's fingerprints weren't found on the gas can he allegedly used, and that after Hobley's appellate lawyers learned of a second gas can possibly related to the investigation, police destroyed it. Last year, the Illinois Supreme Court found sufficient merit to those allegations to order a hearing on them. The court said it was "deeply troubled."

At trial, the lead prosecutor insisted there was no fingerprint report. Now, the state's attorney's office says there was a report and believes the defense was notified of that before the trial.

But the questions surrounding Hobley's conviction go further.

In a befuddling move, Hobley's trial attorneys allowed a suburban police officer to get on the jury. Most lawyers consider police officers the worst jurors imaginable for defendants because of their potential biases in favor of law enforcement. The officer became jury foreman. In an affidavit, another juror said the officer revealed his gun in the jury room and, citing his own experience, vouched for the police's work in Hobley's case.

Hobley was interrogated by police officers under then Cmdr. Jon Burge, whose name would become attached to one of the worst scandals in the modern history of the Chicago Police Department. At the center of the scandal were allegations that in the 1970s and 1980s, police tortured suspects to obtain confessions, using such means as electroshock and Russian roulette.

Fourteen men sentenced to death in Illinois were convicted with what they claimed to be false confessions obtained through torture by Burge's officers. Ten, including Hobley, remain on Death Row as their claims of abuse by a discredited police unit move through the appeals process.

Hobley, who worked for a medical-supplies company and had no prior criminal record, claimed officers wrapped a plastic bag over his head, struck his chest, kicked his shins and pushed their thumbs against his throat. The officers denied it.

Hobley's complaint went nowhere in an internal police investigation. But because so many suspects made similar claims, the department's Office of Professional Standards later conducted a far-reaching review of abuse allegations and, in 1990, found that Burge's officers engaged in systematic torture. Burge eventually was fired.

The police officers working for Burge said Hobley confessed; Hobley denies he did. Detective Robert Dwyer said he wrote down the confession, but testified that his notes got wet and torn, so he threw them away.

An arson detective's initial report indicated the fire started on the ground level. But Hobley allegedly confessed to starting the fire outside his third-floor apartment. At trial, the detective modified his analysis to say the fire could have started anywhere.

Other than the disputed confession, the prosecution's case hinged on a witness who said he saw Hobley filling a gas can shortly before the fire. But certain elements of that witness's testimony contradicted other evidence, and Hobley's attorneys have alleged the witness received special consideration in a pending criminal case in exchange for his cooperation.

Prosecutors put into evidence a gas can found under a 2nd-floor apartment's kitchen sink. They claimed Hobley used it to set the fire. But that can differed in size from the one Hobley reportedly had been seen filling, and Hobley allegedly confessed to throwing the can down a hallway, not into an apartment. In a deposition this year, one of the prosecutors said he doesn't believe Hobley used that can. Three months later, he wrote a letter taking that back and blaming a memory lapse.

Currently an inmate at Menard, Hobley has been on Death Row for nine years.

"I respected the law. I worked," he recently told the *Tribune.* "The only thing I did wrong was I was unfaithful."

PROSECUTOR MISCONDUCT

To win a death sentence, prosecutors in Illinois have repeatedly exaggerated the criminal backgrounds of defendants—turning misdemeanors into felonies, manslaughter into murder, innocence into guilt.

Prosecutors have lied to jurors, raising the possibility of parole when no such possibility existed.

They also have browbeaten jurors, saying they must return the death sentence, or they will have violated their oaths and lied to God.

Death-penalty cases in Illinois have included some of the most sympathetic victims, helping flare emotions at trial. Of the 285 cases since capital punishment's reinstatement, there were multiple murder victims in 104. In 44 cases, at least one victim was 12 years old or younger. In 15 cases, the victim was a police officer.

When the drive to avenge such crimes reaches the courtroom, a prosecutor's worst tendencies can come to a boil and spill over.

More than 10 percent of Illinois' death-penalty cases have been reversed for a new trial or sentencing hearing because prosecutors took some unfair advantage that undermined a trial's integrity, according to the *Tribune*'s review of appellate rulings. The misconduct by prosecutors has included misstating the law or evidence, using inflammatory arguments that appeal to jurors' prejudices, and even breaking a promise to a defendant not to seek the death penalty if he provided a written confession.

In securing a death sentence against Verneal Jimerson, another one of the Ford Heights Four who was exonerated by DNA evidence, prosecutors allowed their star witness to tell what they knew to be a lie, the Illinois Supreme Court ruled.

Jimerson, according to a previous *Tribune* investigation, is one of at least 381 defendants nationwide to have a homicide conviction thrown out because prosecutors concealed evidence suggesting innocence or knowingly used false evidence. That total underscores how questionable tactics marring Illinois death-penalty trials also course through other cases and states.

Although the great majority of misconduct by prosecutors occurs at trial, some prosecutors have run afoul while defending death sentences on appeal.

When Cornelius Lewis was convicted in 1979 of murdering a Decatur bank guard, the Macon County state's attorney obtained the death penalty by portraying Lewis as a career criminal with four felony convictions. On appeal, however, Assistant State's Atty. Jeff Justice and Assistant Illinois Atty. Gen. Neal Goodfriend discovered that was only half-true: One felony charge had been dismissed and another reduced to a misdemeanor.

But neither prosecutor notified Lewis's attorney or the courts that false evidence had been used to help secure Lewis's death sentence, according to court records. That information surfaced only because Lewis's attorney discovered it on his own. In 1987, a federal appeals court vacated Lewis's death sentence and called Goodfriend's and Justice's withholding of vital information "shocking" and "reprehensible." The court referred both to the state's lawyer disciplinary agency, but neither was sanctioned. At a new hearing, Lewis was sentenced to life.

"These prosecutors just sat on the information. They made a conscious decision not to tell me," said J. Steven Beckett, who represented Lewis on appeal. "What were those prosecutors thinking? That's advocacy taken to an extreme."

Another way that many prosecutors have bent or broken the rules in death-penalty cases has come at the trial's outset—when picking the jury.

Juries are supposed to represent a cross-section of the community, because people of different backgrounds, races and genders often have experiences and perspectives that can benefit a jury's deliberations. For example, an African-American from the Englewood neighborhood on Chicago's South Side might be more skeptical of a police officer's disputed testimony than a white resident of Schaumburg.

Having different races represented on juries would figure to be especially important in capital cases, where, in Illinois, nearly two-thirds of the defendants sentenced to death have been black or Hispanic.

Although the Constitution bars racial discrimination during jury selection, prosecutors often have flouted that prohibition. And reviewing courts, with rare exceptions, have let them, even after a 1986 U.S. Supreme Court ruling that was meant to crack down on the practice.

At least 35 black defendants condemned to death in Illinois since 1977 were convicted or sentenced by an all-white jury, the *Tribune* found. That accounts for 22 percent of all blacks sentenced to death.

Of 65 death-penalty cases in Illinois with a black defendant and white victim, the jury was all white in 21 of them, or nearly a third.

In the Death Row cases where blacks were convicted by an all-white jury, prosecutors frequently used their discretionary strikes to remove African-Americans from the jury pool. Such strikes allow attorneys on both sides to excuse an allotted number of jury pool members, usually without giving a reason.

In the 1983 trial of Andrew Wilson, who was convicted of murdering two Chicago police officers, Cook County prosecutors removed 20 African-Americans from the jury pool. In the 1979 trial of Farris Walker, who was convicted of the murder and attempted robbery of a retired lawyer, prosecutors struck 16 African-Americans. In the 1979 trial of Hernando Williams, who was convicted of kidnapping and murdering a natural-childbirth instructor, prosecutors struck 11 blacks.

Despite the long string of cases where prosecutors have removed an inordinate number of blacks from jury pools, only one conviction in an Illinois death-penalty case has been reversed because of a finding that prosecutors discriminated on the basis of race during jury selection.

QUESTIONS BRUSHED ASIDE

In addition to tolerating such widespread practices as racial discrimination during jury selection, reviewing courts have, at times, shown a willingness to uphold individual death sentences despite a host of troubling questions about a trial's integrity.

William Bracy was convicted and sentenced to death in Cook County in 1981 for the murders of three drug dealers in Chicago. The prosecution's chief witness was a man who had admitted taking part in the crimes and who, in exchange for his testimony, received a lenient sentence.

Presiding at Bracy's trial was Thomas Maloney, who would become the only Illinois judge ever convicted of fixing murder cases. He was sentenced in 1994 to nearly 16 years in prison for fixing three murder cases in the 1980s.

To represent Bracy, Maloney appointed Robert McDonnell, a convicted felon who became the only Illinois lawyer ever disbarred twice. McDonnell was then between disbarments, reinstated despite concerns about his emotional stability and drinking, lawyer disciplinary records show. The prosecutors were Michael Goggin and Gregg Owen, a team that repeatedly committed misconduct during trials, racking up 35 instances of wrongdoing in one case alone, court records show.

The jury included the wife of a judge who had sentenced Bracy to prison in an unrelated case. In addition, the jury was all white, according to an affidavit filed by one of the trial's lawyers.

Several aspects of Bracy's case gave reviewing courts pause, but none reversed. Misconduct by the prosecutors was deemed harmless. Issues concerning the jury's makeup and McDonnell's competence were raised and rejected. So was an argument that Maloney was motivated to make pro-prosecution rulings in order to protect his law-and-order reputation and to deflect suspicion that he was on the take in other cases.

When a federal appeals court denied Bracy's appeal in a 2-1 decision in 1996, dissenting Judge Ilana Diamond Rovner wrote: "I do not know which I find more shocking: the base quality of justice that Bracy and (co-defendant Roger) Collins received in the Illinois courts, or our holding today that the Constitution requires no more."

A fair trial requires an impartial judge, but "the State of Illinois placed the fate of William Bracy and Roger Collins in the hands of a racketeer," Rovner wrote.

The U.S. Supreme Court has since granted Bracy's attorneys the opportunity to find evidence showing Maloney penalized defendants who didn't bribe him. Maloney presided over nine cases in all in which a defendant received the death penalty, the second most of any Illinois judge.

Six of those defendants have received new trials on appeal: Two were acquitted, two were convicted again but sentenced to life and two await retrial, although prosecutors have told the Illinois Supreme Court that convicting them again will be difficult.

The other three defendants remain on Death Row.

String of Errors, Reversals

In Illinois, errors by judges, ineptitude by defense attorneys and prosecutorial misconduct have been so widespread in death-penalty cases that a new trial or sentencing hearing has been ordered in 49 percent of them, the *Tribune* found.

That so many convictions and death sentences have been vacated shows that the Illinois Supreme Court, unlike the reviewing courts in some states, has not been a rubber stamp in capital cases. At the same time, the Illinois Supreme Court has upheld scores of death sentences while forgiving trial errors that benefited prosecutors, dismissing the errors as harmless.

In a chilling illustration of the death penalty's frailties, the very courts that have granted a new trial or sentencing hearing to nearly half of Illinois' Death Row population rejected the appeals of Anthony Porter, an innocent man who came within two days of execution.

Wrongly convicted in 1983 of shooting to death a couple as they sat in bleachers at a park on Chicago's South Side, Porter was saved not by the justice system, but by journalism students. Working with a private investigator, they proved Porter's innocence earlier this year by obtaining a videotaped confession from the real killer, who recently pleaded guilty.

Porter's appeals were denied even though his trial was seriously compromised. A juror was acquainted with one victim's mother and had even attended the victim's funeral, but she didn't disclose her potential bias during jury selection. In addition, Porter's attorneys tried the case on the cheap, failing to capitalize on available evidence that could have punched holes in the prosecution's case. They conducted a limited investigation, and in a sworn affidavit, one attorney even accused the other of having a judge sentence Porter instead of a jury to save time and money.

In words that now ring hollow, reviewing courts chose to excuse the shortcomings in Porter's trial, deeming such errors harmless because the evidence against Porter was so strong. "Overwhelming," the Illinois Supreme Court once called the evidence of Porter's guilt.

In Illinois, the majority of death-penalty cases reversed for a new trial or sentencing hearing have been attributable to errors by trial judges, such as inadequately screening jurors for bias or allowing prosecutors to present such dubious evidence as what a defendant supposedly muttered while sleeping, according to the *Tribune*'s review of appellate records.

Judges have sweeping responsibilities. They are gatekeepers of trial evidence and instruct jurors on the law. At trial, there are numerous junctures where judges can commit errors affecting the outcome or leading to reversal.

Some judges have misstated the law to jurors, while others have demonstrated a profound ignorance of how capital trials are structured, sometimes depriving defendants of the right to have a jury impose the sentence instead of the judge.

Although many rules of death-penalty trials are unique, no specialized training is mandated in Illinois for the judges who preside over them.

Some of the most puzzling work by judges has been performed during Death Row appeals when cases have been returned to the circuit court for hearings on new evidence or various legal issues.

In Cook County, Judge John Morrissey mocked efforts by lawyers for Death Row inmate Ronald Jones to have DNA testing performed.

"What issue could possibly be resolved by DNA testing?" Morrissey asked.

Over the objection of Cook County prosecutors, the Illinois Supreme Court later allowed the tests, which exonerated Jones for the 1985 murder and sexual assault of a South Side woman and led to his being released from Death Row earlier this year.

The pervasiveness of reversible errors in Illinois capital cases has imposed substantial costs in court time and taxpayer money.

In Cook County, Dennis Emerson has been sentenced to die no fewer than three times for the 1979 murder of a woman during a tavern robbery on Chicago's South Side. A blend of errors by the trial judge, prosecutors and one of Emerson's attorneys has twice caused appeals courts to order a new trial or sentencing hearing. Now, 20 years after the murder, the appeals process for Emerson's third death sentence is just beginning.

And in a twist that adds police error to the mix, new evidence suggests Emerson may have committed a different murder that Chicago police pinned on an innocent man. James Newsome served 15 years of a life sentence for a South Side grocer's murder before being exonerated in 1995 by new technology that showed his fingerprints didn't match the gunman's. Instead, those prints belonged to Emerson, according to police.

Prosecutors had sought the death penalty against Newsome. Had they succeeded, Newsome would have pushed the state's number of exonerated Death Row inmates to 13—assuming he hadn't been executed first.

CALLS FOR REFORM

The growing list of innocent men who have been sentenced to die in Illinois has attracted attention worldwide and become a rallying cry for opponents of capital punishment.

The Illinois Supreme Court and Illinois General Assembly have created committees to study the death penalty, and the reforms being considered include the dramatic step of creating minimum standards for prosecutors as well as defense attorneys in capital cases. But so far, the state's judicial and legislative officials have passed few rules or laws to shore up the capital-punishment system.

And in Cook County, where seven of the state's 12 exonerated Death Row inmates were convicted, the string of wrongful convictions has barely stirred officials.

Compare the fallout from the cases of Dennis Williams and Guy Paul Morin.

Both were convicted of murder with jailhouse-informant testimony and hair-comparison evidence. And both were exonerated by DNA evidence—Morin in 1995, Williams in 1996. But while the crime pinned on Williams took place in Cook County, the one blamed on Morin occurred in the Canadian province of Ontario. Morin, convicted of murdering a 9-year-old girl, had received the country's maximum penalty: a life sentence.

Following Morin's release, top province officials appointed a special commission to investigate the case and recommend ways to prevent future miscarriages of justice. The inquiry lasted nearly two years. The commission called 120 witnesses, including criminal justice experts from around the world.

After reviewing thousands of documents, the commission issued a 1,200-page report, calling Morin's conviction a tragedy. "The system failed him—a system for which we, the community, must bear responsibility," the report said. The commission urged significant restrictions on hair and jailhouse-informant evidence, calling them generally useless or inherently unreliable. Ontario's government then turned the recommendations into policy.

Cook County, meanwhile, settled Williams' wrongful-arrest lawsuit for $12.8 million, thereby avoiding a trial and a public airing of the alleged misconduct by law-enforcement officers.

County officials have extended Williams an apology, but so far no reforms to go with it.

William Greider

Of all the sweeping political, technological, and economic changes of recent years, corporate globalization has proven particularly challenging to journalism. As corporations merge, converge, concentrate their resources, and begin to look and act more and more like governments, journalists are often left to rehash press releases and read the tea leaves of stock-performance reports.

William Greider—who in defiance of a conventional career path has moved from the respectability of the Washington Post *to the pop magazine* Rolling Stone *to the relatively small circulation of the left-liberal* Nation*—does not accept the premises of the new economy. Instead, he takes as his beat "the unregulated globalization that tramples human values on every continent, among rich and poor alike." His reporting, reviving both the radical-reform spirit and comprehensive research of Lincoln Steffens, has ranged in its focus from the Federal Reserve Bank to South Asian sweatshops.*

Greider sounds a central theme facing American investigative journalism in the twenty-first century: the fate of democracy amid unprecedented concentrations of corporate power and widening inequality of wealth.

These Dark Satanic Mills

From *One World, Ready or Not,* 1997

On May 10, 1993, the worst industrial fire in the history of capitalism occurred at a toy factory on the outskirts of Bangkok and was reported on page 25 of the *Washington Post.* The *Financial Times* of London, which styles itself as the daily newspaper of the global economy, ran a brief item on page 6. The *Wall Street Journal* followed a day late with an account on page 11. The *New York Times* also put the story inside, but printed a dramatic photo on its front page: rows of small shrouded bodies on bamboo pallets—dozens of them—lined along the damp pavement, while dazed rescue workers stood awkwardly among the corpses. In the background, one could see the collapsed, smoldering structure of a mammoth factory where the Kader Industrial Toy Company of Thailand had employed three thousand workers manufacturing stuffed toys and plastic dolls, playthings destined for American children.

The official count was 188 dead, 469 injured, but the actual toll was undoubtedly higher since the four-story buildings had collapsed swiftly in the intense heat and many bodies were incinerated. Some of the missing were never found; others fled home to their villages. All but fourteen of the dead were women, most of them young, some as young as thirteen years old. Hundreds of the workers had been trapped on upper floors of the burning building, forced to jump from third- or fourth-floor windows, since the main exit doors were kept locked by the managers, and the narrow stairways became clotted with trampled bodies or collapsed.

When I visited Bangkok about nine months later, physical evidence of the disaster was gone—the site scraped clean by bulldozers—and Kader was already resuming production at a new toy factory, built far from the city in a rural province of northeastern Thailand. When I talked with Thai labor leaders and civic activists, people who had rallied to the cause of the fire victims, some of them were under the impression that a worldwide boycott of Kader products was under way, organized by conscience-stricken Americans and Europeans. I had to inform them that the civilized world had barely noticed their tragedy.

As news accounts pointed out, the Kader fire surpassed what was previously the worst industrial fire in history—the Triangle Shirtwaist Company fire of 1911—when 146 young immigrant women died in similar circumstances at a garment factory on the Lower East Side of Manhattan. The Triangle Shirtwaist fire became a pivotal event in American politics, a public scandal that provoked citizen reform movements and energized the labor organizing that built the International Ladies Garment Workers Union and other unions. The fire in Thailand did not produce meaningful political responses or even shame among consumers. The indifference of the leading newspapers merely reflected the tastes of their readers, who might be moved by human suffering in their own communities but were inured to news of recurring calamities in distant places. A fire in Bangkok was like a typhoon in Bangladesh, an earthquake in Turkey.

The Kader fire might have been more meaningful for Americans if they could have seen the thousands of soot-stained dolls that spilled from the wreckage, macabre litter scattered among the dead. Bugs Bunny, Bart Simpson and the Muppets. Big Bird and other *Sesame Street* dolls. Playskool "Water Pets." Santa Claus. What the initial news accounts did not mention was that Kader's Thai factory produced most of its toys for American companies—Toys "R" Us, Fisher-Price, Hasbro, Tyco, Arco, Kenner, Gund and J. C. Penney—as well as stuffed dolls, slippers and souvenirs for Europe.

Globalized civilization has uncovered an odd parochialism in the American character: Americans worried obsessively over the everyday safety of their children, and the U.S. government's regulators diligently policed the design of toys to avoid injury to young innocents. Yet neither citizens nor government took any interest in the brutal and dangerous conditions imposed on the people who manufactured those same toys, many of whom were mere adolescent children themselves. Indeed, the government position, both in Washington and Bangkok, assumed that there was no social obligation connecting consumers with workers, at least none that governments could enforce without disrupting free trade or invading the sovereignty of other nations.

The toy industry, not surprisingly, felt the same. Hasbro Industries, maker of Playskool, subsequently told the *Boston Globe* that it would no longer do business with Kader, but, in general, the U.S. companies shrugged off responsibility. Kader, a major toy manufacturer based in Hong Kong, "is extremely reputable, not sleaze bags," David Miller, president of the Toy Manufacturers of America, assured *USA Today.* "The responsibility for those factories," Miller told ABC News, "is in the hands of those who are there and managing the factory."

The grisly details of what occurred revealed the casual irresponsibility of both companies and governments. The Kader factory compound consisted of four interconnected, four-story industrial barns on a three-acre lot on Buddhamondhol VI Road in the Sampran district west of Bangkok. It was one among Thailand's thriving new industrial zones for garments, textiles, electronics and toys. More than 50,000 people, most of them migrants from the Thai countryside, worked in the district at 7,500 large and small firms. Thailand's economic boom was based on places such as this, and Bangkok was almost choking on its own fantastic growth, dizzily erecting luxury hotels and office towers.

The fire started late on a Monday afternoon on the ground floor in the first building and spread rapidly upward, jumping to two adjoining buildings, all three of which swiftly collapsed. Investigators noted afterwards that the structures had been cheaply built, without concrete reinforcement, so steel girders and stairways crumpled easily in the heat. Thai law required that in such a large factory, fire-escape stairways must be sixteen to thirty-three feet wide, but Kader's were a mere four and a half feet. Main doors were locked and many windows barred to prevent pilfering by the employees. Flammable raw materials—fabric, stuffing, animal fibers—were stacked everywhere, on walkways and next to electrical boxes. Neither safety drills nor fire alarms and sprinkler systems had been provided.

Let some of the survivors describe what happened.

A young woman named Lampan Taptim: "There was the sound of yelling about a fire. I tried to leave the section but my supervisor told me to get back to work. My sister who worked on the fourth floor with me pulled me away and insisted we try to get out. We tried to go down the stairs and got to the second floor; we found that the stairs had already caved in. There was a lot of yelling and confusion. . . . In desperation, I went back up to the windows and went back and forth, looking down below. The smoke was thick and I picked the best place to jump in a pile of boxes. My sister jumped, too. She died."

A young woman named Cheng: "There is no way out [people were shouting], the security guard has locked the main door out! It was horrifying. I thought I would die. I took off my gold ring and kept it in my pocket and put on my name tag so that my body could be identifiable. I had to decide to die in the fire or from jumping down from a three stories' height." As the walls collapsed around her, Cheng clung to a pipe and fell downward with it, landing on a pile of dead bodies, injured but alive.

An older woman named La-iad Nada-nguen: "Four or five pregnant women jumped before me. They died before my eyes." Her own daughter jumped from the top floor and broke both hips.

Chauweewan Mekpan, who was five months pregnant: "I thought that if I jumped, at least my parents would see my remains, but if I stayed, nothing would be left of me." Though her back was severely injured, she and her unborn child miraculously survived.

An older textile worker named Vilaiwa Satieti, who sewed shirts and pants at a neighboring factory, described to me the carnage she encountered: "I got off work about five and passed by Kader and saw many dead bodies lying around, uncovered. Some of them I knew. I tried to help the workers who had jumped from the factory. They had broken legs and broken arms and broken heads. We tried to keep them alive until they got to the hospital, that's all you could do. Oh, they were teenagers, fifteen to twenty years, no more than that, and so many of them, so many."

This was not the first serious fire at Kader's factory, but the third or fourth. "I heard somebody yelling 'fire, fire,' " Tumthong Podhirun testified, ". . . but I did not take it seriously because it has happened before. Soon I smelled smoke and very quickly it billowed inside the place. I headed for the back door but it was locked. . . . Finally, I had no choice but to join the others and jumped out of the window. I saw many of my friends lying dead on the ground beside me."

In the aftermath of the tragedy, some Bangkok activists circulated an old snapshot of two smiling peasant girls standing arm in arm beside a thicket of palm trees. One of them, Praphai Prayonghorm, died in the 1993 fire at Kader. Her friend, Kammoin Konmanee, had died in the 1989 fire. Some of the Kader workers insisted afterwards that their factory had been haunted by ghosts, that it was built on the site of an old graveyard, disturbing the dead. The folklore expressed raw poetic truth: the fire in Bangkok eerily resembled the now-forgotten details of the Triangle Shirtwaist disaster eighty years before. Perhaps the "ghosts" that some workers felt present were young women from New York who had died in 1911.

Similar tragedies, large and small, were now commonplace across developing Asia and elsewhere. Two months after Kader, another fire at a Bangkok shirt factory killed ten women. Three months after Kader, a six-story hotel collapsed and killed 133 people, injuring 351. The embarrassed minister of industry ordered special inspections of 244 large factories in the Bangkok region and found that 60 percent of them had basic violations similar to Kader's. Thai industry was growing explosively—12 to 15 percent a year—but workplace injuries and illnesses were growing even faster, from 37,000 victims in 1987 to more than 150,000 by 1992 and an estimated 200,000 by 1994.

In China, six months after Kader, eighty-four women died and dozens of others were severely burned at another toy factory fire in the burgeoning industrial zone at Shenzhen. At Dongguan, a Hong Kong–owned raincoat factory burned in 1991, killing more than eighty people (Kader Industries also had a factory at Dongguan where two fires have been reported since 1990). In late 1993, some sixty women died at the Taiwanese-owned Gaofu textile plant in Fuzhou Province, many of them smothered in their dormitory beds by toxic fumes from burning textiles. In 1994, a shoe factory fire killed ten persons at Jiangmen; a textile factory fire killed thirty-eight and injured 160 at the Qianshan industrial zone.

"Why must these tragedies repeat themselves again and again?" the *People's Daily* in Beijing asked. The official *Economic Daily* complained: "The way some of these foreign investors ignore international practice, ignore our own national rules, act completely lawlessly and immorally and lust after wealth is enough to make one's hair stand on end."

America was itself no longer insulated from such brutalities. When a chicken-processing factory at Hamlet, North Carolina, caught fire in 1991, the exit doors there were also locked and twenty-five people died. A garment factory discovered by labor investigators in El Monte, California, held seventy-two Thai immigrants in virtual peonage, working eighteen hours a day in "sub-human conditions." One could not lament the deaths, harsh working conditions, child labor and subminimum wages in Thailand or across Asia and Central America without also recognizing that similar conditions have reappeared in the United States for roughly the same reasons.

Sweatshops, mainly in the garment industry, scandalized Los Angeles, New York and Dallas. The grim, foul assembly lines of the poultry-processing industry were spread across the rural South; the *Wall Street Journal*'s Tony Horwitz won a Pulitzer Prize for his harrowing description of this low-wage work. "In general," the U.S. Government Accounting Office reported in 1994, "the description of today's sweatshops differs little from that at the turn of the century."

That was the real mystery: Why did global commerce, with all of its supposed modernity and wondrous technologies, restore the old barbarisms that had long ago been forbidden by law? If the information age has enabled multinational corporations to manage production and marketing spread across continents, why were their managers unable—or unwilling—to organize such mundane matters as fire prevention?

The short answer, of course, was profits, but the deeper answer was about power: Firms behaved this way because they could, because nobody would stop them. When law and social values retreated before the power of markets, then capitalism's natural drive to maximize returns had no internal governor to check its social behavior. When one enterprise took the low road to gain advantage, others would follow.

The toy fire in Bangkok provided a dramatic illustration for the much broader, less visible forms of human exploitation that were flourishing in the global system, including the widespread use of children in manufacturing, even forced labor camps in China or Burma. These matters were not a buried secret. Indeed, American television has aggressively exposed the "dark Satanic mills" with dramatic reports. ABC's *20/20* broadcast correspondent Lynn Sherr's devastating account of the Kader fire; CNN ran disturbing footage. Mike Wallace of CBS's *60 Minutes* exposed the prison labor exploited in China. NBC's *Dateline* did a piece on Wal-Mart's grim production in Bangladesh. CBS's *Street Stories* toured the shoe factories of Indonesia.

The baffling quality about modern communications was that its images could take us to people in remote corners of the world vividly and instantly, but these images have not as yet created genuine community with them. In terms of human consciousness, the "global village" was still only a picture on the TV screen.

Public opinion, moreover, absorbed contradictory messages about the global reality that were difficult to sort out. The opening stages of industrialization presented, as always, a great paradox: the process was profoundly liberating for millions, freeing them from material scarcity and limited life choices, while it also ensnared other millions in brutal new forms of domination. Both aspects were true, but there was no scale on which these opposing consequences could be easily balanced, since the good and ill effects were not usually apportioned among the same people. Some human beings were set free, while other lives were turned into cheap and expendable commodities.

Workers at Kader, for instance, earned about 100 baht a day for sewing and assembling dolls, the official minimum wage of $4, but the constant stream of new entrants meant that many at the factory actually worked for much less—only $2 or $3 a day—during a required "probationary" period of three to six months that was often extended much longer by the managers. Only one hundred of the three thousand workers at Kader were legally designated employees; the rest were "contract workers" without permanent rights and benefits, the same employment system now popularized in the United States.

"Lint, fabric, dust and animal hair filled the air on the production floor," the International Confederation of Free Trade Unions based in Brussels observed in its investigative report. "Noise, heat, congestion and fumes from various sources were reported by many. Dust control was nonexistent; protective equipment inadequate. Inhaling the dust created respiratory problems and contact with it caused skin diseases." A factory clinic dispensed antihistamines or other drugs and referred the more serious symptoms to outside hospitals. Workers paid for the medication themselves and were reimbursed, up to $6, only if they had contributed 10 baht a month to the company's health fund.

A common response to such facts, even from many sensitive people, was: yes, that was terrible, but wouldn't those workers be even worse off if civil standards were imposed on their employers since they might lose their jobs as a result? This was the same economic rationale offered by American manufacturers a century before to explain why American children must work in the coal mines and textile mills. U.S. industry had survived somehow (and, in fact, flourished) when child labor and the other malpractices were eventually prohibited by social reforms. Furthermore, it was not coincidence that industry always assigned the harshest conditions and lowest pay to the weakest members of a society—women, children, uprooted migrants. Whether the factory was in Thailand or the United States or Mexico's *maquiladora* zone, people who were already quite powerless were less likely to resist, less able to demand decency from their employers.

Nor did these enterprises necessarily consist of small, struggling firms that could not afford to treat their workers better. Small sweatshops, it was true, were numerous in Thailand, and I saw some myself in a working-class neighborhood of Bangkok. Behind iron grillwork, children who looked to be ten to twelve years old squatted on the cement floors of the open-air shops, assembling suitcases, sewing raincoats, packing T-shirts. Across the street, a swarm of adolescents in blue smocks ate dinner at long tables outside a two-story building, then trooped back upstairs to the sewing machines.

Kader Holding Company, Ltd., however, was neither small nor struggling. It was a powerhouse of the global toy industry—headquartered in Hong Kong, incorporated in Bermuda, owned by a wealthy Hong Kong Chinese family named Ting that got its start after World War II making plastic goods and flashlights under procurement contracts from the U.S. military. Now Kader controlled a global maze of factories and interlocking subsidiaries in eight countries, from China and Thailand to Britain and the United States, where it owned Bachmann toys.

After the fire Thai union members, intellectuals and middle-class activists from social rights organizations (the groups known in developing countries as nongovernmental organizations, or NGOs) formed the Committee to Support Kader Workers and began demanding justice from the employer. They sent a delegation to Hong Kong to confront Kader officials and investigate the complex corporate linkages of the enterprise. What they discovered was that Kader's partner in the Bangkok toy factory was actually a fabulously wealthy Thai family, the Chearavanonts, ethnic Chinese merchants who own the Charoen Pokphand Group, Thailand's own leading multinational corporation.

The CP Group owns farms, feed mills, real estate, air-conditioning and motorcycle factories, food-franchise chains—two hundred companies worldwide, several of them listed on the New York Stock Exchange. The patriarch and chairman, Dhanin Chearavanont, was said by *Fortune* magazine to be the seventy-fifth richest man in the world, with personal assets of $2.6 billion (or 65 billion baht, as the *Bangkok Post* put it). Like the other emerging "Chinese multinationals," the Pokphand Group operates through the informal networks of kinfolk and ethnic contacts spread around the world by the Chinese diaspora, while it also participates in the more rigorous accounting systems of Western economies.

In the mother country, China, the conglomerate nurtured political-business alliances and has become the largest outside investor in new factories and joint ventures. In the United States, it maintained superb political connections. The Chearavanonts co-sponsored a much-heralded visit to Bangkok by ex-president George Bush, who delivered a speech before Thai business leaders in early 1994, eight months after the Kader fire. The price tag for Bush's appearance, according to the Bangkok press, was $400,000 (equivalent to one month's payroll for all three thousand workers at Kader). The day after Bush's appearance, the Chearavanonts hosted a banquet for a leading entrepreneur from China—Deng Xiaoping's daughter.

The Pokphand Group at first denied any connection to the Kader fire, but reformers and local reporters dug out the facts of the family's involvement. Dhanin Chearavanont himself owned 11 percent of Honbo Investment Company and with relatives and corporate directors held majority control. Honbo, in turn, owned half of KCP Toys (KCP stood for Kader Charoen Pokphand), which, in turn, owned 80 percent of Kader Industrial (Thailand) Company. Armed with these facts, three hundred workers from the destroyed factory marched on the Pokphand Group's corporate tower on Silom Road, where they staged a gentle sit-down demonstration in the lobby, demanding just compensation for the victims.

In the context of Thai society and politics, the workers' demonstration against Pokphand was itself extraordinary, like peasants confronting the nobility. Under continuing pressures from the support group, the company agreed to pay much larger compensation for victims and their families—$12,000 for each death, a trivial amount in American terms but more than double the Thai standard. "When we worked on Kader," said Professor Voravidh Charoenloet, an economist at Chulalongkorn University, "the government and local entrepreneurs and factory owners didn't want us to challenge these people; even the police tried to obstruct us from making an issue. We were accused of trying to destroy the country's reputation."

The settlement, in fact, required the Thai activists to halt their agitation and fall silent. "Once the extra compensation was paid," Voravidh explained, "we were forced to stop. One of the demands by the government was that everything should stop. Our organization had to accept it. We wanted to link with the international organizations and have a great boycott, but we had to cease."

The global boycott, he assumed, was going forward anyway because he knew that international labor groups like the ICFTU and the AFL-CIO had investigated the Kader fire and issued stinging denunciations. I told him that aside from organized labor, the rest of the world remained indifferent. There was no boycott of Kader toys in America. The professor slumped in his chair and was silent, a twisted expression on his face.

"I feel very bad," Voravidh said at last. "Maybe we should not have accepted it. But when we came away, we felt that was what we could accomplish. The people wanted more. There must be something more."

In the larger context, this tragedy was not explained by the arrogant power of one wealthy family or the elusive complexities of interlocking corporations. The Kader fire was ordained and organized by the free market itself. The toy industry—much like textiles and garments, shoes, electronics assembly and other low-wage sectors—existed (and thrived) by exploiting a crude ladder of desperate competition among the poorest nations. Its factories regularly hopped to new locations where wages were even lower, where the governments would be even more tolerant of abusive practices. The contract work assigned to foreign firms, including thousands of small sweatshops, fitted neatly into the systems of far-flung production of major brand names and distanced the capital owners from personal responsibility. The "virtual corporation" celebrated by some business futurists already existed in these sectors and, indeed, was now being emulated in some ways by advanced manufacturing—cars, aircraft, computers.

Over the last generation, toy manufacturers and others have moved around the Asian rim in search of the bottom-rung conditions: from Hong Kong, Korea and Taiwan to Thailand and Indonesia, from there to China, Vietnam and Bangladesh, perhaps on next to Burma, Nepal or Cambodia. Since the world had a nearly inexhaustible supply of poor people and supplicant governments, the market would keep driving in search of lower rungs; no one could say where the bottom was located. Industrial conditions were not getting better, as conventional theory assured the innocent consumers, but in many sectors were getting much worse. In America, the U.S. diplomatic opening to Vietnam was celebrated as progressive politics. In Southeast Asia, it merely opened another trapdoor beneath wages and working conditions.

A country like Thailand was caught in the middle: if it conscientiously tried to improve, it would pay a huge price. When Thai unions lobbied to win improvements in minimum-wage standards, textile plants began leaving for Vietnam and elsewhere or even importing cheaper "guest workers" from Burma. When China opened its fast-growing industrial zones in Shenzhen, Dongguan and other locations, the new competition had direct consequences on the factory floors of Bangkok.

Kader, according to the ICFTU, opened two new factories in Shekou and Dongguan where young people were working fourteen-hour days, seven days a week, to fill the U.S. Christmas orders for Mickey Mouse and other American dolls. Why should a company worry about sprinkler systems or fire escapes for a dusty factory in Bangkok when it could hire brand-new workers in China for only $20 a month, one fifth of the labor cost in Thailand?

The ICFTU report described the market forces: "The lower cost of production of toys in China changes the investment climate for countries like Thailand. Thailand competes with China to attract investment capital for local toy production. With this development, Thailand has become sadly lax in enforcing its own legislation. It turns a blind eye to health violations, thus allowing factory owners to ignore safety standards. Since China entered the picture, accidents in Thailand have nearly tripled."

The Thai minister of industry, Sanan Kachornprasart, described the market reality more succinctly: "If we punish them, who will want to invest here?" Thai authorities subsequently filed charges against three Kader factory managers, but none against the company itself nor, of course, the Chearavanont family.

In the aftermath, a deputy managing director of Kader Industrial, Pichet Laokasem, entered a Buddhist monastery "to make merit for the fire victims," *The Nation* of Bangkok reported. Pichet told reporters he would serve as a monk until he felt better emotionally. "Most of the families affected by the fire lost only a loved one," he explained. "I lost nearly two hundred of my workers all at once."

The fire in Bangkok reflected the amorality of the marketplace when it has been freed of social obligations. But the tragedy also mocked the moral claims of three great religions, whose adherents were all implicated. Thais built splendid golden temples exalting Buddha, who taught them to put spiritual being before material wealth. Chinese claimed to have acquired superior social values, reverence for family and community, derived from the teachings of Confucius. Americans bought the toys from Asia to celebrate the birth of Jesus Christ. Their shared complicity was another of the strange convergences made possible by global commerce.

Acknowledgments

Editing this book has been at once inspiring and humbling. My first and greatest debt is to all the journalists whose work appears in these pages. They provided not only the contents for an anthology but a profound education in craft and history.

The insight and judgment of two individuals are central to how this book turned out. Margaret Spillane contributed in more ways than can be named, most of all in the constant reminder that the demands of journalistic deadline are fully compatible with the aspiration to literature. A conversation with Aoife Spillane-Hinks during a long wait at Bradley International Airport brought into focus the introduction and some of the hidden themes embedded in this compilation.

Friends and professional colleagues have made valuable suggestions over the years this project evolved, particularly regarding long-forgotten journalists worth including. I particularly thank: Chip Berlet, David Block, Jeremy Brecher, Tom Brune, Ed Cray, Christopher Hitchens, Lisa Getter, Jack Hitt, Andy Hsiao, Ben Kiernan, the late Andrew Kopkind, Mimi Morris, Victor Navasky, Deborah Nelson, Lisa Sanders, Clancy Sigal, Frank Smyth, Fred Strebeigh, Katrina vanden Heuvel, Jason Vest, Murray Waas, Mike Weber, Steve Weinberg, JoAnn Wypijewski, and others I will regret forgetting to include. The late Frank Donner, civil liberties lawyer and chronicler of the American inquisition, was a muckraking mentor whose understanding of the complex nature of exposure has much to do with this volume. This anthology benefited as well from conversation about the purposes of journalism with Roger Simpson and Frank Ochberg, M.D., my colleagues at the Dart Center for Journalism and Trauma.

This book owes much to the Yale College Seminar Program and the Yale Summer Creative Writing Institute, which have for some years sponsored my journalism classes. I especially thank Jill Cutler, assistant dean of Yale College and the Summer Writing Institute's longtime director.

Michael Barbaro, a young journalist with an enviable talent for troublemaking, was a deft and energetic research assistant. He is among numerous students at Yale College who have been sources of insight and challenge, and I wish space permitted me to name them all. Research and interviews conducted by a few students over the years led directly to selections or biographical background material in this volume: I particularly thank Gaiutra Bahadur, Shella Calamba, Hailyn Chen-Gallagher, Matthew Goldenberg, Samantha Grant, Dylan Howard and Ritu Pati.

At Nation Books, founding editorial director Dan Weaver seized this project with an enthusiasm carried through by his enterprising successor Carl Bromley. Ruth Baldwin began working on *Shaking the Foundations* as an intern at *The Nation*: Without her excavations, the important and moving work of Vera Connelly would still lie forgotten in musty boxes. Later, as an assistant editor of Nation Books she patiently shepherded my selections through the editorial process.

I am grateful to the staff and membership of Investigative Reporters and Editors, the most generous mutual-support organization in journalism. I especially thank the staffs of Yale's Sterling Memorial Library, Mudd Library, and the Beinecke Rare Book Library, as well as the Columbia University library system and the New York Public Library.

INDEX

Permissions

We gratefully acknowledge all those who gave permission for written material to appear in this book. We have made every effort to trace and contact copyright holders. If an error or omission is brought to our notice we will be pleased to remedy the situation in future editions of this book. For further information, please contact the publisher.

Vera Connolly, "Cry of a Broken People." Copyright © 1929 by Vera Connolly. Originally published in *Good Housekeeping* (1929). ✳ Drew Pearson, "The Man Who Stayed Too Long" from *Washington Merry-Go-Round.* Copyright © 1931 by Drew Pearson. Used by permission of Tyler Abell, administrator of the Drew Pearson Estate. All rights reserved. ✳ Carey McWilliams, "The Rise of Farm Fascism" from *Factories in the Field.* Copyright © 1939 by Carey McWilliams. Used by permission of the University of California Press. ✳ George Seldes, "The Suppressed Tobacco Story." Reprinted by the permission of Russell & Volkening as agents for the author. Copyright © 1941 by George Seldes, renewed in 1969 by George Seldes. ✳ Lowell L. Leake, "Hitler Gets Millions for War Chest through Links with American Firms" from *PM.* Copyright © 1941 by Lowell L. Leake. ✳ John Bartlow Martin, "The Blast in Centralia No. 5: A Mine Disaster No One Stopped." Copyright © 1948 by *Harper's Magazine.* All rights reserved. Reproduced from the March issue by special permission. ✳ Marvel Cooke, "The Bronx Slave Market" Parts I, II, and III from the *New York Compass.* Copyright © 1950 by Marvel Cooke. Reprinted by permission of the Marvel Cooke Estate. ✳ Stetson Kennedy "The Klavaliers Ride to a Fall" from *The Klan Unmasked.* Copyright © 1954 by Stetson Kennedy. Used by permission of the author. ✳ Fred J. Cook, from "The Big Ones Get Away" reprinted by permission of *The Nation.* Copyright © 1958 *The Nation.* ✳ Ralph Nader, "The Safe Car You Can't Buy," reprinted by permission of *The Nation.* Copyright © 1959 *The Nation.* ✳ "Anatomy of a Hate Group" by Frank Donner, reprinted from *The Un-Americans.* Copyright © 1962 by Frank Donner. Reprinted by permission of Alfred A. Knopf, Inc. ✳ "And No Birds Sing" from *Silent Spring* by Rachel Carson. Copyright © 1962 by Rachel L. Carson. Copyright © renewed 1990 by

Roger Christie. Reprinted by permission of Houghton Mifflin Company, All rights reserved. ✳ I.F. Stone, "All We Really Know Is That We Fired the First Shot." Copyright © 1968 by I.F. Stone. Reprinted with permission of The Wylie Agency, Inc. ✳ "The University on the Make" from *Ramparts.* Copyright © 1966 by Robert Scheer, Sol Stern, and Warren Hinckle. Used by permission of the authors. ✳ Seymour Hersh, "The My Lai Massacre." Reprinted with permission of the *St. Louis Post-Dispatch.* Copyright © 1969 by Seymour Hersh. ✳ Neil Sheehan and Hedrick Smith, "Vast Review of War Took a Year." Copyright © 1971 by Neil Sheehan and Hedrick Smith. Used by permission of the *New York Times* Company. ✳ "Secret Memo Bares Mitchell-ITT Move," "Kleindienst Accused in ITT Case," and "Contradictions Cited in ITT Case" from the *Washington Post.* Copyright © 1972 by Jack Anderson. Used by permission of United Feature Syndicate, Inc. ✳ "Spy Funds Linked to GOP Aides" and "Mitchell Controlled Secret GOP Fund" by Robert Woodward and Carl Bernstein. Copyright © 1972 The *Washington Post* Company. Reprinted with permission. ✳ "The Prison Business" from *Kind and Usual Punishment: The American Prison Business* by Jessica Mitford. Reprinted by permission of The Estate of Jessica Mitford. Copyright © 1973 Jessica Mitford. All rights reserved. ✳ Mark Dowie, Barbara Ehrenreich, and Stephen Minkin, "Corporate Crime of the Century" from *Mother Jones.* Copyright © 1979 by Mark Dowie, Barbara Ehrenreich, and Stephen Minkin. Used by permission of the authors. ✳ "Steinman" from *Vicious Circles: The Mafia and the Marketplace,* by Jonathan Kwitny. Copyright © 1979 by Jonathan Kwitny. Used by permission of W. W. Norton & Company, Inc. ✳ Penny Lernoux, "Villains Afoot" from *Cry of the People.* Copyright © 1980 by Penny Lernoux. ✳ Allan Nairn, "Behind the Death Squads." Copyright © 1984 *The Progressive.* Reprinted by permission from *The Progressive,* 409 E Main St, Madison, WI 53703. www.progressive.org ✳ Roy Gutman, "Death Camp Horrors." Copyright © 1992 *Newsday* Inc. Reprinted with permission. ✳ Kenneth Armstrong and Steve Mills, "Death Row Justice Derailed" from the *Chicago Tribune.* Copyright © 1999 by *Chicago Tribune* Company. All rights reserved. Used with permission. ✳ "These Dark Satanic Mills" from *One World, Ready or Not.* Reprinted with the permission of Simon & Schuster Adult Publishing Group, from *One World, Ready or Not* by William Greider. Copyright © 1996 by William Greider.